ON THE SEVENTH DAY

THIRTY YEARS OF GREAT SPORTS WRITING FROM THE SUNDAY INDEPENDENT

ON THE SEVENTH DAY

THIRTY YEARS OF GREAT SPORTS WRITING FROM THE SUNDAY INDEPENDENT

EDITED BY JOHN GREENE

MERCIER PRESS

MERCIER PRESS
Cork
www.mercierpress.ie

© Independent Newspapers Ireland Ltd, 2018

Introduction © John Greene, 2018

ISBN: 978 1 78117 652 8

10 9 8 7 6 5 4 3 2 1

Printed and bound in the EU.

CONTENTS

INTRODUCTION

'People's backyards are much more interesting than their front gardens.'

John Betjeman

One December day the phone rang in the office of the *Sunday Independent* editor, Aengus Fanning. Eamon Dunphy was calling from a pub in Croydon. He was in the company of George Best and his wife, Mary. Dunphy had travelled to London with no real plan, other than to meet with Best to see how he was doing and write a piece for that weekend's paper.

Denis Compton had earlier come into the same pub and taken a seat at the bar. He and Best acknowledged each other. Best sent a drink over to Compton, who then returned the compliment. 'Here's one of the greatest footballers of all time and one of the greatest cricketers of all time in a pub in Croydon,' Dunphy recalled years later.

As darkness began to fall on that winter afternoon, Compton joined the trio for a while. It was then that an idea popped into Dunphy's head, and he couldn't shake it. He wanted to call Fanning, whose passion for – and knowledge of – cricket was well known by all who knew him. He found a payphone in the back of the pub and asked Compton if he would say hello to his boss. If this legend of English cricket thought the request strange, he didn't show it, and a short conversation with a thrilled cricket enthusiast back in Dublin ensued.

In the end, the chance encounter made it into Dunphy's piece, which in turn has made it into this collection of articles written for the *Sunday Independent* sport section over the last thirty years. It is without doubt one of the finest pieces I've read about Best, capturing a side to the man that was seldom observed. Dunphy had, in a manner, gone rummaging in Best's back yard and found the innocence and sadness behind the façade; he is full of caring and concern, and maybe even hope for his fallen hero.

Dunphy's piece on Best proves the truth of Betjeman's observation, an observation which makes a good starting point for this anthology – it's a good finishing point too. The last section takes its title from it, and the three pieces (including Dunphy's) which make up the closing pages demonstrate the writer's art of getting to know people better, people who really interest us – people like Best and Rory McIlroy – by looking a little deeper.

The idea behind *On The Seventh Day* is a simple one. We have always respected the intelligence of our readers. This respect manifests itself each week in how we look at the world of sport. The cliché that sports fans are some kind of one-dimensional bozos is largely a creation of people who know little about sport and less about those who are passionate about it. These are the kind of people who have espoused a ban on alcohol sponsorship in sport but not in the arts because, well, the more refined types are wiser to the dangers of alcohol than the ruffian hordes who go to football games. That is why there is a literary quality to the best of sports writing all over the world; a refusal to dumb it down.

In an exchange of letters over several years, later published in a book entitled *Here and Now*, writers Paul Auster and J. M. Coetzee touched on their passion for sport and tried to rationalise how it intruded so much on their literary world. 'Is sport simply like sin: one disapproves of it but one yields because the flesh is weak?' asks Coetzee at one point. In his reply, Auster observes: 'Of the many hundreds of baseball games I have watched – perhaps even thousands – nearly every one has had some small detail or event I have never seen in any other game. There is pleasure in the new, but also pleasure in the known. The pleasure of eating food one likes, the pleasure of sex. No matter how exotic or complex one's erotic life might be, an orgasm is an orgasm, and we anticipate them with pleasure because of the pleasure they have given us in the past.'

And it is this philosophy which has underpinned how the *Sunday Independent* has approached sport for a very long time, giving strong-minded and talented writers the platform to express themselves in a way designed to stimulate readers, who are thus invited to agree or disagree. We have always been keen to entertain, to produce good reads, but never to pander. There is a sometimes devilish quality to the writers, in that they enjoy provoking and challenging people, but not in some kind of cheap, attention-seeking play; it is more to engage readers in the argument, cajoling them to look beyond the conventional wisdom which tends to permeate all sporting reactions. There is also always room for humour, passion and even for a little exaggeration for rhetorical effect. Irreverence is important.

On The Seventh Day is not an anthology of memorable moments in Irish sport over the last thirty years, although some are there. Nor is it intended as a chronicle of those years. It is intended to cast a light on the world of Irish sport in all its forms, which is what the *Sunday Independent* strives to do every week. The pieces have been chosen to reflect this. These are my choices, based on what I think the paper has brought to the sporting landscape over those three decades, how it has criticised, praised, challenged or even cheered. As much as possible, articles have been reproduced as they originally appeared. There may be references or usage of language which appear a little dated, but I felt it was important for the integrity of the book to avoid the temptation of updating them to account for the passage of time, or even allowing the benefit of hindsight to colour my judgement. In some instances, footnotes have been used to explain a contemporary reference, but otherwise every effort has been made to keep the pieces intact.

There is anger, joy, humour, sadness, pity, tragedy, beauty; there are memories, controversies and celebrations; tales of addiction and tales of redemption. The book opens with Paul Kimmage's opus from the winter of 2001 on the story behind Ireland's memorable win over Holland in September of that year, a game that – as it turned out – as good as sealed our place at the World Cup the following year. The central figure in that game, of course, was Roy Keane, who also became the central figure in a different way when storming out of the Irish camp at that World Cup the following summer, and Kimmage's famous interview with Keane, which he conducted in Saipan just before the storm erupted, also features here.

There are only four women writers represented in this anthology, an imbalance that is bound to raise questions. Going through the newspaper archives of the last three decades, it was striking how long it has taken for women to become established in the world of sports writing. Cliona Foley was among a very small group of women who made the first breakthrough in the early 1990s and her insight into a very young Catherina McKiernan is included here, but, otherwise, the remaining contributions from women are from much later. The situation has improved, thanks in part to the emergence of a new and talented group of female journalists, but there is still a way to go to see the same kind of representation in sports writing as we do in other areas.

The belated emergence of more women writing about sport, though, has come at a time when the newspaper industry as a whole is under threat. Fewer people are buying newspapers, which is not the same thing as saying that people are not interested in what good writers have to say. It is just that the habit of buying a paper each day, or on a Sunday, is dying. There was a time, not too long ago, when hundreds of thousands of newspapers were sold in Ireland every Sunday. On the seventh day Irish people had an extraordinary custom, which seemed to set them apart from other nations, of buying several papers and catching up on the week's events in politics, sport and whatever else tickled their fancy. And as the newspapers grew in size in response to their growing popularity, buying the Sunday paper almost became an event. The *Sunday Independent* was the first choice of many and enjoyed a massive weekly sale. There was a stable of writers who were setting the agenda in the national discourse each week, including in sport. In the late 1980s and early 1990s, the voices of the likes of David Walsh, Eamon Dunphy and Mick Doyle led the way; then came Paul Kimmage and Colm O'Rourke; later, into the noughties, Dermot Gilleece, Dion Fanning, Neil Francis, Joe Brolly and Eamonn Sweeney, whose award-winning 'Hold The Back Page' column has been ever-present since 2006, were among the prominent voices.

Despite the changes in the media landscape, and the gravitation of journalism to online platforms, sports fans still have the same voracious appetite to read good pieces and so we continue to produce them. The principles of what we do haven't changed – we are bound to inform and entertain – and the *Sunday Independent* is still the largest-selling weekend paper in the country.

I hope you enjoy this collection from our sports pages. Some of you will be more than familiar with the *Sunday Independent* and our ideology; others may be coming to us for the first time. I hope whichever bracket you fall into that you enjoy reading these pieces as much as we enjoyed producing them. We have always endeavoured to give our writers the freedom not just to express themselves but to have fun while doing so. There has never been a party line. All the writers are free to express their own varied and often contrary opinions. Indeed, it is not uncommon for different writers to put forward diametrically opposed views on a subject in the same issue. There is room in our church for all. As Walt Whitman said, 'Do I contradict myself? Very well then I contradict myself, I am large, I contain multitudes.'

We like to be serious about sport, but not solemn; we like to talk about sport the way Irish people talk about it ... especially on the seventh day.

John Greene

I

INSIDE THE TEAM
THAT MICK BUILT

'Who's Friedrich Nietzsche? What team

did he ever play for?'

INSIDE THE TEAM THAT MICK BUILT (PART 1)

PAUL KIMMAGE

On 1 September 2001 the Republic of Ireland produced one of the most memorable displays in the history of Irish sport. How was this remarkable performance achieved? From the hotel room to the dressing room; from the tunnel to the final whistle; every stride, every breath, every thought … here is the full story.

28 OCTOBER 2001

Barry Murphy was almost there. After a week of reading the sports pages and shooting the breeze with punters in queues, the *Après Match* comedian had placed his finger on the pulse of the nation. Nobody, but nobody, expected Ireland to get a result in the World Cup qualifying game against Holland and the opening sketch during the RTÉ live broadcast on Saturday would have to reflect this. He picked up the script and began to tweak it again. He was almost there. It was almost perfect.

Take One: *Après Match*, 1 September, 14.53.

(*As thousands of Irish fans make their way to Lansdowne Road, one jersey-clad supporter with a strong Dublin accent seeks refuge in a bar and is handed a pint of stout by his friend.*)

'Can we switch on the match?' the friend inquires.

'We're not watching the match, that's why we came here, right?' the fan replies tetchily.

'What are ye talking about, we're not watching the match?'

'We're not watching the match. We're going to get destroyed! We're going to get annihilated! You don't need to see that, right?'

'What are you talking about?'

'Have you seen the team they have?'

'I have, yeah.'

'Yeah?'

'Yeah.'

'And what? You want to watch them stuff us nine or ten nil? What are you, Oliver Cromwell?'

'What are you talking about? The Duffer's in great form.'

'The Duffer's in great form … they've got van Nistelhooks, Kluiverts, Hasselbainks, Overbooks … who have we got, The Duffer! His real name: DAMIEN BLEEDIN' DUFF! Sums up our chances! It will be like watching your man, Gary O'Shaughnessy, at the Eurovision. Do you remember? He got us relegated. I don't want that humiliation, right? I'm not having that blood on me hands.'

(A pregnant pause ensues.)

'Who's Gary O'Shaughnessy?'

'Exactly!'

1

Mick McCarthy has never appreciated his phone ringing on Saturday. Phone calls on Saturday mean …

'He's out.'

'He's injured.'

'He's done his hamstring.'

'His ankle's gone.'

'It's his knee.'

He lost Stephen Carr on a Saturday. He lost Kenny Cunningham on a Saturday. He lost Mark Kinsella on a Saturday. He lost Gary Breen on a Saturday. Saturdays are bad news for international managers and the last Saturday of August would prove the same. A friend, Aidan Kelly, had just sent a text message from the West Ham/Leeds game at Upton Park: 'Hartey injured and doubtful.' McCarthy glanced again at his mobile and tried to figure it out. 'Doubtful'? What did doubtful mean? But he knew. He knew.

2

Ian Harte sat in the dressing room at Upton Park and studied the gash in his leg. The real damage had been done, not in the seventy-eighth minute when Paolo Di Canio's studs had ripped into his ankle, but a week earlier in the 2–0 defeat of

Southampton when the ankle had been badly bruised. He had struggled all week to be fit for West Ham and probably shouldn't have played but it was a Catch-22. Would Leeds release him to Mick McCarthy if he wasn't fit for David O'Leary? That's not how the game was played. So he gritted his teeth and suffered in silence and almost pulled it off.

Gary Kelly and Robbie Keane came over to take a look. Keane knew Harte was struggling even before the game. 'At half-time he was icing his leg in a bucket. I wouldn't be able to do that. I find it hard to get going when I ice my leg but full credit to him, he stuck with it.' The plan had been to fly home from London later that evening but the plan had suddenly changed: Kelly and Keane would be travelling on to Dublin, Harte would be returning for treatment to Leeds. 'I'll see you during the week,' Kelly offered by way of encouragement. But he wasn't sure. The ankle looked a mess.

3

The following afternoon, as Ian Harte spent his first day on crutches, a crowd of 42,632 were streaming through the turnstiles at Villa Park for the first clash of the season between Aston Villa and Manchester United. For 42,631 of them, the winning of the game was all that mattered, but one spectator had come with a different agenda. His name was Stephen Staunton and he would spend the ninety minutes sitting in the stand studying Ruud van Nistelrooy.

Staunton, Ireland's most capped international, wasn't happy that John Gregory, the Villa manager, had left him out of the team. He never is. 'Stan loves playing,' Gregory told *The Daily Telegraph* recently. 'He is always banging on the door saying, "Why wasn't I on the bench? Why wasn't I in the team? I can't believe you've left me out."'

Staunton hates when he isn't involved. He hates it so much that he often feels like registering his protest by staying at home. On any other Sunday he might have, but his pending appointment with van Nistelrooy in Dublin had become an obsession. So he joined the queue of traffic to Villa Park. The Dutchman was good. The Dutchman was very good. There could be no falling asleep with this guy on your shoulder. Staunton drove home and packed his bags for Dublin. The game was six days away but already his pulse was starting to race.

4

Mattie Holland was also learning Dutch that afternoon.

'Magic the shirt heaven algebra, Patrick?'

No, didn't sound right.

'Ma gick je shirt hebban algebreest, Patrick?'

No, it still wasn't right.

The Patrick in question was Patrick Kluivert, the star of the Netherlands football team. The 'shirt' was the brilliant orange tunic he would wear at Lansdowne Road. From the moment Mattie had announced why he was travelling to Dublin, the pressure had come on from his seven-year-old son. Jacob Holland loved Kluivert. He was the star of FIFA 2000, Jacob's favourite Playstation game.

'WHAAT! YOU'LL BE PLAYING AGAINST KLUIVERT! AW DAD, PLEASE, PLEASE, YOU'VE GOT TO GET ME HIS SHIRT.' So Mattie started making plans. He was sure Kluivert spoke English and knew 'May I have your shirt please?' was the easiest path to tread. But what if he asked in Dutch? Kluivert couldn't but be impressed. He started taking lessons.

'Mag ik je shirt hebben alsjebliest, Patrick?'

Hmmm, he was almost there but it still wasn't perfect. He needed to roll it out with a bit more gravel in his throat. It needed more arrogance, more confidence, more … Dutch.

5

Jason McAteer stood staring at his reflection in the bathroom mirror. It was Sunday evening at the Dublin Airport Posthouse Hotel and he was just about to head into the city to meet Damien Duff.

Don't look at me like that. I know what you're thinking. You're thinking 'a night, on the town is the last thing you need.' You're thinking 'he hasn't started a game for Blackburn in yonks.' You're thinking 'Saturday is only six days away, you should be wrapped up in bed.' You're thinking 'Spice Boy! Waster! After all that's happened you haven't bloody changed!' But you're wrong. I have changed. I have. I'm a father now. I'm in a relationship now. I'm older now and harder now and … okay, so I'm probably not as wise as I ought to be but I'm getting there. I'm getting there. I'm trying to be good.

6

Mick Byrne went striding into the lobby like his trousers were on fire. It was Monday morning at the Posthouse Hotel and the team's physiotherapist, psychotherapist and Mother Hen had a million things to do and as much on his mind.

'Has the gaffer arrived yet?'

'I better phone Hartey again.'

'I'd better phone Roy.'

'The first training session is scheduled for 4.00; some of the lads will need treatment and strapping.'

'There's Ciaran. I hope he has organised the drinks and medical supplies. And I see Jason is in. Has Clinton arrived yet? Got to keep working on Clinton. I wonder does he mind us calling him "Brother"? Have to make sure he is feeling at home.'

'Jaysus the rooms! We're moving to Citywest tomorrow. Has Eddie faxed them the rooms I wonder? Did I give him the list? Alan Kelly with Shay Given; Kevin Kilbane with Niall Quinn; Steve Staunton with Dean Kiely; Gary Kelly with Ian Harte; Robbie Keane with Richard Dunne; Damien Duff with Lee Carsley; Jason McAteer with Mark Kennedy; Steve Finnan with Gary Doherty; Clinton Morrison with Stephen Reid; Andy O'Brien with Dave Connolly; Mattie on his own; Roy on his own. Have I missed anyone?'

'Ahh Packie! Great to see you! Gaffer! There y'are. Wait till I tell you about the dream I had last night, it was definitely an omen. I've a good feeling about this week. We owe them Dutch.'

'Jason me oul flower, great to see you son. Come 'ere till I give you a hug.'

7

Damien Duff wasn't sure what hurt the most: the pain in his head from the night on the town with Jason or the look on his twelve-year-old brother's face when he'd informed him he was going out. Jamie had planned a night in front of the telly. It wasn't every weekend his famous brother was home. They could nestle down on the couch with a bucket of cake and chocolate and watch the Spanish League football on Sky, just like old times.

But Damien wasn't having it: he'd scored a brilliant goal for Blackburn against Spurs the day before and fancied a little R&R before answering Ireland's call. But now he felt desperate. His head was pounding like a jackhammer and Jamie was giving him the eye. 'Okay Jamie,' he said, 'I'll make it up to you. Win, lose or draw on Saturday against Holland and I'll come home.'

'Is that a promise?'

'It's a promise. We'll sit down and watch the England game on Match of the Day.'

'Okay,' Jamie smiled.

8

It was a wave. It was a wave that picked me up and carried me on its crest for almost a decade. One moment, I was just an unknown Scouser playing for a bunch called Marine and the next I was sitting in a dressing room in Giants Stadium, New York surrounded by boyhood heroes: Ronnie Whelan, Ray Houghton, John Aldridge and Paul McGrath. We were playing in the World Cup! That's how incredible it was. Six caps for Ireland and I was playing in the World Cup! Sprinting up and down the line against Paolo fuckin' Maldini. And, overnight, I was a hero too.

It was a dream. It was a dream that picked me up and carried me away to a different planet. Planet Popstar. Celebrity fare. Girls throwing their knickers; a mansion with electric gates; shampoo commercials à la Ginola; supermarket openings like Jack. Walking out at Anfield for my beloved Liverpool. Walking out at Wembley to play United in the final of the Cup. Walking up the catwalk in Armani. Peeling off those crisp new bills to Enzo Ferrari … one hundred, two hundred … revving up, slapping them down. Meet Jason and The Three Amigos. Thought it would last forever. Thought it would never end.

It was a crash. It was a crash that knocked the air out of my lungs and brought the world tumbling down around my ankles. We were training at Liverpool one morning and Stan Collymore gave the ball away in five-a-side. 'Don't worry Stan,' Roy Evans, the manager, says. 'Come on, win it back, you'll be alright next time.' A few minutes later I lost possession and was rewarded with an unmerciful bollocking and stormed off the training ground.

The manager pulled me in. 'What's the matter with you?' he asks. 'Fuck you,' I reply, absolutely livid. 'I give the ball away once and you read me the riot act! Stan gives it away all the time and it's "That's okay Stan!"'

'Yeah,' he says, 'but a manager has got to know his players. I know I can do it with you. I know you'll respond positively but Stan will go the other way.' And then he put his arm around me and everything was fine.

I needed that. I needed an arm around my shoulder. I needed reassurance that I was a valued member of the team and could play. And when I got it, I could play and in return I gave it all: 100 per cent commitment, absolute loyalty to the cause.

Everything changed when Gérard Houllier came in. The first time he sees me, he calls me to the touchline: 'What's your name?' he asks. I couldn't believe it. A World Cup with Ireland! A hundred appearances for Liverpool! 'What's your name?'

I was dropped shortly afterwards. Hit me like a bomb. And then things started to slide: transfer to Blackburn, wage cut, broken leg and suddenly my value was falling faster than an IT share. Nobody would touch me. Couldn't get a game. And the only thing that kept me going was the loyalty of family and friends and the faith shown in Ireland.

Mick Byrne and the way he might hug you; Mick McCarthy's defiant belief; Ian Evans and Packie Bonner's prompting on the training ground; Johnny Fallon's tireless grin; Joe Walsh laying out the kit; Tony Hickey laying down the law; Ciaran Murray in the treatment room; Derek Carroll on the bus. Doctor Martin, Father Liam, the inimitable Eddie Corcoran and the lads: Sparky, Duffer, Kells, Alan Kells, Quinny, Carso, Breeny, Stan, Shay, Hartey, Robbie, Dunney, Mattie, Stevie, Kendo, Kev, Kince, Deano and yeah, sometimes even Roy.

9

25 August 1996, Eschen, Liechtenstein.

A reporter places a glass to the wall of his bedroom. On the eve of Mick Mc-Carthy's first World Cup qualifying game as manager, two of his most experienced players are discussing the plight of the team on the other side of the wall …

'So, what do you think then?'

'Of Mick? Well, at least we're playing football. I thought he'd have us lumping it forward like Jack. I thought it would be a lot more direct.'

'Yeah, but what about the results? How many games have we lost?'

'Five.'

'And won?'

'One.'

'Draws?'

'Two.'

'And he's what … five months in the job?'

'Yeah.'

'Not easy is it?'

'No, but it was never going to be. What age is he? Thirty-seven? And how does anyone follow an act like Jack?'

'I can't believe I'm still here to be honest.'

'No, me neither. Bryan Adams concerts! Travelling everywhere as a group! Eleven o'clock curfews on Sunday evenings! For fuck's sake we used to be only driving into town at that time in the old days. It was a lot more fun under Jack.'

'No, I don't mean that.'

'What do you mean?'

'I can't believe he keeps calling me into the squads. As soon as he got the job I was sure "that's me gone".'

'Naah, he needs all of the old boys on board, doesn't he? Look at the ages of some of these kids! What's Hartey? Nineteen? And Shay Given and Keith O'Neill can't be that much older. He's not going to win much with a team of kids. You've got to get the blend right. It has to be a gradual transition.'

'Yeah, I suppose.'

'I do think he's going to struggle with Roy though.'

'In what way?'

'Well, do you remember that row they had in '92? I thought Mick was going to chin him. And look at how it's started: Mick makes him captain for his first game in charge and not only is Roy sent off but he then goes AWOL for the US Cup!'

'Yeah, but what's new? Jack struggled with Roy; Alex Ferguson struggles with Roy. Even Roy struggles with Roy!'

'Yeah, true enough.'

'I tell you what has surprised me – the training and how well organised it is. I didn't ever see Mick as a coach.'

'Fuck me, you can say that again. What about all these cones?'

'The pitch this afternoon was like the M25.'

'There was none of that with Jack.'

'No, you're wrong, there was two at each end to make the goals.'

'Hah, yeah.'

'Have you heard the latest innovation?'

'No.'

'He's showing us a video tomorrow.'

'What? A Liechtenstein game! No thanks, I was here last year.'

'No, an instructional video on how to sing the anthem.'

'You're joking!'

'I'm not. He wants us to act more patriotic. He wants us to show more respect for the shirt. He wants us to learn the words of the national anthem.'

'What? In Irish!'

'Yeah.'

'Naah! Are you sure?'

10

Things were looking up by Monday evening. Roy Keane had picked up a knock at Villa Park but had phoned to say he was fine and would be staying in Manchester for treatment until Wednesday. Kevin Kilbane, Niall Quinn, Andy O'Brien and Shay Given had arrived relatively (O'Brien had a slight foot injury) unscathed from the Sunderland/Newcastle game.

There had been no worrying calls from Manchester, Birmingham, Coventry or Wimbledon where Richard Dunne, Alan Kelly, Lee Carsley and Dave Connolly were involved in evening games. And there was better news of 'Hartey', who was off the crutches and responding to treatment.

Mick McCarthy pulled back the sheets and climbed into bed. The hotel lobby had been humming. He had noticed the tension as soon as he'd stepped off the flight. The way people had looked at him walking through the terminal, the words of encouragement: the desperation to succeed.

'All the best Mick.'

'Good man Mick!'

'This is it Mick.'

Yes, this was it, and yet with just five days to go he had never felt as calm. He smiled and thought of his wife, Fiona, and the prayer she kept pinned to the kitchen wall: 'God grant me the serenity to accept the things I cannot change, the courage to change the things I can and the wisdom to know the difference.' He was trying. It wasn't easy.

Fiona. That's when it started: two years before his debut for Ireland in the summer of 1982. She had relatives living in Portmarnock, it was his first time to visit and they spent the evening in a pub. He can still see them now, gazing in wonder through the smoke-filled haze from a seat in the corner: the guzzling, the laughing, the singing and then, at the end of the night, the strangest part of all, EVERYBODY STANDING BOLT UPRIGHT FOR THE SINGING OF THE NATIONAL ANTHEM!

He had never seen that before. No one ever stood up for the national anthem in England. And just as curious as the act itself was the song and the sound of the words.

Sinne Fianna Fáil, atá faoi gheall ag Éirinn,
Buíon dár slua ...

What exactly did it mean?

For the next fifteen years, the question was to haunt him. He remembers the summer of 1990, leading the team out onto the pitch in Cagliari to play England at the World Cup finals. He remembers the lump in his throat and the tear in his eye; bursting with pride that Jack had awarded him the captain's armband. Bursting with pride for his teammates and the shirt on their backs.

Bursting with pride for Charlie, his Co. Waterford-born father. Bursting with pride for Fiona and their three children at home. Bursting with pride for the fans who had travelled and the people of Ireland. Bursting with pride. And then they turned to face the flag for the playing of the national anthem and he found himself frustrated again. He was bursting with pride but unable to express it.

Sinne Fianna Fáil, atá faoi gheall ag Éirinn

He had tried to learn the words but it didn't sound the same in his broad Barnsley accent.

People wrote letters to him regularly, disgusted that the Irish captain, and most of the Irish team, spoke like 'Brits' and couldn't sing the national anthem. It used to drive him absolutely mad. 'NOBODY HAS EVER GIVEN MORE THAN I GIVE PLAYING FOR IRELAND. A FEW POXY WORDS WON'T MAKE ME PLAY ANY BETTER. I REGARD MYSELF AS A FULL-BLOODED IRISHMAN BUT I WAS BORN IN BLOODY BARNSLEY. AND I'M SORRY IF PEOPLE TAKE OFFENCE BUT THERE'S NOTHING I CAN DO TO CHANGE IT.'

But he knew, deep down, there was.

In the summer of 1996, shortly after he took over as manager, another letter arrived from a 'Liam O'Sullivan'. McCarthy opened it, saw the words 'national anthem' and thought at first it was from another crank. But there was something different about it: the stamp on the envelope, the address inside. Liam O'Sullivan, born in England and living in Coventry, was offering to teach him 'Amhrán na bhFiann'.

Curious, McCarthy decided to give him a call. 'Look, I can teach you,' O'Sullivan assured him, in a thick English accent. 'Believe me, it's not as hard as it seems.' A few days later, a video arrived in the post: 'TEACH YOURSELF TO SING AS GAEILGE: A Cowboy Production for Chancers Video'. McCarthy shook his head in disbelief: 'Oh God, what have I done?'

He slipped the tape into his recorder. Suddenly, the amazing Liam O'Sullivan was grinning at him from the screen with a bunch of cards in his hands. Each card was a line from the anthem and the key to learning it off was to ignore how the words actually looked and sing them phonetically.

'Take the opening two lines: Sinne Fianna Fáil atá faoi gheall ag Éirinn,' O'Sullivan announced. 'Try saying that with your gob and you've got no chance. Or the third line: Buíon dár slua. I mean, dár would be pronounced "duh" in Barnsley when what you've really got to say is "daw". So forget everything you've read and try this instead.

'SHEENA FEE-NA FALL,
A-TAW FAY GALL EGG AIR-IN,
BWEEN DAW SLOO

'Get it?'

The manager got it. And by the time he had reached the last two lines he was thoroughly enjoying himself. He would do it. He would learn the sounds of these words. But then came the twist. 'Now Mick, I'm sorry but you'll have to excuse me,' his instructor announced. 'I haven't a clue about the last two lines because you know what always happens then, don't you? The band plays on and the crowd always shout, "Come on fucking Ireland." But I'll find out for you and let you know.'

Summer kicked on to August. McCarthy brought the video to Liechtenstein and showed it to his players on the eve of his first World Cup qualifying campaign. He wasn't sure how some of the older hands – Andy Townsend, Ray Houghton and Tony Cascarino – would react, but they all really enjoyed it.

A rehearsal was organised in the dressing room before kick-off. When the chorus reached its climax, a deafening roar shattered the singing. It was Keith O'Neill, who said: 'COME ON FUCKING IRELAND.' McCarthy would never forget that moment. It epitomised everything he had achieved as a player and a critical element of what he aspired as a manager to build. A team that never lay down: a team with unbreakable spirit.

When it came to the building of this team, McCarthy didn't start with a blank sheet. On the field, some of the cornerstones of the old regime – Andy Townsend, Ray Houghton, Tony Cascarino, Steve Staunton and Niall Quinn – remained loyal to his cause. Off the field, three of Jack's most faithful servants – Mick Byrne, Charlie O'Leary and Eddie Corcoran – had also been retained. There was no temptation to resort to a big brush and make a clean sweep. Jack's teams had always played with spirit: 'Why change what was good?' But that didn't mean he couldn't make it better.

One evening, his son Michael arrived down for dinner wearing one of his old Irish shirts. Curious, he went upstairs to where they were stored and decided to take a look. There were dozens in the box but he couldn't tell one from the other. Was this Euro '88 or Italia '90? The England game in Stuttgart or the one in Cagliari? When exactly had he worn them? Had he ever worn them? What made them different to those sold in the shops?

One thing that had always struck a chord was the reverence shown in Brazil for their famous golden tunic. More than a vest to sweat in and discard, the Brazilian shirt was an icon universally adored. Just to wear it was a symbol of achievement: 'This is one of the best in the world.' McCarthy, blessed with one such nugget on his team, began to think of ways of enhancing his shirt.

Under the old regime, players had always received their kit in the hotel on the morning of a game. 'You'd pick it up off the bed, sling it in a bag for the trip to the ground and find an empty space on the bench in the dressing room.' But what if the kit was delivered to the dressing room on the morning of the game? What if it was folded neatly under pegs numbered from 1 to 16? And what if the shirt was embroidered with the date of the game and the name of the opposition? Wouldn't that make it unique? Wouldn't that make it more precious?

For sure, it was just another small brick in the building of the team. But try building anything without them.

11

I'm very close to Mick, not just on a football level but as a friend as well. I've had a tough time over the last six months with a few things that have happened at home but he has always been there for me. He reminds me of Bruce Rioch, my first manager at Bolton. Bruce always stuck by me: 'You do well for me and I'll look after you,' he'd say. Bruce got it all from me but so does Mick. I think he likes me to be the chirpy lad about the place. He sat me down one day and told me. So I try, even when I'm not on the team, to be my chirpy self.

From the moment you come in, though, you're looking around, aren't you? Everyone does it, don't let them tell you they don't, everyone looks around and picks the team in their head. And do you know what? I think I've got a chance. I wasn't sure coming over. I'm fit, but I've only been playing in the Blackburn reserves and this is such a massive game I wasn't sure that would be enough. But Stephen Carr is still out, so the question now is who's going to play right-back?

Hartey's injury has given me a real chance. If he doesn't make it, he'll switch Kells over to the left, slot Stevie Finnan in at right-back and clear the right side of midfield for me. If Hartey does play, then the worry for me is that he will play Stevie at right-back and push Kells into midfield. The game with the Under-21s is always a good indicator. We play them tomorrow but I definitely think I've a chance.

Cut my head in training this morning. Was jumping for a ball with Gary Doherty – not a good idea – and came off worse. Blood everywhere. Mick Byrne had to cut my hair to put the fly stitches in. I wasn't best pleased: 'What about my hair? How am I going to look on Saturday?' I moaned. 'Hair me bollix,' he laughs. 'Your country needs you. It's getting cut.'

I'm rooming with Carso who came in from Coventry today. I was supposed to be rooming with Sparky but he did his groin last night playing for Wolves so they've put Carso in with me instead. I like Carso. He's a character. He could be in the army the way he lives his life: up at eight o'clock, teeth brushed by five past, never dressed later than ten past the hour. After training, it's straight into the shower the minute we get back: I'd be still lying on the bed in my training gear and he'd have his boots polished and ready to go next day.

He never calls room service, will always make a pot of tea and he doesn't like a night out, doesn't take a drink. I love rooming with him. He is such a brilliant motivator.

'Looking sharp today Trigger.'

'You played really well in that game.'

'You're buzzin, Trig, buzzin.'

He's probably messin' half the time but it always rubs off on me. And I always feel being with him for the week enhances my chance of making the team.

He has this book he carries around with him that I clocked one time at Blackburn, a sort of secret code of how to live your life. 'Point One: always be positive. Point Two: always play what you see. Point Three: always ...' Er, no, I'd better say no more about it. He doesn't know I've seen it. He'd probably murder me if he ever found out.

12

After a week spent watching videos and consulting with Ian Evans, his friend and first lieutenant, McCarthy arrived in Dublin with two big calls to make: who to play up front? And who to play on the right side of midfield? Contrary to thoughts running through Jason McAteer's head, Ian Harte's injury had changed nothing. From the moment McCarthy had watched him train on Monday, McAteer was in the team.

'I like Jason. I like his personality. I think he has been terrific for us and always has been. Sometimes he gives the ball away and everybody jumps on him but I think that's fuelled by the press who tend to pick on him a bit. I had also made up my mind about Quinny. I told him at the first session what I was thinking and gave him my reasons why.'

Niall Quinn: 'He said, basically, that he felt Damien's and Robbie's time had come and I agreed with him. I wasn't in the best of form. I hadn't done anything at club level. I felt good and my back was fine but I hadn't reached the level of fitness I was to reach three or four weeks later, and felt it was the right decision from my point of view. I also thought it was the right decision for the team: Holland would be doing a lot of work trying to stop stuff coming to me.'

Mick McCarthy: 'I firmly believed it was the right thing to do. I knew Holland thought Quinny was going to play. And I would anticipate they thought we were going to pump long balls into him. They could have handled that. I've watched Jaap Stam play a couple of times this season and thought he struggled against people in and around his feet. I'm a six-foot-two, thirteen-and-a-half stone centre-half: who do I want to play against? Niall Quinn. Who do I not want to play against? Robbie

Keane and Damien Duff. That's why I went with them. But I didn't want everyone knowing. I wanted to spring a surprise.'

Niall Quinn: 'So Mick said – and this was the only little problem I had with it – "I want you to announce that you're playing. I want you to pretend you are playing all week." I wasn't happy with that: I couldn't tell the papers or anyone that interviewed me I was playing when I knew I wasn't, that would have looked really silly come match time. So we reached a compromise and agreed to split the difference: I told Mick that if anyone asked I'd say, "I'd love to play but I'll have no complaints if the two lads do." And that's the way we went with it.'

13

Wednesday afternoon at the Citywest Hotel: the media gather outside a dining room on the first floor and watch as the players arrive for lunch in groups of two. Why groups of two? It's one of the team's unwritten rules: NEVER LEAVE THE ROOM AT MEALTIMES OR FOR TEAM MEETINGS WITHOUT YOUR WINGMAN. For wingman, read roommate, or see the film *Top Gun*.

There are other aspects of the team the public rarely sees. Whereas 'The Team That Jack Built' were card players (almost all), crossword experts (most), womanisers (one or two), and world masters of *Trivial Pursuit*, whose favourite pre- and post-match activity was going 'over the wall' for a pint, 'The Team That Mick Built' are a much more serious crew.

There are still the card schools and the occasional 'Great Escape', and they still do most things as a group, but the games have changed. Take a walk down the corridor of the team floor at night (you'll need a Bazooka, mind, to get past Tony Hickey) and you'll find them gathered in a circle playing 'two-touch-off-the-floor' with Dave Connolly's miniature ball. And any you don't see will be gathered in some other room checking emails, playing Gameboy challenges or swapping DVDs.

But who are these guys? Where have they come from? What are they like? We knew the old team, Aldo and Razor and Ronnie and Kevin and Andy and Cas, like brothers. They were forever brightening up our rainy days with funny stories and inviting us to share their lives. But this new team is a mystery.

14

The Team That Mick Built (fifty-fourth selection v Holland) by Niall Quinn.

Shay Given: Good storyteller, great wit and oozing Donegal charm: women are mad about Shay but he rarely seems to notice which makes him nice to be around. At ten o'clock when the tea and sandwiches arrive, you'll always find him in the middle of the group. But on the training ground nobody works harder. As soon as he came into the team, you could see it was probably going to be the end of Packie, not because Packie had done much wrong, but because Shay had such an appetite for the game and wanted it so badly. Once came to Sunderland on loan for eight games but made such an impression that the staff still ask about him. A good lad.

Ian Harte: Hartey is quiet and very laid back. Sometimes, at training, Mick would be absolutely fuming at him, trying to get him going, but it never seems to make much difference: 'Okay Mick, no problem.' Maybe, if it hadn't happened so quickly for him, and he spent a year or two in the lower divisions, he would understand why the rest of us get so worked up. But then, that's just a sign of his quality and class. Gary, his uncle, is brilliant. Gary absolutely hammers him, leathers him, in front of the lads. He's fantastic. He does his accent brilliantly and poor Hartey just stands there speechless when he starts. But he's a smashing kid, one of those people who never turns down an autograph. And morning, noon and night you'll find him at the centre of the group playing ball in the corridor.

Steve Staunton: Hates the yellow jersey (awarded daily to the worst player) on the training ground with a passion. Never takes it well when the lads vote him in. A key member of the team, he is always offering advice and will sometimes run sixty or seventy yards to tell you what you're doing wrong. Robbie (Keane) does a great impression of him: 'Robbie keep your eye on the ball when you're striking it.' And his desire to win is amazing. In 1988 he was called into the squad before the European Championships. He was only seventeen or something at the time and didn't travel but stayed with the team during their time at the hotel in Lucan. One night, the card school convened and Stan pulled in a chair to watch. Liam Brady was God at the time and as the game progressed says: 'Steve, just pop up and get us some tea and sandwiches.' But he was told where to get off. And that's Stan. Nobody walks on him.

Richard Dunne: So laid back it's unbelievable. Nothing phases Dunney. The lads call him Meatloaf and take the mick something fierce but he never gets upset. You could tell Richard his house was on fire and there wouldn't be a panic to sort it out: 'Alright, no problem.' And, like Hartey, you'll often find him on the training ground, talking about what he was doing Saturday night, when Mick is pulling his hair out trying to make a point. 'Don't worry, Mick, I'll sort it out on the big day,' which, to be fair, he has done every time. I've never seen him in bad humour. Ever. He's great company to be with.

Gary Kelly: Gary is one of the elder statesmen now and very much one of the leaders. The young scallywag who came home from America as one of the 'Three Amigos' has disappeared. He's a very important element to Mick and would have far more influence on most of the lads in the squad than I would. They all look up to Gary. He's the one who makes them laugh and dishes out the stick. A really funny lad and on the go all the time.

Jason McAteer: Trigger. Mad as a hatter and one of the team favourites. He's bubbly, lively, funny and witty – most of which comes at his own expense, which is always the sign of a genuine lad. Jason enjoys the finer things in life but understands how it happened for him and doesn't rub noses in it like some people. Terrible judge of clothes: Jason will spend a fortune on a suit that could never look good and then hammer himself for having bought it. But he's a very good footballer. Things have conspired against him at a couple of clubs but he's a very valuable player.

Matt Holland: A good operator: whatever he does, he does right and a mini-Roy in his determination to win. While the rest of us will have a night out before we meet up, and spend the first three days trying not to get found out, Mattie will be sensibly organising himself. He's unobtrusive off the pitch and definitely not a messer, but another good guy.

Kevin Kilbane: I don't know how Kevin Kilbane ever made it in the game. Sincere, honest and brave as the day is long, he never looks for excuses or points the finger when things go wrong – qualities not normally associated with the profession. Ask him for something and he'll always give ten times more. The cynics would call him soft but he's just a fabulous young man, one of those kids who's a credit to the way he's been reared. The rooms at Citywest are quite big and have a single and a double bed. He put his bag on the double when we arrived but then took it off and went to the single. He was thinking about it. And the day will come soon when he starts acting like a normal footballer and claims the double bed. But not too soon I hope. Just a pleasure to be around.

Damien Duff: Has anyone ever noticed Damien sprint and weave the length of a pitch and then lean over and take deep breaths as if he's about to keel over? Well, that's what he's like when he gets out of bed and walks as far as breakfast. Damien sleeps more than anyone I know and still manages to look knackered most of the time. He was very quiet at first but has really come out of his shell and likes being involved when we're having a bit of crack. He's sharp too, the type who doesn't say a lot but will cut you down in a sentence. And he's a seriously talented player.

Robbie Keane: For all the sleeping that Duffer does, Robbie does none. You might mention to him by mistake that you're really tired and fancy an early night, and he'll get a key and come into your room every hour, on the hour, and turn your bed upside down. He's a disaster, an absolute nightmare, but he's funny. And always playing tricks. When Robbie isn't going around the hotel trying to make fools of everyone, there's something wrong with him. He's not feeling himself. I think the Italian experience hurt him, because he couldn't understand why it went the way it did and for the first time he was being doubted. But he's got it back now. The summer break has done him good, he's found that extra yard, and he looks like he's got goals in him again.

That's the eleven, isn't it?

15

Johnny Fallon left home on Wednesday morning and jumped into his car. Fallon is the team's facilitator. Need a lift? Ask Johnny. Need those tickets picked up from Merrion Square? Ask Johnny. Need a perfect-fitting Ireland kit for your nineteen-month-old son? Ask Johnny. Everybody loves Johnny. He's the Jason McAteer of the backroom team.

His mission, this morning, took him across the M50 and down the M1 to the airport roundabout. At 9.45 a.m. he approached the security checkpoint and was ushered onto the arrivals road where he parked, opposite the taxi rank to the right of the main exit. He was pleased about that. Thought it would cost him at least a ticket. Flight EI203 wasn't due for another thirty minutes. He turned on the radio and started watching the exit. At 10.25 a.m. his mobile went off. He knew the accent immediately. Cork. Irritated. 'Johnny! Where are you?'

'I'm here!' he replied. 'I'm parked just outside the exit on the other side of the road.'

Before he had even hung up, Roy Keane was bounding towards him dressed in jeans and a casual top. The drive to the team hotel at Citywest took forty-five minutes. Keane checked into his room, changed into a tracksuit and was taken to the training ground in Baldonnel where the team were playing the Under-21s. Ian Harte was due in later that evening. Gary Kelly was playing at left-back. Keane watched the game from a seat on the perimeter wall. His groin strain had eased. He was ready for combat.

The team returned to the hotel and adjourned for lunch. At the table, nobody chastised Roy for arriving without his wingman. Roy doesn't have a wingman: not on this team; not at United. Follow the team upstairs to their rooms after lunch and you'll find twenty-one players with their door almost permanently open and one with his door almost permanently closed.

The boys often smile that the most they see of Roy during international week is the ninety minutes of the game. But no one ever complains. And no one ever questions his commitment. He turns up for every training session. He respects all of the rules. He gives 110 per cent in every game and plays like a colossus. But everything else is on his terms. And for the manager, and the team, that's absolutely fine.

And yet, although not a sentiment ever expressed, there is no escaping the sense that they wish it could be different. Think about it. You share a dressing room with one of the best players in the world. Every time you follow him onto the field it's playing on your mind. Every time you pass him the ball you want to win his praise. Every time the media questions, you express your admiration.

'Roy is a great player.'

'Roy is an inspiration.'

'Roy is a giant.'

When what you'd really love to say is, 'Roy is a friend.'

Jason McAteer: 'I always find you get two Roy Keanes when you come away. There is Roy Keane the person and Roy Keane the footballer. I like Roy. I admire him immensely. I think he's a great professional, a great footballer, but he is such a complex person.'

Niall Quinn: 'If Roy is buttering jam on toast it has to be perfect: woe betide the person who's not pulling his weight and giving him margarine instead of butter. As cross as you see him on the football pitch, if Mick Byrne says he'll call to his room at 10.00 to give him a strapping and he's not there at two minutes past, you'll hear this roar in a Cork accent: "MICK". And we all scramble out of the way and make sure we're not in the firing line.'

Jason McAteer: 'We didn't see eye to eye (in 1994) when I first came into the squad. There was me, there was Phil (Babb), there was Gary and there was Roy and we didn't see eye to eye. Roy hated the Three Amigos thing, hated it with a passion. I think we were just completely different. Roy wasn't cheeky. But he hated us for it, hated the three of us. Now there is no Three Amigos. He has become the player he is and I have become the person I am. We've grown up a lot since.'

Niall Quinn: 'Roy is a deep character. Success means so much to him. It's the whole engine room for him. He doesn't suffer fools. He is single-minded. And when you are as gifted as him and have achieved what he has achieved I suppose it has to be like that. It's too much to ask for Roy to be the joker of the pack AND be the player he is. He's not somebody I feel awkward with. I think he's fascinating to be with.'

Mick McCarthy: 'I think you'll find in every walk of life – musicians, artists, singers, songwriters, dancers – that the great performers are different. They're all – I'm not sure eccentric is the word – but they've all got their own characters, all got their own little things they do. The problem they have, because they are great performers, is that everybody wants to have a look.'

Jason McAteer: 'I remember one time, I couldn't tell you where it was, but I got into trouble on the pitch and he was there, fighting my cause. And I remember when he was sent off at Lansdowne Road and I was there, fighting his cause. That's what happens when this team comes together: sometimes I think we're a right bunch of weirdos but we all look after each other.'

16

Thursday is cinema night: a long tradition with the team. The visit used to be compulsory under Jack but with Mick you can stay or go as you please. Tonight the venue was Blanchardstown and it was chocca, an absolute nightmare. The choice was Rush Hour 2, *a Jackie Chan film that I'd already seen, or* Blow, *the story of a bloke who established the American cocaine market in the 1970s – at least I think that's what it was about. Got there late as usual: queued for popcorn and missed the first twenty-five minutes. And of course, you know what happens, don't you? As soon as I sit down, nine hands ransack the bucket and I'm left with nothing at all! Waste of bloody time. I'm useless.*

Apart from the film review, there's not a lot else to report. Hartey came in last night and his foot looks very nasty. Don't think he's going to make it. Definitely think I'm going to play. You can always tell when he hands out the bibs on Thursday and I think I've got a great chance. But I'll still get butterflies tomorrow morning at Lansdowne when he calls out the team.

My new laptop is giving me problems. Did I not mention that? I'm a gadget man. I bought this new digital camera before I came away and took some photos of Harry, my son, but I'm not sure the two are compatible. I can't load him onto the screen. Spoke to Johnny about it. Tomorrow, when we come back from the ground, he's taking me to PC World.

17

By Friday evening the stage was set. Ian Harte had passed a fitness test. Mick McCarthy had informed the players of the team. Roy Keane had made a surprise, but welcome, appearance at the press conference. And Jason McAteer, his laptop sorted, had been reunited with his son.

Tension was starting to build as the team came together for dinner. Mick McCarthy brought two videos into the dining room: Holland's 2–0 defeat of England two weeks earlier and the 2–2 draw with Ireland at the start of the campaign.

Ian Harte: 'Normally, when we're eating our food Mick would stick the video on. You can either watch it or don't watch it.'

Robbie Keane: 'You tend to watch it because it's on, it's there isn't it?'

Niall Quinn: 'The lads hate watching videos. Anyone who asks a question gets ticked off by the rest for not letting Mick get on with it so we can all get out of there as quickly as possible. And any team I've known has been the same: woe betide the person who asks a question – he gets battered.'

Damien Duff: 'I didn't need to watch it. I knew everything about their players – they're world famous. I was more worried about my own performance. I was looking at their defenders and wondering whether I'd do the business the next day. Everyone knows what Stam's about: I was thinking "Fucking hell, how am I going to cope against him?"'

Steve Staunton: 'I hadn't seen the game. Everyone was on about how good the Dutch were but the one thing that stood out when you watched it – not one tackle was made.'

Mick McCarthy: 'I wanted to make the point that I could have played for Holland in that game! There wasn't a tackle made! They were just passing it and strolling around. It was a nothing game. Holland looked great but wouldn't we all look great if the other team just sat back and said, "Come and attack us."'

Shay Given: 'They won 2–0 but they could have won by a lot more. So maybe they were coming to Dublin thinking it was going to be easy. Mick just said, "We've got to get close to them, don't give them time to play."'

Kevin Kilbane: 'We watched the first half of the Holland–England game and then Mick just let our game against Holland run while we were having dinner. I think the point he was trying to make was, "Look how well you've played against this team. Look how comfortable you played in Amsterdam." And I think that made some of the lads sit up and take notice.'

Robbie Keane: 'The gaffer said, "If you can play this well away from home, how well can you play at Lansdowne Road?" It was good watching the tapes because it gave us two different views of them. We set our stall out and we knew what to do.'

Jason McAteer: 'It was good management. He made us watch it to give us a boost, to prove to ourselves we could do it again. We played well that night. We footballed them off the park, not that I needed to see it again. I've watched that game about 300 times, could tell you every pass. I was sitting right by the telly and I remember turning around at one point and most of the lads had gone. I think we'd all seen enough at that stage. I think we were all mentally prepared.'

INSIDE THE TEAM THAT MICK BUILT (PART 2)

PAUL KIMMAGE

4 NOVEMBER 2001

We all have our own special memories of the day. For the former captain, Andy Townsend, who watched from the Lower West Stand, it was a moment during the first half when the ball cannoned into the crowd and he jumped from his seat and headed it back to a cheer and a round of applause. What he is reluctant to reveal is that he couldn't see a thing for the next twenty minutes. 'The ball was like a brick.'

For the Middlesbrough defender, Curtis Fleming, who refused to bother anyone for a ticket and watched the game in a Dublin pub, Bruxelles, it was the scoring of the winning goal. 'I was with Keith O'Neill, Johnny McDonnell and Graham Kavanagh. We all jumped up when Jason scored and I looked out the window to McDaids across the road and you could see all of these people with their arms in the air. And in every pub and house in the country it was probably the same.'

For the ball boys from Broadford Rovers who officiated at the game, it was every time the ball went into touch. For Noel O'Reilly, the Ireland Under-18 coach, it was the moment of the final whistle and 'the feeling of sheer joy'. And for certain sports writers (who must remain nameless), it was the editor's voice screaming down the telephone for copy as they struggled to find words for what they'd seen.

But what was it like beneath the West Stand? What was it like on the journey to the ground? What was it like Inside The Team That Mick Built? Was it truly, as it seemed, the stuff of dreams?

1

Dreams? No, not on Friday. It's never the stuff of dreams on the eve of the game, because in order to dream, you have to sleep. And in order to sleep, it helps to have a full day's labour weighing on your bones. Or a few pints of lager washing into your blood. Or a short dose of amnesia tickling your brain. Yeah, a short dose of amnesia would be fine.

It would be nice to be able to forget, at least for a couple of hours, that my name was Jason McAteer. That I was FORMERLY of Liverpool. That I've hardly started a game for Blackburn this season and hardly scored a goal in almost a year. That World Cup 1994 was seven years ago! Oh yeah, and that I was marching out at Lansdowne Road to face Holland in twelve hours' time. But I don't. So I'm tossing and turning.

Carso's in the other bed sleeping. And not only is he sleeping but he's dreaming. And not only is he dreaming but he is enjoying his dreams. And not only is he enjoying his dreams but he is enhancing his chances of playing well tomorrow should Roy or Mattie get kicked or pull a hamstring and he is suddenly sprung from the bench. But that's Carso for you. Carso always sleeps positive and does what's best. If he was playing tomorrow, you'd still find him lying here enjoying his ZZZs. But he's not. And I am. Wishing I could forget.

Forget all that counting sheep, it's the butterflies you've got to watch for, the butterflies that do you down. You tell yourself to relax. You put yourself in situations. The FA Cup final at Wembley. The World Cup in New York. You try to remember how it was before. You tell yourself: 'I can do this. I have been here before.' And suddenly you start to feel less anxious. And suddenly you start to believe. 'Yes, I CAN do this. Yes I HAVE been here before.' And what happens? The butterflies kick in and you're ready to play. And you want to play now. YOU WANT TO START THE GAME NOW!

But it's three o'clock in the morning, so there's nothing you can do but turn over one more time. Trying to remember. Trying to forget. The game. The butterflies. The sound of Carso breathing.

2

Joe Walsh kicked his legs out of bed at 6.30 a.m. It was his fifth early wake-up call since the team had come together on Monday but the kit man wasn't complaining. How could he? Millionaires would pay to swap places. He was about to spend another day with them. He was about to journey with them from the hotel room to the dressing room. He was about to live this day of days as a member of the inner sanctum! But first there was work to be done.

He washed and shaved and made his way to the kit room to check the skips he had packed the night before. At 7 a.m. he boiled a kettle and was joined in the room by Ian Evans, the assistant manager, Ciaran Murray, the physiotherapist, and Derek Carroll, the driver, for a cup of tea. It took forty-five minutes to tiptoe past the players' rooms, with the five skips, eight bags, two beds, fifty towels, ice buckets, Gatorade and crates of water. They loaded the equipment onto the bus and hit the road.

Traffic was light on the journey into the city. By 8.20 a.m. they had arrived at

Lansdowne Road. The skips were unloaded and taken to the dressing room. Murray set up the therapy beds and medical supplies in a corner. Walsh and Evans began unloading and arranging the kit. Each player receives a slip (underpants), socks, shorts, a light top, a heavy top, a rain jacket, a tracksuit bottom and a long- and short-sleeved jersey.

The jersey of preference (Roy Keane never wears long-sleeved, Damien Duff rarely wears short) is hung on a peg. The replacement is folded neatly on top of the other garments below. The numbers are laid out in order. Because the goalkeepers always sit together, 1 and 16 are pegged side-by-side, and then it's 2, 3, 4, 5, 6, etc., across the wall.

Most players will sit where their shirt is pegged. Niall Quinn, however, always walks to the furthermost corner where Mick McCarthy and Packie Bonner sit. Quinn says it stems from an old habit that goes back to his debut when he was 'shy and just wanted to get out of the way'. McCarthy says the striker has been around so long 'he considers himself a member of the coaching staff'.

The last of the garments arranged, Walsh opened the skip with the studs, pliers and shin pads and pulled it into the middle of the floor. It was 9.30 a.m., and there was just one final detail to be sorted before the door was locked and they returned to Citywest for breakfast. He reached into a bag for the pennant and the armband and hung them over the number six peg.

3

Shay Given decided to skip breakfast. So did Mattie Holland. The first compulsory duty, the traditional pre-match walk, wasn't scheduled to begin until 11.30 a.m. and they decided to take advantage and lie in. The walk has changed since the team shifted its base to Citywest. Once a thirty-minute stroll on Malahide beach, they now stretch their legs on the hotel golf course.

The pressure was starting to build with every minute. When it was time for the walk, players chatted in twos and threes but the mood was a lot more sombre than usual until they happened upon a two-ball playing the ninth: one a seasoned practitioner, the other obviously struggling with his game. At first, the seasoned practitioner was spared as his friend's wayward drive was greeted with howls of derision on the tee. But by the time they had reached the green the support had shifted. There was, they collectively decided, something a bit 'flash' about the seasoned practitioner. It was easier to identify with the guy who was struggling. And when he took the hole with a putt from twenty feet, he was cheered as if he had just won the Open.

'Never met the bloke before,' says Niall Quinn, 'and probably never will again. But it was great, a bit of a laugh, and it just got us away from the match for a second.' The team returned to the hotel for the pre-match meal. There were three hours to kick-off.

4

They all sat on separate seats on the journey to the ground. And they all locked themselves away in private places. Steve Staunton is in a TV studio being grilled under lights. To his left, Ruud van Nistelrooy has answered every question. So has Patrick Kluivert, standing to his right. Eamon Dunphy is about to throw his pencil. 'Goodbye Mister Staunton, you are the weakest link.'

Mick McCarthy is sitting in an empty dressing room. Thirty minutes to kick-off. The players are warming up. He pours himself a cup of tea but doesn't feel like drinking. He picks up a match programme but can't focus on the words. Outside he can hear the roar of the crowd. He feels lonely. Helpless. It's the one moment of the day he dreads.

Alan Kelly is standing outside The Beggars Bush with a pint in his hand. A fan is beating a bodhrán. Another starts a chorus of 'The Fields of Athenry'. A police siren announces the team's arrival. Kelly raises his pint as the coach whizzes by: 'YEEESSSS! COME ON YOU BOYS IN GREEN!' Always wanted to be here. Always wondered what it was like.

Niall Quinn is sitting on the substitutes' bench at Highbury. The manager has left him out again. Niall has the hump, has spent twenty-four hours cursing George Graham. Burning nervous energy. Didn't sleep a wink. Never even considered that he might get a game. 'What's that Boss? Perry Groves is injured! He can't be injured! We've only played four minutes!' Learnt a valuable lesson that afternoon. Played absolutely shite. The Substitutes' Code: rule number 1, 'Always prepare to play.'

Robbie Keane is in Tallaght. His parents are out. His brother is babysitting. It's the summer of 1994 and Ireland are playing Italy in the World Cup. For eleven minutes they watch transfixed until, incredibly, Ray Houghton scores. Big brother jumps out of his chair. The hall door is flung open. The next five minutes are spent jumping up and down with the neighbours on the road.

Gary Kelly is in Lansdowne Road. He has been there most of the week. There's this guy in an orange 11 shirt who keeps asking him questions.

'How's the foot blisters Gary?'

'Still on the subs' bench at Leeds?'

'Remember the last time we met at the Nou Camp? Was it four or five that night?'

'And weren't you playing regularly then?'

Go on Gary, tell the people what it's like to be one-on-one with Marc Overmars.

5

The walk is when it starts for me. The walk is when Jason McAteer-Nice-Guy becomes a nasty bit of work who can't be arsed. I can't be arsed to get match tickets. I can't be arsed to sign autographs. I can't be arsed to pose for photographs. Sorry family, friends and fans, no disrespect intended, I just can't be arsed. Want to get out of there and get to the ground. Want to switch that mobile off and pull those shin pads on. Want to play. NOW!

There was a huge crowd in the lobby as we made our way to the coach. Picked a seat at the back. Went looking for myself. Curious what I found. Couldn't remember anything in a Liverpool shirt. Thought about a game I played once as a kid: the final of a five-a-side tournament. Scoring the winning goal: everyone mobbing me. Floating home on that massive high.

Thought about the coach ride to Giants Stadium. Gazing out the window. Listening to the songs. Looking for myself on the way to the game. Not the Italy game that everyone remembers but the 0–0 draw with Norway. Norway meant more to me. Norway was huge. Norway was the official seal of approval, a starting place on the team.

Twenty minutes to get to the ground! That has to be some sort of record. Follow Stan into the dressing room. Take my seat beneath the number 7 peg next to Roy. Listen to Mick's speech. 'Passionate hearts are great,' he says, 'but calm heads will win the day.' Struggling with his advice. Take a leak. Take another leak. Take another fucking leak. Can't stop going to the toilet. Can't stop fidgeting and jumping up and down. And Roy, sitting there, cool as a breeze. Seen that Kit Kat ad? That's exactly what he's like.

Almost time now. Mick Byrne tours the dressing room with final hugs. Alan Kelly wishes me luck. 'Just watch me Kells, I'm going to run and run and run.'

Follow Robbie Keane into the tunnel. Find myself in line with their subs: Jimmy Floyd Hasselbaink, Pierre van Hooijdonk, Giovanni van Bronckhorst. My opposite number, Zenden, is staring at me. Arrogant bastard. Know exactly what he's thinking. 'Who the fuck is this?'

6

Three o'clock at Lansdowne Road. The moment had arrived. From the kick-off, the Dutch moved the ball back to Edwin van der Sar who took a touch before pumping it forward towards the centre circle. As it dropped for Marc Overmars, the winger was felled by a crunching tackle from behind. There was thirty-eight seconds on the clock. The enforcer was Roy Keane.

A free kick. The ball was played to the wing where Boudewijn Zenden was obstructed by a strong challenge by Ian Harte. Patrick Kluivert immediately retaliated with a kick on Kevin Kilbane. The game was less than a minute old but the tone had been set.

Mick Byrne: 'The first tackle Roy made. I knew, *I knew*, this was our day.'

Mick McCarthy: 'Yeah, I think it probably was a statement, but he would be like that anyway, that's the way he plays.'

Jason McAteer: 'The tackles were flying in … van Nistelrooy had a go at Hartey.'

Steve Staunton: 'Overmars got a wallop, van Nistelrooy got a wallop – not a wallop in the sense that he was taken out, but a hard physical challenge.'

Kevin Kilbane: 'I was tackled by Kluivert and he lost it a bit. There was a bit of a brawl but I just smiled and walked away. I think they realised then they were in a game.'

Steve Staunton: 'You could see they were rattled. "This isn't supposed to happen. We're supposed to be allowed pass the ball and move." Every time the boy, van Bommel, tried to turn there was someone rattin' around his feet.'

Ian Harte: 'We got stuck into them.'

No question, but within less than a minute it was Ireland who were feeling the strain.

Gary Kelly: 'My biggest strength at right-back is my pace. Make bad decisions and your pace will always get you out of trouble. When you are playing someone quicker than you, you have to be on your game.'

But what do you do when your game has been blunted by a prolonged spell on the substitutes' bench? How do you defend against the quickest winger in the game?

As the match entered its third minute, Kelly headed the ball down on the halfway line and was chasing it back towards his goal when he came under pressure from Overmars and was dispossessed by Kluivert.

Gary Kelly: 'I was caught in two minds, whether to go back to Shay or to come inside. I tried to play it across the line and it just cut out. After that, everything seemed to be in slow motion. Kluivert picked it up, I was coming back, everyone was chasing.'

Shay Given: 'Kluivert was coming through. It's one-on-one so I'm just trying to come out and close the angle. He hit it to my left, I've dived to try and get it but it's gone wide of my hand. I looked at it going towards the post. I could see it all the way. It was only a matter of a couple of inches.'

Gary Kelly: 'It never went in. For some reason it just hopped outside Shay's left-hand post. I don't know how it didn't go in. I've thought about it a few times since. It must have been my sister, above.'

Mick Byrne: 'I bring my rosary beads with me. Every five or ten minutes I put my hand in my pocket. I call on everyone to help us.'

Mick McCarthy: 'They should have scored.'

Kevin Kilbane: 'We knew we'd been let off the hook. Nine times out of ten he'd have hit the back of the net. It was a lucky break and we had to capitalise on it.'

But the nervy start continued. Shay Given was tested early with a shot from van Bommel. Zenden nipped between Staunton and Dunne but failed to finish. Up front, Robbie Keane and Damien Duff were struggling with the surface (Keane: 'It was difficult. The grass was quite sticky. The ball was catching under your feet.') and the Dutch centre-halves, forcing them to drop deep. And it wasn't until after the twenty-fourth minute, when Arthur Numan was momentarily sidelined after a clash with Jason McAteer, that Ireland settled and began creating chances. And the last fifteen minutes before the interval were easily Ireland's best.

The only blight was a thirty-seventh minute booking for Gary Kelly, for a challenge on the ever-troublesome Overmars. 'It was always going to be difficult for our two full-backs,' says McCarthy. 'We wanted Jason and Kevin to tuck in and play narrow, so that was always going to leave them a bit exposed. We're talking about Overmars and Zenden, two of the best wingers in the world. And yeah, they got past a couple of times, but I thought the boys were handling it well.'

The second half began as positively for Ireland as it had ended. Roy Keane went close with a header. Ian Harte forced a save from van der Sar from a free. In the fifty-fifth minute it was the Dutch manager, Louis van Gaal, who was forced to make the first tactical switch – Hasselbaink replacing Zenden on the wing.

The Dutchman had hardly caught a breath when he was reunited with a former colleague at Leeds.

'I got tight,' Harte explains. 'He started swinging his elbows and I ended up ripping his jersey.' And conceding a free.

7

The game was fifty-seven minutes and thirty seconds old and about to reach the first of its three major turning points. From the free, the ball was played across the park to Numan and then short to Overmars, who was chopped from behind by Gary Kelly, leaving the referee with no option.

Steve Staunton: 'Oh no.'

Jason McAteer: 'Shit creek.'

Johnny Fallon: 'Despair.'

Mick Byrne: 'I nearly died. Don't do this on us, ref. You can't do this.'

Steve Staunton: 'Tackle from behind. He has to go.'

Gary Kelly: 'I never actually thought about getting sent off. When I got the first booking, I never thought of getting another. It's not in my nature to go in and lash someone from behind. But if you are going to tackle from behind, you're definitely going to hit them with something, even if you do get the ball. After the game he shook my hand and said, "I should have stayed on my feet, I should have got up," which was nice of him, and fair play to him, but it was a bit fucking late. To be sent off in front of your friends and family.'

Ian Harte: 'I was gutted for him.'

Mick McCarthy: 'Instantly I thought, "Let's change this, I'll get Stevie Finnan on, go four-four-one and see if we can hold on."'

Robbie Keane: 'I thought: "It's either me or Duffer off here."'

Damien Duff: 'I thought: "One of the strikers is gonna have to come off, I wonder who it will be?"'

Jason McAteer: 'I nearly shit myself. I turned around and looked at the sub and thought "Fuck it's Finn! Fuck I'm off!" I thought he was going to bring me off.'

Damien Duff: 'I saw Robbie's number go up, which was hard for him. He'd done well. He'd done brilliant.'

Robbie Keane: 'You're never pleased to be taken off, especially in a game like that. I was enjoying it, I felt good, felt sharp. I'm not going to lie and say I wasn't disappointed but I knew one of us had to go.'

Damien Duff: 'I thought, "Right, you have to do it on your own up front now." I had played against Portugal up front on my own but had been dropping too deep, I learned a lesson from that.'

Robbie Keane: 'I went and sat in the dugout. "Oh shit we've got ten men. Oh my God, we're playing Holland and they've got an extra man!"'

8

Three minutes after Kelly had made the lonely walk to the touchline, Steve Staunton was chasing back and about to intercept a ball chipped towards van Nistelrooy, when he crossed wires with his oncoming goalkeeper. The result was almost calamitous.

Steve Staunton: 'I was waiting for Shay to come but didn't think he was coming. And then, as I was ready to head the ball back, he shouted and I thought: "I've just got to touch this cos van Nistelrooy's right on my shoulder." And as I've headed it, I've looked at Shay and it's gone under his body.'

Shay Given: 'The ball came over the top and I remember running out and shouting to Stan "KEEPER'S!" Or "LEAVE IT!" I'm sure it was "KEEPER'S" but the noise was so loud I'm not sure if he heard me. Or else he heard me too late. I was only a yard away from him and he has headed it past me. I thought, "I've got to try and get the ball," but it was past me. I could see van Nistelrooy coming. He was going to tap the ball into an empty net! I put my body in front of him to try and shield the ball and his momentum took me down. Obviously he was looking for the penalty.'

Steve Staunton: 'I never even thought of a penalty. Honestly. It never even entered my mind. All I could see was the ball rolling towards the post. All I was concerned about was that I was about to score an og. And then I saw. I think it was Hartey and Kevin running back, and I knew it was okay.'

Kevin Kilbane: 'Hartey got to it first and put it out for a corner.'

Ian Harte: 'I just laugh every time I see it. I was chasing back and tried to get a touch on it and nearly put it in.'

Matt Holland: 'I'll talk you through this one. I'm running back towards the goal. The referee is, I think, maybe ten metres behind me. I see the scrap for the ball and I'm thinking, "There's going to be a whistle in a minute." I'm waiting for the whistle, knowing the whistle is coming. I'm running back, jogging back, still waiting for the whistle. No whistle! The ball goes round the post and there's still no whistle. I look around and the referee is pointing at the corner. I thought: "We got away with that one."'

Jason McAteer: 'Very clever play by Shay Given. He knew exactly what he was doing. But my first reaction was not a penalty.'

Damien Duff: 'Penno. It looked like Shay had chopped him in half.'

Niall Quinn: 'You could see van Nistelrooy sniff the fact that Shay and Stan had got mixed up and try to go past. And you could see that he was fouled to stop him getting there. We couldn't have argued about a penalty there. You could look at it over and over again, it was a penalty.'

Gary Kelly: 'If mine's a sending off, that's a penalty. Would I have given it? Definitely. And if you give the penalty, you have to send him off. Maybe the referee said, "I can't send two off, I'll be fucking lynched!" But you don't know, do you?'

Johnny Fallon: 'Relief.'

9

With thirty minutes to play, van Gaal decided to make a second tactical switch: van Hooijdonk on for Numan. As the substitution was made, the ground vibrated with a familiar call from the Lansdowne faithful, 'COME ON YOU BOYS IN GREEN'. Never had the chant been rendered with such passionate desperation.

Stephen Staunton: 'The intensity of the crowd really came through when we went down to ten men. I know they've been brilliant down through the years but I've never experienced anything like that before. It was as if another hundred thousand people walked in through the gates.'

Alan Kelly: 'When Gary was sent off, it definitely went up a level. The sound was absolutely amazing. I think the crowd thought, "We need to get behind these lads. We need to make a difference."'

Niall Quinn: 'Gary getting sent off added to the stakes and got everybody giving that bit more. Obviously the team react to it first, and the team didn't drop their heads. It was "Roll-up-your-sleeves time, backs-to-the-wall." There was also a sense that they weren't enjoying it too much. The two lads up front (Kluivert and van Nistelrooy) started arguing with each other and it was great for our lads to see that.'

McCarthy urged for calm heads from the touchline. Backs to the wall, the team were starting to buckle under the challenge but cometh the hour, cometh the Roy.

Matt Holland: 'Roy was immense. I thought he was absolutely fantastic. One minute he was breaking up the play, the next he was running forty yards taking the pressure off us. I thought he was immense. And he drags you along with it.'

Damien Duff: 'He was running around like a lunatic. It just inspires everyone else. I've had an evil eye off him but if you run your socks off for him, you'll have no problems. You try and do the business for him. He's a legend.'

Johnny Fallon: 'You take so much for granted with Roy in a way. "Roy'll do it, give him the ball, don't worry." I don't know how he does it, to be able to take the ball and make it look so easy. And what a relief for fellas to have. John Giles against Italy in 1971 was the greatest display I've ever seen in an Irish shirt. But Roy's performance has to be up there on a par.'

10

If Keane's (once again) was to be the outstanding contribution, he was about to lose the headlines to an old amigo. The game had reached its sixty-sixth minute and Ireland had broken the siege and won a corner.

Jason McAteer: 'I walked towards the corner flag, made a "come on" gesture to the crowd and put the ball down. I'd taken a few good corners in training on Friday and just went through the routine and swung it in. But he's managed to punch it clear.'

Damien Duff claimed the rebound and passed the ball to Ian Harte, who side-stepped a tricky challenge from Hasselbaink and laid it off for Keane.

Damien Duff: 'Roy made a burst down the left, cut inside and gave it to me. Steve Finnan was out on the right, I played it across to him.'

Jason McAteer: 'I'm jogging in now. Just jogging in. Didn't have a clue what was around me, could have been a man behind me for all I knew. Then the ball went out to Finn who turned back on himself.'

Damien Duff: 'Steve's a good player. I knew there was a chance of him getting a cross in. He cut back to his left and crossed it. I was trying to flick it on.'

Jason McAteer: 'It skimmed Duffer's head and dropped in front of me.'

Matt Holland: 'Jason was in acres. I thought, "Have a touch, bring it down, you've got time." But he doesn't know what's behind him so he hits it first time.'

Alan Kelly: 'It's funny, but the week before, we've both been bombed out of the first team and we're training together. The ball drops for him five times, in similar situations and it's save, save, wide, save, wide. So we're walking off the training ground and you know what his head is like: "Fuck it," he says, in his thick Liverpool accent, "I'm never going to score."'

Jason McAteer: 'It was instinctive. The ball bounced up and I've just got a whip on it. I could do it ten times and never hit the target again, but it just went in.'

Johnny Fallon: 'Joy.'

Mick McCarthy: 'Absolute joy.'

Ciaran Murray: 'I jumped and embraced Packie.'

Mick Byrne: 'I jumped six feet in the air.'

Joe Walsh: 'The elation was just unbelievable.'

Shay Given: 'I went into supporter mode for maybe a minute. I didn't even know it was Jason at the time. People were hugging each other and just going mad. The atmosphere was electric.'

Damien Duff: 'It was just unbelievable. He went sprinting off but I was too tired to run after him, so I went across to Stevie and congratulated him cos he's done brilliant for the goal.'

Niall Quinn: 'It was a great moment. Alan Kelly was beside me and we're all over each other. Just can't believe it.'

Steve Staunton: 'I clenched my two fists but didn't sprint after him. I had to save my energy.'

Matt Holland: 'Don't ask me why but I'm always one of the first to congratulate whoever scores. I ran straight over. Kevin Kilbane was with him in the corner. I held my arms out and waited and he jumped into my arms.'

Jason McAteer: 'I always end up with Kevin Kilbane after a goal. We hugged each other. That's when I remember the crowd going mad. I ran across the pitch but wasn't really out of breath. Looked at the bench and gave them a gesture, "That's for you." I turned round and looked at the clock. There were twenty minutes left.'

Joe Walsh: 'There's a clock behind the dugout. I kept looking at the clock.'

Johnny Fallon: 'I was worried about my ticker. I thought, "I'll never get through this."'

Robbie Keane: 'It was the longest twenty minutes ever. When you're playing, it's different, but when you're sitting on the bench watching!'

Gary Kelly: 'Try being sent off!'

Robbie Keane: 'I'm no good at watching games. I get too nervous.'

Kevin Kilbane: 'We had to defend with our lives.'

Ian Harte: 'We couldn't get out of our own half.'

Ciaran Murray: 'It was like the Alamo.'

Shay Given: 'It was just attack after attack after attack.'

But the Dutch were feeling the pressure even more and at a time when he needed to stay calm and detached, van Gaal buckled and made his worst decision.

Joe Walsh: 'When they put up Overmars' number to take him off I thought it was a mistake. I knew then that we had them. It was like winning the lotto. Taking Overmars off!! Their best player! I couldn't believe it.'

Steve Staunton: 'When we went down to ten men, they really didn't know what to do. They took Overmars off; I thought, "That's good." They took Zenden off; I thought, "That's great." He put Hasselbaink on; I thought "Please don't have him playing through the middle." He went over on the right. He played van Hooijdonk down the middle; I thought, "Yeah, we can handle this."'

Alan Kelly: 'The tactics were just: Hasselbaink, who couldn't cross a ball to save his life, playing right wing! This technically brilliant team just went long ball!'

Mick McCarthy: 'Strange decisions. It was almost as if he didn't want to take one of his star strikers off. "We'll put as many strikers on as possible and we're bound to get a goal" but you need people creating them. Their shape was lost completely. With fifteen minutes to go I thought, "Meat and drink to us." We'll cope with this.'

11

As the game entered its final phase, Matt Holland chose a break in play to approach Kluivert – the hero of his son Jacob's Playstation game – and pose the question he had been practising all week. 'Mag ik je shirt hebben alsjebliest, Patrick?' The striker looked at him, visibly surprised. An opponent asking for his shirt in Dutch? Now that was a first. 'Yeah, no problem,' he replied.

And it probably wouldn't have been if Holland hadn't immediately undone his good work by outjumping Kluivert as another hopeful ball was pumped into the Irish box. But Ireland's cause was greater. And for those last fifteen minutes it was shoulders-to-the-wheel for all as the siege continued.

Shay Given: 'For the last twenty minutes it was onslaught after onslaught. There was one save at the end, a weak header from van Nistelrooy, and it was just a basic dive to my left. But I remember the ball going away from me by a yard and being hard to grip because I was sweating so much. My gloves were just drenched in sweat.'

Gary Kelly (watching on an RTÉ monitor in the tunnel under the stand): 'As I was walking off I thought, "Jeez, if we get beaten four or five–nil I'm going to take some stick." And then Jason scored: "Great! Hold on now."

'With twenty minutes to go Larry Mullen (U2's drummer) came down; I think he was getting a helicopter to head back up to Slane. We were watching it and it was like, "Oh Jesus!" And we just kept hanging on and hanging on.'

In the eighty-seventh minute, McCarthy made his second substitution – Niall Quinn for Damien Duff. 'It felt odd, because I was asked to come in and be a centre-back,' Quinn recalls. 'And it seemed to last a lot longer than it should, but then he played a few minutes of injury time as well. I think I could have been on the pitch for nearly ten minutes. Ten minutes of frantic activity all round, and desperation. I must have headed the ball about a dozen times. It was ridiculous.'

After ninety nail-biting minutes, the fourth official posted three minutes of injury time to be played: van Nistelrooy again went agonisingly close to scoring and then McAteer had a chance: 'Roy put me in. I thought: "Do I go for goal or do I go for the corner?" I decided to be the model professional and made a sharp burst for the corner flag and kept it for a couple of seconds before being robbed. I got cramp in both calves as I was running back. I was gone.'

In the ninety-second minute McCarthy made his final substitution, sending Andy O'Brien on for the exhausted winger.

Jason McAteer. 'I remember coming off, couldn't believe it. Mick Byrne and Ciaran have come over to me: "Right get the ice on your calves." So I take the ice and one of them says, "Get yourself into the dressing room." I said, "Are you fucking sure?" I went to the bench and threw on a jumper. It was almost over. I was thinking: "Don't score. Don't score. Blow your whistle."'

And then, finally, as Richard Dunne hoofed another missile clear, the referee did.

Gary Kelly: 'I thought, "Thank fuck, got away with it." I didn't fancy Mick going through me. After that, I was just looking forward to getting away from there, just looking forward to the flight back to Leeds.'

Shay Given: 'One memory from the day? The final whistle. It was immense. It was the best atmosphere I've ever known in an Irish shirt by a mile. I could have stayed on the pitch for a couple of hours, but emotions were running so high a lot of what happened is a blur. I can't remember who came to me first: I think Stan was there and then Packie came on ... Mick Byrne. Mick McCarthy. They were all shaking my hand.'

Jason McAteer: 'For some reason you get all this energy again – my calves were suddenly fine. I was back running on the pitch. I remember Mattie coming over, grabbing Mattie.'

Matt Holland: 'I went to Kluivert to get his shirt. He said, "In the dressing room." I thought, "If he's going to be like that, leave him to it." Then I just remember hugging everyone, near enough, on the pitch.'

Damien Duff: 'The best thing was being out on the pitch. A few of the boys went down to the end and clapped the fans – they were brilliant. I wasn't sure where my family were sitting so I couldn't wave to them or anything. And then it was back to the dressing room.'

Niall Quinn: 'The final whistle was brilliant. The excitement on people's faces. Stan was the first one I went to. Nothing was said. We just looked at each other: "We're still here. We're still proving them wrong." Stan especially, because he had played from the start and was magnificent. It's a lovely feeling. You get your kicks from stuff like that.'

Steve Staunton: 'The Big Fella came over. We've been together since our Under-21 days and have come through a lot since. We'd proved people wrong? I didn't have to prove a thing to anyone. I just don't like letting people down; my family, the manager, the rest of the team.'

Alan Kelly: 'I was standing by the bench with Lee Carsley. All the photographers came round very quickly to get pictures, so we were looking over them. Jason had shot off towards the East Stand. Mick Byrne was doing a jig and Roy then walked past. Roy doesn't hang around. He gets off the pitch straight away. We followed him in and then I saw Andy.'

Steve Staunton: 'I've always been sharpish off the pitch. There was a big melee in front of me. I walked straight round it and headed for the tunnel. I was walking down the steps with my head down to make sure I didn't slip when I heard this familiar voice from above: "Stan! Stan!" I looked up and it was Andy. He was even more excited than I was.'

Andy Townsend: 'There haven't been many games since I've stopped playing which have had my pulse racing, but this one, I was kicking every ball. Cursing the linesman. I was so excited when the whistle sounded. I just had to get down to shake the boys' hands.'

Mick McCarthy: 'I saw Andy. He was all choked up. It was nice to see him; he has always been one of the good guys, from my point of view. I invited him to the dressing room, but he declined.'

Andy Townsend: 'It wasn't a case of not wanting to go in. I was very much aware of the fact that when I played, and when we had some success, it's a wonderful feeling that's to be enjoyed by everybody in the camp. And only everybody in the camp. It was a special moment they should share.'

Mick McCarthy: 'People have no idea. You're out on the pitch enjoying it and everybody is buzzing, and you come off and walk down the stairs and there's this TV camera and they want an interview! It brings you down very quickly.'

Johnny Fallon: 'The thing that really stood out for me was van Gaal's face at the end, the disbelief. He was shattered. It was as if his whole world was wrapped around his ankles. And I know I'll probably get shot for saying this, but I felt for him.'

Steve Staunton: 'There were only a handful in the dressing room when I went in. Roy was there. He said well done. But to be honest, we just sat there.'

Niall Quinn: 'You look at Roy, and he's giving out to somebody about what they did twenty-five minutes into the game and everybody's going: "What's he on about?" But that's typical. That's Roy for you.'

Jason McAteer: 'Roy is sitting there like he is before it – doesn't say a thing. He shook my hand but would never give you a hug. I looked at him and thought, 'I'm happy I scored. I'm happy we're in this together. I'm happy I've done my bit for you.'

Kevin Kilbane: 'Everyone was waiting for Trig (McAteer) to come in. We piled on top of him in the dressing room. It was fabulous, absolutely fabulous. The best atmosphere in a dressing room I've ever encountered. Niall and Stan have played in the World Cup and know what it's like, but for the rest of us, it was the stuff of dreams, what you dream about when you're a kid.'

Steve Staunton: 'Everyone was so excited. It was everything you could imagine, but I was tired. I was mentally and physically drained, probably more mentally than physically. People don't realise it, they think it's all physical, but the build-up to an international game is mentally draining.'

Alan Kelly: 'I remember going up to Stan, he looked shattered. A lot of people were physically and emotionally drained.'

Mick McCarthy: 'They were sitting with bags of ice on them, absolutely knackered. There were no Champagne corks popping or anything: it was a very weary dressing room, but a very happy and content one with what we'd achieved.'

Steve Staunton: 'The best bit was when Mick Byrne arrived in: "WE OWED THEM EFFIN DUTCH," he roars, smashing the door open. And it nearly came back and hit him in the face. That would have been funny. I would have enjoyed seeing that.'

Mick Byrne: 'Everybody was hugging everybody. "WE DONE IT! THIRTEEN YEARS WE'VE WAITED! WE'VE WAITED THIRTEEN YEARS. AND YOUSE FUCKERS HAVE DONE IT!" It was great to be part of it.'

12

United as never before in the dressing room, the team dispersed almost immediately afterwards, some to Slane, some to Leeds and some for a night on the town. A week before, Damien Duff had promised his twelve-year-old brother Jamie that, win, lose or draw, he would be home after the game. It was a promise he intended to keep.

Damien Duff: 'I walked across to the Berkeley Court Hotel to get a lift off me ma and da. There were loads of people there. We stayed for a half an hour and went home. I was tempted to go out, but I'd promised. Mam and dad went out celebrating. I stayed in, watched the England game and ate lots of crap.'

Gary Kelly: 'I had four people over for the game from Leeds, but I couldn't bring myself to go and see them afterwards. You feel like you've let everybody down. I didn't know what to do. I didn't know whether to stand outside the dressing room, sit in the dressing room or get on the bus. I couldn't wait until the bus came. I was embarrassed. I was ashamed. I just wanted to get back.'

Jason McAteer: 'Gary was very quiet, very distant, as if he had let the lads down. He didn't want to be a part of anything, which was wrong. He had his bags packed and was ready to go. I felt sorry for him, but because I was getting pulled from pillar to post, I didn't get a chance to say anything.'

Ian Harte: 'I would have liked to have stayed for the party, but we had booked flights back that night and I was in first thing Monday morning for treatment.'

Shay Given: 'I met me da in the players' lounge (Wanderers Pavilion) and he said well done. A couple of friends came in as well and they were all obviously delighted. I think me da and his friend had money on me keeping a clean sheet with a bookie in Lifford, so that helped.'

Alan Kelly: 'My cousins had organised a minibus. We were going up to Slane to see U2. I don't know how they did it, but it was parked outside the players' bar. We had a few drinks and then piled into the back of this Fiat minibus.'

Shay Given: 'My sister, her boyfriend and a friend from back home had come up and we'd arranged to drive to Slane. We came out of the ground and started walking to her car. I was dressed in normal clothes and wearing a baseball cap. The pubs were packed, there were loads of people outside drinking, but I think I was recognised just once, when I went into a shop. Outside of that, nobody recognised me, which I thought was quite funny.'

Jason McAteer: 'I had arranged during the week to meet John Aldridge and a friend, John McKenna. I changed in the hotel and shot into town with Dave Connolly and was with them in a bar when I got a call from Joe O'Herlihy, the U2 sound technician, asking me down to Slane to go on stage with Bono. If I could change one thing about the day, that would be it. I wish I'd gone down.'

Kevin Kilbane: 'I was out with my wife and saw a lot of supporters. Everybody was just buzzing, you just couldn't take the smile off their faces. Everyone I came into contact with was absolutely ecstatic with it all. I had a couple of pints and by ten o'clock I was just so tired; drained like I've never been before. I could hardly walk home. My bones were aching, my body was aching, I just wanted to go to bed.'

Mick McCarthy: 'I came back to the Airport Hotel, went downstairs with Fiona, watched about ten minutes of the England game and had a Chinese meal. I had a load of pals over. We had a pint. At one o'clock I went to bed. I was bolloxed. Completely.'

Niall Quinn: 'I stayed in the players' lounge and let the crowd head off. I had family and friends in. We caught a couple of taxis, had dinner at the Lemongrass restaurant in Naas, and then came back into town to meet up with the lads in Lillie's Bordello.'

Jason McAteer: 'We ended up in Lillie's Bordello. It could have been a very late night, but at about two o'clock in the morning I hit a brick wall and took a taxi back to the hotel.'

Niall Quinn: 'They were all in the Piano Bar in Lillie's and there was a singsong. Liam Brady, John Giles, Joe Kinnear and Eamon Dunphy were there. Roy arrived later with a couple of friends. All the barriers came down. Everybody was in great humour. We all had a go at something. Robbie Keane sang all the Boyzone and Westlife numbers.'

Robbie Keane: 'I can't help it if they want me to sing. You either have it or you haven't.'

Ian Harte: 'He's on *Pop Idol* next week.'

Gary Kelly: 'Louis Walsh is looking for him.'

Robbie Keane: 'I think I'll stick to the football.'

Niall Quinn: 'It was just a great night. It must have been bright when we left.'

Alan Kelly: 'It was a good day for Ireland.'

Joe Walsh: 'One memory? At the end of the match the players throw their tops, T-shirts, socks and underwear into a pile in the middle of the floor. Johnny (Fallon) usually gives me a hand to collect it. So they'd all gone, the dressing room was empty and we're going through "the rubble", as Johnny calls it. In the middle of the pile is Jimmy Floyd Hasselbaink's jersey! And it's funny, but I had seen him with it on before the game and he looked magnificent. But here it was now among the dirty T-shirts and jocks, the neck and waistband ripped, all wet and limp. And for me that just summed up the day and how Holland must have been feeling.'

13

'What if a demon crept after you one day or night in your loneliest solitude and said to you: "This life as you live it now and have lived it, you will have to live again and again, time without number; and there will be nothing new in it, but every pain and every joy and every thought and sigh and all the unspeakably small and great in your life must return to you. ... The eternal hourglass of existence will be turned again and again – and you with it, you dust of dust." Would you not throw yourself down and gnash your teeth and curse the demon who thus spoke?' – Friedrich Nietzsche

14

Who's Friedrich Nietzsche? What team did he ever play for? One thing's for sure, if he had been wearing the number 7 shirt at Lansdowne Road on 1 September 2001 he would never have written that tosh. Although, in fairness, he definitely would have described it better.

Me? I'm still struggling to find the words: the ball dropping at my feet like manna from heaven, the net bulging before I've even had a chance to think, and then the joy, the indescribable joy. Arms outstretched and running towards the corner flag. Kevin running over, Mattie running over, Roy running over. Yeah, Roy running over with a smile on his face, now that's worth money.

And the scenes afterwards. The photographers chasing me round the pitch. The messages on my phone. The interviews on TV. I was a player again. A real footballer. It didn't really hit me until the dressing room when I was alone in the shower.

Don't know what came over me. Thought about Lisa and Harry and the rough ride we've had lately, Lisa's parents dying, the hassle at Blackburn, and just broke down. Cried my eyes out.

Watched the game again tonight. Don't think I'll ever tire of it. Went to bed with a smile on my face.

And if that demon did creep up and say: 'This life as you live it now and have lived it, you will live it over and over again' there would be no gnashing of teeth. I'd say, 'Thanks very much mate, look forward to it.' And I would. I've loved every moment of it. I would not change a thing.

II

A NATION'S HEARTBEAT

If you get it hard in life, you'll have the resolve to keep going.

THE BALLAD OF SEAMUS O'ROURKE

DAVID WALSH

He was once told that he was from Leitrim and he would always lose. But he didn't see it that way.

21 AUGUST 1994

On a winter's night six months ago Seamus O'Rourke left Peter Donohue's public house in Carrigallen. He'd taken a few pints and the night drained him of his last pounds. By the time he got home, O'Rourke's spirits were low.

He didn't feel like going directly to bed and went outside. There he sat in the darkness and thought about Druminchin, his part of Leitrim. As the thoughts came, he tried to sort them.

Maybe it was his mood but the images were plentiful and he easily found the words to express them. As he sifted and sorted, he chose the words that sounded right.

A carpenter by trade, O'Rourke wouldn't have dreamt of writing anything down. But the intensity of the exploration brought its own reward. By the time he was ready to go to bed, he felt better.

For days and weeks afterwards he would recall the lines which flowed that night. He called his little poem, 'Druminchin Hills'.

Seamus O'Rourke was big for his age. And talented too. On the football field, he cruised when others ran for their lives. As an Under-16, he was judged the best player in Leitrim and knowing men said 'this O'Rourke is going to be a good one'.

His first game for the Leitrim seniors was a challenge against Meath in Kells. It was 1983, he was seventeen and picked at centre field. At half-time someone said: 'Do you know the man you're marking, O'Rourke? That's Gerry McEntee and you're destroyin' him.'

One year he played for the Leitrim minors, Under-21s, juniors and seniors. Those who watch these things say he is the only Leitrim man to have played for all four teams in the same year.

But Seamus O'Rourke didn't believe what they said about him. And anyway, Leitrim men did well not to get carried away. Friends said Seamus lacked a bit of confidence.

He remembers going home one evening after playing for the county Under-16s. It was his fourth game for the team and the fourth consecutive defeat. He didn't understand why they always lost and he complained to his father, Jim.

'I'll tell you why you always lose,' Jim said. 'You're from Leitrim, that's why.'

At the time, Seamus O'Rourke didn't see it like that. The tide would turn. But it didn't. And as one defeat followed another, the boy saw the sense in what his father said.

He was nineteen when his club Carrigallen went to New York. It was a short trip but Seamus stayed on. There was plenty of work in the Big Apple and he could earn good money.

Early the following year he was asked to come home and play with the Leitrim Under-21s. He remembers the Galway man he worked with: 'Ye mean you're prepared to leave a job, twenty dollars an hour, to go home and kick football for Leitrim. Are you mad or something?'

Seamus didn't answer. He just went home.

A stone heavier, he reassured himself if Leitrim got a run in the championship, he would regain his old fitness. If …

Within a few years they were saying it was a pity about O'Rourke. So much ability as a minor. Never really made it. Inclined to get heavy, they said. He played his best when some fellow hit him a box. Not determined enough.

Seamus heard all that and it bothered him. In his mind, he went onto the pitch full of determination. He thinks he lacked belief, in himself and in Leitrim. And if you didn't believe things were going to get better, things didn't get better.

As a footballer, he began losing hope at around twenty. He played for four or five years with the Leitrim seniors. They did no good and that was no surprise.

Seamus knew he was losing it. At twenty he wasn't as good as he had been at nineteen, at twenty-one he was worse than he was at twenty. The extra pounds picked up in New York in 1985 survived the rigours of football in Carrigallen and Leitrim.

Cathal Farrelly decided to get an early night before the day of the Connacht final. But the phone rang a little after midnight. It was his close friend, Seamus O'Rourke. Typical O'Rourke.

'You know we're goin' to the match tomorrow,' said O'Rourke.

'Yes?'

'You wouldn't mind if Sean Donnelly and Tommy Battles travelled with us as well?'

'No, I wouldn't.'

'But one thing, Donnelly says he won't come if I put bacon in the sandwiches.'

'Tell him he can starve.'

'You're right. By the way, you wouldn't come down and join us for a pint?'

'No, I wouldn't.'

Farrelly did a strange thing that Sunday morning. He brought his car down to Paddy McCann's supermarket in Carrigallen and had it washed. In the way that a man might wash his car on the morning of a wedding.

O'Rourke, Donnelly and Battles were supposed to be waiting outside the Kilbracken Arms at twelve o'clock. One of them was there, the other two were dragged from a pub further up the street.

Donnelly sat in the front passenger's seat, holding a Leitrim flag out the window and, along the way, they discussed the match. All but Tommy Battles were hopeful. Battles thought little of Leitrim's chances, ever.

'Weeds of men, you get in Leitrim,' he'd say. 'Never win anything with them. You need the bigger men you find in Meath.'

The lads knew Tommy wasn't against his own county, it was just that he wanted to prepare himself for any disappointments the day might bring.

Farrelly and O'Rourke had stand tickets, Donnelly and Battles were on the sideline. Two Mayo men sat beside Farrelly and O'Rourke; one of them was a priest home from Peru. The Mayo men felt no great affinity with their representatives and, a long way from the end, were telling the Leitrim men they deserved the victory that was coming their way.

Cathal Farrelly thought they didn't know Leitrim. As a child, his father had taken him to the Connacht finals of '57, '58, '59 and '60. Each time Leitrim was beaten by Galway. And now he still expected something would happen to keep Leitrim in its place.

'We'll go down to the pitch,' he said to O'Rourke when the last whistle sounded. He met faces he recognised from other championship games. 'People,' he said, 'that had gone grey since you last saw them.'

Seamus O'Rourke stood on the pitch and didn't know what to think. The breakthrough that he never expected had happened.[1] He talked with Noel Maxwell,

---

1 Leitrim's victory over Mayo in the 1994 Connacht final on a scoreline of 0–12 to 2–4 was only the county's second provincial success, and came sixty-seven years after the first, in 1927.

exchanged a thumbs-up with Jimmy Ward, both former Leitrim players. O'Rourke saw in Maxwell and Ward the same emotions he himself was experiencing. 'I reckon it was a strange thing for anyone who had played for Leitrim. You were delighted this had happened and a little sad that you weren't part of it.'

They got back to the car and hoped Donnelly and Battles would show up. They did. It was time for the 7UP and bacon sandwiches. The other three waited to see what Donnelly would do with the bacon sandwiches.

He ate them.

The journey home was hell.

No agreement could be reached on where they would stop. Carrick would be too packed, no comfort. Sean Donnelly was for Lanesboro, which had the advantage of being near. O'Rourke and Battles were inclined to go with that.

Farrelly wanted to get closer to Drumlish in Co. Longford. 'There'll be a great feckin' atmosphere in Drumlish alright,' said Donnelly, mustering up as much contempt as he could. But the driver decided and their first pint was in O'Reilly's of Drumlish.

Donnelly was right about the atmosphere and, around seven, they left Drumlish, giving themselves enough time to get to the Breffni Arms in Arva for *The Sunday Game*. Arva is in Co. Cavan, a couple of miles over the border from Leitrim and just three miles away from Carrigallen.

It was no accident they chose Arva for, as Leitrim men, they didn't mind their Cavan neighbours seeing them on such a night. Soon the Breffni Arms was filling as Leitrim folk returned from the game.

Philip and Sean McIntyre, uncles of Declan Darcy, joined the company now rich with Carrigallen people. Eamonn Grey, owner of the pub, was one of the last to get back from the match and he put up a drink for every person in the bar. Leitrim's win was being celebrated.

Someone called for a song and Farrelly did 'The Fields of Athenry'. The pints were flowing and the night flying. Men from Longford and Cavan wore Leitrim colours and Tommy Battles said Down would win the All-Ireland, he couldn't see them bet.

Sean Donnelly sang 'Will You Go, Lassie, Go':

Oh the summertime is coming
And the trees are sweetly blooming
And the wild mountain thyme
Grows around the blooming heather …

That captured the mood. Life couldn't have been better. And Seamus O'Rourke was savouring every moment of it. He liked especially when someone sang and there was quietness. It gave a man the chance to think about the day, the achievement. He tried to figure out why it was so damn important. And he put it down to this: Leitrim's win allowed the county to take its place with all the others, to be considered no different. That was all it ever wanted.

It was around two o'clock in the morning when Farrelly called on him to recite 'Druminchin Hills', his little poem about his part of Leitrim. Philip and Sean McIntyre were still in the company and, from the townland of Curraghboy, they knew Druminchin well.

Many others wouldn't have known but they sensed they were about to hear a man's heartfelt thoughts about his home area. A silence descended before Seamus began to recite, not the silence before a song but the silence before something more serious.

Seamus began:

Lie down flat you Druminchin hills
For there's damn-all for you to see
And there's no one looks at your rushy sides
Or your mossy bottom down at Kelly's drain
And what sod you have can go to sleep
For hungry sheep would rather wait to die
And young men pass by and walk on to prouder, flatter land
In parts of Cavan and up near Mullingar
Aye, and I'll sit beside you now
And sing songs of times gone by
When young men made hay with the fork
And drank tae from a bottle
And hid their joy in your drauchy camouflage
What right have you to stand so proud
Among the whin and the whitethorn bush
What crop did you ever yield
That wasn't washed away in the autumn flood
What good could your God have meant
When backs were bent lifting watery spuds
And cattle walked knee-deep in your daub and mud
In your unsheltered fields

You're as auld as the hills, Druminchin
And you'll be there for ever more
Crushed between Kilerrin and the walls of Newtowngore
No foreigner shall ever plant his trees in your channelly ground
Not a rood of your unsheltered fields shall be sold for a Government pound
You're as auld as the hills, Druminchin
You're my Druminchin hills.

It was left to O'Rourke to drive the others home. Farrelly, they would decide the next day, had played a good first half. Late in the night, he wilted. Battles and Donnelly stood up well.

As for O'Rourke himself, he couldn't have been more satisfied. Leitrim was no different to the rest.

He got home to his Druminchin hill and went directly to bed.

REAL WORLD IS FAR FROM THE MADDING CROWD

DERMOT CROWE

Tradition and toil keep the flame alive for the GAA in every corner.

25 JANUARY 2009

Every GAA follower will have had a relationship with their club, and many will take another, the latter grouping rendering the recent sponsorship slogan of 'one life, one club' somewhat unsound. In the twenty-five years since the GAA's centenary there have been massive demographic and social changes that require clubs, the prized lifeblood of the Association, to respond and adapt, or face possible ruin.

The most telling impact has been the movement of people east, to Dublin and its surrounding hinterland, flooding the capital with greater playing resources and impacting profoundly on the existing club matrix. Over forty per cent of the population of the Republic resides in this area, a breeding ground for new clubs and a fresh challenge to those already established. Old clubs that catered for country players have folded and the once redoubtable bastion of Dublin purity, St Vincent's, won an All-Ireland last year with almost a third of the team from the country.

Whereas it was once regarded as an act of hideous betrayal to leave home and sign for another club, this is now a great deal more commonplace and socially acceptable. The demands of work and the contraction of leisure time, in what has been described as a time-poor modern society, have contributed to this need for versatility and compromise.

And yet, still you will find young men and women leaving their jobs in Dublin and other scattered parts to drive through the evening traffic so that they can serve the home club. For them, nothing will surpass the visceral thrill they achieve by pulling on their own native colours and following, perhaps, in the footsteps of a father and grandfather whose exploits are still recalled.

Clubs are faced with all sorts of modern pressures: competing in the larger urban areas for players; competing with other sports; denied their best hurlers and footballers because of the overbearing demands of the county team; competing with the dire and shocking instability of the annual fixtures schedule.

For many years club players had too few games, and now the chronic problem is that there are too many gaps in their playing time and competitions are left unfinished. County boards are grievously failing in their duty to provide a dependable service on that score. Too many club players cannot plan a life around their playing duties with any degree of certainty.

The future welfare of the clubs, the new GAA director-general Páraic Duffy has claimed, is the most important issue for the Association. That will come as a great comfort to the thousands for whom it is their chosen outlet and source of infinite joy. The club is the starting point and the finishing point for most players, supporters and members of the GAA. Long may it stay that way.

NO PLACE LIKE HOME

To appreciate true sacrifice, a winter match near Keel Beach on Achill Island is recommended. Faced with wind gusting in over the grey Atlantic and temperatures dipping unsympathetically, it is no place for fancy-dans and those of a delicate disposition. The goalposts are wooden, stripped bare and without ornamentation, and still they qualify as the venue's greatest extravagance. There are no dressing rooms and, on this wild late afternoon in January, no pitch marks or trace of life, past or present.

Last year when Davitt Park, the main pitch near the island's mainland bridge, wasn't available, the local team hosted two matches at Keel, dragging visitors from Shrule and other parts of Mayo further away from the civilised world. Packie McGinty, chairman of Achill GAA club, remembers matches played here among the island's village teams for the Scanlon Cup, a competition that started in the 1950s and is now defunct. It featured scores of emigrants home for a few months after Christmas to work the land, before heading back to London or America by Easter.

Achill has long grown accustomed to its young men heading away for work. In the Scanlon Cup, sport cut its cloth to measure. Packie's father was away from home for most of his life, working in London, from where he would send back money. Much of the finance needed to develop Davitt Park came from emigrant pockets. The McGintys' experience was not unique; the majority of families at one time did not see their fathers during their working lives except for Christmas and a short time after. The GAA provided some distraction from those realities, even when, as Packie says, the players were so blue from the cold at Keel that they could not take off their boots.

One Sunday in the 1960s, Packie played in a county minor final and the next day, aged seventeen, he was on his way to London to find work. He's home and settled now, with a grown-up family, having spent ten years in London as a carpenter and then a little more time in the Middle East and Dublin to help finance the building of a new home in his native place. Holiday homes have flourished in Achill in the last twenty years and that has kept him in regular and local employment. He doesn't drink. The club is his indulgence, his means of winding down and forgetting his ills and ailments.

It is all relative, of course. Early in the current decade, in much better times economically, the club decided it needed to roll up its sleeves and turn its fortunes around. Playing Division 5 football brought them to Clare Island for a match, which was a stark reminder that they needed to take stock. Around that time one of their players noticed a local newspaper poll showing the top forty clubs in Mayo, and Achill didn't feature. He stored it away but highlighted the omission when they won the junior football championship in 2007 with a stirring display of football.

Nothing comes easy for Achill, even in better times. Most of their players are dotted around the country and they all made selfless commitments to be back on the Friday nights for training in 2007, availing of the floodlights installed a few years ago, the first in Mayo. The lights meant they could train late after eventually getting through the Friday evening traffic and arriving at their westerly destination. No one asked for travel expenses. Most of them grew up together and that day in Castlebar when they won the junior championship they all bundled into a giddy and delirious heap for the victorious photograph. Packie McGinty says it was his proudest day as an Achill GAA man.

His brother, Hughie, is the club treasurer. Achill isn't, he admits, Chelsea. They have to earn every cent through the weekly lottery and other fundraising ventures to raise the €40,000 or so that is needed annually to break even. To register every team costs money. They are also obliged to sell tickets for the county board to pay for McHale Park's redevelopment. Being where they are means travelling to matches can weigh adversely on the annual balance sheet.

Of a family of seven, all of the McGintys, like their father, emigrated, although four are now back in Achill or living close by. After London, Packie threw himself back into the club. London had its charms. "'Where do you play?" they'd ask you, and a lad would say "I can play anywhere" – they'd be using that for work,' says

Hughie. 'It (football in London) was a great outlet but at the same time it wasn't like here. There was no identity.'

Packie met his wife, a Wexford woman, in the Galtymore in Cricklewood.[1] They celebrated their fortieth anniversary recently. 'You always thought with so many Achill men in the one area in Cricklewood, if they were all back home, how many titles could we have won? I came back at twenty-seven and played till I was forty-two.'

Hughie: 'I was away for twenty years, I will never forget the day I came home: 10 March '95.'

Faced with a drain on resources, Achill had to find some way of getting by. 'It was survival,' says Packie. 'Sometimes on a Sunday you would have no more than eleven players, you were playing lads just to make up the numbers. There were great people in the club who held it together.'

Founded in 1941, Achill had a tradition of football among the different villages on the island, which measures fifty-seven square miles. They played one year at senior and there is one survivor from the team which followed the first junior title in 1942, John Cooney. Most of their time since has been spent in junior ranks. Last year they were squeezed out of the intermediate championship quarter-finals on score difference. They believe they are capable of winning one.

The McGintys recall the teams they had at underage in the 1960s before most of their players moved away. 'Didn't matter what team (we met) in the county,' says Packie. 'Castlebar was the strongest that time; we played them thirteen times, and I think Achill had the seven and Castlebar the six.' Michael McNamara, a local councillor and schoolteacher, managed the Achill team that won the Mayo junior championship in 2007. They reached the Connacht final but lost by a few points in Ballinasloe, hitting a feast of wides. Last year they won the All-Ireland junior sevens. The ambition that exists now is unprecedented.

'We started training in January and I'd say we'd have trained three times a week and they (players living away) would have travelled at their own expense. About a dozen might be present on a Wednesday night and you might be lucky if there were half of those on the team,' McNamara outlines. 'Our main trainer would have come from Galway. Others from Limerick, Athlone, Dublin; we were lucky in that they were nearly all single lads. One older lad in his thirties did travel from Clonee (in

---

1   The Galtymore was an iconic dance hall located in Cricklewood, north London. First opened in 1952, it was a popular draw for Irish emigrants throughout the following decades. The venue closed its doors in 2008.

Meath); he has a family. He played with Thomas Davis for most of his adult career but he joined us two years ago and commuted up and down.'

Packie recalls the day the pitch was opened in 2002 after a drainage job on the surface and the construction of a new stand, installation of floodlights and improved changing facilities. Dublin arrived down to play Mayo in a challenge.

'They parked out there,' signals Michael McNamara from a local hotel room, 'and the poor lads from Dublin thought they were going to get drowned. The tide was in.'

Afterwards, they adjourned to the same hotel for refreshments and Shane MacGowan walked in with his mother after visiting the locally based House of Prayer. He gave an impromptu performance for twenty minutes. Packie jokes that Achill GAA had him booked specially for the event.

The population has stabilised, Michael McNamara believes, though the current recession may create more uncertainty and reawaken familiar challenges. If the weather is too hard for Achill men, they have the use of a large gymnasium, and if Davitt Park is over-used and needs rest, there is, like the last place on earth, Keel.

The club is benefitting from the hard work of the last ten years.

Colm Cafferkey has been on the Mayo senior panel for a few years and they are expecting up to three club men on this year's Under-21 panel. In the past, players from Achill have won All-Ireland minor and Under-21 medals for Mayo.

'I have to say my dream would be Mayo to win Sam Maguire and there's an Achill man on the team,' says Michael McNamara. 'That would be fantastic, that would be fantastic for the club.'

And as the winds roar over Clew Bay, the McGinty brothers nod in agreement. There's no place like home.

THE FIRE REMAINS LIT

In a large farmhouse in Cavan, Peadar MacSeain, whose father was a founding member, rallies to the cause of the once opulent Cornafean. A winner of a record twenty senior football championship titles, renowned as the famous Reds, they now languish in junior ranks: a fortune squandered. Peadar was on the last team to win a senior title in 1956 and proved a conspicuously vocal presence when following his sons in later life, enjoying their junior success in 2000 in which three took part.

They are still way ahead on the senior football roll of honour, but a series of factors have conspired to consign them to the more humble company they keep today. The club was founded in 1908 and a year later won its first championship. John Joe O'Reilly played for Cornafean for a brief spell before moving to the

Curragh with the army, and his brother (Big) Tom was a long-serving hero, still talked about in reverential tones.

Some fine players came from the outskirts, from Killeshandra and Arvagh, to play for the Reds in those days of plenty because they had a senior team and it offered blow-ins a route to the county team. When Cavan reigned supreme, so too did Cornafean, but after 1956 they began the slow decline into what the author of the club history, local schoolteacher George Cartwright, would label frankly the 'years of despair'.

In Peadar MacSeain's house, it is easier to extract stories about the good times than the hard ones that followed. Rural depopulation, averaging twenty-six per cent for parts of rural Cavan around where Cornafean is located, depleted playing resources, whereas the neighbouring clubs improved, became more independent and held on to their footballers. All of this helped erode Cornafean's invincibility. When Cartwright was growing up in the 1960s, he can remember the opening of the local pitch and Galway arriving as guests at a time when Cornafean was still a strong contender. But the decay had started. MacSeain's sons refer morbidly to 'the Seventies' when asked what qualified as rock bottom, a time when their fortunes went into freefall.

In his book on Cornafean, an excellent production entitled *Up the Reds*, Cartwright admits that the club felt a sense of 'hopelessness' during its gradual decline from the mid-1960s into the next decade. In 1972 Cootehill met them in the first round of the senior championship and won 4–19 to 0–5. Cornafean had always found players; now they were paying the price for not having initiated a proper underage strategy.

They spent their last year in senior ranks in 1974, and in 1978 against Belturbet in the first round of the junior championship they barely scraped together fifteen players. The next year they were beaten by thirteen points in the first round at junior level and in 1980 they lost by fourteen. One of the club's legends, Paudge Masterson, said in an interview that players would laugh off a twenty-point defeat whereas in his day Cornafean men would cry their way off the field after a one-point reversal against Cavan Slashers.

They don't have good footballers falling off every tree like they had then. In the place of football success, the less celebrated pastime of Scór has provided some solace and brought titles to Cornafean, driven by a local enthusiast, Paddy McDermott.[2] The

---

2   Scór is a competition among clubs organised by the GAA, featuring a number of events focused around traditional dancing, music and singing.

exploits of local athlete Catherina McKiernan have also given them something to shout about. Her brother, Peadar, was the last Cornafean player to represent Cavan in the championship around twenty years ago.

And for all that, you don't win twenty championships and not retain some measure of self-esteem for the rainy day. Peadar MacSeain is unflinching: he talks unstoppably about what makes a good team, the value of determination, and why Cornafean wore their red colours with such resolute pride.

'The Reds were the Reds and no white,' he says, meaning that any modern white cuffs or trimmings would amount to sacrilege, a betrayal of their tradition; it simply wasn't up for negotiation. He gave a grandchild a gift of a Cornafean shirt some time ago and made sure it was all red – pure and unspoilt, like the old days.

For the '56 county final against Bailieboro, there was the prospect of a clash of colours and Cornafean would not give way. 'We said we wouldn't change, we were going to play with red jerseys,' says Peadar. 'We'd have played in our skin, we wouldn't put any other team's jersey on – that's the truth.'

Those in surrounding areas may shake their heads at the enduring confidence in Cornafean long after they were a force in the game. They will accuse them of profiting from players from outside their borders. They'll joke how they now have a lovely ground and no players, whereas in the past it was the other way around.

In 1933 and '35, Cornafean had four players on the teams that won Cavan All-Ireland titles, and in 1947 in the Polo Grounds the Cavan centre-back and captain John Joe O'Reilly further embellished the Cornafean story. Footballers were on every road. As a boy, George Cartwright used to get his hair cut by neighbour Josie Martin, who played for Cavan and won nine senior club championship medals.

Also close to where Cartwright lives is Sean Masterson, now eighty, an amiable and soft-spoken farmer who was another member of the '56 team. He takes a break from feeding cattle on this miserably windy and cold January day to talk about days past and the players he saw and admired.

He welcomed the junior championship nine years ago but admits that back in his time it would have been barely acknowledged. 'They won a junior championship in Cornafean way back and the presentation of medals was up in the hall. And they got a crate of stout and went away over and lay down on hay and they drank the stout and they didn't go near the presentation. It didn't mean a thing.'

His hero was 'Big' Tom O'Reilly and he has paid tribute to him in verse. 'Like, Tom was streets ahead of John Joe. Big Tom played his heart out for Cornafean. He could catch it one hand on his shoulder.' And then he recites in a mellow Cavan lilt: 'I remember the great men, a pity they grew older; I remember Big Tom with one hand, bring the ball down on his shoulder.'

Most of the old footballers have passed away, but in people like Cartwright, Masterson, MacSeain, and those who still love Cornafean and what it represents, the fire remains lit. 'Look,' says Cartwright, 'I know that Cornafean would have been despised in the county because they won so much and there was an arrogance about them. That is a legacy of too much success. Everyone loves the underdog.'

To paraphrase Brendan Behan's wife: they've seen the two days.

FOREVER YOUNG

In the Faughs clubhouse lounge in Templeogue, you can pay homage to a famous past in between buying rounds. Part social hub, part museum, the odour is old world. Among the exhibits is a trophy cabinet containing the All-Ireland hurling trophy that preceded the MacCarthy Cup, won in 1920 by Faughs when representing Dublin; photographs of triumphant Faughs teams stretching back to the nineteenth century; and long-serving chairmen saluting you from wooden panels where their names are respectfully carved.

This is an ancient order. The GAA's formation and that of Faughs go almost hand-in-hand, only a year dividing them, and Michael Cusack bore witness to both landmark events. It was in his Civil Service academy headquarters in Dublin, now the location of the Dergvale Hotel, where the Faughs club was founded and the name agreed. The inaugural year, 1885, is displayed defiantly on the clubhouse exterior, like a declaration of immortality.

Through many of the key moments in Ireland's emergence as a nation Faughs was present. Harry Boland, later killed in the Civil War, and friend to Michael Collins, won championships with the club, hurling at full-back, and later served as chairman of Dublin County Board. Over the generations that followed, numerous esteemed hurlers found a home at Faughs when their work took them to Dublin.

But for such a long existence, it wasn't until 1981 that the club could say it had a permanent home. That year they moved to their current location and began developing facilities and looking to the future, realising that the world in which Faughs lived for generations had changed a great deal. Unless it changed, it would die. Other clubs that served the city's rural settlers fell by the wayside but Faughs has managed to adapt to ensure its survival. Eamonn Rea had almost given up hurling when Faughs and he converged in 1970 and he went on to win championships on teams that formed a rainbow coalition of players from different counties. In the next decade, the current chairman P.J. Newman arrived from a junior club, Delvin, in Westmeath. P.J. remembers training in Terenure and having to play their matches away before they finally got a settled home. For most of the club's lifetime moving about has been par for the course.

In Rea's playing days, there were two adult hurling teams to look after and no underage structure but that had to change. Over the past twenty years the transition from being a safe house for capital-based rural hurlers to a club rearing its own talent from the local neighbourhoods has been in full swing.

Benefiting from a thriving GAA coaching programme in Dublin, Faughs have adapted to the modern era and now cater for kids from six all the way up to their adult teams. The senior hurling team is now evenly split between country and home-grown talent. As the years move on, the balance will tilt more towards locally produced hurlers, as Faughs look to add to their record thirty-one senior hurling championship title wins, this year marking the tenth anniversary of their last success.

'I used to travel home to Delvin for matches,' says Newman, 'but my brother had been with Faughs and I eventually signed. I settled in, I enjoyed it. I felt at home. I never really missed going back to play with Delvin after that. It was only culchies and rednecks who played hurling in Dublin then, but you go into the city now and see lads walking around with hurls and it's now cool to play hurling.'

Rea, winner of an All-Ireland medal with Limerick in 1973, played with O'Toole's initially after coming to Dublin just over forty years ago. He can't recall exactly why he then moved to Faughs but he went on to add sixteen years' service as club chairman. He talks of his first championship won with Faughs, against St Vincent's, the Dublin thoroughbreds, and the good relations that have existed between the clubs. They made a point of going for a drink in the clubhouses at away games and invite others to do the same when hosting matches at their own headquarters.

Even in this clubhouse where the legacy is so visible, there is nothing stuffy or conceited about the men who welcome you in. That has been the success of Faughs and it promises to lead them back into the good times again. Already their underage work is bearing fruit, with hurlers being grafted onto county development squads and successes posted at minor and Under-16 B level. Further down the age graph, they are competing at the top tier. They are a purely hurling club, although there is an early Dublin football championship holding up their large stash of honours.

Some of the parents of their young players have no GAA background and Rea tells of one rugby man from Terenure who has, as all are encouraged to, become immersed in the club's activities. He is talking high stakes, about winning an All-Ireland club.

Fittingly, the cup awarded to the All-Ireland club champions perpetuates the memory of the Faughs chairman, Tommy Moore, who served in that role for almost forty years, a publican from Kilkenny whose influence is fondly recalled and warmly appreciated.

Next year Faughs will celebrate 125 years in existence. They hope to mark the milestone by bringing Marcus de Burca's history of the club, published in 1985 for the 100th anniversary, up to date. In the time since, the aspiration of establishing a viable juvenile structure has been fulfilled and Faughs continue to remain a colossus in the tradition of GAA clubs. Forever young.

05

YOU HAD TO SHOW WHO WAS BOSS

MICK DOYLE

Paddy 'Bawn' Brosnan is one of the true legends of Gaelic football – and in more ways than one.

28 JUNE 1992

I was a fairly handy sprinter. I gave up drinking once, for a fortnight, before the Dingle sports. I came last. I had a good feed of pints that night and challenged the lads to another contest the next day. I won. From that day, I never gave up the drink before an event. Dr Eamon (no, not the Bishop) allowed me three pints a day during serious training. He knew what he was at.

So speaketh Paddy 'Bawn' Brosnan this week in sun-drenched Dingle, where near-naked tourists were flaunting it on bikes and the locals were daring them. The barony of Corca Dhuibhne never looked so good as we drove around Slea Head. The fishing boats, the white beaches, the familiar salutations of the locals and the smell of fresh seaweed re-awakened dormant dreams and evoked the promiscuous promises of a longer visit in the near future.

The convivial surroundings of O'Cathain's in Ballyferriter, Quinns of Ventry and the warm embrace of Ventry Bay unlocked the memories and made my day with Paddy Bawn a truly memorable one.

I have much to tell you but the gist will have to do.

Paddy Bawn is one of the true legends of Gaelic football and in more ways than one. He and the late Tom Clifford have much in common – physique, mental and physical ruggedness, gentleness and good humour. Both were great sportsmen. I feel as if I have known Paddy Bawn all my life.

I remember long-gone summer heatwaves and sitting round my grandfather's radio in Dan Sullivan's yard in Currow village with the men and other young boys listening to the incomparable Michael O'Hehir's stirring commentaries as he brought the games to life with the deeds of Joe Keohane, 'Gega' O'Connor and Paddy Bawn.

My youthful fantasies were given substance when I saw him play in Currow's sportsfield against a Tom Shanahan-inspired Castleisland team around 1951–52. Only five foot ten-and-a-half inches and fourteen stone four pounds, Bawn was a huge physical presence on the field, lording over all and prowling the square like a stalking lion with tawny blond mane, protecting his patch and his goalie.

I have clear memories of regular melees in the square with the ball disappearing for minutes, and it didn't matter, shouts of approval heralding Paddy Bawn's emergence, ball clutched to his chest, body hunched forward in a straight line, like the prow of a fishing boat scattering mere mortals left and right like helpless wavelets.

'There was glamour and pride in full-back lines in those days,' said Paddy. 'And you had to show the forwards who was boss. Dr Eamon had us looking after our own zones and we never ventured too far upfield. The goalie was fair game and we had to protect him. With the catch and kick game, the ball moved very quickly so you couldn't be running around much. The game has changed a lot … and not all for the better.'

Brosnan was born in Dingle on 16 November 1917, to Timothy Brosnan and Ellen Johnson – the fourth of eight children, four boys and four girls. His primary and secondary schooling was in Dingle where 'the Brothers hardened me up a lot. I got it easy though, because I was playing,' he admits.

Between 1933 and 1936, he won many schools/colleges medals but lost the senior cup to North Monastery – a game which also starred budding Taoiseach Jack Lynch.

In 1937 he served as solicitor's clerk to Paddy Fitzgibbon for six months, but the lure of the sea propelled him to fishing on 'the *Rory*' – his father's boat.

'We used to land our catches on Valentia Island early the next morning,' said Paddy, 'and I'd spend a while kicking a ball around till it came time to go out fishing again that evening. I brought the ball along always. I was fishing off Galway one Saturday with my uncle Paddy, rough weather almost drove us into the Shannon estuary, but I told the uncle I had to get home for a county championship match the following day. We made it home – just about.'

He worked his own boat – the *Ros Dubh* – a fifty-foot trawler, from 1951 to 1962, crewed by his brother, Timmy, and two local men, Tadhg Brosnan and Tim Devane. It is now in Arklow, he thinks, still working.

'Gega' O'Connor, Joe Keohane, Sean Brosnan and Bill Casey were among his contemporaries in Dingle. 'Gega was the fittest player I ever saw,' he says. 'He had a gym at home above the pub and he would skip a mile and back each day collecting the cows. Back in the forties, the boots were heavy and ignorant, with two caps like steel. The ball became heavy as lead when it rained, there were no showers only a cold tap, and tracksuits were for fairies. We had only one ball to train with in Dingle and sixteen of us would play backs and forwards for hours.

'Unless you were a good fielder, you didn't get a kick. I believe the art of high fielding is a rarity today; the fact that there are almost as many balls as players at the training sessions, the real close contact is missing and training is simply not competitive enough.

'There is too much toe-to-hand ball carrying and too much fouling as a consequence. The free taker has too much influence. The ball will always travel faster than it can be carried, you get less nasty fouls and a far better game.'

Brosnan's first game for Kerry seniors was at left full-back against Clare in 1936 in the league; Keohane was full-back. He played full-back against Galway in 1938 and in the All-Ireland championship which Kerry lost. Injury kept him out in 1939 but in 1940 he played left wing-forward to 'Connor' (centre half) and Johnny Walsh (my late friend Father David's brother) making up a fiercesome trio against Galway in the final which Kerry won, and repeated the feat in 1941. In a career spanning fifteen years (1937–52) he won (and lost) three All-Ireland medals, three Railway Cup medals, twelve Munster and six county championship medals.

In 1949 Paddy married a Dingle girl, Eileen Johnson; they had two sons, Pat and John, and a daughter, Maire, who keeps him on his toes. He has six grandchildren. Eileen was much involved in his career and 'gave him the hip' many a Sunday morning to get him up for early Mass on a match day. She died seven years ago and he misses her a lot – naturally.

He gave up fishing in 1965, took to golf like a duck to water and goes to most major GAA occasions. As you would expect, he has definite views of the game and many players. Paddy Kennedy and Mick O'Connell were the best midfielders he has seen and Tom Langan of Mayo the best full-forward he played on. Mick Higgins, Tony Tighe and Joe Stafford, all of Cavan, were great footballers. Sean Purcell of Galway was another to command his admiration.

His best Kerry team was the 1937–41 side which won four All-Irelands, with the recent four-in-a-row side a close second. Pat Spillane, 'Bomber' Liston, Mikey Sheehy and 'Ogie' Moran were favourites of his but, for Paddy Bawn, John Egan was 'the best of them all'.

He has incredible respect for Dr Eamon O'Sullivan, who got the squad of twenty-two together for two weeks before the semi-final and final. 'He was the first real coach in Ireland and a brilliant planner. He was a blackboard man, you learned what you had to do in each position and you did it.

'Kerry is coming again, the depth is there in the youth, Mickey Ned has a good body-building programme going and pride is coming back with a bang. Limerick taught them a lesson.'[1]

His eyes misted over momentarily as he talked about the glamorous All-Irelands and the supporters arriving in their thousands on Sunday morning by 'ghost train'.

'They used to arrive into our bedrooms in Barry's Hotel, just off the train on Sunday morning, and we had to give 'em our beds – an' we playing in the afternoon! Be Jaysus, it wouldn't happen today.

'But supporters then were more a part of the team – they were knowledgeable and we talked with them for hours – we learned a lot too and didn't get swelled heads. I'm not too impressed with today's followers – they are not true supporters.'

Comparisons with different eras can often be a bit fruitless, but I have to agree with Paddy Bawn – 'unless players now have total commitment and jobs that allow them to train regularly all year round, they won't be picked. Many good footballers, because of their occupations, will miss out. Athletes are the in thing.

'But all the impressive work in training in the gym and on the track still won't make a racehorse out of a donkey. Fellas like me wouldn't be picked these days probably.'

As Willie Duggan did in a recent article, Paddy Bawn points out that the fundamentals of high fielding, accurate kicking and fair shouldering have been left behind: 'Television has reshaped the new game and has dictated to the new players. The Man of the Match does nothing for a team.

'In 1952 Kerry "retired me" for the Tipp match without my knowing it; they picked me to play against Cork in the Munster final without my knowing it either. After the match I made off to the nearest pub in my playing gear and had three quick pints. I went back to the hotel and told the County Board that I was now retired for good, in my own time.'

Today, at seventy-five, he is a fine man who enjoys his friends, his pint and his golf. He is obviously proud of the friendships he made across the whole spectrum of

---

1   Although Kerry had beaten Limerick the previous Sunday in the Munster semi-final, for the second year running, it had been a close call. A few weeks after this article was published, Kerry were shocked by Clare in the Munster final.

sport and life. It is the length and breadth of him, the life and soul of him, the pride and manliness of him and the quiet feeling of confident invincibility that make Paddy Bawn so important to me and countless others.

Up Kerry.

06

MORE THAN SPORT:
IT'S A NATION'S HEARTBEAT

EAMONN SWEENEY

In the GAA, everything begins and ends with the club. The country's club championships contain a multitude of stories, generating wild extremes of heartbreak and sorrow – and this is the time of year when the weak become heroes.

7 OCTOBER 2007

If you ask the genuinely committed followers who backbone the GAA whether they'd prefer their county to win an All-Ireland or their club to win a county title, chances are that he or she would plump for the latter option.

Everything begins and ends with the club.

The nation's various club championships contain a multitude of stories. Last weekend, at one end of the spectrum, Crossmaglen Rangers won a remarkable twelfth Armagh senior title in a row. Meanwhile, Clongeen were qualifying for their first ever Wexford football final.

Today more clubs will be trying to achieve almost unimaginable feats and send the small communities they represent into raptures. In Down, Longstone are looking for a first ever senior football title as they take on serial title winners Mayobridge. In Offaly, Shamrocks are also trying to make history with a first football title against Tullamore, who've won a quarter-century of them.

A couple of hurling semi-finals also present the chance for teams to perform once-in-a-lifetime feats. If Killenaule overcome Drom-Inch in their Tipperary hurling semi-final, they'll be in their first decider since 1942. And if the famous Tulla club can get past Clarecastle in the Clare semi, they'll bridge a seventy-four-year gap between final appearances. This is the time of year when the weak become heroes.

I've chosen one county final to represent all the club championship matches which generate such wild extremes of sorrow and heartbreak. It is last Sunday's Longford senior football final between Colmcille and Dromard.

There are few counties where interest in club football reaches the fanatical level which pertains in Longford. The passion which fuels the county championships in the GAA's second-least-populous county has long been a source of both wonder and envy to neighbouring counties such as Westmeath, Leitrim and Roscommon.

Longford's attendances at the blue riband game are usually around the 6,000 or 7,000 mark, a remarkable achievement for a county of 30,000 people. There have been deciders in Cork and Dublin which attracted no greater crowd. And the North Longford area which borders Cavan is the county's football hotbed.

So when I heard that Dromard and Colmcille would be battling it out in this year's Longford final, it seemed too good an opportunity to miss.

Here was a classic local derby, between neighbouring parishes whose pitches are only four miles apart, between a team trying to end a long famine and one which had overcome adversity on and off the pitch this year, between players who all went to the same secondary school, several of whom are bound by ties of blood and marriage, and between two clubs who hail from parishes which number not much more than 700 houses between them, yet have done some remarkable things.

COLMCILLE

Colmcille is traditional football country. The club won the first ever Longford county final, in 1890, and followed up with victories in the 1930s, '40s and '50s. It is the home club of Eugene McGee and of his brother, Fr Phil, a legendary figure in Longford GAA and the driving force behind the establishment of Moyne Community School, the fine football nursery which the players in Sunday's final attended. For good measure it's the ancestral parish on his mother's side of Mel Gibson, or to give him his full name: Mel Colmcille Gerard Gibson.

Yet since 1958 this football-mad parish, centred around the village of Aughna-cliffe, has suffered one heartbreak after another in its attempts to win another county title. Seamus McKeon was full-back on a team which reached six county semi-finals and seemed at times to be jinxed.

'Between 1988 and 1995 we lost several semi-finals by a narrow margin and we could have won all of them. Then we reached the final in 1994; we were six points up at half-time against Longford Slashers and we lost to a goal in the last minute. In 1995 we were two points up in the semi-final against Killoe and they got a penalty in injury time and scored it. It was the last kick of the ball. That was the worst one of all because they walked the county final afterwards. I'm delighted the club are back in the county final, it stops people talking about our team.'

The 1994 heartbreaker was Colmcille's last final before this year's decider. Their championship run was notable for being achieved without a home pitch to train on. 'We developed an all-weather pitch this year and it wasn't ready for the team, so we've been training on the pitch at Shroid outside Longford and at Longford Rugby Club, and we've done a good bit of training in the gym in Longford,' notes Chairman Seamus Treacy.

Perhaps it wasn't surprising that Colmcille weren't among the championship favourites at the start of the season (someone tells me he got them at 8/1 in the bookies back then). But they're favourites now, after a series of sparkling displays which have seen them average sixteen points a game and clock up a 4–11, a 2–15 and a ten-point win over Dromard before their neighbours came in the back door. Former Cavan star Ciaran Brady, from neighbouring Gowna, has worked wonders in his first year as manager.

The sense that forty-nine years of hurt may be about to come to an end is palpable in the clubhouse. They know this is a talented bunch of players. 'A lot of them were on the team that won the club's first Under-14 championship in 1994. They won a county juvenile title and three Under-21 counties in-a-row,' says Treacy. This is Colmcille's Golden Generation.

Yet the club members are taking nothing for granted. McKeon remembers going to a meeting in 1978 when it was proposed to disband Colmcille altogether, emigration having demoralised the club to such an extent that a total of five players had turned up for a training session. And then there's the local dimension. The rivalry between the parishes is so keen, someone jokes, that they've started calling a road between Dromard and Colmcille 'The Gaza Strip'.

'We might never play Dromard again in a county final, it's like Cork playing Kerry in the All-Ireland,' muses McKeon. 'The result will be felt for a long time by whoever loses,' adds Treacy.

The thought of defeat seems to momentarily dampen the spirits before Pearse Daly, club delegate to the County Board for the last fifty-two years, invokes club tradition.

'There's a link with 1890,' he says. 'Our top scorer Donie McKeon is the great grandson of a player from that team.'

So it goes with GAA clubs. No matter how forward-looking they are, the past is always there to give them sustenance.

DROMARD

Dromard is the most impressive GAA club I've ever seen. I've seen some great ones but none quite like this North Longford outfit, based in a parish where there isn't even a pub let alone a village and apparently determined to maximise the effect a club can have on a community.

There's Páirc na nGael for a start, a superb pitch which boasts a covered stand with seats on one side and the kind of graduated terracing more commonly seen in inter-county grounds on the other. There's a fine clubhouse too and a crèche on the club grounds, run by the community, which looks after fifty local kids. But the most impressive thing of all is that Dromard are only getting started.

Club chairman Joe Murphy explains: 'We're looking to build a youth café where young people can come, play a bit of pool, listen to music, do their thing, without having to go to the pub. We'll also have an Astroturf pitch, a couple of five-a-side pitches, a gymnasium and a place for the aged, where they can maybe play bowls. We're planning to invest €750,000 to start, and when it's all fitted out and furnished there'll be over a million spent.'

It kind of beggars belief that a club based in a sparsely populated area like Dromard could pull off something like this. Then again, they've done it before.

'We used to have an old pitch that was very wet. We tried for years to buy it off the farmer but it didn't work out,' explains vice-Chairman Paul Hourican. 'We got this piece of land from the County Council. It was a pure hill with a twenty-five or thirty foot drop on it, we said there was no way we'd put a pitch here.'

'People thought we weren't right in the head when we started in 1992,' adds Murphy. 'All our players were going away, we'd bring them through to Under-16 and minor and then they'd go to England or America. But we did all kinds of fundraising, we even bought twenty-five heifers at a local mart and gave one each to local farmers. They raised them till they were a suitable age for sale as springers. We had a lot of fun.'

As often happens, doing the right thing off the pitch led to success on it. Dromard won their first senior title since 1946 in 1999, two years after opening the new pitch, with current manager Seán Hagan playing a starring role. They added a second one in 2005. In normal circumstances they'd be going into the final as favourites. But this hasn't been a normal year. In fact, it's been something of an *annus horribilis*.

Before the championship they were told that key defenders Cathal Conefrey (injury) and Eugene McNaboe (exam commitments) would miss the whole season. Then, in their second-round clash with Clonguish, county full-back Diarmuid

Masterson broke his ankle. There was the tragic death in a road accident of T.P. Pettit, promising inter-county referee and brother of senior wing-back David, to cope with as well. Most clubs would have written off a year like this.

But Dromard aren't most clubs. As Murphy puts it: 'If you get it hard in life, you'll have the resolve to keep going. If you have everything handed to you on a plate you don't respect it as much. Hardship hardens you up as a person. It comes through in your play. We don't lie down.'

Conefrey is back from his cruciate ligament injury months ahead of schedule. There's even a suggestion that Masterson, who suffered ligament damage as well as a break, might appear on Sunday. Dromard have won two games by a single point and another by two. Everyone I speak to in Longford agrees that Colmcille have looked far better than their rivals all season. Yet there is admiration for Dromard, summed up in the words of one county board official I speak to: 'Dromard will always keep coming on.'

What keeps them coming on becomes apparent to me as Hourican shows me around the clubhouse. There are thirty-odd kids playing traditional music. Hourican explains that the club started lessons a couple of years ago and some of the children have progressed sufficiently to win national titles. On a Thursday some of the older people in the parish come in and listen to the music, have a cup of tea and chat to club members.

I don't think any other sporting organisation in the world contains clubs who see it as their duty to perform a social function like that in their community. That is what makes the GAA different. And it is what makes Dromard an exceptional unit in the GAA. They're just after launching a €50 ticket draw. Buy one, if you're asked. You couldn't give money to a better club.

MATCH DAY

The atmosphere on final day is every bit as electric as I'd been led to expect. People talk about Martin McHugh helping out Colmcille and Kieran McGeeney doing the same with Dromard. Dromard live up to their image as a family club by bringing six kids around with them during the parade. Captain Pádraig Jones carries his three-month-old son, Killian, in his arms. Then we're off.

It takes Dromard forty-three seconds to notch the first score. Their full-forward, Francis McGee, is the leading scorer in the championship and he shows why with a point from a fifty-five-yard free.

Yet the predictions that Colmcille's Champagne football will simply sweep aside their neighbours look well founded early on. They equalise, and in the fifth minute full-forward Declan Farrell tears through the Dromard defence. Longford keeper Damien Sheridan makes a great save but the rebound goes in off wing-forward Anthony Gormley. Colmcille are 1–2 to 0–2 up by the tenth minute.

For all the physical intensity and local pride involved, sheer quality proves vital in the twelfth minute when McGee collects a through ball and races clear of the Colmcille full-back line, at which point most players would sprint as fast as they can and hit the ball as hard as possible. McGee follows his own counsel, slowing down to let two of his pursuers skid past him and then rolling the ball subtly and precisely into the bottom corner. There will be no runaway victory.

By half-time Colmcille are 2–2 to 1–4 up, Pádraig Murtagh having slotted home a penalty after their own brilliant number fourteen had wreaked more havoc. Yet there is unease among the supporters of the favourites. The doughty Clonguish veteran beside me, who had predicted a comprehensive Colmcille victory before the throw-in, now suggests that Dromard will win it. 'Those boys will win any game that's close coming into the last ten minutes.'

The crocked Diarmuid Masterson appears for Dromard early in the second half. His mobility is extremely limited but his presence in the full-forward line clearly lifts his teammates. With thirteen minutes left Dromard lead by 1–8 to 2–3. Entering the final ten, Sheridan makes a miraculous Gordon Banks from Pelé-style save from Thomas Doyle. Colmcille keeper Gavin Tonra points the fifty. A point in it and ten minutes to play. Everything to play for.

Colmcille reach deep within themselves for one last mighty effort. Enda Farrell is a colossus at midfield, wing-back Gary Murtagh is piling through challenges which should fell him. At one stage Tonra soloes the ball into enemy territory and there are no players at all left in the Colmcille half. The recovered Cathal Conefrey and the skipper Pádraig Jones perform miracles in a besieged full-back line.

Six minutes to go and Colmcille win a scorable free. Donie McKeon drags the ball inches wide. Two minutes to go and they have a free forty yards out. This time Tonra takes responsibility. Inches wide again. In the last seconds Noel Farrell takes on a free sixty yards out. The shot from his hands is prodigious, clearing the throng gathered round the square, but it tails off at the end.

Dromard have won.

AFTERMATH

I've seen few sights in sport as sad as that of the Colmcille players and officials dejectedly trooping to their team bus in the car park. I was neutral at this year's final but I sincerely hope they win next year's. Fifty years seems a propitious period of time for this great club.[1]

Pádraig Jones is tired and happy; his speech was a model of dignity and eloquence though his voice cracked and wobbled when he spoke about T.P. Pettit, 'the little man who left a big hole in Dromard, Longford and the GAA'. He had his own problems too; he tells me that the first few weeks of little Killian's life were very worrying indeed. We're at the door of the dressing room. Inside you can hear cogs bouncing off the concrete and players chanting, 'championes, championes, are we, are we, are we'.

Jones says this moment can't be put into words but he does his best. 'We were so down to have lost to our neighbours by ten points the last day, we couldn't let it happen again. We lost Cathal and we lost Diarmuid but it's not always the leading lights who see you through. The last ten minutes were just basic, get stuck in, batten down the hatches and see that it works out.

'Ah, it's a country area and the club is the gel that holds us together. You've been out in Dromard, you saw it, it's nothing much except for a great pitch, a clubhouse and a crèche. But there's a community spirit there, you go to the big towns and they don't have it. That's what's behind us and that's what got us through.'

---

1   Colmcille did, in fact, win the championship the following year, beating Longford Slashers on a scoreline of 0–13 to 0–07.

07

IN THE FIRING LINE

KEVIN KIMMAGE

'If you are going to bow the knee all the time to people who intimidate you, you might as well be dead anyway. You can't go through life that way.'

18 JANUARY 1998

Martin (not his real name) is a member of the Tír na nÓg GAA club in Portadown. Has been, since the day it was founded in the 1940s. He was a minor footballer back then. Loved the game. Played it until age crept up and weakened the limbs. Eventually he hung up the boots and started helping from the sideline.

As a manager he took the club to a county junior and intermediate title. As a committee member in the mid-1980s, he helped negotiate the club's transfer from a barren piece of land on the Moy Road to a four-acre site just off the Garvaghy Road. He's not so much a member of the club as an integral part of it.

He grew up in the town alongside his Protestant neighbours. Used to enjoy the pageant of the Orangemen's traditional march from Drumcree Church in July: no resentment here. When the Troubles began in the 1970s, and the mounting cycle of murder increased sectarian hatred and bitterness, Martin never let it seep into his bones. To this day he would tip the hat to any Orangeman he met in the town as quickly as he would to a nationalist. That was always his way.

Martin wasn't there on the day, back in 1994, when loyalist terrorists drove into the Ballyoran estate, peppered the Tír na nÓg club walls with bullets and sped off. It was a shock for the members, and security was reviewed and tightened afterwards, but the thought of not returning to the club just did not enter Martin's head. Nothing could keep him away from Tír na nÓg. Until Billy Wright was murdered.[1]

---

1 Billy Wright was a prominent Ulster loyalist paramilitary leader. Initially a member of the Ulster Volunteer Force (UVF), he later helped form the breakaway Loyalist Volunteer Force (LVF).

In the dying days of 1997, Wright was shot dead by the INLA (Irish National Liberation Army) while incarcerated in the Maze prison. The Loyalist Volunteer Force's threat of revenge caused a wave of fear right across nationalist areas of Northern Ireland, but the Tír na nÓg club had greater reason for anxiety. Wright lived in the Brownstown estate in Portadown, less than two miles from the club.

The following day, Martin was approached by his son and daughter. They pleaded with him not to continue travelling down to the club. He asked why, and they told him that they feared for his life. Every time he visited the club they would worry until he was home safely. Touched by his children's fear, Martin agreed not to return.

For seven days he kept his distance, but not even the fear of death could erase the love of a lifetime. One week later he returned. He has come down almost every night since. 'I came back because I love this club, I love the game. If you are going to bow the knee all the time to people who intimidate you, you might as well be dead anyway. You can't go through life that way.'

After Wright's murder, the club members met to review security. Extra cameras were placed in the yard, and the gates, previously open all day long, are now locked permanently. From seven in the evening until closing time seven days a week, a watchman stands in the hall behind the front door, monitoring those seeking entrance to the club.

At night, all the bar staff lock up and leave together. On away trips to matches, the schoolboys' team buses carry six and seven adults, just in case. Everything that can possibly be done to secure the club members' safety has been ... and yet every member knows that, when they walk out the gates, behind every gust of wind, every movement in the shadows, lies the possibility of a gunman ready to take a life. 'There is not a GAA man in the six counties who doesn't look over his shoulder when he walks home now,' says the club secretary.

On the same day in 1994 when the Tír na nÓg club was raked with bullets, a bomb was discovered hidden in a beer can at the gates of the St Enda's clubhouse in north Belfast. Designed to go off when the gate was opened, the bomb was discovered and safely defused, but the members of St Enda's have not always been so lucky. For their club, situated high up on the exposed Cavehill mountain, in the mainly Protestant suburb of Glengormley, is an easy target for hard-line loyalists who see it as a symbol of hate.

Since the Troubles began, the club has suffered five bomb attacks, three gun attacks and eight arson attacks. It bears the dubious distinction of being the most attacked sports club in the six counties. In 1991 Colin Lundy, a member of the

Under-16 team, perished with his mother in a sectarian-inspired petrol bomb attack. Two years later, the club president, Sean Fox, was tortured and shot dead in his house, a couple of hundred yards from the club.

When their younger members play a game of hurling, they have to be picked up at their door before the game and left back there afterwards, because to be seen walking through the streets with a hurley in your hand is to invite the possibility of attack. The club has had members as young as eight beaten up while walking home from games.

And yet, despite persecution and the handicap of a small population to draw on, the club has maintained more than a token presence within the GAA. Last year, the senior team finished fourth in the Antrim Senior Football League. The year before that, it reached the semi-finals of the Antrim championship. With a new clubhouse worth almost half a million pounds recently completed and a brand new pitch to look forward to playing on, the senior team manager, Gerry Devlin, had big plans for 1998.

But Gerry Devlin never lived to see the turn of the year. On a Friday evening, 5 December last, he arrived at the clubhouse to pick up his brother. A gunman stepped out from the bushes and shot him four times in the head.

Last Wednesday, seventy-five members of St Enda's attended the club's AGM. It was an evening of mixed emotions, for the meeting was held in the new clubhouse. The shock and sadness at the loss of Gerry Devlin has not abated, and yet, they know they must move on. 'It was Gerry's brother, Kevin, who said at the funeral that we just had to keep going. We could not let them (his murderers) drive us out, because that is what they want. And we knew that if Gerry had been there, he would have said the same thing,' says a club member.

Moving on, however, is easier said than done. Today, the club's senior team meets for the first time since Gerry's death. For them, concentrating on football will be hard in the short term and the club has still to appoint a manager. But to survive, the club must look ahead. On May Day this year, the club plans to open the new pitch. They hope to do so with hurling and football matches featuring Antrim against two of the top county teams. 'We'd love to give it a big kick-off, get a really big crowd in to see those games. We've written to a couple of county boards in the South, so we're hoping for a positive response.'

There are grounds for optimism for the future. The club's old pitch and clubhouse are to be flattened and a 400-house estate is to be built. This is likely to be filled by young Catholic families.

It is another reason for not giving up. 'If anything, the death of Gerry Devlin has made us dig in deeper. That is a natural reaction. If you put anybody under the pressure that we are under, they are never going to give in, because all they do is think of our members who died for this club. This is our Irish national game, a game we enjoy. I grew up playing hurling, I enjoy it, always have. Do I have to stop playing and does the club have to die because some people can't tolerate everything that is Irish?'

08

SURVIVOR'S GUIDE TO THE CLUB DINNER DANCE

COLM O'ROURKE

The highlight of the social calendar, the great annual meeting of local tribes is a bonanza for hotels.

After the games themselves, the single biggest occasion for most clubs is the Annual Dinner Dance and with hundreds of GAA clubs in the country, Friday nights in January and February are a bonanza time for hotels. A couple of hundred meals and no shortage of drinkers means a tidy sum for these establishments at a fairly slack time of year. This is the users' guide and perhaps survivors' guide to this great annual meeting of the local tribes.

The planning takes place in the back end of the year when the games are drying up and the monthly committee meetings are running out of topics to debate. At this stage the chairman will be heard to offer the opinion, 'We had better be thinking about the Dinner Dance.' This is the cue for the social committee to be wheeled out.

This particular committee will have had important matters to attend to during the year, like making sandwiches for the odd visiting team and organising soft drinks for the juveniles after winning their first match (for two years). Now, however, their hour is at hand.

The first major decision is the choice of hotel. An immediate enquiry takes place on the vegetable soup, the roast potatoes, vegetables, not to mention the quality of the turkey and ham from last year's function. After much debate from those with a more sophisticated palate, a decision is made to return to the same hotel and menu.

At that stage a committee member is delegated to meet the hotel manager and discuss the price (better than last year) without making any commitment. This means in reality that the meeting with the manager will ensure that the price will be slightly dearer this time and the date will be booked.

The other important item to be sorted out at this stage is the music. Somebody else gets this brief. The orders are 'not too loud, but with a good variety'. This rules out Westlife, the Spice Girls, U2 and Madonna. Big Tom and The Mainliners are not around any more, so a local group is signed up. Everyone knows that all the young people will slip out to the nearby disco around midnight, so the issue of music is not critical.

Of greater importance altogether is who the committee might deem worthy of a special presentation on the night. As the club has not won a championship for sixty-three years and only one tournament in the last twenty, there is a general feeling that something must be done on the night to take the bare look off the evening, not to mention having a few flashy trophies at the top table.

After much discussion it is decided that the club's junior team, which was beaten in the divisional semi-final years ago, should be honoured for outstanding commitment. The fact that there were only four teams in the competition at the time is completely overlooked. Another factor which would make this presentation even more appropriate is the fact that nearly all the team are now dead so, with only four trophies to present, it would save the club money. At a time when the finances are badly strapped, this is a vital consideration.

Everything is going swimmingly until someone suggests making another presentation to one of the younger players who was a sub for a while on the county minors. This involves heated debate and the chairman decides to move on quickly when it is pointed out that this gentleman had decided to go playing soccer on the day of the local derby which consigned the club to the Fourth Division of the league for the first time in its history. An old timer suggests that a 'kick up the arse' would be far more appropriate in the circumstances for him and many more like him than wasting the club's money which was hard earned in a pound raffle.

The guest list is the next item and this is a tricky one with all the political and diplomatic skills needed to balance out the conflicting views. The problem is that nobody on the committee likes anyone on the county board as they all agree that they were wrongly blamed for starting eight 'all in' melees during the year. This resulted in a few heavy suspensions and a fine which has yet to be paid. In the end it is agreed to check out all the big clubs in the county who are holding their dinner dance on the same night and find out who they have invited from the county board. Knowing that a board member would not go to a junior club function when there was a senior one on the same night, they could issue all sorts of invitations knowing full well that no major official would show up. A lesser light from the board would substitute and everyone would be happy.

Someone then suggests that a celebrity should be invited to make a presentation but immediately a problem arises as there is general agreement that no one would attend without getting a few quid. Again a simple solution is arrived at, with the chairman's blessing. The club will give a piece of glass and twenty pounds for petrol. No one could expect any more than that.

* * *

The night. The meal is scheduled for 8 p.m. sharp but everyone knows that if it is up and running at a quarter to ten it will be a minor miracle as you would need a whip to beat most of the players out of the bar. Eventually a semblance of order is imposed and the parish priest, who also doubles as president of the club and spiritual advisor, says grace before the meal and the show is on the road.

By half eleven the speeches start. The chairman tells everyone that there won't be much chat as things have run on longer than expected. He then goes on to welcome everyone at the top table which takes several minutes and then lashes out for another twenty at the lack of commitment to the club. He blames, among other things, loose women, tight haircuts, drink (naturally), discos, lack of respect for the selectors (himself), bad company and too much money too soon. He finishes off by saying that he sees a very bright future for the club this year as there are a number of good young players coming through.

The county board representative starts off with the statutory twenty words in Irish. Nobody understands them, or the English that follows, as most of the audience switched off halfway through the chairman's outburst. The applause is polite as everyone likes this particular county board official as he has helped to fix a few referees' reports in the past on behalf of the club.

The presentations are then made to the men of the past. They shuffle up proud as punch for their moment of glory. Their daughters and granddaughters flash their disposable cameras before an old-time supporter of the club suddenly realises that one of the recipients never played on that team at all. Such a minor hiccup should not be allowed to spoil a great night's entertainment and the information is kept under wraps. It will be one of the trick questions at the next table quiz that the club runs in the local pub, the same pub that sponsors the team and the one which the chairman particularly thanks before launching his tirade on the demon drink and late-night cavorting in bars.

The speeches finish at a quarter to one and the band strikes up an old-time waltz. Nobody under the age of twenty-five has lasted the pace. The chairman closes proceedings by thanking everyone for coming and proclaiming that it has been such an outstanding success that he is already looking forward to next year's Dinner Dance.

09

CASTLES CAN'T PROTECT THE HEARTLAND

JOHN GREENE

Croke Park has always been a go-to spot for sport, religion and culture – even more so since it was completely rebuilt.

30 JULY 2017

More than simply a sports venue, Croke Park is the national home of the country's largest sporting and cultural organisation, it has been shaped by and sadly played host to the momentous events of Ireland's history, and stands as a testament to modern stadium design and the work of an Association that built it and made it a success.

Mike Cronin and Roisín Higgins
Places We Play: Ireland's Sporting Heritage

It was in ways the perfect marriage. An Irish wedding; a gathering of the tribes. A pristine band in a pristine venue. A celebration of Modern Ireland, with all the rough edges dutifully hidden away; a night of nostalgia to momentarily reflect on where it all went wrong before dusting down a thirty-year-old album and proudly proclaiming in one voice, 'We're back, Baby.' This was a different sort of homecoming.

This was a night for the VIPs and the corporate boxes; for the €200 tickets and the car passes. It was the night when the roar of approval from the Squeezed Middle for that old rocker Michael D., perched high up in the Hogan Stand, might have persuaded our president that another seven years in the Park is on the cards. It was the night when Ireland came out to play.

It was nothing like 1987, the last time *The Joshua Tree* was aired in Croke Park. U2 had some rough edges then, the rickety old stadium had even more. Back then it had taken two June nights in Croke Park to satisfy the country's needs, along with separate shows in Belfast and Cork in what was presumably a nod to how difficult it once was to get around this island.

In the year U2 released *The Joshua Tree*, Charlie Haughey became Taoiseach again after the Fine Gael–Labour coalition collapsed, Johnny Logan made history when he won a second Eurovision, and the Republic of Ireland qualified for a major championship for the first time. It was also the year of Enniskillen, and hospital closures, and job losses – and it was the year an All-Ireland hurling semi-final was played in Dundalk in front of fewer than 5,000 people. Ireland still hadn't found what it was looking for.

The Ireland of today is a different place. We can move around easier thanks to our road network, and a show that once took four nights can now be condensed into one.

This was U2 now. And it was the GAA now – a reminder of how far, and how fast, the Association has travelled in thirty years as proud owners of Ireland's last great cathedral. It has welcomed super powers from the world of soccer and rugby, and the British Queen. Mass has been said there; Bruce, Beyoncé and One Direction have performed there.

Croke Park has always been a go-to spot for sport, religion and culture – even more so since it was completely rebuilt. As Mike Cronin and Roisín Higgins point out, the stadium is 'an iconic site in Irish life' and the country's 'most historically significant' sporting venue.

I once asked a sport historian from Boston, whose only experience of a game in Croke Park was an All-Ireland semi-final in the late 1970s, what were his memories of that day and, apart from the stench of urine, he remembers the stadium being massive, primitive and alive. When he visited again last year, it took his breath away. The GAA just doesn't do 'rickety' any more. Most of its principal county grounds are now fit for purpose after an ambitious programme of upgrades over the last twenty years or so, coinciding with a period when clubs all over the country have also enhanced their facilities.

Ironically, on the day Bono lent his support to Ireland's bid to host the Rugby World Cup in 2023 – which would see the final played in Croke Park – the new Páirc Uí Chaoimh hosted its first major game. In total, nine of the twelve venues which have been included in the rugby bid belong to the GAA, and the Cork venue may play host to a semi-final. It has been completely rebuilt, just as Croke Park was, at a cost of €80m or so. Next up is Casement Park in Belfast, which is also part of the bid. The £80m redevelopment has had numerous planning setbacks but the GAA remains confident that it too will be ready in time for 2023, should Ireland's bid be successful.

The GAA now owns and operates twenty-two of the country's twenty-five biggest grounds, and when Casement Park is finally rebuilt it will own the largest stadia in this island's three largest cities.

Not that all is perfect. Structural issues with a stand at Pearse Park in Longford must be dealt with and are in hand, but counties like Meath, Louth, Kildare and Waterford are lagging behind. Yet the question has to be asked: have these counties missed the boat, and is it time for the GAA to change its focus for now? Should the Association now say, 'What we have, we hold'?

Problems around club fixtures and the high drop-out rate among adult players have been well highlighted, but these are not the only threats to the GAA's position in the Irish sporting hierarchy. Soccer has been gradually moving towards a summer programme, while rugby has also been infiltrating so-called GAA heartlands with clever development strategies, especially in Leinster. A recent report found that there are twenty fewer GAA clubs in Leinster, outside of Dublin, than there were forty years ago, despite a massive population increase in the province.

A major advantage both soccer and rugby have at grassroots level is their ability to provide certainty to players about when and where games are played. They can set out fixture programmes for a season which are largely adhered to and which can make them a more attractive proposition to many people. The GAA is not doing likewise.

Ultimately the GAA is in the business of providing games to men and women, and boys and girls, and perhaps it has now reached the point where investing in facilities – and especially in major, costly redevelopments – needs to be put on hold in favour of bolstering its presence on the ground.

Perhaps games development, and not ground development, is where the GAA's money should be directed for the time being, and if that means a few high-profile venues are left hanging for a few years then so be it. Given the quality – and quantity – of venues across the country it's not really a burning issue in the Association at this moment.

The GAA's burning issues lie elsewhere: reconnecting with the grassroots; re-structuring championships which are clearly not fit for purpose; making football and hurling accessible to all, and so on. This is where the GAA needs to focus more of its attention, and its money. The rest can wait.

10

HURLING MAN – A BREED APART

EAMONN SWEENEY

Anyone who has ever followed the GAA has met him along the way, but if you haven't, here's some help to spot him.

7 APRIL 2013

In the first half last Sunday at Walsh Park, Galway corner-forward Davy Glennon slipped past his marker, Waterford corner-back Stephen Daniels, and looked set to score a goal. Which was when Glennon hauled him down. Over in Nowlan Park, Kilkenny's Colin Fennelly suffered a similar fate as he cut inside Cork full-back Brian Murphy.

It's a reasonable bet that had Fennelly and Glennon not been fouled they'd have scored goals. Instead their teams were awarded penalties, neither of which produced a goal.

Watching the fouls on Fennelly and Glennon, it struck me how common this particular type of offence is in hurling. We've been watching forwards being wrestled to the ground just as they were about to pull the trigger for a long time now.

It's probably because penalties are more difficult to score in hurling but this blatant rugby-tackling of an opponent through on goal isn't anything like as common in football. There's nothing manly or honest about it, it's simply a cynical act of the kind which prompted the introduction of the red card for a professional foul in soccer. The very type of offence, in other words, that the new black card rule is designed to stamp out in Gaelic football.

Yet during the debate about the introduction of the black card it was stated again and again that hurling didn't need such a rule. Cynical fouling, we were told, is absent from hurling. Now, having seen many hurlers hauled down as they were about to score, I was puzzled by the difference between rhetoric and reality. But then I realised that these statements were coming from Hurling Man, a creature ordinary mortals like ourselves do not possess the power to fully understand.

Hurling Man is not to be confused with the hurling fan. He is a different bag of sliotars altogether, a self-important colossus who resembles a cross between Mat The Thrasher from *Knocknagow*, Comic Book Guy from *The Simpsons* and one of those TV wine connoisseurs who could detect fruity wood notes in a bottle of Blue Nun. Anyone who's ever followed the GAA has encountered him along the way but, just in case you haven't, here are a few pointers to help in the identification of the species …

1   Hurling Man doesn't know why you bother with that aul' football at all at all. You can change all the rules you like but it'll always be a terrible spectacle on account of its bastard origins.

2   Hurling Man can debate at length the competing claims of Christy Ring and Mick Mackey to be regarded as the greatest player in the history of the game, even though he never saw either man play.

3   Hurling Man was talking to a man who knows a man who knows a man who's involved with the team and told him that the manager has definitely lost the dressing room.

4   Hurling Man thinks the All-Ireland hurling final should be played in Thurles because the sod is much better.

5   Hurling Man is always unhappy with whatever system the GAA have come up with for the National League because he doesn't think any of the strong hurling counties ever deserve to be relegated or forced to play against Kerry.

6   Hurling Man is convinced that there's a plot to do away with the Munster hurling championship, so when the first exciting incident happens in the Munster final he shakes his head and says to everyone within earshot, 'And to think they were going to get rid of this.'

7   Hurling Man believes there's little point in trying to promote hurling in the weaker counties because they just don't have the tradition.

8   Hurling Man believes that if hurling was promoted in the proper way it could spread to other countries and become a major worldwide game.

9　　Hurling Man gets great enjoyment out of an Internet forum discussion on the efficacy of different brands of helmet, even if it's a while since he wore one.

10　　Hurling Man thinks Liam Griffin's statement that hurling is the *Riverdance* of sport is one of the great profound statements of Western civilisation. And so is the Mícheál Ó Muircheartaigh thing about neither of Seán Óg Ó hAilpín's parents coming from a hurling stronghold.

11　　Hurling Man has a lot of favourite Mícheál Ó Muircheartaigh quotes, which he'll tell you if you come back here for a minute.

12　　Hurling Man isn't sure about Galway.

13　　Hurling Man believes *The Sunday Game* should be anchored by someone with 'a feel for hurling'. Someone like Hurling Man.

14　　Hurling Man derived much of his knowledge about the game from those Raymond Smith books he used to get at Christmas but is embarrassed by this and pretends he derived it from the giant folkloric collective unconscious.

15　　Hurling Man knows the right way to spell Paddy Rutschiztko. Which is Paddy Ruschitzko.

16　　Hurling Man believes that the referee should let the game flow. Unless Kilkenny are doing the fouling.

17　　Hurling Man felt personally let down by Lar Corbett's behaviour in last year's All-Ireland semi-final and will never forgive him for that affront to the spirit of the game.[1]

18　　Hurling Man believes there should be more ground hurling.

1　This refers to Tipperary's tactic on the day to have Lar Corbett track Kilkenny's Tommy Walsh. Tipperary lost the game by eighteen points.

19   Hurling Man gets an orgasm if someone doubles on the ball in the air.

20   Hurling Man knows they hadn't a lot of ball work done when the teams met in the league.

21   Hurling Man is not the best person to meet on a long train journey. But he's better than the man who has a theory about how an Open Draw system could be made to work.

22   Hurling Man will occasionally say things like, 'I seen he done well on Sunday', because it adds a folksy down-to-earth flavour to the conversation. What are you, a snob?

23   Hurling Man thinks Henry Shefflin took the wise option by pointing that penalty in last year's All-Ireland final. He'd have thought the same if Henry had gone for goal.

24   Hurling Man knows that it's not the 4–9 from the full-forward line which won the game but a particular clearance by the right half-back in the eleventh minute.

25   Hurling Man just loves the Christy Ring quote about sticking a knife into every football east of Bandon. Or is it Kinsale? Hilarious.

26   Hurling Man likes to get his All-Ireland ticket the night before in a hotel bar after falling into conversation with someone who's got one to spare.

27   Hurling Man will tell you the stories about the Tipperary hurler, the Kilkenny hurler and the Limerick hurler, and then tell you there's no truth in any of them.

28   Hurling Man thinks that hook there should be repeated for the benefit of any kids playing the game. It's a dying art.

29   Hurling Man thinks a black card rule would kill the game though it might survive in isolated pockets like the handful of survivors in *The Walking Dead*.

30 Hurling Man is concerned that the game is in trouble in Cork City.

31 Hurling Man is delighted to see the hurling revival in Dublin as long as they don't win anything of real significance.

32 Hurling Man says we shouldn't forget Billy when we're talking about the Rackards.

33 Hurling Man has doubts about Eoin Kelly's temperament. The Waterford lad, not the Tipp one.

34 Hurling Man mourns the loss of the North Mon and Farranferris.

35 Hurling Man believes inter-county players who've given a lot to the game should be allowed to choose the manner of their departure from the county team.

36 Hurling Man believes players should never be paid but should be looked after in some undefined way.

37 Hurling Man thinks no one is going to complain if the ref makes a draw of this one.

38 Hurling Man saw no malice in that pull. Or any pull.

39 Hurling Man wonders if you can follow the flight of the ball there, you being from a football county.

40 Hurling Man misses Carrolls' All-Star wall charts in pubs and signed that 'Bring Back the James Last *Sunday Game* Theme Tune' petition.

41 Hurling Man enjoys the aul' banter.

42 Hurling Man thinks that in fairness the moderator is being a bit paranoid about libel.

43 Hurling Man wouldn't expect anything better from you, it's yourself you're showing up you ignorant hoor.

44 Hurling Man's nightmares are dominated by a green plastic Wavin hurl.

45 Hurling Man once met an American who told him they had no game like this in the States and couldn't believe the players were amateurs.

46 Hurling Man can remember the precise contents of the first *Our Games* annual bought for him.

47 Hurling Man admires Antrim's long struggle to keep the game alive despite British oppression, and thinks the 'B' championship is the place for them.

48 Hurling Man uses anecdotes from ghosted autobiographies and pretends they come from his personal experience. If challenged he'll say, 'That's an old story. I can't believe you didn't hear it before.'

49 Hurling Man believes that in the Amazon rainforest, the Western Sahara and the depths of Siberia, native herders and tribesmen are awed by the fact that hurling is the fastest field sport in the world.

50 Hurling Man knows you're all only jealous.

III

A LAW UNTO HIMSELF

Because you don't get on with a person doesn't mean you dislike them.

'I HONESTLY DON'T THINK THEY WANT THE SAME AS ME'

PAUL KIMMAGE

When Roy Keane left Saipan and walked out on the World Cup, the nation was split. On the day before he quit Ireland, he gave this interview, and all was not well.

26 MAY 2002

In March of 2001, a few days before his monumental performance against Cyprus, I pressed the stop button of my tape recorder after a two-hour interview with Roy Keane.

There was one more item on my agenda. A few months earlier I'd heard a rumour he was considering writing a book and I wanted to throw my hat in the ring. 'I don't care if the deal is already done,' I said, 'I just want you to know I would kill to do it.' My hat wasn't quite big enough but I meant every word: I'd have given just about anything to have spent six months trawling through the crevices of that fascinating head.

So you can imagine my spirits last Wednesday afternoon in Saipan when, a few hours after he had almost quit the team, I was afforded the first interview. The hour we had wasn't quite six months, but I certainly wasn't complaining …

This isn't quite the same interview we had planned earlier in the week but here goes. How are you feeling?

Not bad, could be better, could be worse.

Okay let's start from the top. We arrive here on Saturday afternoon after a long and tiring flight and you go to your room?

Yeah.

And you're rooming on your own?

Yeah.

What do you unpack in terms of comforts of home?

One or two books. A DVD that I've just purchased. Photographs of the kids and of the wife.

What books?

I'd rather not say.

Music?

Bit of Bob Dylan … a bit of Tupac, who is a rapper … Phil Collins … some Irish pub songs … some Irish rebel songs which I try and save for before kick-off.

Really? Irish rebel songs?

Yeah.

And what would be your favourite? In a piece about the Holland game last year it was suggested that Simon and Garfunkel's 'I am a Rock' might be your private anthem. (You hand him a copy of the words.)

I am a rock
I am an island.

(He reads it and laughs.) Maybe I am an island.

Does it come close?

Yeah.

Two photographs from the Holland game stand out: the photo of the joy on your face when Jason McAteer scored and the photo of you shaking hands with Mick McCarthy as you walk off the pitch. The contrast has always struck me as very odd.

Well, obviously … it's a job done. I'm not really into hugging and kissing and the hoo haa about it. Obviously I'm delighted, don't get me wrong but just get off the pitch and get into the dressing room. I think sometimes there is too much carry-on on the pitch regarding results. For other people it might have been a shock but I always felt we would get a result. And my emotions are different, I suppose. I react differently.

A lot of people interpreted the photo with Mick as proof that you don't get on.

Emm.

They say the camera never lies?

Because you don't get on with a person doesn't mean you dislike them. Of all the people I've been around in football, there are none I would regard as a personal friend. Maybe the closest would be Alex Ferguson. So with Mick … I don't expect to be pals with Mick. I played with Mick, I wasn't pals when I played with him and I certainly don't want to be pals when I'm playing for him. I mentioned Alex

Ferguson because he's someone I feel close to but we're not pally-pally. I wouldn't send him a Christmas card.

Does that mean you dislike Mick?

No, I don't dislike him.

What about your teammates? Who are you closest to here?

None of them, but that's been the case for many a year which, I suppose ... it's not a problem over two or three days but over a length of time it does (bother me).

That same photograph was the first time I noticed your tattoos.

Yeah, very painful.

What are they?

I've got my kids on my right arm: Shannon, Caragh, Aidan and Leah. And on the left (arm) it's just a standard cross. The wife did ask me why didn't I get hers (name put on) and I said, 'they'll always be my kids but you won't necessarily always be my wife,' which she wasn't too pleased about (laughs).

The other interpretation of that photo would be 'I want to get out of here as quick as possible.'

Yeah.

And that's difficult when you come to a place like this and have a blowout with your teammates like yesterday, isn't it? Because I would suspect that happens regularly enough at Manchester United, that you lose the head with your teammates? But the difference this time was you couldn't get into your car and drive home?

Yeah. If I could have got a flight yesterday I wouldn't be here now.

Let me take you back to the Iran game and the problem with your knee.

Well, again I was having problems. I never played for three weeks before the first play-off match. I spoke to the manager, our own manager at Man United, and the deal was, and there was a deal done before the match, that if we got a positive result – and 2–0 to me is positive – I wouldn't jeopardise it by doing any more damage. First of all with the flight and obviously by playing two matches in four or five days which I hadn't done for maybe three and a half weeks. So after the match I felt my knee again and on Sunday morning the manager (Ferguson) rang and said, 'We class 2–0 as a positive result.' And that was it, I decided to go home. In my eyes the game was over. I couldn't see us losing 3–0. And of course (that leaves) you open to criticism again.

What criticism?

That I was being put under pressure (by Manchester United), but I couldn't play the second match. And, as you get older, you have got to be more selfish regarding your body because I've played in hundreds of games when I probably shouldn't have played, especially when there was something at stake. But I weighed up everything: we're 2–0 up going to play a team where I think we will get a result. If it was 1–0 or 0–0 it would have been different but I couldn't see them scoring three and us scoring none.

Okay but you're the biggest player on the team and …

Well I don't see it that way. And I'm not being humble. People are entitled to their opinion but I think it's so exaggerated, it's untrue.

So who is bigger?

We're all the same. No one is better or worse.

The point I am trying to make is that Ireland without Keane is a much lesser team and that the Iranians were handed a psychological advantage the moment you didn't check in for the flight.

What was the score again?

1–0.

And we qualified?

We qualified … okay, point taken. Another criticism was that you left the hotel in Dublin that morning without wishing your teammates luck or telling them you weren't travelling.

I can't remember what happened. It was a Sunday morning and I booked the flight and I think they might have gone training or gone out for a loosener. Obviously I spoke to Mick and Mick Byrne and, in between, obviously I spoke to the manager who rang me on my mobile. But I felt the job was done. There was no way I could see us losing the game.

Your relationship with Mick and with your teammates would suggest that you play for Ireland on your terms? Is that fair?

No, probably not.

It's not fair?

No. I am always one or two days late (joining up) but I feel I travel more than most of the players in the squad because of my European commitments with the club. And I don't like being away for long periods of time. I've got four young children. I know the other players have kids but I don't worry about them, I look after me. And there's no doubt it must piss them off. But when I'm here I work as hard as any of them. If there is a player who prepares better than me I'd like to meet him. And that's what it's all about. I love the ninety minutes playing for my country. I love it as much as the next man. And people go on that I keep blasting this and blasting that but all I want is what's best for me and for my teammates. And if that's a crime, I'm guilty.

Did you watch the second leg in Iran on TV?

Yeah. At home. I was flicking.

You were flicking?

Yeah.

Why?

Because it wasn't a great game. It was pretty dire.

And when we qualified?

It was no big deal. I felt we qualified on the Saturday before.

So there was no sense of elation?

No. I remember in '94 going bloody berserk and I remember all the scenes, but this was completely different. I think as you get older you accept it.

Did you enjoy it more then?

In '94? Yeah, without a doubt.

Why?

I wish I had an answer. Maybe it's because I was younger. As you get older … I've got more balance in my life. In '94 it was more of a rollercoaster. I'd be up (if we won) and then down the following week if we were beaten. But now I'm trying to take the good and the bad along the same level. And the fact that I wasn't there (in Iran) obviously makes it different. I was at home and obviously pleased but, again, I was convinced we had qualified on the Saturday.

What does it mean to play in another World Cup? And what did it mean first time round? There has been a sense of you really driving the team to get here this time?

Hopefully I try to do that in every match. Obviously when you get that bit older you are more mature about things and take things a bit more in your stride. And I feel without doubt that I'm a much better player. '94 was a bit gung-ho. I don't think my preparation was the best for all sorts of reasons and I feel this year … I feel this year will be a lot harder than '94 because of the teams we're playing and the fact that we are so far away.

You say you enjoyed it more in '94. Does that mean you don't enjoy it now?

No, I do. I love training when I'm fit. And I love winning, although it's not been a great season for us this year. The team has not played well and I've had one or two injuries and not played particularly well. But I love training. And I love being around people who have the same targets as me and at United that's generally the case, although sometimes maybe not. But I've got people around me who want the best and that's what I think we should try and do. I look after myself a lot better. My recovery after games is a lot better and I feel a hell of a better player, but I still feel I can improve. I'm thirty-one this summer and the games are getting faster and players are getting stronger so you need to prepare right. And you shouldn't be looking for a pat on the back for it. Everybody should be pulling the same way, which probably pisses me off with Ireland sometimes when I don't feel it's quite there. Some people have a laugh and bite their tongue and accept it but I don't.

That side of you that refuses to go with the flow.

The only thing that goes with the flow are dead fish.

Very good. I bet you read that?

Some friend of mine told me it recently, but that's not … every few months, especially last season, it was Keane blasts this and Keane blasts that. I don't blast anything. I love my teammates. I love what's best for them and for the Irish team. I think all of the lads are nice lads on the Irish team. They are all genuinely good lads. They train hard, they play hard and good luck to them. And it's the same at United. 'Keane blasts this.' All I want is what's best. And no one has ever disagreed with me. Ever.

Okay, but this side of you that refuses to go with the flow. With a bit of work, you could easily be the most popular sportsman in Ireland but you make no effort whatsoever to do anything for yourself in terms of PR.

There's enough people who do that. There's enough people out there who enjoy things like that. And I think, eventually, people see through that. Most people I meet, United fans and Ireland fans when I go back to Cork, are generally quite nice and polite to me and I don't need to. There are enough people out there looking for photo opportunities and to become pals with certain people. I don't need it.

But the flip side is that you only appear in the papers when there's a controversy or you're in a rage. There's an imbalance there?

Maybe so, but I don't want to be … even last week when people said, 'Oh you should have turned up for Quinny's night' but what do I need to do? Make a statement every time there is some sort of accusation. Or justify why I might have been late when I told the people who were important. And today is the same. They wanted me to speak to the press today but I'll speak to the press when I'm due to speak to them at a press conference in two days' time.

I don't believe you don't care what is written about you.

Of course I care. I care what my parents think and what my family think.

And how it affects them.

Of course. And I do accept criticism when it's constructive, but I'm coming over on the flight (to Dublin) the other day and reading 'Roy Keane was disrespectful to

Niall Quinn and should have been in the stand with a shirt and tie on.' But why the fuck should I have been sitting in the stand with a shirt and tie on when I'm not fit. It's Niall Quinn's night, not Roy Keane's! That was Quinny's night and good luck to him. 'Disrespectful.' That's not nice, but did I send out a statement the next day to correct it? No, because I'd be making statements every day of the week.

There's no history between you and Niall?

No.

But this is a guy who has gone out and made this fantastic gesture for charity. He is Ireland's record goalscorer. Why not do him a favour? Why not say, 'Okay, this doesn't suit me but he's my teammate and I'll go along?'

To do what?

As a gesture of support. To be there because you're Roy Keane.

I was flying out the next day for four or five weeks ... now do you want me to sit in a stand or stay at home with my wife and kids? I went to the pictures with my wife. Did you want me to sit in the stand and be pestered by people who are drunk? Do you think it would have made a difference?

I bumped into Eamon Dunphy recently and we spoke about your book (Dunphy is ghosting the Keane autobiography) and one of the things he mentioned was that you don't have any friends in the game.

No, that would be right.

And that won't hurt you when your career has ended?

No.

But you like dogs?

Yeah, I've got my dog.

What is it?

A Labrador retriever.

What's his name?

It's a she. Triggs.

Why dogs?

Loyal.

They don't let you down?

Yeah.

They don't turn you over?

No.

Okay, let's rewind the tape now to the start of this trip. It's Friday 17 May, we've just played Nigeria and we're about to depart for the World Cup. And seasoned Keano watchers are wondering 'How is he going to handle a month away from home?' (He grins.) So you arrive at the airport to check in and straight away there's the media circus with Bertie and it's obvious from your demeanour that you're not very impressed.

No, but none of the players were. And did you not see the (chaos at) check-in? And then we go into this lounge and there's two guys dressed as leprechauns (promoting) *The Sun*, telling me to cheer up. They want me to pose for a photograph for *The Sun* newspaper! And we're in a lounge getting ready for a long haul flight with the Irish football team! It's a laugh, isn't it? It's a great laugh.

But you're not laughing?

Certainly not.

Because you hate all that?

It's crazy. It's absolutely crazy. And all of the players feel the same. They were all complaining about it on the plane. And then eventually we do get into some sort of lounge but we're still getting all sorts of people coming up to us and you're thinking, 'How the hell did they get in here?' And it's not losing touch with reality it's … We're getting ready for a World Cup. We're going to be travelling for over twenty hours. And I've got two bloody leprechauns telling me to 'Cheer up Keano.' I thought, 'I'll fucking knock you out, you stupid c**t.'

And did that put you in bad humour for Bertie?

No, but again, the Bertie thing. I've met Bertie before. I think there was an election that day, was there?

You mean you didn't vote?

No. But all that should have been organised before we left the hotel. The president came out the night before and it's well and good them all wishing us luck, it's great, don't get me wrong, but there are always hidden agendas, always, always, hidden agendas. Bertie is a bloody nice bloke. I've met him a few times, he's a big United fan, I know all that but it's just … it should have been better organised.

Okay, so then we fly to Amsterdam and you have a go at a couple of journalists at the airport?

No, no, I didn't have a go. If that's having a go …

So that was mild?

(Laughs) Very mild. I was dead relaxed about it. It was them that got carried away.

It was just a mild bollicking?

It wasn't even a bollicking. I just thought … And I was annoyed with myself afterwards because I felt I had lowered myself … But it was because of what I had read on the way over. Philip Quinn (*Irish Independent*) said I was disrespectful to Niall but they need to know their facts. And Billy George! Billy works for the *Echo* or the *Examiner*, which I despise anyway for some of the things they have written about my family so … I felt annoyed at that. But that's history now.

And when you get annoyed like that, how difficult is it to control?

Sometimes I don't find it a problem but other times enough is enough. But I haven't had a confrontation with a reporter for a long, long time.

Okay, so we arrive in Saipan and there's a meal and a team meeting that evening and Mick announces that the training kit hasn't arrived.

Yeah.

And it pisses you off?

Yeah. But it doesn't surprise me.

So is that his fault or the FAI's?

It doesn't matter, does it?

So you go training next morning and you tog out in runners and stuff and the pitch is bad and that's really irritating for you, the ultimate pro.

Yeah, for any pro.

And there's a barbecue with the press later that evening?

Yeah, which I can't understand … But then again, some of the players are best mates with the press so why not go out with them? And the same with Mick and the staff.

It's called good public relations?

Yeah, but a lot of them are hypocrites. And you want me to sit there and have a barbecue with a guy who three or four years ago wrote an article encouraging people to boo me at an international match? Am I supposed to enjoy that? Am I supposed to feel comfortable with that? I probably shouldn't have gone but sometimes I do make the effort.

And yet, despite these irritations, by Tuesday afternoon you're in good form. Jason says he has spoken to you more in the last couple of days than in the last couple of years. Relations within the team are good.

Yeah … but again … they're all decent lads, to be fair to them, although I wouldn't take too much notice of what Jason says. Jason has a big mouth.

Even when he says nice things about you? Even when he says, as he did last week when you were getting it in the neck from the papers, that people never hear about the Roy Keane that goes to visit sick kids in hospitals?

Naah … Jason is just being Jason … he's probably hoping I'll find that out. He also said a few months ago that I was a grumpy bastard, but the day I start worrying about what Jason says will be a sad one. But he's a nice lad.

Despite that?

Yeah.

And then we get to the training session and Stan (Steve Staunton) makes a joke about Packie (Bonner) justifying his job and you have a laugh about it. And you run out to begin the session with a smile on your face and everything appears to be normal until the five-a-side when suddenly it is announced that the goalkeepers have finished for the day. What happens next?

Well you ask any footballer in the world, whether they are playing Sunday league or right at the top … when you finish training with a five-a-side you need 'keepers. Ask any player. Ask any of the Irish lads. We all felt the same. But they (Packie) felt the 'keepers had worked hard enough. But we've done just under three hours training since we've come here and I think we've come to work. It's not our fault that Packie started (the training session with the three 'keepers) a half an hour earlier. We had done our shooting earlier for their benefit and that's where the team comes into it – even if you are fucked you just stand in the goal. And that did piss me off.

And so you had a word with Taff (Ian Evans, the assistant manager) about it?

Yeah I mentioned it to Taff and he's gone 'Oh well they're knackered' as if we all felt great. We were all tired.

So the game starts with Niall Quinn and Richard Dunne improvising in goal but not allowed to use their hands. And what was interesting watching it was the intensity with which you played. As if winning that five-a-side was life or death.

Ehh … I wouldn't go that far. It was probably more important than that (laughs). No, I suppose there was an element of 'let's just get on with it', but inside I was fuming.

Because there were no goalkeepers?

Yeah. But also because of the whole combination of things … Fail to prepare, prepare to fail. From day one it has been negative. And that's my opinion. And I'm entitled to my opinion. And people are saying, 'It's Keane as usual', but all the players are feeling the same but some show it in different ways.

With the game tied at 4–4 you lose to a penalty and you walk off and have a go at Packie.

Not really, no.

Okay, you have a lively discussion with Packie?

A lively discussion, but I'd have hundreds of thousands of them with the lads at United.

Except that you can get in the car and drive home afterwards?

Probably, yeah.

And then you have a go at Alan Kelly?

I didn't have a go at Alan Kelly. Alan Kelly had a go at me.

What did he say?

Well, I'm not going to get into the gory details but obviously I felt the 'keepers should have been there. And Alan said, 'Well, we've worked really hard.' And I said 'Well what are you here for? And will you be working as hard tomorrow on the golf course?' We've (only) done three hours work since we got here! And I know it's a relaxing break and the sun is going to do you good and that you can't train too hard but you've got to step into it. Alan felt we had done enough work and I felt we hadn't.

And the argument was heated.

Yeah, the one between me and Kells (Alan Kelly) was … but again, I'd had hundreds of thousands of them with teammates at United.

And what about when he shook his head and told you to shut up and you said, 'Are you going to make me?' What if he had said, 'Yeah I fucking will'? Would you have hit him?

(Smiles) You never know, he might have hit me … Naah, he told me to calm down.

He told you to calm down?

Yeah. And I said, 'Are you going to make me calm down?' As if that was possible; I was pretty angry.

But why were you so angry?

It was a combination of the training kit and no footballs the first day and the pitch. I think it would be softer training on the car park! I genuinely believe that. And there's got to be people responsible for that! Is it asking too much to travel twenty hours on a flight for a training pitch that hasn't even been watered! It's not right. And by nature I can't accept it. I am what I am, warts and all. I have no problem with Kells. Kells is a good lad. He is probably one of the lads I would speak to a lot on the trips (laughs) so I've ruined that one. I'm going to have to speak to Jason again … fuck sake.

But that wasn't the time or place to discuss it, was it?

No, of course not. But everything is great in hindsight. You don't pick these moments.

But what about the control, Roy? That it would almost come to blows? And that you would be prepared for it to come to blows? That isn't rational behaviour from a man of your stature?

Yeah, but I was giving my opinion and I felt he was wrong. And he has the right to be wrong, I'll have to remember that. But when he starts going 'Ahh we've worked hard', I'm thinking 'Well what did you come over here for? You're supposed to work hard.' You've got to make sacrifices for your teammates. Do you think when you're tired you can just walk off? And that's when you wonder: do these people want the same as me? And that's when the doubts set in and I honestly don't think they do. Whether it's the players or the staff ... it makes me wonder.

But the goalkeepers' work is particularly physical?

They're not going to die. They looked all right at the barbecue the other night. They won't be too fucked on the golf course today.

Okay, take me through the process of what happened next. You returned to the hotel and had a meeting with Mick. Was that your call or his call?

My call.

You told him you wanted to see him?

Yeah.

And what happened?

I told him I'd had enough.

And how did he respond?

Are you sure, blah, blah, blah. And I said yeah.

Now that meeting took place almost as soon as you had returned from training so you hadn't thought about it for very long.

Yeah, well ... I did have a cold shower before I met him but I'd had enough. And it's not just been this trip, it's been a combination of things over the years. International football if anything has been a nuisance to me. I love the ninety minutes but it's the rest of the crap. The negative stuff I've had off people over the years regarding rooming on my own and hanging about with the lads and all that, and I just thought, 'Naah, I don't need it.' And I wouldn't be here now basically only for other people. If it was down to me, I'd be gone.

And is that it now for international football after the World Cup?

Yeah.

Definitely?

Yeah.

Okay, so you tell Mick you're gone and go back to your room.

Yeah.

You didn't speak to anyone before you spoke to Mick?

No, because I'm convinced they would have said I was doing wrong.

Who did you call first?

My wife.

What did she say to you?

She said do whatever you think is right. She told me that Michael (his solicitor Michael Kennedy) wanted to speak to me because the press had got hold of certain things … which amazed me because only one or two people knew about the conversation (with Mick). So I spoke to Michael and he said the manager (Alex Ferguson) had been ringing and wanted to speak to me. So I rang him and I'm glad I did. Because he is somebody I would listen to and trust.

You also went for a walk last night on the beach?

Yeah.

And did anything on that walk change your mind in any way?

It was a long night. There was a lot going on. I felt the same this morning but after I spoke to the manager and he gave his opinion on what I should do, I decided to stick it out.

I'm not sure what he said to you but I would imagine it was something along the lines of 'For fuck's sake don't do this. You will be destroyed.'

(He looks puzzled) How would it destroy me?

You were prepared to walk out on your country and on your teammates on the eve of a World Cup?

Naah … I think you're reading it wrong. I'm sure they would have thought 'Well he must have a damn good reason.' And I think if I did walk away people would, well, maybe not agree with me but say, 'Fucking hell, that must have been bad.' But I wouldn't have worried what they thought of me in Ireland but I've got my mam and dad and family over there and it would have been a lot harder for them so.

There are a lot of guys on the technical staff who have enormous affection for you: Mick Byrne and Johnny Fallon stand out. Would nothing they said have changed your mind at all?

No.

When you decided you were staying how did you notify Mick and the rest of the team?

I don't really want to go into that.

Did you feel awkward, having announced you were going home, facing your teammates at training this morning?

Em … I hadn't announced it. I had spoken to Mick. I hadn't announced it to anybody else.

Eamon Dunphy announced it on Today FM.

Well, you know Eamon … but they would have had to book flights so it could have been a combination of anything.

You didn't speak to Eamon?

No. But they were trying to book flights so … Did I feel awkward? No, I just decided to put my head down and get on with it.

Did you make it up with Alan Kelly?

We spoke yesterday.

So has there been nothing positive about this week? The fact that you can float around the hotel without getting hassle isn't a plus?

Yeah, yeah, I had two walks yesterday and it's great but there's only so much walking you can do. It's different if you have a dog with you or somebody ... I could spend an hour on the beach but I get bored after half an hour. And I've got books but there's only so many books you can read. I've got my three brothers and my cousin coming out next week, so that will give me a bit of breathing space I suppose. People I can talk to. And feel relaxed with. People I can trust.

Is Theresa (wife) coming out?

No, with four kids it's too far.

Okay, where does it go from here? We play Cameroon next week. What's your take on this World Cup?

Well, a lot of people think we should qualify but I think it's going to be very hard. We have an important week and a half ... and no matter what happens, and no matter what I think is not going right, I'll make sure I'm right. Cameroon next Saturday at three o'clock will be bloody hard physically, because the conditions will play a factor. We need a positive result but I'll try and enjoy it and make my mark.

In the World Cup?

Yeah.

And is it going to be hard for you to stay within the team?

I don't really care. I'll just get through it and we'll see what happens.[1]

---

1 Two days after this interview was conducted in Saipan, Keane famously left the island and returned home after a very public row with Mick McCarthy, playing no part in the World Cup.

A LAW UNTO HIMSELF

EAMON DUNPHY

From journeyman pro to World Cup winner and Irish national hero, throughout his long and often abrasive journey Jack Charlton has remained stubbornly and defiantly his own man.

Post-war England: battle-scarred, bleak, ration books; professional footballers earning £12 a week. Young Jack Charlton left the mining village of Ashington in Northumberland to join the ground staff at Leeds United.

Football was in his blood. His mother was a Milburn, daughter of a goalkeeper, 'Tanner' Milburn, and cousin of 'Wor' (our) Jackie Milburn, the legendary Newcastle United goalscorer, a hero on Tyneside and beyond. His father was a miner, his thirteen-year-old brother Bobby already renowned as a prodigy destined, everyone agreed, to play for England. Jack turned professional with Leeds in 1953.

Bobby was a natural, bound for Manchester United, then England's most glamorous club. United, managed by Matt Busby, had won the FA Cup in 1948 playing inspiring, imaginative football that captivated a generation of youngsters growing up in the austere post-war world. Bobby Charlton remembers listening to the 1948 final on the radio and deciding that United was the club he wanted to join. The magic of their 4–2 victory over Stanley Matthews' Blackpool could be felt, imagined, even though in those far-off days all people would ever see were the clips of *Movietone News* on their cinema screens weeks after the event.

Brother Jack's Leeds United was not a glamour club. Ten years after leaving Ashington, Jack Charlton was still a journeyman pro, centre-half at Leeds, an unremarkable club in a city which preferred rugby league. Jack was perhaps best known for being Bobby's older brother. The team he played for was sliding down the Second Division.

English football was changing. A revolution was fermenting. Players had traditionally been slaves, bound to their clubs by lifelong contracts, freed only when the employer decided that they were too old to be of much use to anybody else. Until 1961 there was a maximum wage of £20, and among professional footballers, the more enlightened of them certainly, a sullen sense of grievance lingered about their serf-like terms of employment. They were filling stadiums, yet earning a pittance. They could break a leg and be out of work tomorrow, cast aside by callous bosses who'd stick a few pounds in their pocket and send them into the world ill-equipped for any other work.

Don Revie was the Leeds manager. Men of Revie's generation began to think about this injustice. Jimmy Hill assumed control of the players' union, the PFA, and after a bitter campaign of threats and agitation, the clubs were forced to remove the maximum wage a man could earn. The victory had a profound psychological effect in the dressing rooms of English football. For the first time players felt that they could earn what they were worth. Success would be rewarded, where previously there had been no difference between winners' and losers' wage packets.

Having thought about this, men like Revie began to think more about winning. And also about creating for players a new sense of belonging to the club, not as a serf but as a valued member of what Revie called 'the family'. Leeds United would be, he vowed, 'a family' for his players.

At Christmas there was a club party for wives and children. Players' wives would receive flowers at their bedside when they gave birth. Revie's door was always open to a player with personal problems. In this, the age of burgeoning sexual promiscuity among young people, with all the attendant worries for parents of young lads leaving home, Leeds United engaged a chaplain to counsel their players. But even more tangibly Revie, unlike more experienced Football League managers Matt Busby and Bill Shankly, took full advantage of the removal of the maximum wage to reward his men as handsomely as he could. In return he demanded more. Leeds would be fitter, more committed, in terms of thought and physical preparation, than any other side in the game. A spirit of them and us was fostered. Leeds felt themselves to be different from other clubs. A real team in a game still favouring and indulging the gifted individual.

As Revie's radical approach to club management bore fruit, Jack Charlton emerged as a key figure and became one of the finest central defenders in the game, winner of a World Cup winner's medal, partnering Bobby Moore at the heart of England's defence in 1966. But in the early 1960s Revie almost let him go.

Jack had his own ideas about things. He wasn't particularly enthusiastic on the training ground. He resisted the clubmanship ethos. Jack, the rebel, was sceptical of the 'all for one and one for all' idea.

Jack remained an occasionally truculent dissident, tolerated, on the whole, fondly by the squad of outstandingly gifted players with which Leeds became a feared and potent force in the English game for the decade beginning 1964. The team, now fielding young players Terry Cooper, Eddie Gray, Peter Lorimer, Paul Madeley, Allan Clarke alongside Giles, Hunter, Bremner and Charlton, became one of the best in the history of the game. Individually brilliant, collectively they were fiercely competitive to the point of callousness.

Extraordinary though the comparison may seem, for in terms of talent there is no comparison, it is accurate to say that Leeds were regarded as the Wimbledon of their era. Revie's team became synonymous with all that was bad in the game, being known not for their abundant gifts but the brutal physical intimidation of opponents which frequently degenerated into aggression for its own sake. Giles, Bremner and Hunter were the chief enforcers of Leeds' first principle, which too often seemed to be get your intimidation in first.

Always in contention for major honours, Leeds' decade at the summit of the English game yielded just one FA Cup and two Championships. They were runners-up in the First Division five times, fated, many felt, by their paranoia, a unique mean-spiritedness, never to fulfil their footballing potential.

In Revie's team, Jack Charlton made a dramatic transformation from middle-aged journeyman, brother-of-Bobby, to accomplished international defender. His distinctive, giraffe-like gait, which suggested awkwardness, belied a keen intelligence, pace and deftness in the tackle. Jack was naturally gifted in the air, a quality that Leeds exploited to telling effect at set pieces. Harassment was a favoured Leeds tactic and the sight of Big Jack discomforting opposing goalkeepers is an enduring memory of Revie's Leeds United.

The one dimension of Leeds' style that Jack Charlton didn't approve of was the naked aggression, which too often resulted in bloody feuding with the opposition. They would retort that instead of moaning at them, Jack, ideally positioned as a defender to do so, should be getting stuck in to even the score.

'They're kicking our forwards, why aren't you kicking theirs?' was the cry. However, Charlton always had a commendable dislike of the kind of physical intimidation for which Leeds are remembered more often than the quality of the football they played.

It is ironic, therefore, that when the football establishment's wrath finally fell upon Leeds, it was Jack Charlton who found himself in the dock. He had only himself to blame. In a careless moment of bravado Jack referred publicly to a 'little black book' in which he claimed he had written the names of a number of opponents marked down for retribution. The story made headlines in the tabloids and the ensuing controversy, during which Jack was severely reprimanded by the Football Association for 'bringing the game into disrepute', blemished the reputation of one of the fairest defenders in the Football League. The view in the Leeds dressing room was that the little black book never existed. Jack merely wished to convey the impression of toughness.

The supreme moment of Charlton's playing career came when England won the World Cup final, beating Germany 4–2 at Wembley on an unforgettable afternoon in June 1966, a triumph shared with his more distinguished brother, Bobby. Jack Charlton was finally vindicated, no longer merely the brother of England's greatest player. Sadly the relationship between the two had cooled. They are no closer today.

Jack believes that Bobby 'changed' after the Munich air crash, which claimed the lives of eight young Manchester United players in 1958. 'He was,' the older brother claims, 'never the same lad afterwards.'

Others who know both men well offer a different explanation. 'I think Jack used to embarrass Bobby,' one former colleague of both speculates. Bobby is every bit as tough as Jack, but more reserved and thoughtful. Controversy in the tabloids, such as the 'black book' affair, or the projection of Jack's favoured professional Geordie image would be anathema to Bobby.

Charlton the younger was renowned then, as now, for epitomising English dignity: the cool, clean graceful hero as depicted in *Boy's Own*. As their respective careers progressed, the incompatibility between Jack and Bobby might best be defined not as a case of people at odds, but rather as a matter of conflicting public personas. Bobby courteous, the ambassador for English soccer, ever diplomatic, heading via the BBC and his seat on Manchester United's board for football statesmanship; Jack, indubitably ITV, unreconstructed Geordie calling a bloody spade exactly that and upsetting anyone who stands in his way. Jack the lad, Bobby the gent.

Professional footballers lead a cloistered existence. As you train, travel, rest in hotel rooms, the outside world becomes remote. Family and friends are 'out there' somewhere. You exist in a cocoon surrounded by other players, the manager, the trainers and retainers there to pander to your every worldly whim. This preparation for the thing that really matters, the ninety minutes of extraordinarily intense experience, the match, can seem rather like a prison. In this all-male environment you become very close to the other inmates, familiar with their quirks and insecurities.

For Don Revie's Leeds United the natural sense of isolation was accentuated by the manager's insistence that they leave home to stay in a local hotel the day before home games. Their success over a period of almost a decade meant that Leeds competed in Europe every season. Inordinately close bonds were formed. These men knew each other more intimately than most.

Within this unique family, each carved out a role for himself, a character part, usually at odds with the public's perception of the man. John Giles of the quiet, cerebral public persona, the ultimate pro, was privately the joker, his astute appreciation of the human condition allowing him to spot vanity or insecurity and, whenever possible, in the long boring hours of rest or travel, exploit such foibles as existed for amusement.

Billy Bremner was as wildly impetuous off-stage as on, a 'live-hard-play-hard' Scot with a cruel sense of humour. Peter Lorimer, explosive on the field, was a different kind of Scot: cool, sardonic, composed, cat-like, vigilant. Peter was a heavy gambler, trusting horses more than people. Norman Hunter, the most feared defender in the English game, a potent presence on any battleground, was, in civvies, a pussycat: open, honest, naive, trusting, a gentleman in a world where fear had corroded many spirits.

Jack Charlton was the registered eccentric in this group. Jack was Jack, a law unto himself in all things. Among these smart late 1960s lads with well-cut suits and longish hair, Jack, plain, straight Jack, stood out. A man from the previous decade. He was by several years the oldest of the team – a former playing colleague of Revie – and this showed in many ways. His hair was thinning, his dress sense a source of some amusement. While the others carried their smart suits in hangers over their shoulders, Jack would arrive at the airport or railway station with his old anorak in the same conveyance. This inspired much hilarity. Why bother hanging it up, Jack?

Teasing Jack was the first resort on quiet days. Monday morning in the dressing room, a bitter cold wind is blowing outside. A laugh is badly needed. Jack has a ritual of going to the toilet with his *Daily Mirror*. As he sits, contentedly browsing, Giles and Bremner steal into the adjoining loo with a bucket of cold water. The water is deposited over the partition. A sharp intake of breath indicates that the water has found its target. Moments later, the victim appears at the dressing-room door. The room is hushed, no eyes meet Jack's. Jack knows the guilty men but can't prove anything. 'You fucking bastards,' he seethes, looking at Giles and Bremner. 'Fucking, childish bastards,' he continues. 'I'll tell you what, nobody is going to have a crap in peace in this place from now on. I'll fucking have you lot,' Jack vows, to general protestations of innocence.

The figure that greets the eyes which now look up to see what the fuss is all about is drenched. The thinning hair hangs in damp strands down his neck and forehead, his tracksuit is dripping, his *Daily Mirror* soggy. 'Bastards ... never grow up ...' he mutters as he turns to leave the room. But first a parting shot: 'Anyway you missed!' The room erupts, the day is off to a good start with a vintage Jack performance.

What makes this moment so delightful to the perpetrators is not the drowning of Jack, so much as his assertion that they missed. Despite irrefutable evidence to the contrary, Jack would not be wrong, could not concede, would always have the last word. Jack was abnormally stubborn. But he didn't bear grudges, people did subsequently 'have a crap in peace' as the incident was quickly forgotten.

In the Leeds dressing room Jack was regarded as an odd but essentially decent older brother to the more delinquent inmates. Traits that would not be tolerated in other men were, in his case, excused. He was careful with money, a capital offence in most groups. He'd cadge fags, borrow a fiver and forget to pay it back, and never rush to the bar to buy the first round of drinks. He was never at fault for a goal conceded, always tracing the cause to an error made elsewhere. He was irascible, but not sly or unduly self-regarding, unforgivable crimes in this male community.

Leeds reached the FA Cup final in 1972, Jack's testimonial year. This was a rare opportunity to make some money, especially for the players in the squad who weren't on the highest wage scale. All squad income, from tickets (many of them traded on the black market) and commercial product endorsement, was traditionally 'pooled' and shared equally among the squad.

In 1972 Jack demurred. As a World Cup hero, Jack was among the more coveted commercial endorsers, certain to earn a tidy individual sum. Rather than donate this to the 'pool', Jack insisted that it be earmarked for his testimonial fund. A row ensued. A vote was called. Jack found himself in a minority of one. He stuck to his guns and that was it. Don Revie's intervention made no difference.

A singular man, but genuinely so, Jack – a certain selfishness and insensitivity notwithstanding – was, and remains, fondly regarded by those whose lives he shared. The petulance and obstinacy fundamental to his character was more readily tolerated by the group on the important issues to do with the game.

Jack was a significant contributor on the field. Curiously, despite his later prominence as coach and commentator, he remained a relatively uninfluential voice on matters of a tactical nature.

Jack was a coach. While still a player he'd been to Lilleshall to acquire his coaching badge, signalling that he wanted to stay in the game when he finished playing. Lilleshall was a controversial place, especially at the highest levels of the game where natural ability was cherished as the supreme currency. Lilleshall: the word was uttered with contempt. What the fuck do they know at Lilleshall? In the opinion of most of the better players and many of the deepest thinkers, Lilleshall was a weird laboratory where mad boffins, schoolteachers and others who'd failed to make it in first-class football, tried to rationalise soccer as a game bad footballers could play and schoolteachers could understand.

Had Matt Busby been to Lilleshall ... or Shankly ... or Bill Nicholson ... what would they say about George Best at the college that taught football? Some of this criticism was harsh, some irrational, but the core criticism, that what was essential to the creation of great football could not be passed on by a hierarchy of theorists, was valid. Coaching as understood by the Lilleshall establishment remains a controversial topic, for it places tactics – the coaches' view of the game – above the natural gifts of footballers. Coaching, at least bad coaching enforced by men with sterile imaginations and little faith in players, blights the English game.

Yet in 1971 the coaching philosophy received impressive testimony when Arsenal, coached by Don Howe, won the Double – Championship and the FA Cup – only the second team to do so in the modern game. Spurs, managed by Bill Nicholson and led by Danny Blanchflower, had done the Double ten years earlier playing the kind of fluent, imaginative football of which Howe's Arsenal Double side were the very antithesis. Significantly the present Arsenal manager, George Graham, was a member of that Arsenal team.

In very simple terms this coaching was, and is, more about destruction than creation. Players are harnessed to a system rather than freed to play the game, their own talent being the primary resource. The more insidious problem with coaching is that it vests power in the man with the badge, wearing a tracksuit, power that ought to be vested in footballers.

Coaching attracts bullies, opinionated bullies who fall in love with the power and the jargon of coaching which they employ to convey the notion that football is not the beautiful accessible game of the streets but some higher calling that can be learned, like geometry, from a book. The recently departed England manager, Graham Taylor, was the quintessential Lilleshall coach. The football played by George Graham's Arsenal is the game as preached at Lilleshall.

When Jack Charlton returned to Elland Road with his coaching badge he got short shrift. Lilleshall cut no ice in a dressing room full of outstanding footballers who, intuitively, knew the game. Billy Bremner was the player closest to Don Revie, John Giles the most influential voice in the dressing room. Jack was a noisy distraction.

Significantly, when Revie resigned to become England manager, he recommended Giles to the Leeds board as his successor. It should be noted that in the early Revie years Leeds had been the masters of negative football, a well organised, ruthlessly destructive unit designed to suppress the creativity of better sides. By the early 1970s Revie's team had, however, evolved. It was now one of the greatest (though ill-starred) club sides of all time.

Jack Charlton retired in 1973. He was thirty-eight and had enjoyed a magnificent career during which he'd won almost every honour the game has to offer. Only the European Champions Cup had eluded Jack. A career that began in 1953, the year Hungary beat England at Wembley, was distinguished by a World Cup winner's medal and thirty-four appearances for his country.

Jack had been a late developer. The last decade of his career had seen him grow from journeyman to renown as one of the best central defenders ever to wear an England shirt. He was a one-club man, playing 629 Football League games for Leeds United. From a team whose reputation would always be more than a little tarnished for the dubious tactics it too often employed, Charlton emerged unblemished. To the rule that Leeds were bad, Jack Charlton was the exception.

In the years after England's World Cup victory, Jack had become a popular hero. Television made him. Soccer was now fashionable.

Television paid more attention and engaged experts to analyse the game for a growing audience. Jimmy Hill was the first TV pundit, rendering football's mysteries understandable to all. ITV expanded this service by forming a panel of experts, respected characters from the professional ranks, to deconstruct the happenings on the field. Jack Charlton was a founder member of the first TV panel. Malcolm Allison, then football's leading coach, was another. Paddy Crerand of Manchester United and Scotland, Bob McNab of Arsenal, and John Bond joined Jack and Malcolm for television's first football brains trust.

This radical broadcasting development proved immensely popular with viewers. The old, bland BBC commentary, the banal leading the blind, was exposed for what it was … trite, conservative and condescending to the public. The panel soon became an indispensable element of television's football coverage. The opinions expressed by these knowledgeable football men were vivid, pungent, uncompromising, gave credit where it was properly due and placed responsibility for matches lost … and goals conceded … where it properly belonged.

This was sensational stuff, a wholesome diet of football talk, which the audience hungrily consumed. For the first time the fans, whose devotion was football's *raison d'être*, were privy to the kind of genuine argument and debate professionals used to conduct behind closed doors.

Allison, Charlton and their fellow panellists spoke with real authority, telling it as it was, sparing no player or manager, or coach, who failed to do the business. Feathers were ruffled. It was Allison, 'Big Mal', and Jack Charlton, 'Big Jack', who cut to the heart of things. These two were hard. But fair.

But the panel could not sustain the show. Egos got out of hand. Controversy was now contrived; good football talk deteriorated into showbiz. Brian Clough appeared on the scene at some stage. The game was up.

The lads became performers. Jack was the exception. He was a natural performer. He spoke the language of the common man without apparent affectation. The Geordie dialect was perfect. And he was good on the game. He got to the point rather than engage in abstract stuff about what might have been.

Jack saw the game from a defender's perspective. Goals were scored, chances created because defenders were 'hurt'. The way to hurt defenders was to get the ball in behind them. Teams played well when they hurt defenders, badly when they didn't.

By the time he retired from playing, Jack, 'Big Jack', was an established English character. The unvarnished, northern 'Man of the People'. He belonged with Geoffrey Boycott, Arthur Scargill and Brian Clough, men who were respected for being distinctly of their place. Tough, uncompromising, plain-speaking fellows who probably ate chip butties for tea.

Jack Charlton accepted the position of manager at Middlesbrough in 1973. This was a shrewd move. Clever, ambitious football managers are always on the look-out for what are known as 'sleeping giants'; clubs with potential that are currently underachieving. Clubs that, with sensible management, 'can only go one way'.

Middlesbrough was not exactly in that category. Rather, it was a club with First Division credentials, a good squad of players, with a few 'bob' to spend to secure promotion from the Second Division, which had narrowly eluded them for several seasons.

Jack seized this first opportunity to put his theories to the test in magnificent fashion. He bought Graeme Souness from Spurs reserves and Bobby Murdoch, a veteran from the Celtic team which won the European Cup in 1967. Around those two gifted players Charlton built an outstanding side that won promotion by a record number of points in their first season.

Jack's Middlesbrough team was arguably the best ever to gain promotion from that division. Certainly, no side in my experience of the Second Division dominated as Jack's did. The team I recall playing against (my last game for Millwall, in fact) was fluent, tough and well organised. They won the title by fifteen points, an unheard of margin in what was traditionally the toughest league of all.

Alas, Middlesbrough made no impression in the First Division. Murdoch aged, Souness demanded to go (to Liverpool) and the vicissitudes of club management began to get to Jack, who'd always claimed that he didn't need football. If you don't need it you'll never stick it.

Managing a football club is only partly about football. Players are human, have problems, need cosseting and cajoling, insecurities must be cared for. Haggling over wages is perennial. Players' wives become disenchanted. That's your problem too, if you're the manager.

'The club house (still a feature in the 1970s) isn't quite right, wife's not happy boss.' 'We can't settle (in the north/south/east/west).' 'I want away.' 'Why have I been dropped, played out of position, treated unfairly?'

Every day one of those problems will land on the boss's desk. Jack didn't need that. He was earning a handsome income outside the game. Television offered punditry and more: his own Channel 4 series on his favourite hobby, angling. There was the ghosted newspaper column in the *Express*. And Jack Charlton was in great demand as an after-dinner speaker.

He was, is, a superb turn at the brandy and port stage of those dreadful functions popularly known as 'sportsmen's evenings'. Everyone is full of bonhomie and booze, everyone feels sentimental, though the food is lousy. Then Jack stands up. He's a great raconteur. The anecdotes about the World Cup, 'our kid' (Bobby), the hard men of Leeds are delivered deftly. He is funny, sometimes wickedly indiscreet. The room smiles benignly upon him ... and he on it: all men together, sportsmen, great stuff, all agree. Good old Jack.

And no pressure. No whingeing players ... or bitter players' wives. No directors or sceptical, tiresomely ignorant journalists. Still, Jack persevered with 'Boro until 1977, in the end leaving them, as he has said himself, 'better off' than when he arrived.

Middlesbrough simply didn't have the money to complete their grandiose plans for Ayresome Park and buy good players. The board opted for expansion off the field rather than invest in the team.

Jack went to Sheffield Wednesday in 1977, a sleeping giant that had lapsed into semi-consciousness. Wednesday were buried in the Third Division. Another club that had put money into a splendid stadium, Hillsborough, instead of players. Sheffield was traditionally a passionate football city, Wednesday, rather than United, the team. Jack couldn't go wrong. He didn't. Between 1977 and 1983 he took Wednesday into the Second Division where they became a force always there, or thereabouts, in the promotion race. Jack's Sheffield Wednesday gave expression to his now well-developed footballing philosophy.

One night in Brussels, towards the end of the Sheffield period, I met him in the bar of Ireland's hotel. He'd come to look at a Belgian player in that night's World Cup qualifier. We fell to talking about English football. In such circumstances Jack was genial company as long as you kept him supplied with beer and left your cigarettes on the table.

'You need a good goalkeeper, a big, aggressive centre-back, someone to win the ball in midfield and a good target-man up front,' he expounded. This was not a particularly original theory, a strong backbone has always been the foundation of successful teams. Yet, as Jack elaborated, it was clear that like nearly all players of his generation, and mine, he believed the English game was 'gone'.

'The players aren't there' is a fair summary of the conclusion we agreed upon. Of course, this meant the coach was more important, the task being to devise a system of play that placed a premium on discipline and organisation, and didn't demand of players skills that they didn't possess. In this Jack Charlton was a realist and, given that he was manager of Sheffield Wednesday, his views made sense.

In 1983 he ceased to be Wednesday's manager. Talking to him in Brussels, other irritations had surfaced. Freedom of contract for players had made club management very difficult. Building a team was virtually impossible. Players could leave at the end of their contract, appealing to the Independent Tribunal, who invariably awarded the selling club less than your man's true value.

One sensed in Jack, and indeed in most other managers of English clubs who spoke about the contemporary game (men reared in a different era when players were serfs), an abiding frustration with the circumstances in which they were obliged to work. Ironically, Wednesday gained promotion shortly after Jack departed.

After a spell out of work devoted to the lucrative business of being a celebrity, Jack returned to the fray the following year. Another sleeping giant, Newcastle United, had just been promoted to the First (now Premier) Division. Jack's boyhood club, the scene of 'Wor' Jackie Milburn's legendary deeds, meant an emotional return to his Geordie roots. Sadly it also ended in tears.

A few months into the job Jack walked out. According to George Best, Jack 'bottled' the challenge of managing good players such as Chris Waddle and Peter Beardsley in the big league. (George is, however, hardly an objective witness for there was no love lost between him and the Charlton brothers. Jack the pundit had excoriated George for his various lapses down the years.)

Chris Waddle suggests more plausibly that Jack's commitment to management was by this time questionable. As evidence, Waddle tells of a morning before an important Newcastle game when Jack and his players are on the training ground. A car pulls up alongside, the driver one of the boss's fishing companions: 'Jack, Jack, there's trout in the Tweed.' Exit boss and mate.

Hostility from Newcastle fans who chanted 'We hate you, Charlton' was the last straw for Big Jack. If Waddle's story smacks of the apocryphal, it merely confirms the impression Charlton has always striven to convey that there is more to life than being messed around by footballers, or any other of the game's attendant irritants, such as directors or journalists.

Best's reference to Jack's 'bottle', his capacity to take pressure in the form of criticism or supporters' expectations, tends to reinforce the recollections of those who shared the Elland Road dressing room with him. 'Jack hated pressure,' one Leeds colleague recalls, 'his bottle would go when things got rough.' Newcastle seemed to signal the end of Charlton's career in management. He was back to punditry and the after-dinner circuit, with time for his fishing and shooting, answerable to nobody.

Until 1986, that is, when the ultimate sleeping giant, the Irish soccer team, began looking for a manager to replace Eoin Hand. Ireland's last competitive game under Hand was a disastrous 4–1 home defeat by Denmark. Lansdowne Road was virtually empty and travelling Danes made up much of the attendance for this World Cup qualifier. Ireland were humiliated.

A squad including Paul McGrath, David O'Leary, Mark Lawrenson, Frank Stapleton, Ronnie Whelan, Kevin Moran and Liam Brady had become weary and demoralised through the course of the qualifying campaign for the 1986 Mexico World Cup. By the time Ireland played Denmark, the team was hardly functioning at all.

To say Ireland was disorganised would be a considerable understatement. Yet Eoin Hand, with the active support of his pals in the press box, seemed by no means certain to end his seven-year reign as Irish manager. Who else was there? The players were to blame. 'A manager can do nothing once the teams take the field' was a popular line touted by journalists, who would subsequently deify Jack Charlton for working miracles for Ireland.

Facing bankruptcy and a relentless campaign from a couple of dissident journalists, the Football Association of Ireland grasped the Hand nettle, answering the question 'Who else?' by conducting a series of interviews with England-based candidates. From this process, driven by an enlightened minority in Merrion

Square, four candidates emerged in public: Jack Charlton, Liam Tuohy, John Giles and Billy McNeill, then managing Manchester City.

Privately the majority on the FAI Council were plotting a coup to install the most successful manager in English football history, Bob Paisley, recently retired from Liverpool. The idea, a dodgy one, was that Paisley would manage part-time with an Irish assistant, thereby allowing the FAI to retain maximum control over what might be best called 'events'. This was going to be a repeat of the Hand era.

Of the four publicly acknowledged runners, Charlton and Tuohy were least favoured. McNeill seemed the ideal choice. Giles, a return to a previous frowned-upon regime, was informed that he was the FAI's favourite, for which blessing he was invited to come to Dublin on D-Day, prepared to assume command.

This was a shabby charade. The Paisley plot did not include a role for Giles. Deviousness and ineptitude, characteristics common to football legislators the world over, produced a surprise result on that Friday in February 1986: Jack Charlton was to be Ireland's new manager.

The plot to install Paisley failed when one of those involved in the secret ballot reneged. As a consequence, the Liverpool manager fell one vote short of the ten required to prevail. Paisley got nine votes, Giles, Tuohy and Charlton three apiece (McNeill had been forced to withdraw by Manchester City), and so it went to a second ballot. 'Some rat threw a spanner in the wheels,' a conspirator later muttered.

Giles was despised by too many in the boardroom, while Tuohy suffered the disability of being liked and respected in the Irish football community, 'one of our own'. So Jack cruised home on the final count. Bob Paisley, waiting by his telephone in Liverpool, was shocked to learn that he would not get the 'nixer' of managing Ireland. Nobody could find Jack Charlton's phone number. Despite frantic efforts to contact the victor charged with waking the sleeping giant, it was the following day before Jack learned of his good fortune.

The press conference at the Westbury was crowded. RTÉ was out in force, every journalist in Dublin seemed to be on the case when Jack was formally introduced to Ireland. He was superb. Funny, amenable, promising every co-operation with the media, willing, astonishingly, to give all present his home phone number. He was delighted to have the job. He knew the quality of the Irish squad and although he promised nothing specific, he was optimistic that Ireland could become a force in the international game. A warmth enveloped the proceedings, a sense that this indubitably professional character, large and football wise, would enable the Irish soccer team to fulfil its fabled potential.

All queries satisfied, Jack – 'Mr Charlton' as one eager (for the first exclusive) hack addressed him – prepared to go. Peter Byrne of *The Irish Times* begged one final question, not of Mr Charlton but of Des Casey, President of the FAI, who, along with the rest of his committee, sat proudly by their chosen man.

The question, innocuous but valid, concerned the shambles of the previous Friday night. Casey shifted uneasily in his chair. Details of the failed coup were not yet out. And this would hardly be the time or place for that to happen. A frisson of embarrassment could now be felt. An unwelcome vibe.

Casey hummed and hawed for a moment or two. Jack, Big Jack, began to flush as he is prone to do when he is about to get 'the needle'. 'Hold on a minute,' Charlton exclaimed, fixing Byrne with a stony look, 'what's this got to do with anything? The past's the past, I've been appointed. He,' (a nod in Casey's direction), 'doesn't have to answer any questions from you.'

Byrne, later to become Big Jack's Boswell (*World Cup Diary 1990*), was in big trouble. He had caused offence to the man who'd come to save Ireland, this genial, journalist-friendly, famous World Cup-winning, footballing fisherman.

Byrne and I were hardly friends (he thinking, aloud, that I was not 'a proper journalist'), yet I felt compelled to intervene, to offer a modicum of support. Byrne was absolutely within his rights on an issue, the shambolic administration of football, of acute public interest. When I argued this with Charlton, Byrne was off the hook. I replaced him on it.

Big Jack now gave me the treatment, 'I know you … you're a troublemaker.' I insisted that journalists had rights which he couldn't proscribe, and anyway this argument was not with him, or his appointment, but with the boys in blazers beside him. My conciliatory tone did not mollify Jack. Sensing that the mood in the room favoured him, he made to rise with the words: 'Do you want to settle this outside?' I declined.

The assembled elite of Dublin journalism then did something quite remarkable. There was a burst of applause; like a wave, it engulfed the room. They were applauding him. The Charlton era had begun.

Wales beat Ireland 1–0 in Lansdowne Road in Charlton's first game in charge. Ian Rush scored on a cold, windy afternoon. Although defeated, Ireland looked like a team that day. There was a shape and sense of purpose about the side that had been woefully missing under the previous regime. Nobody minded about the scoreline. What was obvious and reassuring was the discipline, coherence and enthusiasm of the players, who looked as if they understood what they were trying to achieve.

In June Ireland were due to play in a friendly international tournament in Iceland. David O'Leary was surprisingly omitted from the squad chosen to travel to Reykjavík. O'Leary had been an outstanding player for Ireland over the years. He was an important member of the Arsenal side, one of the best in the First Division. Although Paul McGrath, Kevin Moran and Mick McCarthy were available as alternative central defenders, O'Leary's omission from the squad was strange. Especially as Mark Lawrenson had indicated that he would be unavailable for the trip to Iceland, preferring instead to take a holiday with his Liverpool clubmates after their strenuous season.

O'Leary, though disappointed, was philosophical. He is not the demonstrative type. There were no complaints in the tabloids. David booked his own family holiday. Then, for one reason or another, but mainly because the three Liverpool players – Lawrenson, Jim Beglin and Ronnie Whelan – decided to do what O'Leary had done, a crime for which they were never subsequently punished, Jack's squad was seriously depleted at season's end. He decided David was needed after all, and phoned the Arsenal centre-half to request his presence. O'Leary declined on the grounds that he didn't want to disappoint his family at such short notice. The seed of Jack Charlton's first telling major controversy was sown.

Ireland won the Reykjavík tournament. A modest but not insignificant portent of better things to come. The best, most desired, of those things was qualification for the 1988 European Championship finals in West Germany. Ireland, having failed narrowly to do so on a number of previous occasions, regarded qualification for the finals of a major international tournament as deserved vindication of the talents of our team.

The first match of the European Championship series was against Belgium in Brussels in September 1986. The Belgians were a good side, old adversaries who usually got the better of us. But not on this occasion. A Liam Brady penalty scored a couple of minutes from time earned Ireland a 2–2 draw. That was an excellent beginning, the point won being well-deserved after a convincingly spirited performance.

Back at the hotel where the Irish party was lodged, a small group of us gathered in the early hours of the following morning. The players were in bed or out on the town. A number of Irish journalists and a few fans were joined in the residents' bar by Jack and his assistant, Maurice Setters. A singsong was in progress, the mood jolly, as other, less encouraging nights were remembered. Nights of ifs, buts and maybes, losing nights, when the moral victories that Ireland was famous for were all we had to celebrate. Fuck moral victories, this was better. We drank to that. And sang our songs.

Jack received the noble call. Without hesitation, he obliged. His song, a moving, melancholy English ballad, commanded order of a kind extended only when such renditions are heartfelt. And well performed, as this one was. When he finished Jack was close to tears, some long-buried emotion touched at this moment, in this hotel room, late at night in the company of strangers.

Wiping a tear from his eye he laughed: 'If any of you tell anyone about this, I'll bloody well have you.' This was the private man, the character remembered fondly by his colleagues at Leeds, forgiven his idiosyncrasies because behind it all there was a soul more tender than the face the public saw.

Ireland were in a tough qualifying group. As well as Belgium there was Scotland and Bulgaria; Luxembourg were the fodder. But the sleeping giant was beginning to wake up, become formidably professional. Jack Charlton's team was designed to compete on its own terms, to play the British way, to contest every yard of space, denying European opposition time and room to develop their own rhythm, to compose themselves, especially at the back where their defenders liked to stroke the ball around as a prelude to launching swift, incisive attacks.

Having been to the 1986 World Cup finals in Mexico to assess potential opponents, such as the Belgians, Charlton decided that aggressive disruption of their pattern of play, as it began in their own half, was the way to rattle players accustomed to a more leisurely approach.

Managers of international teams from these islands had for too long been seduced by styles of play that British players were not familiar with. In this process the quintessential qualities of players from these islands were sacrificed. Trying to ape Europeans and South Americans, we – and here no distinction need be drawn between Ireland and England – had betrayed the virtues that were fundamental to our nature: resilience; determination; physical endurance; power in the air; above all, a willingness to battle harder and longer than our more technically gifted adversaries.

A certain conviction about values that were inherently British/Irish distinguished Jack Charlton's approach to the task of managing Ireland. This conviction was very welcome, reminiscent of Alf Ramsey who managed England's World Cup-winning team that Charlton played in. And Ireland's progress through the European Championship qualifying series bore witness to this conviction.

The compromise involved seemed at first acceptable: with the two best central defenders in Britain at his disposal, Charlton chose to play Paul McGrath and Mark Lawrenson elsewhere, in midfield or at full-back. Mick McCarthy was a fixture at centre-half. David O'Leary was banished from the squad for being disloyal.

A great victory over Scotland at Hampden Park should be recalled as, perhaps, the definitive expression of the remarkable compound of pragmatism and conviction Jack Charlton uniquely possessed. McGrath played right-back, Lawrenson in midfield, Ronnie Whelan as stop-gap left-back. A magnificent Irish performance vouched for the courage and discipline of the players and the manager's inspirational leadership.

After the years of glorious failure, this was an occasion to savour. Reservations about McCarthy and the injustice of O'Leary's enforced exile seemed inappropriate.

Other disturbing matters were not addressed, lest the optimism of the 'New Era' be in any way undermined. There was, for example, the brutal treatment of Liam Tuohy, Ireland Youth team coach. Tuohy had been a great player in the wonderful Shamrock Rovers teams of the 1950s and 1960s. The 1950s team, led by Paddy Coad on and off the field, was part of Irish soccer folklore.

The League of Ireland in its most glorious period was Irish football at its most captivating, witty, imaginative, an enthralling blend of deftness and power, the original game of streets rendered magically glamorous by the smell of liniment, the dazzling colours and the vast crowds that in the 1950s thronged to Dalymount, Tolka Park, the Mardyke in Cork, Limerick's Markets Field, Waterford's Kilcohan. But nowhere was magic more intoxicatingly tangible than at Glenmalure Park, the home of Shamrock Rovers, The Hoops of green and white legend.

The names still reverberate down the years, the memories as vivid now in middle age as when we were kids waiting anxiously on College Green after Sunday lunch to claim a place on those packed CIÉ special buses. They were special all right, transporting us to a scene of incredible drama, a pageant that nurtured our dreams. Paddy Coad, Liam Hennessy, Ronnie Nolan, Mickey Burke, 'Maxie' McCann, Paddy Ambrose, Christy O'Callaghan in goal, Noel Peyton and Liam Tuohy.

As long as soccer is played in Ireland those names will be revered, those times talked about, our Golden Age, the drab 1950s, poverty redeemed in splendour by a love affair with this beautiful game, played by these extraordinary men. In their finest hour The Hoops went to Old Trafford to play the Busby Babes in the European Cup, losing 3–2. The Manchester crowd, who had seen Real Madrid and all the great European sides, saluted this group of working men, accessible heroes, our heroes, from the streets of Dublin.

This was Irish soccer, the guile of the streets, the dreams of urchins, given life and expression. Between that world and the Charlton era there were bonds that were precious, that gave resonance, true meaning to the Lansdowne Road thing. Ronnie Whelan's father, the late Ronnie Snr, played for St Pat's in the Golden Age.

Christy O'Leary, David's dad, was around; his close friend 'Bunny' Fullam, Drum's legendary full-back, had spent what seemed like a lifetime kicking Liam Tuohy. The Gileses – Dickie, John's dad, his uncle Christy – were real Dublin football people, steeped in the lore of the game.

John Giles, the greatest son ever conceived in that beautiful culture, remembers Sunday evenings outside Fagan's – and other venues – sitting in Dickie's old car eating Tayto crisps and drinking orange. We all have memories out of which our infinite love for soccer was forged. Mine are of other working-class heroes who played in Drumcondra's gold and blue in Tolka Park on Richmond Road, where I was born and reared. 'Bunny' Fullam, 'Rosie' Henderson, Johnny Robinson, Baldy Johnny, Paddy Neville, a goalkeeping giant.

And others, gifted working men, poets from the streets, 'Kit' Lawlor, Ben Hannigan, Shay Gibbons, 'Ollie' Conroy, Terry's older brother, 'Ginger' O'Rourke, who played like Gibbons for Pat's with Ronnie – Whelan's dad. The Bradys were also members of Dublin's football aristocracy. Ray, Pat, Eamonn, Liam's brothers from whom the gift was passed on, as it was to Ronnie Whelan, David O'Leary, John Giles.

This is Irish soccer, the legacy Jack Charlton inherited, knowing nothing about it of course, knowing least of all about the distance from Lilleshall to the back streets of this old garrison city where the 'foreign game' was life, miserable life redeemed, as in the slums of Glasgow, Liverpool, Naples and the shanty towns of Brazil by the magical whimsy of a ball.

Preaching Irish football, Liam Tuohy had been very successful with the Irish Youth team. He had taken his boys to the equivalent of the World Cup semi-final at their level. It was, however, good habits rather than the need to win that Tuohy tried to instil in his players. This good-humoured, knowledgeable man was perfect for the task of introducing young lads to representative football.

One evening shortly after he assumed command of the senior side Charlton went to Elland Road to watch the Irish Youths play. The first half proved difficult for the Irish youngsters. At half-time Charlton breezed into the dressing room, in itself a serious breach of protocol, and insisted that Liam Tuohy sit down while he read the riot act to the players. This was outrageous, the behaviour of an insensitive bully. Tuohy was completely undermined. He did the right thing, resigning soon afterwards.

This rather unpleasant exercise of authority did not make news. The senior team's improved results were beginning to render criticism of Charlton dangerous. In the hysteria engendered by later success – or what presumed to be success – expression of alternative opinions became life-threatening!

Misgivings about the glorious new age continued in relation to David O'Leary's absurd exile from the Irish squad. This also passed without much comment. Quite simply the journalists assigned to the Irish case were afraid of Charlton's wrath.

Cap in hand, shifting impatiently, his replies were curtly dismissive. Occasionally he would erupt indignantly, 'I'm not answering that,' fixing a glare on the unfortunate hack doing no worse than his job. At the very least this conduct was unprofessional, some might argue intolerable. Here the print and broadcasting media were sympathetic to the point of obsequiousness.

The name of David O'Leary, raised the odd time by brave souls, provoked seething anger. 'I'm sick of hearing about David O'Leary,' he retorted on more than one occasion.

Ireland qualified for the 1988 European Championship finals thanks to a goal scored by the Scotsman Gary Mackay one minute from the end of his country's away game in Bulgaria. We deserved our good fortune.

John Aldridge and Ray Houghton had been successfully integrated into the side. Packie Bonner made some magnificent saves at vital times. Paul McGrath scored a superb goal to salvage two points that looked threatened at home to Luxembourg. Lawrenson and Whelan contributed hugely. Liam Brady was a better player in the disciplined Charlton set-up than previously under Eoin Hand. Tony Galvin and Kevin Sheedy were similarly better players in a resilient, well-balanced team.

The creation of harmony in the dressing room is the hardest task facing an international team manager. Charlton succeeded in forging a common identity rare at this level of the game.

When Ireland beat England in Stuttgart in the opening game of the Championship the country went crazy with delight. People who never before took notice of 'the foreign game', some who despised it, joined the national celebration. This was more than sport, Orwell's 'mimic war', an ancient score settled in the most satisfying manner possible. Olé, Olé, Olé … Olé.

Defeat of England was followed by a superb performance against the Soviet Union in Hanover. Fluent and inspiringly determined, Ireland took the lead through a stunning Ronnie Whelan goal. John Aldridge should have converted a chance created by Tony Galvin, the climax of a lovely bout of football. The Soviets were lucky to snatch a draw in the memorable game.

Three days later we lost to Holland, the reigning European Champions, by the narrowest of margins. Drained by the heroic efforts of an historic adventure, Ireland played indifferently, before losing 1–0 in Gelsenkirchen.

The Irish fans, 15 to 20,000 of them, had transformed the usually grim ambience of major soccer championships, the familiar aura of incipient violence, into a wonderful carnival of good humour. The streets of German cities resembled a small Irish town at Fleadh Ceoil weekend, with music, song, banter, the generous good fellowship of a Munster final day radiating around an international event more closely associated with security and hooliganism.

At the end of the game in Gelsenkirchen, Ireland made her exit from these championships in style, joining with their Dutch counterparts to salute the teams in an inspiring display of sportsmanship. We were proud of our team, their gallant endurance, their behaviour in victory and defeat, which was a tribute to their manager, and with good reason we could be proud of our country which, through the gloriously natural humour and dignity of the Irish supporters, had reminded Europe that international sport could be a festival of unsullied joy.

In an age when it is idly alleged that winning is everything, the Irish had proven that it was not. For services rendered to sport and the nation, the Irish team, Jack Charlton's Irish team, was welcomed home by half-a-million people. A tribute richly deserved.

After Stuttgart this was no longer a football story. Jack and his valiant team, and the good-natured army of supporters who travelled to make carnival wherever they played, offered this nation a glorious image of itself with which we fell in love. Even the most rigorous mind was seduced by the symbolism: after centuries of oppressive defeat the English had been vanquished. And at their own game.

That Ireland was the most enthusiastic member state in the European Community was no accident. No nation longed more profoundly than Ireland to be, in the patriot Robert Emmet's words, free to take 'her place among the nations of the world'. Our presence at the European Championship finals, the victory over England, the valiant performance against Holland, who went on to win the tournament, all of this represented something more than sporting achievement.

In the modern world, nations much more powerful than Ireland look to their sportsmen and women, as if at a mirror, to understand more the state of their own spirit. In Britain, the USA and the old Soviet Empire, performance in the international sports arena was the barometer by which decline – or prosperity – was gauged.

When Ireland reflected on its condition in the summer of 1988, the image of the Jack Charlton team and its now legendary supporters offered persuasive evidence that we had matured, taken our rightful place in the international community, yet lost none of our capacity to celebrate life, to sing, tell stories and laugh our way through the long, dark night.

Around this pleasing image a nation gathered to worship. Every Irish match drew people from their homes to pubs, clubs, village halls, to follow the story. Offices closed, no work was done on the sacred occasion of The Game. Families came together, as they would at Christmas, or a wedding or christening, to share the joyous experience of following this football team. Neighbours who'd not previously done so, spoke warmly to each other. Even in the stuffiest suburbs, protocol dissolved, ladies and gentlemen cast away their inhibitions and started chewing.

Proof that Ireland had truly arrived to take her rightful place among the nations of the world was provided when we qualified for the 1990 World Cup finals. 1988 had not been a fluke, some gloriously deceptive illusion; Jack Charlton really had delivered the vision first proposed by Robert Emmet. Charlton was no longer a coach, rather a character of legend.

There were now two stories unfolding, though the story that was about football was ironic and not particularly inspiring. As Italia '90 illustrated, international soccer was sadly impoverished. No great player emerged in the tournament, no Pelé, no Bobby Charlton, no Franz Beckenbauer. Maradona, supreme in Mexico in 1986, was now influential only in spasms, a great player, spirit and body bruised beyond repair, playing from memory. That was enough to see Argentina through to the final, a memorably mediocre contest which the Germans won by default. Italia '90 will be remembered by the international football community as a moment when cynicism prevailed at the expense of the game's most inspiring virtues. Italia '90 was banal.

Ireland will never forget Italia '90, the draw with England, honour salvaged when Kevin Sheedy took unerring aim to score an equalising goal, the dreadful draw with Egypt which revealed a telling lack of ambition in the Irish team. Jack Charlton set out to expose an imagined weakness at the heart of the Egyptian defence. A succession of long, hopeful balls, missiles designed to unsettle the opposition, failed to do so. Having refused the challenge of the day, which was to deploy the creative talents of his team rather than resort to bullying the Egyptians physically, it was Jack Charlton, the coach, who lay exposed at the end of this game.

But Charlton was beyond reproach, in this instance rational football analysis. Purists who dared to cavil at this perverse betrayal of the gifted players in Charlton's squad, who raged at this failure to honour soccer as it had traditionally been played in Ireland, were swept away on a tide of national indignation. How dare they criticise Jack and the boys for this momentary lapse into impotence, how dare they sully this glorious chapter of Irish history with prosaic talk of tactics and team selection?

It was the manner of Ireland's failure against the Egyptians more than the result itself – a 0–0 draw – that ensured a confrontation between football facts and cultural fantasies. This duel, between myth and reality, which would prove decisive, was resolved within days. Holland, the European Champions, were Ireland's next opponents. Surviving the concession of an early goal to the 'Dutch Masters' of tabloid hyperbole, Ireland fought back with immense skill and courage.

Then, with the end in sight, as the Irish nation prepared itself for the shattering blow that defeat now would represent, Niall Quinn pounced on a goalkeeping error to score a stunning equaliser. Opportunism was never more divine. A nation at prayer had been heeded. God was now on the team, Charlton his earthly apostle.

After Holland, Ireland faced Romania in Genoa for a place in the quarter-finals. The tense, evenly balanced game went to a penalty shoot-out. In Genoa weary players grouped in the centre circle dreading the ordeal, praying that they would not be the one to miss. Back home the nation fell silent: cars pulled to the side of the road, the occupants unable to drive and listen to their radio; watching big screens in pubs, village halls and offices, people urged each other 'hush', as if the noise from Ireland might break the concentration of the heroes in Genoa.

The shots from both sides were accurate. Then Packie Bonner guessed correctly, diving to his right to foil the fourth Romanian marksman. David O'Leary (restored to favour as an extra-time sub) strode forward; if he scored Ireland were off to Rome to take on Italy. The irony that Ireland now depended on a man banished by Jack was not lost on the watching millions back home. Nor, indeed, as he subsequently confided in me, on David.

He struck with calm conviction. The ball, curled with the inside of his right boot, hit the top of the net, a yard wide of the Romanian 'keeper's desperate left arm. Those at home, and the millions scattered round the world, the diaspora which has embraced this team with particular fervour because so many of the players are sons of exiles, symbols of the comforting thought that Irishness survives the sorrow of exile, for them the O'Leary goal is a moment that will never be forgotten. It is no exaggeration to say that in the same way that other generations remember where they were, how they felt, the moment news broke of Kennedy's assassination or the Munich air crash – so the Irish remember the O'Leary goal.

That night, O'Connell Street filled with revellers, while elsewhere people around the country spontaneously took to the streets to celebrate the team. Why? It's hard to put it into words. One image endures: the late John Healy, the *Irish Times*' legendary political columnist, was a Mayo man, a lover of Gaelic games, a debunker of myths, a dealer in harsh truths. Above all a registered cynic. There is a piece of film showing Healy as he watched the penalty shoot-out. The face is stern, the posture worldly, sceptical. As O'Leary's shot hits the net the hard-bitten old hack begins to sob. The tears follow, tears of joy, tears of relief, the tears of a man from the barren West of Ireland where poverty and despair are rooted in the rocky soil.

Healy knew about emigration, failure, false dawns, and hated the stereotype Irish of myth, feckless beggars at the world's door. Now on a football field in far-off Italy he saw an Irishman step confidently forward to claim the prize. For once prayer was answered, no longer the solace of the defeated. Knowing nothing about soccer, Healy was, however, only too familiar with Irish history, the real context for the story of Jack Charlton and his team.

Taoiseach Charles J. Haughey flew to Rome for the game against Italy. So did U2 and 20,000 fans who couldn't afford the trip but couldn't bear to miss the occasion. Ireland lost 1–0. After the game the Irish sang and cheered as Haughey and Big Jack did a lap of honour round Rome's Olympic Stadium.

C. J. Haughey has gone the way of all politicians, Jack Charlton is more re-nowned than ever. Last month he was conferred as Freeman of Dublin City, an honour he shares with Nelson Mandela and Mother Teresa. He plays the role of national hero to perfection. He was well prepared by the years of after-dinner speaking, the creation of the Big Jack persona for ITV and Channel 4. And of course his own entirely natural eccentricity.

When the Irish team returned from Italy, the twenty-minute drive from Dublin Airport took three hours. An estimated half-a-million people turned out to greet the heroes. But the football statistics of Italia '90 might confuse a Martian or an American – witnessing Ireland's national celebrations in the light of the numbers. Ireland played five matches winning none of them. Only two goals were scored, both of them desperate equalisers.

The unpalatable football fact is that although the Irish team was undoubtedly courageous, disciplined and highly motivated, attributes for which Jack Charlton deserves immense credit, they should have done better, and would have if different players and tactics had been used.

Three of the best Irish players made no contribution to Italia '90. Liam Brady had retired from international football before the World Cup finals, having been rather cruelly humiliated by Charlton at Lansdowne Road the previous September. Brady was not sympathetic to Charlton's long ball tactics. He was also independent-minded, a bold sceptic rather than a wilting instrument of the coach's plans. Jack had Brady earmarked for demotion.

The problem was that Brady had adjusted himself to Charlton's tactics and was playing as well as ever for Ireland. Brady was hugely popular with the Irish fans. Journalists who would never have dreamed of criticising the national hero might have bridled at Brady's omission.

Identifying a looming problem, Jack acted when Ireland entertained West Germany in a friendly at Lansdowne Road. This was certain to be a difficult game. Brady was selected. He and Ireland played well to take an early one-goal lead. After thirty-five minutes the Germans equalised. Jack immediately substituted Liam Brady.

The inference was clear. Brady was at fault for the goal conceded. Asked shortly afterwards by an acquaintance why he'd substituted Brady, Jack alluded to his need 'to get Brady out of my hair before the World Cup finals'. The substitution was a pre-emptive strike against a Brady-for-Italy campaign. It worked.

Ronnie Whelan went to Italia '90 as captain of Ireland. He returned home without playing a game. A thigh injury kept Ronnie out of the England and Holland games. He declared himself fit to face Egypt. Jack, pleased with the way things were going, decided to keep faith in the lads who'd already played. Fair enough. But after the Egyptian debacle he again declined to include Whelan for the games against Romania and Italy. Whelan had made the mistake of going public with his declaration of fitness before the Egyptian game. Jack resented what he deemed to be a challenge to his authority.

The assessment football analysts had to make was how much better an Irish team containing Brady, Whelan and O'Leary would have performed at the 1990 World Cup finals.

If soccer lovers in Ireland, those who cherished the game as traditionally played by Brady, Whelan, O'Leary and the old heroes who charmed these men's fathers, stood aside from the celebrations of Jack and his team, it was not because of begrudgery, rather a matter of taste. Winning, or drawing, at all costs had never been the Irish way.

Remarkably and happily, the football story has now in 1994 begun to justify the hype of the last six years. The definitive judgement of Jack Charlton the coach will be made this summer in the US and in 1996 when England host the European Championships.

Two factors have had a profound bearing on the saga. Since 1990, a number of exceptionally gifted players have emerged and, wisely, been nurtured by Charlton. Men like Denis Irwin, Terry Phelan, Roy Keane, Gary Kelly and Jason McAteer have added distinction and vitality to the squad. Paul McGrath now plays in his best position.

The second factor is a change in the way the team plays. In 1993 a new FIFA law decreed that the ball could no longer be passed back to the goalkeeper's hands, unless headed. Effectively, this new law forced Ireland to forswear one of Charlton's primary attacking preferences: the long ball aimed high by Packie Bonner into opposition territory. It was, for example, by that route that Ireland scored the equaliser of legend against Holland in Palermo. But it was also that method that rendered men like Liam Brady and Ronnie Whelan redundant. Now defenders are obliged to turn and play old-fashioned football, the game as it should be played and always had been pre-Jack in Ireland.

The coach of narrow conviction is a complex character. Bloody-minded and stubborn Jack may be, yet he is the supreme pragmatist and has therefore adapted with zeal to the new FIFA law. Ireland's style has changed radically as a result of that, the results have improved dramatically. The perfect balance now exists between discipline and resilience, the English qualities Charlton has infused into his Irish teams, and those quintessentially Irish characteristics, wit and imagination.

Asked recently by journalists about the changes, Jack denied that much had changed, an echo of that long-ago day in the Leeds dressing room when, standing drenched in the doorway, he told his tormentors that: 'Anyway, you missed.'

As the Irish party landed at Kennedy Airport last Monday, the Aer Lingus chief hostess bid them farewell with words that were as sincere as they were moving: 'We wish you well, you carry the hopes and dreams of our nation with you.'

Should Ireland contest the closing stages of USA 1994, a career that began over forty years ago will reach an extraordinary climax. Jack Charlton will join the ranks of the great football managers. He will probably deny that it has happened.

DARKNESS AND LIGHT

You don't think about the consequences until you wake up and it's happened.

DAY THE GAA WORLD STOPPED

DERMOT CROWE

The nation felt a family's pain as Cormac McAnallen was laid to rest.

They flocked in their thousands to Brantry for a final glimpse of Cormac McAnallen, stewards shuttling them in from the Jordan Engineering plant nearby: a who's who of the GAA firmament united – and baffled – in their grief. On Thursday night the crowds grew more dense by the minute, routed through an adjoining marquee specially erected. There they stalled to sign a book of condolence, then moved past the open coffin.

In aching proximity sat the Sam Maguire Cup, which the Tyrone footballer had brought back just five months before – two journeys ending as one. At around 9 p.m. on Thursday, the Bishop of Armagh, the Most Reverend Seán Brady, arrived to pay his respects. Cormac's fiancée, Ashlene Moore, stood by the coffin, heartbroken, holding the hands of the man she had planned to marry sometime next year. For a few moments the queue paused for prayer.

Over the surreal days since his sudden death on Tuesday morning, at twenty-four, mourners filed into Eglish parish to offer their sympathies to the family. It is impossible to say for certain how many. Some, like GAA president Seán Kelly, said they had never witnessed a funeral of this magnitude. Surrounding roads were closed to traffic and, somehow, the local stewards ferried everyone through.

Later, as Cormac's family, along with his fiancée, returned to the house, the full moon shone brightly in the sky as it had the night before. But by now the crowds had dispersed and the first traces of normality revisited their lives. They began opening some of the hundreds of cards and letters that had arrived. It was a helpful distraction.

'There's one from Barney Eastwood,' said Donal, Cormac's elder brother.

He looked shattered, not having slept for twenty-four hours after his brother's death, and managing only a short rest on Thursday night. Yet the dignity and courage he and his family displayed under unimaginable strain was incredible.

He spoke about how Cormac and Ashlene had bought a site up the hill in this tranquil rural setting where they were to set up home. They'd met in 1999 when Cormac was studying at Queen's and she was attending Jordanstown. Donal recalled how much he'd wished for all the family to live there, close at hand.

His late brother had turned twenty-four on 11 February. 'I look back with regret,' said Donal, 'not having given him more of a present. But what can you give to a man who has everything?' There are moments he'd liked to have shared with his brother … but many more which he did and which he'll cherish forever.

We are sitting in the house and every now and then he gets up to check television news reports of the funeral earlier in the day. There is a large, framed photograph of him and Cormac from the victorious Tyrone dressing room last September after the county won the All-Ireland. They are holding the Sam Maguire and both are beaming: a moment of unrestrained joy.

He looks at this photograph and says that it will be one of the memories he will treasure of them together. When the final whistle went on 28 September he was seated in the bottom row of the Hogan Stand. His girlfriend, Katie, was beside him then, as she is now: 'I have never seen anyone clearing a barrier as quickly,' she smiles.

There was pandemonium on the pitch, people spilling in from all angles, as he raced towards his brother. 'I think as I got there, two other Tyrone players had just joined him. I don't think he realised it was me, and I said, "Hey, it's Donal. Donal!" He grabbed me by the hand and dragged me towards the presentation area, but we got separated in the crowd.

'But I managed to get into the dressing room and they weren't letting many in. That's when that photograph was taken. I know it looks staged but it was totally spontaneous. That will be one of the great memories I'll have of us together.'

* * *

There was football in the family before Cormac's ascension to greatness. His mother Bridget's brother, Peter, was on the Tyrone panel in 1986 that reached the All-Ireland, losing to Kerry. Her uncle, Joe, played for Donegal in the 1941 Ulster championship. Cormac's father, Brendan, was secretary of the Benburb club in the 1960s and his own father helped establish a club in Brantry.

In 1956 St Patrick's GAA club in Eglish was formed and the Brantry players became part of the new entity. They won only one senior championship, in 1970, but in the 1980s and 1990s minor titles were claimed, back-to-back in both decades.

Donal recounts how his uncle Peter was a major early influence on the boys. 'Whenever he called to the house we'd be out messing with a ball. It was always a thrill when he'd arrive. On the odd occasion he had Plunkett Donaghy with him.' Donaghy was a legend, an empowering symbol of Tyrone football from the last generation.

Fergus, the youngest of the three brothers at twenty-two, didn't show the same level of interest in football as the other two boys. His primary passion is rallying and for some time it looked that if anyone was going to play for Tyrone in the McAnallen household, it would be Donal.

A year older than Cormac, he grew a lot quicker. When they started playing together Donal manned central positions like midfield or centre-forward; Cormac was positioned at corner-back with a limited mandate. Nobody can say that they saw a future All Star in the earlier years of his career.

Paddy McIntosh, a local carpenter who arrived in Eglish from Dungannon almost thirty years ago, watched him blossom – saw the transition take place. He took charge of the local underage teams and had the boys from the time they started up to the county minor wins of 1996 and 1997. By then Cormac was a county minor and had played in an All-Ireland final.

'He was a small tubby lad,' he recalls, 'a wee round face. The only thing you'd have picked out at that time was his determination, but you could say that about a lot of young fellas. Around about fifteen he lost some weight.'

But there were early signs of resolve. Like the time he was stranded in Donegal on a family holiday, anxious to make it back for an Under-14 challenge match in Co. Down. McIntosh rewinds: 'We gathered here in Eglish and they were on the bus when I arrived and I said to Donal, "What about Cormac?" He said, "Oh, he'll be here, I was talking to Mammy. Before I left they were in Letterkenny, he was getting new boots." We waited over half an hour. Then we could wait no longer but decided to start the journey and take a route through Armagh which meant we might meet their car coming home. Donal and I were sitting up at the front of the bus watching out for it.

'We didn't see it so we drove on without him. We arrived there and went into the dressing room. I'd totally forgotten about Cormac and anyway you could understand; family holidays came first in those days. We were out on the field ready to start, a man short, and then I saw him running up the sideline pulling on his jersey. For any lad of that age to be able to persuade his parents to drive from Donegal to Down was amazing.'

Cormac was sixteen and full-back when Eglish won the 1996 county title. His brother Donal recalls that day as the point where their career paths diverged. They had played on the same teams for all but one of their years in school together in St Pat's, Armagh and also on many of the underage teams for Eglish.

Donal failed to make the Tyrone minors in 1996. When the county final came up afterwards he was eager to prove a point, but it didn't go well and he was substituted. His brother took the man of the match award. 'After that, I just got left behind. And it was hard for me to take for a while.'

* * *

Mattie McGleenan, 'Big Mattie' as he is known here, has taken charge of the Eglish team this year. He recalled how Cormac showed up unexpectedly for a challenge match in Armagh against Cullaville a week ago. He tried to cover every assignment.

'On Sunday we got a whisper that he was coming, but you had to tell Cormac sometimes, because he was so busy, that, "Listen, you've had enough." He'd be apologising for not coming to games. Benny Donnelly rang me to say Cormac wanted to travel and he arrived with Ashlene – they were joined at the hip.'

On Thursday night the Cullaville players turned up at the home to pay their respects. 'They said how, after the game, he shook hands with them and wished them all well.'

James Muldoon, who played with Cormac up through the ranks of underage football in Eglish, recalled the challenge match – Cormac's last. 'He just turned up out of the blue. One of the fellas I was marking said: "He must give you some commitment to turn up on a Sunday morning like that." I just said: "That's Cormac, like."'

McGleenan faces a tough challenge in lifting his team, who have their first league match on 28 March. 'This is a whole new world for me. He was someone I will never forget. I will try to do my best for the club. I hope this will give us a new sense of urgency and we can have an attitude of: "Let's do this for Cormac."'

Former Eglish chairman Canice Murtagh was more downbeat. 'Up to the weekend I would have said we had as good a chance as any in the championship. But I'm afraid that has now taken a very severe dent. It's going to take strong men and strong hearts to get us through. You saw him coming through Eglish yesterday and you filled up. There's no short way out of it. You know the old saying: big men do cry. He was a brilliant lad, we owe everything to him. He put our club on the map a long time before today.'

Cathal Murtagh, who played football with the McAnallens and was on the same Scór quiz teams, remembered how Cormac had said that they could win a county championship this year. That was a fortnight ago, after they won the semi-final of the county Scór. Earlier in the day McAnallen had captained Tyrone in the McKenna Cup final.

'He drove to Omagh from Ballybofey for the Scór after having the meal with the team,' says Murtagh. 'I mean, he had to sit around for a couple of hours in Omagh before the quiz started.' Donal recalls how they had tried to persuade Cormac that they might manage without him but he wouldn't hear of it.

'He was very competitive and liked to be involved. We talked about getting Mammy to stand in but he wanted to take part. We won the quiz and I was annoyed at the same time because I felt we might have won without him. But I'm glad we won together now.'

* * *

During the week it was suggested that Cormac McAnallen would have made an ideal GAA president: he impressed on all fronts. These virtues placed a high demand on his time outside of football. In recent months he had been to several counties for GAA functions. The tributes that have flowed since his death underlined his remarkable legacy. A large part of this was because of his achievements as a footballer. But it went beyond that. He had human qualities that touched many people in the GAA, cutting across sporting and other divides. 'An honour to have met you and played with you. For once, all of the clichés about greatness and humility are true,' stated the Wexford hurler David O'Connor in one of the online books of condolence set up after his death.

Kieran McGeeney's words were especially moving in light of their recent rivalry: 'Like all great athletes he had the lot, real courage, unbelievable focus, an unwavering dedication and commitment to his sport, true loyalty to his teammates, the ability to never give up, integrity, honesty and, above all, the mark of all great leaders, the ability to really listen and the modesty to learn.'

The Derry coach John Morrison brought a signed Mass card with the names of the Derry panel inscribed on it. Derry and Tyrone are poles apart in many ways, but this tragedy made no sense of it. 'You see the tributes you read?' says Morrison. 'They're meant.'

They came in huge numbers to Eglish. Names that resonate around the GAA fraternity – Jack O'Shea, Colin Corkery, Pádraic Joyce, D. J. Carey, Dessie Farrell, Brian Cody. It stands alongside any of the great GAA funerals for size and impact.

Muldoon says that when the body came back from Belfast to Eglish from the autopsy on Wednesday the finality of his death hit home. He was one of the stewards co-ordinating traffic and that night he stopped a car containing Colm O'Rourke and Seán Boylan. The last time Muldoon saw O'Rourke was when they had a coaching session with him in Meath as Under-12s.

The high for him though was when Cormac came back with Sam last September. It is the same for Edward Daly. 'The sensation was just unbelievable,' he says. 'Even for Peter Canavan. We call him God. But for our own clubman to win an All-Ireland medal and then on top of that to get an All Star … I was so proud to even know him. It was a joy. There's emptiness. Why? I don't know; he must have been too perfect for this world.'

While McAnallen achieved an abundance of riches in twenty-four years, invariably there are thoughts of what might have been ahead were he given the chance. Daly believes that, having won the All-Ireland, Cormac, like the team itself, would have relaxed more and played even better football.

He watched them in the McKenna Cup final win over Donegal a few weeks ago. The football they played was, he says, 'like music'. He was stewarding at Jordan Engineering on Wednesday when the hearse passed. 'You began to realise you had lost someone special.'

* * *

The McAnallens have redoubtable energy and that fans out from the family home. Cormac's parents, Bridget and Brendan, are deeply immersed in local cultural and historical events. And they have been through the grieving process before. In 1997 Paul McGirr was on the same minor team as Cormac and died freakishly on the playing field.

Before Christmas Cormac was in Ballintubber in Mayo for a GAA presentation. The club asked if Eglish would bring down a juvenile team to coincide with next week's league match involving Tyrone and Mayo. One of Paddy McIntosh's final dealings with Cormac was being alerted to the request and asked to see it through. The death made him have a rethink, but Mickey Harte's advice to him outside the McAnallen home during the week was unambiguous.

'He said to me, "You have to move on. You know what he'd say himself." And I know if Cormac was here he'd say, "Paddy take those kids down to Ballintubber."'

* * *

Friday night in the McAnallen home. Bridget, Cormac's mother, is bringing us tea and discussing family history. The McAnallens talk like the Spanish; they hardly ever stop. They live it to the full. It is no surprise that they raised a son like Cormac.

Donal remembers the two of them playing basketball after walking home from school and how they carried the coffin down the same road. His mother sang a song she used to sing for Cormac when the doors were closed before his remains left the house. Her father Charlie, Donal says, is eighty-seven and plays the fiddle, often – he jokes – unrequested.

In conversation Donal will frequently speed off on tangents, new ideas and associations popping off in his head. They are too vibrant a family to stop doing the things they love to do.

Donal regrets not having travelled to Cullaville to share in the last available piece of football action Cormac experienced. Missing something like that went against the grain and you sense that this is what irks him most.

It has been a harrowing week. He recalls the moment around 3 a.m. last Tuesday when their lives changed. 'I heard this noise upstairs and it escalated in volume and got more repetitious. I went to the bottom of the stairs and said: "What's going on up there?" And the thing continued. Then I went upstairs and realised the noise was coming from Cormac's room. He was lying slightly on his side and staring straight ahead and he had some sort of mucus on his upper lip. He had descended into his last couple of gasps. That will haunt me for the rest of my life.

'I went out of the room and Mammy was dozing. I ran to her. Daddy heard the shouting, but there was no life out of him after that. I can't work out how he died in his sleep. You think you might have been able to do something if you got there a little earlier.'

14

SPURNED AND MAIMED BY HIS OWN KIND

JOE BROLLY

Peadar Heffron hoped that joining the PSNI would help to build peace. He was wrong.

19 OCTOBER 2017

'Get fucked into them lads, fucked into them.' The man beside me in the main stand at Queen's playing fields is shouting and waving his fists.

Neil Blevins, a midfielder with the PSNI Gaelic football team, has just done his best to decapitate a big Garda, who crumples to the ground. I laugh at my companion as he roars. He turns to me, suddenly sees the funny side, and bursts into laughter. 'It was off the ball, too late, and too high, Joe,' he says, 'but it needed to be done.' Peadar Heffron is a big, strong, robust man in his early forties. He is in a wheelchair.

After the game, we go to a café and he tells me his story. 'It was Friday the eighth of January 2010. There was ten inches of snow on the ground when I backed out of the driveway to go to work at Grosvenor Road Station in Belfast. A half-mile from the house, I felt a bang and the car spun off the road. I looked down and my legs were on fire. I thought, "Fuck, I have to get out of the car." I tried to climb out but for some reason my legs wouldn't work. I pulled myself out by my arms and rolled onto the ground on my back. I felt no pain. I just couldn't feel my legs. I kept thinking, "Why can't I feel my legs?" When the ambulance men arrived, they turned me over, and it was then that they had the "Oh fuck" moment.'

His wife, Fiona, also a police officer, was first on the scene. They had been married just four months earlier, on 9 September 2009. '999,' says Peadar, 'we thought that was funny.'

After Peadar had been lifted into the ambulance, she went to look at the car with another officer. When they saw the hole in the driver's seat the size of a football, going through to the ground, they knew immediately what had happened.

In the ambulance, Peadar was strapped down. Fiona said: 'It was a bomb, Peadar. An under-car booby trap.' Her husband went into a terrible rage, shouting: 'The bastards got me, they got me.' He fought violently to break free of the straps, causing mayhem in the crowded ambulance. They got to Antrim Area Hospital within a few minutes; he was injected by the trauma team and went into a coma.

His arse had been blown off. Literally blown off. At that point, it seemed certain he would die. The snow and ice had staunched the haemorrhaging as he lay on the road, keeping him alive until the ambulance appeared. But now the blood was pumping out; 140 units (a unit is roughly a pint) were transfused into him. It went in one end and out the other. His ruined right leg was amputated. The surgeons at the Royal Victoria filleted the bone from the flesh, discarded the bone, and used the flesh and tissue to make a new arse for him to sit on. Like stitching a rubber ring to his waist. For three weeks, he hovered between life and death. Then the doctors brought him out of the coma.

'I joined the PSNI as soon as it was formed because deep down, naively, I thought this was the little bit I could do … you're not allowed to laugh when I say this Joe … to help this island become one again. I thought if policing here was normalised, we could in due course join with the Gardaí and then further down the line, who knows …'

Peadar had hurled and played Gaelic football for Creggan Kickhams near Randalstown since he was a child. He was fanatical about the games. He also loved the Irish language. As a fifteen-year-old, he snogged one of my sisters at the Gaeltacht, maybe both of them. By twenty-one, he was the established full-back for the Creggan senior footballers, and that year helped them to win the Antrim intermediate championship. He repeated the triumph two years later.

When he was twenty-five, he applied to join the new police force, established as a result of the Good Friday Agreement. The hated RUC, an overwhelmingly Protestant force, had been disbanded and the PSNI promised a new beginning. He was worried about having to tell his teammates, but not overly.

First, he told his parents, Frank and Ethna, who laughed, thinking he was joking. But when they realised he was serious they said they would support him. A few days later in Joe O'Boyle's bar, one evening in January 2002, at the first team meeting of the new season, he waited until everyone had spoken, then stood up and told his band of brothers that he was joining the new force. 'It must have gone down like a bomb,' I say.

'I'll pardon the pun. It did.'

The gathering was stunned into silence. Two of the team leaders rounded on him, saying what the fuck was he thinking of and that he couldn't go through with it. No one supported him. After the meeting, no one said a word to him. His boyhood friends never spoke to him again.

He went to the first training session, and when he went into the changing room the chatter stopped. Out on the field, the manager ignored him. When teams were picked for training games, he was left standing. A stubborn bastard, he simply joined in with one of the teams and played as a spare man. No one passed him the ball or acknowledged him. Then, posters started going up around the parish, warning the young people against joining what they described as the PSNI/RUC. One was posted opposite his family home on the phone box. He trained on, never missing a session.

After one session he spoke to a club official as he left the field. 'I need your backing on this. It's supposed to be a new beginning.' 'I can't son. I can't do that.' After another session, an official approached him and said he was putting the club in a very awkward situation. He said a well-known club in Tyrone with a very strong history of republicanism had rung him, said they'd heard Peadar Heffron was joining the PSNI and they'd like to come up and play Creggan in a 'challenge' match. Then, after ten weeks or so, one Sunday morning in April, as he was togging out for training in the changing room, four local republican activists came through the door. They approached him, eye-balled him, and pointedly handed him a leaflet warning against the dangers of joining the PSNI. 'I got into my car, drove home and never came back. It had gotten too personal. Too serious. It was an awful wrench. I never recovered.'

When Peadar says this to me in a café in North Down, fifteen years later, he sits in silence for a long time, clenching his teeth and rubbing his right shoulder with his left hand over and over. 'Fucking pricks,' I say eventually.

'Fucking pricks,' he says.

Peadar joined the PSNI a month later in the first wave of recruits and immediately worried he had got it all wrong.

Peadar: 'We had to introduce ourselves to everyone else in our class. All the others were RUC reservists, or ex-soldiers, or from bank or office jobs. There was no one from my background. Not a single other GAA man. I was a fish out of water. Even the accents were different. I was in a world I had never been exposed to before.'

Me: 'Martha Wainright's song "These are not my people, I should never have come here"?'

Peadar: 'That's exactly it. Exactly it.'

He bulled on regardless. Stubborn bastard. He helped form the PSNI Gaelic football team and became automatic choice at full-back, marking himself out with the ferocity of his play. Their first game was played against the Gardaí in 2002, behind closed doors in Dublin with the names of the PSNI team anonymised.

In 2006 they played their first game against a club team, against my club St Brigid's. There was a huge fanfare around the game and heavy security. Peadar was marking me and responded to the throw-in by letting me know he was there. Afterwards, in the Harlequins clubhouse, we had pints and a laugh. It seemed to herald a new era, where our lads in the PSNI would be able to enter a league and play as normal.

I strongly backed the game, and shortly afterwards graffiti went up around the city. SHAME ON YOU JOE, SHAME ON YOU and other guff of that type. Turned out not to be a breakthrough at all. Just over three years later, people from his own community set Peadar up for assassination. Crawled under his car in the dead of night and planted a bomb to free Ireland.

Just over a year later, Ronan Kerr, another young GAA man who had joined the PSNI, was murdered by a similar booby trap. I won't forget standing with his distraught mother in her kitchen, beside the coffin that couldn't even be opened, under a framed photograph of Peter the Great kicking his great winning score against Armagh in the 2005 All-Ireland semi-final. Things no one should ever have to see.

In Eric Bogle's great anti-war song 'The Band Played Waltzing Matilda', the young hero was a free rover who travelled the outback. When the war came, he fought at Suvla Bay against the Turks and was hit by a mortar. When he was shipped home to Sydney:

I looked at the place where me legs used to be
And thank Christ there was nobody waiting for me
To grieve and to mourn and to pity

When Peadar was in a coma, I spoke to Damien Tucker, the first manager of the PSNI team. He said, 'I wouldn't be surprised if he becomes the first Gaelic footballer to take the field with a prosthetic. I never saw spirit like it.'

Well, the prosthetic wasn't possible. There was just too much damage. But he plays wheelchair basketball and tennis. And he plays at full-back for the Ulster wheelchair hurling team, who play round-robin games against the other provinces twelve times a year.

What, though, about his anger? 'I am a very bitter man. After the bomb, not even a letter from the club. Two of the committee visited my parents' house when I was in a coma. My father Frank played for Creggan, was the club referee and the treasurer. They said to him when they arrived, "We are not here on behalf of the club, only in a personal capacity." I'd be fairly certain guys I played with passed on my details to others. People I knew well were arrested and questioned about the bomb but there were no prosecutions. It's hard, with pricks like you defending them.' As he says that, he raises the middle finger to me.

He was finally released from hospital after eleven months, in November 2010. He pisses through a urostomy bag. He shits through a colostomy. He has a mobile seat cover that prevents him rolling over when he sits. He was invalided out of the force. For the last eight years, pieces of foam from his car seat and shrapnel from the car have been making their way out of his body, most recently in December past when a rusty lump of metal was removed from his pelvis by the surgeons.

I ask him what he makes of it all now? 'When I joined we were promised peace. A new beginning. I thought I'd remain part of my community, a community I loved. I thought I'd play football for Creggan and drink pints in O'Boyle's. That we'd have children and I'd take the underage teams. Now I'm in a wheelchair. I live in North Down. It wasn't supposed to happen. It wasn't supposed to happen.'

We sit for a good while after that, sipping tea, saying nothing. Then he chit-chats about his wife, Fiona, and the football. We arrange to go out for a meal together over Christmas. This is the first time he has spoken publicly about his life. As we are about to leave, I ask him, 'What's your life like?'

He says, 'It's a life. But it's not my life.'

15

'I KNOW WHERE I GET MY HIGHS NOW AND IT'S FROM WINNING'

MARIE CROWE

Kieren Fallon has put his demons behind him, but he hasn't lost his determination to succeed.

18 APRIL 2010

12 NOON, BISHOP'S STORTFORD

It's twenty-seven years since Kieren Fallon left home. The champion jockey picks me up just outside the town of Bishop's Stortford and pretty quickly he's the one asking the questions. He has just come from a concussion test, but there seems to be only one thing on his mind now: home.

He immediately begins recalling his favourite memories, detailing the nights spent playing outside the pubs of Tubber listening to the strains of Joe Cooney as his parents went for an evening drink. He remembers going to the Ennis market on Saturdays to sell collie puppies and the day-long drive to Dublin in the summers to visit his grandmother.

Perhaps caught up momentarily in the memories, a few wrong turns follow as Fallon tries to navigate his way out of unfamiliar territory. He assures me he has an excellent sense of direction, always had, and we eventually set off on the right road to Wolverhampton.

There's a hint of sentimentality about his reminiscences for Clare but it would be wrong to stretch this to a longing to return. 'I miss home,' he admits, 'but there's nothing there for me.' And there's the rub. 'It wouldn't be possible for me to come back because the way I ride over here suits me – with lots of racing. Ireland is more of a National Hunt country.'

Nor does it help that the country he left behind to go in pursuit of winners has changed, he says, beyond all recognition. 'There used to be a nice easy-going way of life there but things have changed and changed for the worse I think.'

The jockey's life now seems far removed from his childhood in Crusheen, but on closer inspection it has almost gone full circle. When he left Ireland, Fallon set himself big goals, he knew he wanted to be the best. Fast-forward twenty years and Fallon is off the rollercoaster his life had become and he wants to put the past behind him and be the best again. He's starting afresh.

'My demons are gone, I don't have them any more so I'll never resort to them. I now look forward to racing again, to getting up in the morning and finding good horses, to the big days like Epsom and Chester. I was starting to get lazy towards the end the last time but now I want it again and I appreciate things.

'I have to put everything that happened in the past to bed. It's boring and people are bored of it. It's going to be exciting, it's going to be tough and obviously I will have days when I will be disappointed. I have to try and move on but if I can't win today then I will the next day; it's what keeps me getting up. I know the consequences and I know where I get my highs now and it's from winning.'

As we wind on towards Wolverhampton, he nibbles on a few sweets, manages half a packet of Walkers crisps and a few gulps of Lucozade, and that concludes his food quota for the day.

'I can eat and drink what I like if I'm riding eight or ten times a day and the weather is hot but right now I'm a little fat. When I was seventeen and dressed, I was five stone. Now I'm about 8–3 and I need to get it down.'

4 P.M., WOLVERHAMPTON RACETRACK

The busy Friday traffic and roadworks have made the journey longer and more frustrating than usual but we still have time to spare. He has ridden here countless times but still Fallon surveys the scene before him. With the first race still over two hours away, Fallon's only ride of the night, for trainer Linda Stubbs, is almost three hours away.

He may be a former champion jockey, and one of the most gifted of his generation, but on this quiet Friday night in Wolverhampton one ride on a horse without a win in a year is his lot – for now, at least.

It is seven years since he won the last of his six British jockey titles. Ryan Moore won it on 174 last year; Fallon has had 200 four times. It's getting the good horses and the rides that is the problem. The recession is hitting everyone and, as a freelance jockey just back from an eighteen-month ban, it's even harder. When Fallon arrives at a stable to ride out in the morning, there could be three or four top jockeys there all hustling for the rides.

'I would like to say I can see myself winning the jockeys' title but I don't have the same ammunition behind me as Frankie Dettori or Ryan Moore, but I do have more determination. It's important to me, but it's more about doing well and getting back the confidence and trust of the trainers and the owners. And getting back to where I was before and riding in all the big races. If you don't have a good horse to ride, it's not the same. I'm used to riding good horses, championship winners. If I wasn't it might not be too bad. I'm still riding winners but if you don't have a good horse you almost feel empty.'

It was a rocky road back to the track for Fallon. There was a big part of him that wasn't sure if he would make it back this time. The charges pertaining to race-fixing allegations dragged on for over two years and Fallon's freedom hung in the balance. He was eventually exonerated but the ordeal took its toll. He abstractly refers to the fear that gripped him, the thought that he may spend time in a cell, locked up in a small space. It was a dark time and he resorted to extreme means to block it out. The result was catastrophic in its own way – an eighteen-month ban for failing a drugs test in France.

He was with Coolmore at the time, riding the best horses and living every jockey's dream when his world came crashing down again. It took the support of all those around him to get him back on track. In his last week there, Aidan O'Brien told him what he needed to do.

'Aidan told me that it will be a quick eighteen months and what I needed to do was take a year to get my head right and six months getting myself fit and back riding. He is a very clever man, and his approach was the right one to take. I couldn't see it then. I couldn't see myself getting back riding again. He was able to see what I couldn't.'

And Fallon stuck to the plan, riding every morning for Michael Stoute, working out in the afternoons with a personal trainer and playing squash in the evenings. In the process, he discovered something that he loved, a possible career option for the future, managing horses in a big stable.

Once he got his licence back last September, he rode fifty winners in the space of a couple of months, reigniting the old determination and hunger that had first forced him to leave Ireland and to reach the heights he did. He has regrets, many of which will haunt him for the rest of his life. He doesn't think he will ever ride for Aidan O'Brien again but he definitely wants to.

'If I was lucky, and if there is a God, I would love to ride St Nicholas Abbey but that's Aidan O'Brien's and Johnny Murtagh rides him. There might be hope but I'd say I'm tenth on Aidan's list to ride him.'

Fallon knows that the desire to succeed, and the control and calmness he displayed under pressure in big races, never extended to his personal life. His bad judgement and easy-going nature frequently landed him in trouble, and still, through it all, he rarely faltered on the track. Winning the Arc in 2007 on Dylan Thomas the day before the start of the Old Bailey trial was typical of him. He also knew about the drugs storm that was coming down the track.

'I look forward to the big days and I ride better on them too. If you look at my Classics record, you can see that. I like the pressure of the big stage. I concentrate better. I always set myself high goals; if I could just pick up where I left off, I'd be flying it. I love the spotlight, everybody does, there would be something wrong with you if you didn't. I have a lot of confidence in myself. I just love the excitement of the big day. I feel great and hopefully it transfers to the horse. If you can get that combination right and get it flowing, you can walk on water.

'The reason I coped with the pressure of everything that happened to me was because I know there are always people worse off than me. All I have to do is turn on CNN and see the pictures from the Third World and then I appreciate what I have. I think people get cornered and have no escape but I look at myself now and I thank God that I'm all right. It's about trying to get a perspective and that works for me.'

Fallon finishes a disappointing eighth on Five Star Junior in a race won by a 33/1 outsider. Fifteen minutes later, as we leave the track, his disappointment is evident. Back in the jeep, he goes over the race again, piecing it together, figuring out why he didn't win. 'There was no pace in the race, and that annoys me because if there was I could have won. I would have liked to have won it for the owner – she is a nice lady.'

We get back on the road again and Fallon is still brooding. This is the side of racing you don't see. The relentless driving from yard to track, track to yard, the pressure of trying to keep everyone happy – owners, trainers, agents – and the disappointment of not winning. The whole day was spent getting to the track for one race, the day before was the same but Fallon missed the start by one minute and had to turn around and go home without making a penny.

As the traffic stretches out ahead of us, Fallon reveals the extent of his determination. Going to the races for one ride will cost him money. The six-hour round trip will leave him out of pocket and tire him out. But he wants to be on these horses again, to have his chance when the big day comes. So he has to make the sacrifices now, show his determination and build back up the confidence of the owners and trainers who have supported him since he came back. He knows that not everyone is on his side. Walking into the weighing room to face the jockeys was one of the hardest things he had to do on his comeback. Rejoining his counterparts, people he will take rides and winners from, was never going to be easy. He knew some weren't happy to see him back.

'The most difficult thing was getting that eighteen-month ban and coming back riding the first couple of days, having to face everyone again not knowing what they were thinking. I can imagine how Tiger Woods felt with all the crowds. Tiger had it all round him for five miles or whatever it is at Augusta. He had people watching him all around the course. I can hide away, try to get my head right instead of having people asking me why I couldn't lead a plain and simple life. Tiger had to go around the four miles of Augusta with crowds following his every move. When you are in the situation, you don't think about the consequences until you wake up and it's happened and you have to face the repercussions. It's hard really when you think about it, other people suffer besides you. Friends and family suffer but you don't think about it at the time.'

Fallon has learned the hard way. He still lives in Newmarket, but keeps to himself more now and doesn't really go out. In a way, he can't. 'If a lad was out in the pubs around Newmarket and then didn't ride well in a race, you would have other lads saying that it was because he was pissed the night before and I don't want to have to deal with that any more.'

As we drive through a deprived part of Wolverhampton, he reveals how lucky he now feels. 'I have choices. The people that live here, what options do they have? Despite everything that has happened, I know that I'm the lucky one.'

The return leg of the journey is littered with phone calls as he looks to organise his morning ride-out. It will be a 6 a.m. start as usual but he just needs to find out where. Fallon is subdued on the drive back, he still doesn't eat as he wants to ride light in the morning. He forgot his back brace and goggles, they are left in Wolverhampton; more calls are made to get them dropped somewhere that he can pick them up at the crack of dawn. While waiting on a call from Luca Cumani, the trainer he does most of his work for, Fallon recalls some recent advice he got from his old boss Henry Cecil.

'I met him a while back at a stable and he asked me who I was going riding for. When I said Luca (Cumani), he told me I was mad. He picked up the paper and flicked to the racing pages, he went through all the trainers and prize money and Luca had nothing. He told me that I'd be crazy if I joined that yard. But the way I look at it is I've been lucky. When I went to (Jimmy) FitzGeralds and Coolmore, they were on a bit of a downturn but when I got there they picked up again, maybe that will be the case with Luca. I hope the next time a journalist asks me a silly question like "what's the worst piece of advice I ever got" that I can tell them what Henry Cecil said to me.'

10.30 P.M., STANSTED AIRPORT

Fallon still has no confirmation of his morning start time. He is tired but all that's left for him to do is head home and start the process all over again tomorrow. 'My kids always ask me why I don't smile,' he quips, 'they don't understand that this is my work.'

And his work is riding winners. 'It's tough at the moment. The last few days cost me money to go all the way to Wolverhampton but I want the rides and if I refuse them and someone else gets on the horse then I've lost my chance for when the big day comes around.'

The following day he rides a winner at Lingfield, dashes off to Wolverhampton again for the evening meet and rides two more winners. Life goes on for Kieren Fallon.

16

DARKNESS AND LIGHT IN DISUNITED STATES

NEIL FRANCIS

America, a country of extremes, can be summed up by its mind-boggling gun culture, amazing attitudes to steroid use and the behemoth that is the NFL.

GUN NATION

There have been many atrocities committed around the world for many reasons over the last ten or twenty years. The one that stands out for me was the massacre of the innocents at the Sandy Hook Elementary School in Newtown, Connecticut. The massacre took place on 14 December 2012. I happened to be in the United States at that time and witnessed the blanket coverage of the outrage. It had a profound effect on me.

Some time before 9.30 a.m. a withdrawn and disturbed twenty-year-old named Adam Lanza murdered his mother with her own Bushmaster XM15, which is a semi-automatic assault rifle. Lanza then drove in his mother's car to the Sandy Hook Elementary School where, at 9.34 a.m., he gained access to the building. Approximately five minutes later, Lanza ended his own worthless life with a Glock pistol shot to the head. Prior to this he managed to shoot and kill twenty children – eight boys and twelve girls aged between six and seven. He also shot six female staff who had tried to protect or hide the children from this monster.

It goes beyond easy understanding how somebody can do such a thing. Nobody can legislate for this sort of volatility, for the machinations of the criminally insane and the random and fickle nature of crimes like this. What is beyond any doubt is that these children were just old enough to comprehend what was happening and what was about to happen. The teachers, there to protect and educate, knew the gravity and the awfulness of their predicament from the first gunshot. This moment in time should in any structured society have been a staging post for change.

In the immediate aftermath the American President Barack Obama openly wept on national television when trying to address the nation. Most right-thinking people guessed the reason for his outpouring of grief had much to do with the hopelessness of the situation and the grim reality of his impotence in terms of introducing sweeping reforms on gun control.

Three weeks later, I read in one review on the crime in the quality press that sales of the Bushmaster XM15 had soared in that period of time and had done so for two reasons: firstly, there were fears that the weapon would be banned – dealers realised there would be a profit to be made if something could not be purchased through normal channels and they bought up large numbers of the weapon; secondly, the weapon itself – and you have to take a good deep breath here – had done such a good job that some people felt compelled to buy it. There are no words.

In the months that followed, federal and state legislation was proposed, banning the sale and manufacture of certain types of semi-automatic firearms and magazines with more than ten rounds of ammunition. President Obama signed twenty-three executive orders and proposed twelve Congressional Actions regarding gun control. His proposals included universal background checks on firearms purchases, an assault weapons ban and limiting magazine capacity to ten cartridges. This proposed legislation in the first session of the 113th Congress was defeated in the Senate on 17 April 2013, mere months after the atrocity was committed.

After noticing that there were about twenty-five gun magazines in the Barnes & Noble bookstore close to me in Florida, I was drawn to see what I could actually buy in the pages of these magazines and was shocked to learn that virtually any type of sub-machine gun could be purchased with the minimum of hassle. I walked into a local firing range and was amazed at the choice of weapons available for sale or to use at the firing range, including a Bushmaster XM15. To buy, this would set me back $3,500 (€3,300), but I could get 250 rounds of ammunition as a special deal to purchase this gun. All I required was a driving licence. I did not need a letter to say that I did not suffer from any psychiatric or mental illness or that I was in any way an unfit person to purchase such a weapon. I assured the young lady at the counter that I did not have a criminal record. That would be that, job done!

As the young lady put the gun back on the shelf I noticed that right beside the dozen or so Bushmasters there were also about a dozen Armalite automatic and semi-automatic assault rifles. These were a bit cheaper, ranging from $1,500 to $2,900 (€1,400–€2,700). I was asked if I would like to try that weapon for size and so I got to know what it feels like to have an Armalite in my hands. I asked if there were any ballot boxes that go with this weapon. She didn't understand my question and asked would I consider buying the gun. I told her that there were some sitting members of parliament in Dublin who would be able to get me a far better deal than that.

'How so?' 'Apparently they can do a bulk discount.' Two rows down, there was an AK47 section; these were considerably cheaper at $700 (€660) a unit – clearly these are for lower-end users. In the United States, there are roughly 112 guns per 100 people. You can empathise with Obama's sense of helplessness with this situation. As Donald Trump takes office, it isn't going to get any better.

STEROID NATION

A survey by the National Institute on Drug Abuse (NIDA) estimated that half a million eighth- to tenth-grade students (the equivalent of second year to fourth year in Ireland) were using anabolic steroids. Another study estimated that close to 1.5 million Americans between the ages of eighteen and thirty-four have used anabolic steroids. They are some pretty serious numbers.

Now, that information is over a dozen years old so I suspect that numbers have subsequently risen and not decreased. There is no reason to presume otherwise. I bought a magazine called *Flex*. It is for bodybuilders. It was positioned right beside the gun magazines. I have no interest in bodybuilding but I do find the whole concept humorous and I have watched a number of documentaries on the subject. I do like to keep abreast of what these guys are taking. (It's a bit like saying, 'I buy *Playboy* for the features.') I buy these bodybuilding magazines to look at the advertisements and see what they are using.

Quite often what is good for bodybuilders doesn't necessarily translate into increased efficiency and strength for rugby players and athletes. Bodybuilders are what they are and when you see any of the pages in these magazines you can tell straight away that many of these people ingest enormous amounts of steroids. The tell is in the face. It is an homogeneous face – they all look the same. Unfortunately, they all die the same too – in their forties or early fifties.

In terms of where the trend is going, products like Creatine are so passé – they are the last millennium's muscle bulkers. Where we are now and what the labs can produce is light years away from where we were even ten years ago. One of the products that causes me huge concern are these 'pre-workout' supplements which you take an hour or two before a weights session. So as not to receive any letters of complaint from manufacturers I won't name them, but these products, I believe, are more dangerous than Creatine.

They contain, amongst other things, methylhexanamine and industrial dosages of caffeine. None of these supplements are 100 per cent safe from contamination or cross-contamination and anybody using them could be banned because they are on WADA's [World Anti-Doping Agency] proscribed list. I suspect quite a number of seventeen- to twenty-five-year-olds in amateur rugby and other athletic pursuits in Ireland are regularly using these products without any notion of how dangerous they can be.

In the US it is illegal to sell androgynous anabolic steroids without prescription but it is not illegal to take them and so sourcing and sending are the occupational hazards of the dealers. If there are that many users in the US taking that much, then the Feds are only picking up a very small percentage. It is very easy to deal at the gyms and workout stations around the country and that is probably the easiest way to source the product. I am sure the dark net is another forum but it still means that the product will have to be distributed through orthodox channels.

There are, quite unbelievably, a number of steroid sales sites on the Internet where you can pick up everything from about 110 registered androgynous anabolic steroids through to twenty-five variations of testosterone or human growth hormone. Steroid takers will do what they have to do and it's somebody else's problem if they are caught.

What really concerns me, and it is a problem which is either in its infancy or widespread, is the issue of steroid alternatives. The products being sold here are not anabolic steroids per se but what is termed as their 'legal equivalent', and their manufacturers say it is a 'completely legal and safe substitute for steroids without the common side effects'.

So, for instance, if you were a serious athlete and taking an anabolic steroid like Dianabol, you can choose to take the real anabolic steroid and all its consequences, or else use a product called D-Bal – the product which claims to do exactly what the real steroid does but is legal and claims to have no side effects.

This is no cottage industry. Remember in Dublin a few years ago you had head shops which sprang up to give people 'legal highs'? It might be a good idea to check out the validity of these legal steroids manufacturers' claims. A lot of American boys are using them. Who's to say there aren't Irish boys doing the same?

There has been much emphasis on concussion injury and CTE [Chronic Traumatic Encephalopathy] as a cause of suicide amongst professional athletes. Maybe it has or maybe it has not been taken into account, but most of the athletes who killed themselves were also steroid abusers and the ones who had CTE are just a small percentage in relation to the number of steroid abusers who do eventually kill themselves or die prematurely.

RUGBY NATION

Before the season kicked off, the Pro12's CEO, Martin Anayi, raised the possibility of including an American franchise in an interview with WalesOnline. I thought at the time that the likelihood of this happening was remote. I did, however, think that the incorporation of a professional American rugby championship would be very good for the game. If there was no NFL and America's sport was rugby, they would be world champions year after year.

As with all of these ventures at the embryonic stage, getting your structures in place is very important but at all stages money is prime. Douglas Schoninger was the promoter behind the venture and initially they had hoped for a twelve-team competition and that competition would be called Pro Rugby USA.

For a variety of reasons they only managed to get five teams in its inaugural year: the Denver Stampede, Ohio Aviators, Sacramento Express, San Francisco Rush and the San Diego Breakers. On 7 October, Steve Lewis, Pro Rugby's chief operating officer, left and a few weeks ago the San Francisco Rush were expelled from the league for a variety of reasons. A week before Christmas the whole league collapsed amid recriminations between Schoninger and the American Eagles.

All of the players had their contracts terminated and, apart from the players, there are quite a number of creditors and employees who have not been paid in a few months. As usual, money, or lack thereof, is the issue here. Sparse attendances are not really of consequence if you have television revenues coming in. Unfortunately, that did not happen and, despite Schoninger promising that he would give it three years to succeed, the figures were extrapolated and they did not make financial sense. As usual when an entrepreneurial element meets with an institutional element, there will be wrangling of sorts, and prior to the collapse there was bickering and grandstanding from both parties. Nobody knows whether there will be a divine resurrection.

Whither the Pro12? It would seem that the concept of inviting an American franchise to partake was a little premature, or maybe even a little bit of thinking aloud from its CEO. Rather than thinking that the venture is done and dusted, would now not be the time to investigate whether a team could be included in the absence of the Americans not being able to put their own league together?

With 100 players and a few former superstars out of contract, surely there would be an opportunity now to ask the question? I feel if the Americans got some form of a franchise up and running it would be a matter of no more than ten years before they picked up some real talent from some of those un-drafted college superstars.

Remember, once college players leave their universities and don't make it into the NFL or CFL there is no amateur league. A pro rugby league would be a serious alternative. Either way, the days of America turning up to World Cups and getting thumped by professional teams will have to stop.

FOOTBALL NATION

I have been to more than a dozen NFL games in my time. The more I see, the closer the gap becomes between enjoying watching rugby union and NFL.

There are a number of themes which are constant in this game, namely the military, race, money and talent. There is always a strong military presence at these games, particularly in the last ten years. I watched the New England Patriots play the Miami Dolphins at Hard Rock Stadium in Miami on New Year's Day. Quite apart from the national anthem being sung with extraordinary fervour – led by a serving Sergeant at Arms in Afghanistan – there was a pitch-size American flag covering the field which was conveyed onto the pitch by a corps of service people. There were regular intermissions to pay homage to soldiers throughout the game and, as the final strains of the national anthem were played out, two large military helicopter gunships flew over the stadium. It is all-pervasive. The mix of sport and military are good for each other in America.

A football game is the perfect place to see how polarised society is in America. It was quite noticeable how jersey sales went along race lines. For the New England Patriots, the vast majority of Tom Brady, Rob Gronkowski and Julian Edelman jerseys (white players) were worn by the majority of white people and the LeGarrette Blount and Randy Moss (since retired) jerseys were worn by the majority of black people – the same applied for Miami.

At the start of this season, Colin Kaepernick, the San Francisco 49ers quarter-back who played in a Super Bowl a couple of years ago, refused to stand for the national anthem because he believed that the USA oppresses black people and other minorities. This brought forward a storm of disapproval/approval, again drawn on race lines, and quite a number of other black athletes chose the same course of action.

I have to say it was a brave decision by Kaepernick and one which would have brought him a whole load of unnecessary opprobrium, but he stuck to his guns all the way until the end of the regular season. The problem here is that money supersedes race or any sense of inferiority and any action taken to stand against that prejudice. The issue comes down to a time and a place for such a stance. The 49ers had a shocker of a season with a 2–14 record – the second worst in the league. Head coach Chip Kelly was sacked on the final day of the season and his general manager got the boot too.

Conversely, the New England Patriots, the best team in the league at 14–2, had none of these issues. Bill Belichick is the best coach currently working in the NFL and when he finishes he will be looked back on as the greatest of all time. When I looked at the Patriots' roster – which was right in front of us – at the game, all of their players stood for the anthem, not because they are patriotic but because they were there to do a job. Belichick, as befits a successful coach, has zero tolerance for any matters non-sporting or which distract from a team's performance, and that is why he is so successful and why the Patriots are 14–2. Belichick's attitude would be: 'That's fine boys, do it on your own time.'

Finally, it was a pleasure to watch Tom Brady perform seventeen years after I had watched his first game for the Patriots. He is without doubt the greatest quarterback of all time and it was a privilege to see him give a masterclass in passing and field intelligence as the Patriots ensured home field advantage for the play-offs. At thirty-nine, Brady is still as nimble mentally and athletically as he was seventeen years ago. His arm is still strong and the speed and accuracy of some of his passes took my breath away. Brady has a net worth running into the hundreds of millions and is set for life financially, yet his desire for the game is undiminished and his skill levels and drive demonstrate that. As they say, 'In it for the outcome not the income.'

WE'RE OUR OWN WORST ENEMIES

JOE BROLLY

Sometimes humans have to be protected from themselves.

Is it good enough that a young man be beaten to death in a cage for our amusement? Is it good enough that as he begins the slow process of dying, lying on the canvas like a tranquillised cow in the abattoir, Conor McGregor, our most famous sportsman, is giving high fives all around, laughing and beating his chest? Is it?

Before he died in poverty, living upstairs in his decrepit gym, sleeping on a camp bed and heating his beans on a primus stove, the legendary heavyweight champion Smokin' Joe Frazier said, 'The stuff we deal with is life and death. Boxing is the only sport you can get your brain shook, your money took and your name in the undertaker book.'

He fought Ali in Manila in a fight that is held in awe. Both men went to the boiler room of the damned that night. If the brain is a computer, they ripped each other's out and smashed them with gloved fists. When Frazier was pulled out before the bell for the fifteenth, he was blind and suffering severe internal injuries. His trainer, Eddie Futch, stopped it because he thought another round would kill him. What he didn't know was that Ali was about to quit. As Ali put it: 'I had gone through the trap door. I was close to dying.' Ali, diagnosed soon after by Dr Dennis Cope of UCLA with 'Parkinson's Syndrome, secondary to pugilistic brain syndrome' slowly disappeared inside himself, leaving only a hologram. Frazier loathed Ali forever with a hatred that consumed his life. The voice message on his answering service was, 'Joe Frazier, still floating like a butterfly, stinging like a bee. Not like someone I know.'

I used to love the boxing. I was a bad amateur boxer myself, eventually expelled from the St Canice's club for kicking an opponent during a bout. Henry McAuley said to my da, 'He may stick to the football, Francie.'

When my clubmate Paul McCloskey turned pro, he turned to me for advice now and again. I sat at his fights in terror and watched him knock out a series of opponents to become European champion. The atmosphere was hateful, spiteful and inhuman. When he fought the ex-soldier Dean Harrison in Widnes, the venue was thronged with powerfully built squaddies, tattooed and drunk. There were only a handful of travelling supporters and when Paul was announced, the soldiers began to chant: 'You murderin' Irish bastards, you murderin' Irish bastards.' We tiptoed out of that place, feigning English accents.[1]

The end of it for me was the night Paul fought Giuseppe Lauri to defend his title at the King's Hall. BoxRec described it afterwards as 'an all-out war'. By the tenth, they were in the boiler room and the crowd was going insane. I thought I might vomit. Halfway through the eleventh, Paul threw a murderous right which seemed to go straight through Lauri's head. He was unconscious as his head bounced off the canvas and as he lay there, eyes dead and body twitching as if he were having a fit, the girls in the row beside me celebrated hysterically.

There's the rub. Something deep in us thrills to serious violence. Up to the end of the nineteenth century, public executions were the premier spectator sport in England. At Tyburn in London, seats in the grandstand (named Mother Proctor's Pews) were expensive and highly sought after. There was a fine house overlooking Tyburn with large balconies, from which the sheriffs of the City of London and Middlesex watched the executions with their invited guests. A sort of corporate box where you could hobnob with the executioner. Maybe get his autograph.

When Henry Fauntleroy, a gentleman fraudster, was hanged at Newgate in 1824, the crowd was estimated at 100,000. If a smart promoter like Barry Hearn had been alive then, he'd have hired Michael Buffer to say, 'Let's get ready to haaaaaaaaaaaaaaang ...' and got a half-naked dolly bird to hold up notices between executions.

The violent professional sports lobby reacts violently to criticism, like the US gun lobby. They say, 'The fighters want to do it. It is their escape from the ghetto. Their means of expression.' When the young Welsh boxer Johnny Owen died in the ring, Hugh McIlvanney, one of those great writers who, like Norman Mailer, mythologises fighting, said, 'It is his tragedy that he found himself articulate in such a violent language.' As though nothing could have been done about it. He was fucking dead, Hugh. Dead! Do you comprehend what that means? For him? For his family?

---

1   McCloskey won the fight with a fourth-round stoppage.

The fact that there are young men with violent tendencies who are prepared to put themselves on the line is neither here nor there. As a young fighter said in RTÉ's recent documentary on MMA: 'I like to hurt people.' Put it this way. If an American hedge fund millionaire started 'Ultimate Combat', where the fighters use weapons and the battle is to the death, he'd have a queue of men wanting to sign up. They could sign consent forms. He could put them in an amphitheatre and he would most certainly fill it to overflowing. Come to think of it, that's already been done. In Ancient Rome. And didn't it work brilliantly? The new sport would sweep the planet. We'd all be glued to our screens. PPVs [Pay Per Views] would break all records. Young men would die. But hey, it's their tragedy if they find themselves articulate in such a dangerous language.

The promoters would become richer than Trump. The fighters would mostly die, or be disabled, or die in poverty. Just like they do now. They would take to crime and drugs, or alcohol, like Jermain Taylor, or Kelly Pavlik, or Riddick Bowe, or Mike Tyson, or Arturo Gatti, or so many other ex-world champions. And that's the cream. The truth is that violent sports are a rich man's plaything, where poor men try to put each other into a coma for our amusement. When Joe Frazier took on George Foreman in Jamaica, promoter Don King drove to the fight in Frazier's cavalcade, sitting with the champ in his vast limo. Foreman knocked Frazier out and when he got back to his dressing room, the new champion was warmly embraced by King. When Foreman's cavalcade pulled out to return to the hotel, King sat beside him. An example of switching limos mid-stream.

When the knockout artiste Gerald McClellan came to England to fight Nigel Benn for the world title in 1995, it was two fighting dogs ripping each other to bits, only legally. McClellan said beforehand, 'You go to war and you win or you go to war and you die. I'm not afraid because it's my job.'

He knocked Benn right through the ropes in the first round. But Benn recovered to win in the tenth. McClellan didn't die, but he was beaten into a coma. He is penniless and lives in a small bungalow in Freeport with his sister, Lisa, who has devoted her life to him. He is blind. He can barely hear. He is in a wheelchair. His face is puffy and happy in the way that people with severe brain damage often look. He likes to be hugged and touched constantly, because he is afraid of the dark. When a visitor is introduced to him he squeezes their hand and shouts, 'Get him a cookie, Lisa.'

Benn (like McClellan, a juvenile delinquent) said later: 'They brought him over here to bash me up – look at him now.' Benn never recovered either. He himself suffered brain damage, found God and became a preacher.

In 1991 Benn's nemesis, Chris Eubank, almost killed Michael Watson. Watson spent forty days in a coma and had six brain operations. After regaining consciousness, he spent over a year in intensive care and rehabilitation, and six more years as a wheelchair user while he painstakingly recovered some movement and regained the ability to speak.

Just a fortnight ago, Eubank's own son, Chris Junior, almost killed Nick Blackwell after a 'brutal war'. Blackwell was left in a coma but is gradually recovering. The extent of the brain damage is not yet known. Our own Barry McGuigan saw the horror too. Young Ali couldn't withstand the heavy knock-down from those orangutan arms. He was in a coma for five months before the life-support machine was unplugged.

Ray 'Boom Boom' Mancini was the glamour fighter of his era. The fellas' favourite slugger. A sixth Beatle for the ladies. A world champion by twenty-one, in 1982 he fought the South Korean Duk Koo Kim for the WBA lightweight title. It turned out to be a night of unmitigated savagery. Ray had come into the ring handsome as Chachi calling at the door to pick up Joanie. By the second round, Ray's ear was badly damaged and his face was already a mess. The commentators may have worried and the spectators squirmed. But Ray was loving it. He boomed away regardless and by the last quarter of the fight the South Korean was wilting. The boiler room of the damned.

By the twelfth round, Ray was bludgeoning his man. But Kim somehow stayed on his feet as the fistic swarm descended upon him, so the referee Richard Green did not intervene. In the thirteenth round Mancini delivered thirty-nine consecutive head shots. In the fourteenth Kim was finally despatched to the canvas by a thunderous salvo. He never got up again. Lying in the ring, he fell peacefully into a coma and died a few days later in hospital.

Before leaving his hotel room for the fight, he had scrawled 'Live or Die' on the lampshade. Kim's mother travelled from Korea to be with him in the hospital, holding his hand to the bitter end. Then, heartbroken, she committed suicide by drinking weedkiller. A few months later, the referee Richard Green took his own life. Ray himself fought on for a short while, but his boom was gone and he quit when he was twenty-three, coming out of retirement several years later for two fights no one remembers.

These violent life-and-death sports are fun. They bring us to somewhere primitive inside us. It is why the spectators in the Colosseum gasped and cheered as the knife was thrust home. Or why the toffs on the balcony at Newgate paid big money to watch the hangman pull the lever. It is why young, penniless men are queueing up to try to murder each other in cages and boxing rings. And why Conor McGregor high fives and beats his chest as a young man dies.

It's not the fighters' fault. Nor the referees'. Nor the promoters'. Nor the audiences'. The law permits it. And it shouldn't. Time to ban these violent pro sports. Sometimes human beings have to be protected from themselves.

18

THAT GOAL TURNED MY LIFE INTO A NIGHTMARE

TOM O'RIORDAN

Seven years after making history in Croke Park Seamus Darby talks about the aftermath.

12 FEBRUARY 1989

Time is ticking away. The 63,000 crowd await the inevitable moment when Kerry will make history by winning their fifth successive All-Ireland final.

Then the call comes from Eugene McGee. 'Get ready Darby, you are going in.' There are only seven minutes to go and Kerry's two-point lead seems like a mountain for Offaly on that September afternoon in 1982.

Seamus Darby's arrival hardly causes a ripple as Kerry hold control. Exactly ten years previously Seamus played in his only other All-Ireland final and that day contributed three points in Offaly's win over Kerry in the replay.

Just before he replaces John Guinan, Darby is told by McGee to go into the corner and wait his chance. 'It was remarkable him telling me that,' recalled Seamus last week. 'Because I could see our forwards were going out too far trying to get the ball and the Kerry defence were able to clear without much pressure.'

For three minutes Seamus Darby does not touch the ball. Tim Kennelly then makes a long clearance from defence and is heard to say: 'Lads, I think we are going to do it.'

The rest is history. Thirty seconds later Liam Connor floated the ball high into the Kerry danger zone. Darby finishes the story.

'As Tommy Doyle went for the ball, it seemed to dawn on him that he had gone too far. He tried to rectify himself but as he did so I hit him with my hip and in doing so I also held my ground behind him. With the ball in my hand I thought of just one thing, a goal.

'In my mind's eye I knew where Charlie Nelligan was, just left of centre.

Normally I might have turned to my right but this time I said I would rely on my left leg. To this day I can still feel the sting in my leg as I kicked the ball. I have no hesitation in saying that in all my years kicking football, I never connected better. Six inches under the bar near the corner; perfect, beautiful, a dream goal.'

Unfortunately for Seamus Darby that dream goal turned his life into a nightmare, to such a degree that it led to the loss of his business, the near ruination of his marriage, his family and his home. It led to long bouts of wining, dining and boozing up and down the country until it reached the point where his family and friends wished he had never scored that goal.

'It went from one extreme to another, from being a virtual nobody to a bit of a personality and I just could not control it,' he revealed to me in a refreshingly frank and sincere interview. 'From the moment I stepped outside Croke Park, at 6.00 that Sunday evening, the rounds of celebrations started, and they went from one extreme to another.'

He admitted that scoring that goal, which changed the course of history, opened up a completely new scene for him. 'I could safely say that I was out every night of the week for the best part of a year afterwards, drinking here, there and everywhere. There seemed to be no end to it. I used to say that it would die down after a couple of weeks of bringing the Sam Maguire Cup to towns around the county. Instead of slowing down, it got worse.'

At the time Seamus owned a shop in Edenderry in which he sold both hardware and sports goods. 'Having the shop only added to my problems. It meant that I always had ready cash in my pocket. Even then the shop was not going that well, but I did not try and cash in on our victory. Instead I used what cash I had for socialising with friends or, indeed, anyone I met.

'Perhaps if I had been on a set salary it would not be so bad, but I never planned for paying bills. They could wait for another day. It was always another day, just like another drink did not seem important at the time. Eventually I found it increasingly difficult to get credit and the stock was no longer there for the public. Things went from bad to worse and I lost control of myself completely.'

The invitations he received to present medals, attend dinners or just be present as a personality in his own right, were legion. 'I went to virtually every town in the country, from Strabane to Fethard-on-Sea,' he recounted. 'All the time, it was socialising and late-night drinking. It got to the stage where I could not get drunk, even if I drank a barrel of it.'

He would be promised travelling expenses, but sometimes he would return home without collecting them and that added to his financial strain.

Seamus Darby has always been a proud man. That, too, meant problems. If he walked into a pub for a quiet drink and was joined by the inevitable group of 'hangers on', he could not leave without buying his round. 'I wanted nothing for nothing and I always wanted to show I could be as good as the next person. But then I always had the bit of spare cash, at least during the months after the final.'

On many occasions he admitted that because of the late nights he would not get out of bed until lunchtime. 'I often attempted to go back to the shop for the afternoon, but ended up going on another tear. It was not that I wanted drink, but it was the company, the crack and the hype. I was on a "high" for weeks and months after that goal and even to this day walking down the street I'm conscious of it.'

Only five days after that great victory his wife, Veronne, gave birth to a son; naturally he was christened Seamus. However, Darby admits that his domestic life was under considerable strain subsequently. It was said in family circles that it would have been better for Seamus if he had never scored that goal. Things were that bad.

'I should have been more disciplined. But with the shop going so badly, the bills mounting, I began to get very depressed and turned to drink even more. Mentally I went through a very bad patch. At times it was awful.'

He was married young but recounts that after Offaly's victory in the 1972 All-Ireland he was still only twenty-one and did not have the money to really enjoy himself. 'Then I was dropped off the Offaly panel in 1976 when McGee took over and I promised myself that if I ever got back on the team, and we managed to win something big again, I would really let my hair down and enjoy myself.' He was true to his word.

The day the creditors closed in and Seamus was faced with the grim prospect of having his home sold over his head, he began to face up to life.

'I had no choice. The shop was closed. There was no income. I was on the verge of losing my house and everything I had cherished. I had been out drinking every night of the week until the early hours. I decided I was in cuckoo land long enough. I knew if the house went I was a goner. So I cut back on all my travel and drinking and began to pick up the pieces.'

It was no easy task. He has since let the shop in Edenderry, where he still lives with his wife and family. Life is normal again. He has managed to secure the sole Irish agency for English-made wallpaper which means that he must travel the country.

'That does not worry me,' he admits. 'Even to this day, though, with every call I make or every shop I enter people will either recall the goal or someone will say, "Do you know this fella?" It can get a bit tiresome at times but I still get a shiver up my spine if that goal is shown on television.'

He admits that he should have retired from football immediately after that game. 'I could never get the same excitement about playing for Offaly subsequently. I just lost interest. It was like winning the Olympic gold medal; everything else was anticlimactic.'

But time changes things. Seamus trained Edenderry last year to reach the county semi-final and intends to make a bit of a comeback himself this year. 'I have not played for two years,' says Darby, now nearing his thirty-eighth birthday, but still looking fresh.

Did he feel sorry for Kerry in 1982? 'Yes, in a way, because they were a fantastic side. But then you dream about scoring goals like that and I suppose I will carry that special thrill with me for the rest of my life.'

Even if it did bring him to the brink of disaster.

19

FOOTBALL'S EXTRAORDINARY POWER TO BREAK DOWN WALLS WITHIN WALLS

RICHARD SADLIER

The positive impact sport can have in the Irish prison system proved to be an eye-opening experience.

1 SEPTEMBER 2013

Imagine being French-kissed by your mother so she can pass you drugs during a prison visit. Consider how it must feel to be denied early parole at the age of seventeen because there is nobody in the world willing to sign for your release. Or picture a mother pleading desperately with prison staff to keep her son locked up because she cannot cope with his behaviour once he's out.

I knew nothing of this world until recently.

Last summer I was invited by Thomas Hynes, PR director of Bohemian FC, to take part in a one-month football training programme with the prisoners of St Patrick's Institution in Dublin. At that time it housed 220 males between the ages of seventeen and twenty. Along with his nephew, Jeff Conway, the plan was to coach ten inmates on a weekly basis throughout the European Championships and give them certificates on completion of the course. It all went well so we repeated it with ten others and we've been doing it ever since.

The highlight came last Sunday when members of Bohs' senior squad played the inmates in a five-a-side game in the exercise yard watched by the majority of the prison population.

Surrounded by high walls and barbed wire, there was a net above our heads to keep out drugs. Bohs won 10–6, but the whole occasion was far removed from the scene that greeted us a year ago. Funnily enough, the only hiccup was the choice of songs by the officer in charge of the music. Akon's 'Locked Up' proved a wildly unpopular choice.

* * *

Our initial involvement in June 2012 was to work either with Dublin-based inmates or with those from around the country. Either the inmates from C Wing or D Wing, but never with both at the same time. 'Segregation' and 'protection' were constantly being discussed, and before long we realised why.

Governor Daniel Robbins has been in the prison service for twenty-six years and St Patrick's is his fifth institution. 'This is without a doubt the most tragic jail I've ever worked in,' he says. 'St Pat's, like all prisons in Ireland, has groups of prisoners that when they come in tell us, "I need protection." We ask why, they'll say, "Cos I'm fighting." Who are you fighting? "Everyone." What's it about? "Everything." That's the sort of answers you get. "He's going to kill me, or I'm going to kill him." And a lot of it isn't true. It comes from not feeling safe.'

This time last year, eighty of the 220 prisoners were in protective custody, kept separate from the general prison population for their own safety, at their own request.

'We looked at a conflict-resolution situation – how best to get these lads off protection,' explains Deputy Governor Donncha Walshe. 'There was a lot of work done to get to the core issues. Then we looked at sport. We saw sport as maybe a tool that would bring people together.'

The prison psychologist and the chaplain had been working for months with the inmates, explains Robbins. 'They said, "Are you really fighting with him or is it more a disagreement over something that can be resolved?"'

We were then asked to take a mixed group for a football session. As Robbins put it, 'People from different sides of the house, people who were ostensibly going to kill each other.'

Ten inmates were brought to the sports hall and immediately formed two groups, changing at opposite ends of the pitch. I decided to mix the two groups. Gym officer Richie Bruce remembers the reaction when one inmate threw his bib back at me in protest. 'They were like "Hang on a minute." It was that bad. It was like a bloody war between the two of them. Then they realised it was just a game of football. Throw a ball in, and they were like "Hang on, here's a game." They didn't give a shite after that.'

Keen to capitalise on this, a four-team tournament involving twenty-four players from both sides of the divide was organised soon after. Seven games played over four days, five hours of football in all. I was the referee and only had to blow my whistle on four occasions, and there wasn't one serious challenge in all. For Robbins, this was hugely significant. 'It just shows you that these lads can resolve disagreements without pulling a blade on each other. They can have robust physical contact and not kill each other, not lose their temper. In other words, the potential is there. It's just how we get them there and how they use that in everyday life, not just out on the pitch. I firmly believe that at some level, with some of them, that will have an impact. It might not reap anything immediately, but at some stage it will.'

There was no split in the squad for the game last week against Bohs. Inmates worked together as a team, choosing their own positions, tactics and substitutions. I barely said a word. 'They lacked a belief in themselves at the start,' observed Walshe, 'but after a while, they looked no different [to Bohs], they played no different, they were no different, because they were playing a game of soccer. That has helped create for themselves a bit of self-esteem.'

After the game the Bohs players were shown around the prison. One of the players objected to televisions in the cells and thought tougher conditions were needed to make prison life an effective deterrent. He believed they had things too easy. 'What do you want us to do?' asks Robbins. 'Throw them into a hole and forget about them? I'm not defending their crimes, but there is a tendency in society to underestimate the impact of losing your freedom.'

It's a view that many people hold. Friends and colleagues of mine have questioned Bohs' involvement throughout the last year. Why coach people who did what they have done? But once you're inside the walls of the prison you see plenty of reasons. 'There is something about sport,' adds Robbins, 'they get a bit of pride in themselves which is a big thing. Some of them haven't really had that other than in a negative way, like "I'm the big fella 'cos I cut him in the face."'

Our preparations for the game were affected by uncertainty over one player's availability. He was due to be transferred three days before but had put in a request to remain at St Patrick's until after the final whistle. The prison could not facilitate his request, but it reaffirmed to Bruce the positive impact of the work they are doing. 'An inmate not wanting to leave a prison because of a game of football! It could be sport in general but it seems to be the football more than anything else. They're already asking when Bohs are in next.'

I had no prior experience or understanding of the prison system. What was originally intended to last for four weeks is still going after fourteen months. From not knowing what we were walking into when we first got involved, working with the inmates of St Pat's soon became the highlight of my week. I was never interested in coaching before but this was always about more than just that. 'You saw them yourself,' said Robbins, 'they were two groups who said they were going to kill each other. The next thing they were playing in a match and you didn't have to pull a yellow card.'

Despite the efforts of the new management, St Patrick's is soon to be shut down. Following damning reports from the Inspector of Prisons, Judge Michael Reilly, it was confirmed in July that the prison is to be closed and that all staff and inmates will be moved to other institutions within six months. 'I am satisfied that the Irish Prison Service can no longer guarantee the safe and secure custody of young offenders detained in St Patrick's Institution,' said Judge Reilly. He also recommended that 'the name St Patrick's should be consigned to history'. The building is to be incorporated into the adjoining Mountjoy prison, and by now most of the seventeen- to twenty-year-olds have been transferred elsewhere.

With all that their jobs entail, and the public criticism of the prison, it struck me to ask the staff last week if they enjoyed what they do. 'I love it,' said Robbins. 'It is a very tragic prison, but it is also a very hopeful prison. The best chance I have as a prison officer of turning anyone around is probably in this place because they're young.'

Despite finding seven inmates hanging in their cells during his twenty-three years in St Pat's, Bruce says much the same. And even then, his focus was on the three who were cut down in time. 'This is the other side. You don't hear about the lads who survive.'

'We have a duty of care to put into place programmes to ensure these guys return to the community to play positive roles. That is our focus and we will continue to do that,' said Walshe. 'People don't like to hear good news stories about prisoners who succeed. Every day in the Irish Prison Service there is good work being done but it doesn't sell newspapers.'

'If you go behind the lads' stories,' adds Robbins, 'it is invariably tragic. There was nobody born to shoot another human being at eighteen years of age.'

There are inmates in St Pat's who will never integrate with others and some whose differences with one another run very deep. The culture of prison life is far too complex to pretend that their situations can be meaningfully improved in any way through sport. There are many inmates in that situation, but the approach of Bohemians was to work with the ones willing to give it a go.

'There's very little job satisfaction sometimes in what we do,' says Walshe, 'but if we can steer two out of six people out of criminality and back to playing a positive role, I believe it's a job well done. Two out of six – and if you achieve that you're doing well.'

A TOUCH OF CLASS

It was lovely to see that emotion,

as though he was going to cry.

WE CAN'T REST ON OUR LAURELS

BRENDAN FANNING

This Grand Slam can be the catalyst to take Irish rugby to a new level.

22 MARCH 2009

Maybe it was the first time that Luke Fitzgerald got involved in the action in Cardiff yesterday that brought it back to mind, the speed with which he moves his hands and feet. Every time you watch him play you have to remind yourself that he's his father's son. Luke can handle himself well enough physically, but he has traded his way to the top of the market by stepping quickly out of trouble.

Des, his old man, used to deal in a more forthright manner, as a tighthead prop on the field and an opinionated contributor off it. They have a bit in common though, beyond the blood and the special relationship of father and son. Both have been present at the crossroads in critical times in Irish rugby. Separated by eighteen years perhaps, but there all the same.

It was 1991 when Des was in the thick of it. In the week before Ireland played Australia in the quarter-final of the World Cup, he rang his friend and mentor, Roly Meates. The IRFU committee man was about to seat some dinner guests when Fitzgerald put the mockers on his appetite.

'You can tell your friends on the union there won't be any Ireland team running out on Sunday against Australia,' he said.

The spectacular mismanagement by the Cork County Board over recent years has inured us to strike action in sport, but back then this was unique. The Ireland players were becoming increasingly militant over a range of issues where they felt – justifiably – that the IRFU was treating them with disdain.

Things had been brewing since before the tournament started, but after that call they moved swiftly enough and the team went out and played. The endgame that day in Lansdowne Road became as much a part of Australia's rugby history as ours. From being within touching distance of the semi-final, Ireland were left picking up their luggage and making the short journey home.

That team, with determined and articulate leaders in Fitzgerald, Philip Matthews and Brendan Mullin, began to break up soon after. The momentum for change was lost. You always wondered, though: what power might they have drawn from victory had they hung on that day? And would it have been used to move Ireland out of the darkness where they would remain until another World Cup, eight years later, would prod the IRFU into action?

Ironically, in our current Grand Slam circumstances, it was their focus on the championship which prompted the slow walk to the start line. Back then the social whirl of the Five Nations was the winter festival of the middle class. Of course it mattered if the game was lost, but not so much that it would spark a crisis meeting. In those circumstances then, the ripples caused by humiliating results on summer tours never made it back to shore.

So Ireland could fly through the night to get to New Zealand and suffer the humiliation of having no one there to meet them on arrival. That was in 1992, and five years later when they went back with a development squad, Sky TV soon pulled the plug on covering the games because the results were so lopsided.

With no urgency about improving, it was small wonder we weren't winning Grand Slams, but even when it did turn around, ten years ago next autumn, still we never managed to come top of the heap in Europe. In the ten Six Nations campaigns since the Lens experience, so memorably described by a senior union source as 'an absolute fuck-up altogether', there have been five Grand Slams shared between Wales (two) France (two) and England.[1] Until Ireland's arrival yesterday.

The frustrating statistic is that we filled the runners-up spot five times, with four wins from five games. Last season's slump to fourth place (only two wins) was the worst of the period and it marked the end of the Eddie O'Sullivan era.

It is inconceivable that the man who turned Ireland around after the hit or miss tenure of Warren Gatland could have watched this season unfold without a nagging pain. For every good wish for players whom he experienced so much with, there was a counter-force sticking in his craw. Why couldn't this have unfolded on his watch?

The answer is that the extra few per cent needed to take Ireland from being contenders to champions was missing. And while O'Sullivan can take credit for getting Ireland so close, he will also take the blame for not getting them close enough.

* * *

---

1   The 'Lens experience' refers to Ireland's 28–24 loss to Argentina in Lens at the 1999 Rugby World Cup.

When Eddie O'Sullivan took over from Warren Gatland on 30 November 2001, he knew exactly what he wanted to do and where he wanted to go. And it wasn't down the road Gatland had travelled, where planning was sometimes fitful. On any given day you wouldn't know whether the team would be beaten out the gate or carried shoulder-high from the field.

O'Sullivan almost got them there. Three Triple Crowns in four seasons was remarkable when set against a record of six in the previous 100 years. With Ireland having woken up at last to the demands of the professional game, O'Sullivan was the right man in the right place to drive it on. But the lack of a top-class structure would be his undoing. O'Sullivan grew more powerful based on his success on the field, and it allowed him to run the show without a set of rigorous checks and balances.

Of course Eddie had to explain to the committee why he was doing what he was doing, but these were not men who knew the parameters of a high performance operation from a dinner menu. If he told them it tasted good, then indeed it wasn't bad at all. O'Sullivan was far ahead of them in how the game was being played, so largely they let him at it.

Nowhere was this 'light touch regulation' more critical than in his relationship with Dr Liam Hennessy. They were friends, going back to Thomond College in the 1970s where they studied physical education. Hennessy's elevation to fitness director in the IRFU had been a critical move in Ireland dealing with the issue of conditioning, which had plagued us over the years. Together they drove it on.

The split came last season with Hennessy preaching the need to get players off their feet, and O'Sullivan looking at the growing list of things to be done and translating this into longer working hours for everybody. Eventually it blew up in a row in O'Sullivan's hotel room in Bordeaux during the World Cup. When that rift was highlighted subsequently in these pages, the coach played it down and the fitness director wouldn't comment.

Whatever the details of this, ask yourself how it could have been allowed to develop in a system that purports to be high performance. Elsewhere in this same system there were provincial coaches – Declan Kidney and Michael Cheika – who were virtually incommunicado with the national coach. Against this backdrop, perhaps Hennessy felt powerless to get himself and O'Sullivan back on the same page, because whatever he did to stop the strands from unravelling, evidently it wasn't enough.

The cock-up in the physical presentation of the team at the World Cup was compounded by O'Sullivan's reliance on too few players, which had negative implications for squad morale and became critical when they lost form, because they were fatigued or whatever. You add all this up and might conclude that it was O'Sullivan alone who cost the team that extra step. Of course it's not that simple: there was a dysfunctional system, and luck, and some very good opponents who at critical times were simply better than Ireland. It wasn't all about Eddie.

* * *

This is where Luke Fitzgerald comes back into the story. Here he is, twenty-one years of age and twelve caps to his name and already a Grand Slam feather in his cap. And like his dad, Luke is at a point where Irish rugby needs to decide what it's going to do with all this, and where we go next.

Straight away there is more money coming into the coffers. As a player, he stands to pick up an extra €15k on top of the €7,900 he has received for each win to date. That's the guts of €55k for the campaign. To help pay for this, tomorrow morning the IRFU will throw an invoice in the post to their sponsors O2 and Canterbury asking nicely for delivery on the performance clause in each contract. And RBS, the tournament sponsors, will be dropping €1.5m into their bank account as well.

Then they will start work on the coffee table book and celebration DVD and the glossy mag to go with it. And if England's experience is anything to go by after winning the World Cup in 2003, the IRFU's supporters' club will swell its numbers with each passing day until the novelty wears off. At €150 per subscription, every signature counts.

Of course there will be a dinner too. It will be more about celebrating than fundraising and this is where you fear things could get too comfortable. For sure this achievement deserves to be acknowledged in fine style, but when the sun rises the next day, it will throw light on a future where Irish rugby moves onwards and upwards, or slips into a round of more dinners to chow down and drink up to a soundtrack of 'We are the Champions'. And if that happens, we may never be the champions again.

It starts with finding the replacements for the stars. And understanding that we may never get another Brian O'Driscoll or Paul O'Connell, but that we need a system that has the optimum chance of doing so. That means producing more players with more skill and keeping them in the game longer. And it's long-haul stuff.

As part of the IRFU Strategic Plan unveiled last September, an Age Grade Committee was established. And in turn its chairman, Louis Magee, said a working party would be set up to focus on the minis game. Good idea: this needs to be overhauled. He said last week that there would be a report ready in May. Then he conceded that the working party hadn't even been finalised yet. Can't wait for that report. When we asked him about the work of the Age Grade Committee higher up the line, he asked that we send him an email. Sorry Louis, have to move on.

The same Strategic Plan has a line in it about delivering, in the professional game, 'a synergy between national and provincial player exposure and development'.

We think this means getting the provinces to give games to players qualified to play for Ireland. And we know that it is not happening nearly enough. Will winning a Grand Slam make us sit back even further, allowing greater numbers of promising players to waste away or leave the country because their route is blocked by overseas recruits?

We might consider developing some of this indigenous talent by giving them latitude in the Sevens game, except that seven is not considered a lucky number in Lansdowne Road.

Already we have the bodies and, even in this recession, the cash flow generated by the Grand Slam will improve. So invest in the short game and we'll benefit in the long one.

The challenge for Irish rugby now is to see off Luke Fitzgerald when his time comes, and point to all the improvements that were made during his Test career. He has been blessed that his time with Ireland coincided with that of a couple of top-quality players who have kept Ireland in the shop window; that he was in the frame when Declan Kidney got on board with a willingness to invest in excellent support and listen to what that support told him; that there was enough luck on Ireland's plate for them to make a meal of it. And isn't he blessed that he's his father's son, and not the other way round?

21

GIANT KILLERS

SEAN RYAN

Paul McGrath, Jack Charlton and Ray Houghton recall a milestone in Irish soccer history.

13 JUNE 2004

18 JUNE 1994 ... a date forever etched on the minds of Irish soccer fans ... a date redolent with glory for Jack Charlton's Republic of Ireland team thanks to their famous World Cup victory over Italy in Giants Stadium, New Jersey ... a date tinged with sadness because of the cowardly killing of six men in a bar in Loughinisland, Co. Down – killed solely for their support of the Irish team.

Ten years on, we recall the events of that day in America through the eyes of three of the principal participants – manager Jack Charlton, goalscorer Ray Houghton and defensive rock Paul McGrath – ever mindful that the ephemeral glory of sport can do little to assuage the hurt of the relatives of the murder victims in Loughinisland.

In their previews the sportswriters had named Ireland's group, which included Italy, Norway and Mexico, as the Group of Death. Little did they suspect that death would come to visit in the way that it did.

In football terms, the first match in the World Cup is always a tense affair. Neither team wants to lose and thus throw an added burden of pressure on the remaining group games, and when the opposition is provided by number one seed Italy, who had eliminated Ireland at the quarter-final stage four years earlier, the enormity of the task for Charlton's men is readily appreciated. Apart from that, in seven previous meetings, Italy had always come out on top, so this was, in effect, the last bogey to be laid.

GETTING READY

Jack Charlton: We were based in the Sheraton Tara Hotel outside New York, an hour's drive from the stadium. As it was an afternoon kick-off, we had a bit of time to kill, so we had a meal about 11.30 a.m., went for a stroll and then had a lie-down before setting off.

The heat was about 90[°F] but it didn't bother us that much because of the preparation we had been through in Orlando. Still, the Italians live in that sort of temperature and we don't, so that caused me to take precautions on how to handle the game. It was essential that we take a little breather every now and then.

So I said to the lads that, even if they were on the halfway line, not to be frightened about using our goalkeeper. Pass it back to Packie, let him take his time, move it around the area, and wait till he was challenged before knocking it up to their penalty area. That gives the other players a bit of a rest and they are in position for the ball when it's knocked down and they play from there. It was important to give us a break because the work rate we usually produced wasn't possible. It was always going to be a difficult game, but we handled them well.

Because of the heat I decided that there was no point in doing the usual warm-up of twenty minutes out on the pitch. Instead, I told them they were warmed-up and to conserve their energy to burn when it was time to go out and play.

DOUBLE WHITE

Paul McGrath: Ever since my mother bought me my first Chelsea outfit, which had white socks, white has been my favourite colour to play in. It was a mental thing from then on.

So, when I was handed a white jersey I was delighted, and I was walking around the dressing room thinking to myself 'you look good'. Then all of a sudden we're in the tunnel and I'm looking at the Italians – and we're all wearing white. We had to go back and change to our other, green strip. At the time I thought it was a bad omen, and I was a bit panicky, more than anyone, because I love the white socks especially. It's a vanity thing, they make me look better – the white against my dark skin.

Team talks generally went in one ear and out the other with me. Instead of listening to the manager I'm thinking of who I'm going to face, in this case Signori, Baggio, Baresi and Maldini, players I admire and heroes of mine.

I'm telling myself to make sure I don't slip up, don't dive in on Baggio or he'll make you look foolish, so while Jack talked, I concentrated on the job ahead. At 2.30 p.m., half an hour before kick-off, I go into a certain area where I don't listen to anyone and ignore the backslapping encouragement of others, because I'm focused on what I have to do.

As Jack wouldn't let us out to do our warm-up – the first time that had ever happened in my career – we got our first view of the stadium when we walked out to play the game. We only got to know then how many Irish fans were there, and that was the biggest boost because we had thought the Italians were going to buy up all the tickets.

When we saw all the Irish flags and banners all around the ground, it was like playing a home game. That gave us a great lift, we stuck out our chests and we felt that we were going to make it our day. That support deserved a victory.

To be honest, I shouldn't have been playing. I had a shoulder problem, which happened suddenly the night before the League Cup final and put my place in the World Cup squad in jeopardy. Jack said that if I wasn't ready by a certain time he'd have to bring someone else.

To play in that cup final, Jim Walker, the Aston Villa physio, gave me injections and I was crying with the pain, telling him to give me more. I cried with the pain for two weeks after, and it was only thanks to the tremendous work of Jim Walker and Mick Byrne that I made that game.

I was playing more by instinct than anything else. I was about sixty per cent right. My left arm was useless and, as a result, I had to go about five paces to get into my stride. I remember once Signori was five paces behind me going for the ball and I knew he was going to catch me so I jumped as high as I could and just caught it with my toe to push it back to Packie.

Jack Charlton: It was never a gamble to play Paul. He wants to play all the time and he is such a good player that the rest of the players want him there. As long as his ankles and knees are okay he can play.

RAY'S GOAL

Jack Charlton: Ray has never chipped a ball with his left in his life, but he did that night. It probably bobbled as he was attempting to hit it. Now, they had to come at us.

Ray Houghton: The ball broke to me off Baresi. I chested it down and ran across the goal. My first thought was to pass the ball to Steve Staunton but, as the ball hopped up, I decided to shoot. I don't favour my left foot but I caught it just right and it dipped over the goalkeeper.

I turned towards the stand because I knew my wife, Kira, and the kids were there. It was a fantastic feeling.

It meant so much to play in this game, and to score the winning goal was extra special.

Paul McGrath: Knowing Ray Houghton, he went for broke – that's what he would do. In his mind, as he chested the ball down, he's thinking, 'What am I going to do, I've no support on the right, and if I carry it I'll have to beat one or two Italians to get in a shot.' I'm sure he thought, 'Why not hit it?' It was like slow motion watching it – go on, go on, you're saying. I thought it was going to go over the bar but I felt tremendous when it went in.

And you can see the emotion in Ray's face when he did that, looking in the crowd for his wife and kids. It was lovely to see that emotion, as though he was going to cry.

And then my mind started to race. 'Now you've annoyed them, what did you do that for? Things were going along nicely and now they'll come at us in waves.'

Jack Charlton: A glance at the clock in the stadium tells me we've only played thirteen minutes and I think: 'We've scored too early, they're bound to come back even stronger at us.' But we've got the start none of us could have dreamed about. We can still get a point which, to be honest, I'd have settled for before the game.

When we get to half-time, the players lie on the floor of the dressing room instead of sitting on the benches, sipping liquid slowly to replenish their fluid levels.

I expected the Italians to have a go, but never to over-commit to attack, which is what happened. We defended well and there were few moments of stress for us, with Packie making a good save from Roberto Baggio, and Denis Irwin timing his tackle well on the same player.

In fact, if there was to be a second goal it should have come from us. Ray Houghton had a chance just before I took him off, and then Roy Keane got to the end line and laid it back for John Sheridan. Of all the players, I would back John to put it away from twelve yards, but instead of hitting the net he hit the crossbar. That was by far the best chance of the game.

When I was sending on Jason McAteer for Ray Houghton, I said to him, 'You have a habit of running past people with the ball, but Maldini is good going forward but not so good defensively, so kick the ball past him and run him and you'll find you'll get past him more than you might expect.' He did as he was told, and he had a right good game.

PAUL'S DAY

Paul McGrath: It was one of those days, even to the end, when everything went right for me. I remember the Italians coming forward late in the game and they got a corner or a free kick and it was played short. As soon as the player whipped it in, I genuinely knew I was the only player who was going to head that ball. I ran forward, jumped as high as I could and knew that no one could beat me unless they fouled me.

I was practically in shock afterwards because those days don't come too often, especially against the team that had knocked us out in 1990.

I can't remember who I swopped my jersey with. I remember Maldini and Baggio being nice and decent, but I was disappointed with Baresi. I might have got a snub off him.

Jack Charlton: The Italians were very quiet afterwards, they didn't say much. They shook hands with me at the bus. It was good, there was no aggravation whatsoever. They accepted the fact that we deserved to beat them.

Coming off the field, I noticed the police had a kid – I didn't know whether he was Irish or Italian or whatever – and they had a hold of him. They were a bit solid with him and I didn't think they should be so rough. I intervened, but the police know how to tell you where to go.

Paul McGrath: About forty-five minutes after the game we went to a local racetrack for a reception to let the hair down. I stayed in the bus, on my own with the driver. I didn't feel like getting off, so I just sat there taking it all in – the Irish people with their flags dancing around outside.

I was loving it and happy to let everyone else get the enjoyment from the occasion. It was a nice peaceful moment for me. I was glad it happened that day, because it didn't happen too often.

We were supposed to go straight back to Orlando but Tommy Coyne was in a serious way. His game was all about moving people and keeping moving. You couldn't work at the rate he normally worked in that heat or you'd end up in a hospital bed.

Jack Charlton: I didn't know about Tommy Coyne's problem because I was flying down to Washington to see Norway play Mexico. When he was taken to give a sample he couldn't pee, so they kept giving him something to drink and flooded his kidneys. He was quite ill and was taken onto the plane in a wheelchair.

Paul McGrath: A lot of people come to me and say that that game made them proud to be Irish and that it was my best game for Ireland. I'm not obsessed, but I've watched the video three or four times and I still get goosebumps because I think one or two of the things I tried aren't going to come off.

Jack Charlton: Because the papers in America gave very little coverage to Ireland, we didn't find out until the following day about the shootings in Northern Ireland, and then we only heard it second hand. It upset us quite a bit, but it's impossible to make sense of something like that.

When people ask me what my greatest memories are, it has to be when a country the size of Ireland beat Italy in the World Cup. It was unbelievable, really, and yet we deserved it.

22

SHINE ON YOU CRAZY DIAMOND

TOMMY CONLON

Thirty years after winning his first world snooker title, twenty after his second and last, Alex Higgins will be back at the Crucible Theatre in two weeks for the parade of champions.

21 APRIL 2002

He was on the phone to Louis Copeland during the week and he sounded fairly together. In fact, said one of his mates on Thursday, his form is 'dead on'. The cancer is in remission, he's not looking too bad, he's based in Bangor and he hasn't a bob.

But he has always togged out well and he needs a new tin of fruit for the Crucible because he's going back for the first time in eight years. Not to play, of course, but to join the parade of champions who've won world titles at the great arena over the last twenty-five years. It is twenty since he won his last, and thirty since he won his first.

'32-inch waist,' he told Louis.

Four years ago he was seriously ill with cancer of the throat. At fifty-three he has survived that, and a whole lot more. A couple of weeks ago he even played a few exhibition games up North with Jimmy White and Joe Swail.

He will get a rapturous reception in Sheffield on the bank holiday Monday in two weeks' time, the people hungry with nostalgia for the players who were working men before they became stars.

Except Alex Higgins, who was a natural-born star, and maybe the most natural-born predator ever to circle a snooker table. He was also, in the words of Rex Williams, 'the most mixed-up person I have ever met'. A walking, falling debacle for most of his adult life, his behaviour has lurched from wildly comical to downright loathsome, and the casualties along the way deserve better than to be forgotten in the fog of sentimental acclaim that has shrouded the disgraceful actions of many a popular sportsman over the years.

But their stories and scandals usually fade away as they recede from the limelight, into retirement and old age, until eventually all that is left is the greatness that propelled them into the public eye in the first place. Snapshots of the incandescent moments from their sporting lives, distilled and preserved for history after all the impurities of the private life have been burned away. (Unless of course you're O.J. Simpson.)

Higgins is surely, inevitably, destined for a few more lurid moments, but the process will one day overtake him too, leaving nothing but the memories of the febrile brilliance that once upon a time rocked snooker's staid, provincial world.

And, oh dear, what memories.

March 1972, the British Legion club in Birmingham. Day four of a world final that would stretch to sixty-nine frames over six days. Higgins is tied 21–21 with John Spencer, the defending champion, going into the evening session.

'What followed,' recalled the former professional Jim Meadowcroft in the Higgins biography *Eye of the Hurricane*, 'was absolutely incredible. Alex won all six frames. [Alex] had stolen the show in the first five frames and what happened next is still as fresh in my mind today as it was all those years ago.

'Alex took control coming up to the colours in the final frame of the night and potted a tremendous green. Instead of doing it the simple way, the way which would have taken all the pressure off the shot, he wanted to demonstrate just how masterly he was. So instead of just dropping the green in and stunning the white over for the brown, he smashed it in, coming around off three cushions with reverse side. It was awesome. As the applause began on that shot he was so quick to get on the brown that it was still building as he thrashed that ball in with a similar shot. Instead of the cheers dying, they just grew louder and louder as the blue and pink followed in rapid succession.

'By this time the noise was most deafening and then the strangest thing happened. When a cue ball hits the object ball, it makes a loud noise, similar to the one you hear on TV. But by the time Alex got down to complete the most marvellous session of his young career, you simply couldn't hear a thing. I never heard either the white making contact with the black, or the black crashing down. It was magic, pure magic, and as the ball slammed into the back of the pocket, Alex scooped up the white ball and walked off in his own inimitable style to deafening applause.'

Wow.

Higgins beat Spencer 37–32. One of the game's greatest players, Spencer would win his third and final title in 1977, snooker's first at the Crucible. Recalling their '72 epic last week, he said the standard of play was 'unbelievable. I thought I played very well – and I lost.'

Higgins was twenty-three. It was his first attempt at the title. The blade from Belfast had already spent three years playing tournaments and exhibitions around England and had sussed, sensed, that the older generation of master cuemen were vulnerable to his raw, fearless game. His strategy: 'Attack with brute force and frighten them to death.'

He was fast at the table but, as Spencer points out, the fastest part of his game was in his head. 'People thought he was reckless but he had a snooker brain and he saw the shots so quick, and everyone used to say how quick he was playing his shots, but if you watch a video of him, he's not quick. He's quick at getting from A to B – he used to be there waiting for the white to stop – but when he actually played the shots, he was no faster than the average. But going round the table, oh, he was greased lightning.'

The '72 final was played against the backdrop of the miners' strike which was convulsing Britain at the time. Power cuts were a daily hazard and on the fifth day of play, Spencer and his wife were left stranded in their hotel lift for twenty-five minutes on their way to the afternoon session. 'The traffic lights were out, everything was out, and going through the traffic we got a bump in the car on our way to the match.'

To compound matters, the lights over the table kept flickering on and off and when the club's back-up generator kicked in, writes John Hennessey in *Eye of the Hurricane*, 'the temporary lighting threw unnatural shadows at both ends of the table.'

In the ten years that followed, Higgins would lose one wife, a lot of money and a lot of games, including two world finals, to Ray Reardon in 1976 and Cliff Thorburn in 1980.

'I never had any doubts about my ability,' Higgins said. 'The problem was getting into so many scrapes because of my erratic temperament. By my very nature, I would never achieve a great level of consistency. That's my appeal and my downfall rolled into one.'

In 1981 Higgins was well beaten at the Crucible by Steve Davis, who was on his way to the first of his six world titles. Later that year he checked into a private clinic, burnt out and broken down. Snooker, by then, had left the men-only clubs of working-class Britain and entered the brave new world of the Yamaha Organs Trophy, the Lada Classic, the Mercantile Credit Classic, the Dulux British Open, the Goya Matchroom Trophy, the Coral UK, the Tennent's UK, the Skoda Grand Prix and a host of other tinpot tournaments.

One year later he was world champion again, hitting the headlines en route by relieving himself in a plant pot during a late-night practice session, having squeezed through 13–12 against Doug Mountjoy in the second round.

The semi-final, against a twenty-year-old Jimmy White, has gone down in snooker folklore. Leading 11–8, and then 15–13, White needed one more frame to make the final. At 15–14 and 59–0 ahead at the table, it looked as if he would get it too. 'You get the feeling this could be the winning break,' said Spencer, commentating for the BBC. At which point White missed a red with the rest.

Higgins, the tics twitching in that pinched, hurt face, went to work, scrambling for position, improvising on every play, keeping a precarious break alive. His head, his right arm and shoulder jolting in spasm on every shot, just as the white ball was released, then spearing the air with his cue on the follow-through, as if hoping that somehow it might help as he stood there, suspended in a split-second of agony before discovering if the shot had worked out. Every emotion out there to see.

A long black, a wafer-thin cut on a red, a tough blue and later, a red the length of the table to the yellow pocket. 'And another tremendous shot,' said Spencer. One by one, the balls disappeared. Twenty-seven, thirty-four, thirty-five. 'I'm feeling nervous for him,' Spencer gasped. 'I think if he clears this, this will be the break of the tournament.' Now the colours on their spots. Forty-two, forty-four. 'Just has to hold it together for five more shots.' Forty-seven, fifty-one, fifty-six, sixty-two, sixty-nine.

The Hurricane swung away from the table as the roars went up and broke into a smile as he raised his forefinger to the crowd: just one to go. White was a beaten man: 'My head was in a jam jar, I could only sit and watch dumbstruck as Alex finished me off.'

In *The Observer*, the novelist Julian Barnes wrote: 'Shambling and twitching, pockets distended by duck mascots, rabbits' feet and four-leaf clovers, Higgins lurched appealingly around the table like a doomed low-lifer.' Not to mention lashing down vodkas and coke, and sucking hungrily on cigarettes between visits to the table.

In the final he led Reardon for most of the way until the lethal, smiling forty-nine-year-old maestro pulled back a 15–12 deficit to level at 15–15. 'I thought I had him then,' said this old gent. But Higgins toughed it out – he won 18–15, finishing with a 135 clearance in the final frame. Then he broke down, immortalised in those famous images on the floor of the Crucible, pleading for his wife to join him with their baby daughter, oblivious to the crowd, the cameras, the cheque, the trophy.

At the celebrations that night Kirk Stevens, the young Canadian hustler, was heard declaring, as he made big circular movements with his hands, that 'Alex

Higgins has the biggest balls in the world.' Ted Lowe, bless him, would not perhaps have put it quite that way.

In any event, best wishes must go out to the Hurricane on the twentieth and thirtieth anniversaries of his two imperishable moments in time.

Shine on, you crazy diamond.

23

MAJOR EXPANSION BUILT ON STRONG FOUNDATIONS

DERMOT GILLEECE

In five decades, Irish golf experienced some extraordinary feats, but none compare to six Irish Major wins in four years – an occurrence which can be traced back to a seemingly small decision taken thirty years ago.

24 JULY 2011

In mid-November 1990, a quiet passing of the baton took place in Irish professional golf. Three days after Darren Clarke had secured a European Tour card in the qualifying school at Montpellier, Fred Daly died.

Though we couldn't have known it at the time, we were witnessing the emergence of a player whose international successes, especially in WGC events in the US, would help fill the enormous void left by the island's lone winner of the Open Championship. And Daly's demise lent further emphasis to the revolutionary changes which had been taking place here in the development of young talent.

Behind the 72nd green at Royal St George's last Sunday, Clarke's mind guru during a momentous week, Dr Bob Rotella, talked about contagion in an unusually positive sense. 'When you look at your country,' he said, 'do you think the top players aren't identifying with each other and thinking, "He's from Ireland and can do this; I'm from Ireland so I can do it too?" Sure, contagion is there. Oh God yes. No question.'

Mindful of the psychologist's words, you notice that only a year after Daly became the first home winner of the Irish Open in 1946, his great friend, Harry Bradshaw, captured the title. And when the Portrush man savoured an Open triumph at Hoylake in 1947, Bradshaw went close to doing the same at Royal St George's two years later, losing a play-off to Bobby Locke.

In this context, we can but speculate as to the impact an Open win by Christy

O'Connor Snr might have had. The Brad, who knew him better than most, expressed the view to me that, deep down, O'Connor feared that winning the Open would change him into an international player, so dragging him away from the native patch he loved so well. This would also explain why he declined to play in the US Masters where he had a standing invitation from 1955 to 1973 as a current Ryder Cup player, though contemporaries such as Peter Alliss, Harry Weetman, Bernard Hunt and even Neil Coles, who hated flying, made the trip.

Rotella's words can also be heard echoing loudly in the background of a chat I had with Graeme McDowell after he had missed the cut on his US Masters debut in 2005. 'I've been trying to put myself in (Pádraig) Harrington's way as much as possible. Pick his brains. I love the way he goes about things. For me, he's the guy who has it all worked out. He's the guy I want to be.'

News of Daly's death came through to the Grand Cypress Resort in Orlando on what was the Monday of World Cup week. And David Feherty, who was there representing Ireland with Ronan Rafferty, ensured a suitable send-off by relating marvellous stories from his time as Fred's assistant at Balmoral – 'the greatest two years of my life'.

One which I remember with particular affection concerned Garth McGimpsey, who went on to win fourteen championships, including the British Amateur of 1985, and later became a Walker Cup captain. Indeed, he recently captured the Irish Senior Amateur title by the crushing margin of six strokes. Feherty told of an occasion in 1979 when Hal McGimpsey, Garth's father, decided that if his richly promising son was to scale the heights of amateur golf, a lesson from Daly was absolutely mandatory. So they made the pilgrimage to Balmoral, where Hal proceeded to take copious notes for future reference.

Near the end of the lesson, the old pro became seriously animated, swishing the driver vigorously with his left hand through thick grass at the edge of a fairway. 'That's it! That's it!' Daly exclaimed. Whereupon Hal, convinced he and Garth were being made privy to a great golfing secret, eagerly enquired: 'What is it Fred? What is it?' Only to be told: 'That's the damn moss that's destroying our greens.'

As it happened, the 1970s was a rather bleak decade in the Irish amateur game. The glory days of Joe Carr, Tom Craddock and Jimmy Bruen were at an end and a dearth of talent could be seen in only two Walker Cup representatives over the ten years – Roddy Carr in 1971 and Pat Mulcare in 1975. And, of course, it was a time of great torment in the North, when the Troubles were at their height. Attempts at achieving some sense of normality through golf were admirably positive, however, with players crossing the border for championships in both directions. But there were exceptions. Like in 1974, when the interprovincial championship, which should have had a Northern venue, was switched to Royal Dublin, and the Home Internationals, scheduled for Royal County Down in 1979, which were abandoned altogether.

Which brings to mind a story from the 1970s concerning the Connacht players Sean Flanagan and Cyril Devins. Understandable anxiety from Devins about going North for the interpros brought a memorable reply. 'Just think of it,' said Flanagan, a Dublin-based garda with mischief in his eyes. 'Wouldn't it be wonderful to die for Connacht.'

From two Walker Cup players during the 1970s, Ireland delivered no fewer than six a decade later, in Philip Walton, Rafferty, Arthur Pierse, McGimpsey, John McHenry and Eoghan O'Connell. So, what happened in the meantime?

'As far as I'm concerned, the big change occurred when Joe Carr became captain of the Irish team in 1979,' said McGimpsey. 'I first played for Ireland in 1978 and when Joe took over, he brought a freshness and a modern approach to Irish golf.'

Which was, perhaps, entirely to be expected, given how progressive Carr had been during his own playing days in terms of practice, physical fitness, diet and mental preparation.

McGimpsey went on: 'Up to Joe's captaincy, the Irish amateur scene wasn't taken all that seriously. But Joe instituted squad training trips to Spain, which were very significant in the development of young players such as Rafferty and Walton. And I was lucky to be part of it, too. Before that, you were looking at trials in the depth of winter in places like Carlow and Malone, whereas Joe took us away to the sun, where we could play thirty-six holes a day for six days in a row while developing a keen sense of team spirit.'

I happened to be on one of those trips in 1981 when Rafferty set a course-record 67 around Sotogrande Old and Enda McMenamin had a hole in one on what is now the short fifteenth at Valderrama, but was called 'Las Aves' back then, with the nines reversed. That same year, Walton broke new ground by capturing the Spanish Amateur Open title at Torrequebrada, eastwards on the Costa del Sol.

McGimpsey also points to Irish players embarking on scholarships to American universities. Walton, for instance, went to Oklahoma State where he was mixing with such promising American talent as Scott Verplank, Bob Tway and Jeff Maggert; McHenry went to William and Mary, and Clarke had a spell, albeit a short one, at Wake Forest, where O'Connell later did a full degree course.

'I remember Philip joking that he came back with a degree in finger-painting,' McGimpsey went on. 'The important thing was that he became a seriously good player who helped my thinking, along with my putting stroke. His development contrasted sharply with my own, in that I was twenty-three when I first came on the scene. The upshot of it was that Ireland won the European Team Championship at Chantilly in 1983.'

By then, the era of the full-time amateur had arrived in Irish golf. From a time when the top players were career amateurs, our youngsters began to view a professional career in a much more favourable light. No longer would it be necessary, as in the days of Daly, Bradshaw and O'Connor, for a player to have the financial back-up of a club job before trying his luck on the tournament circuit. Amateur internationals Des Smyth and John O'Leary made the move, while Eddie Polland, Eamonn Darcy, Christy O'Connor Jnr and David Feherty progressed through assistant-professional ranks.

Then, as a logical follow-up to squad training in the sun, the GUI [Golfing Union of Ireland] appointed former English Ryder Cup player John Garner as the country's first national coach. To understand the significance of this move, one had only to be at Royal St George's last Sunday evening listening to Godfrey Clarke relate how the newly crowned Open champion received his first golf lessons from Garner.

The Englishman is now coaching in New Zealand, from where he was under-standably quick last Monday to acknowledge his early involvement with Clarke and Paul McGinley. 'Darren came to me back in 1983, when he was a three handicapper on a boys' squad in Belfast and was with me for three years,' recalled Garner. Asked if he ever sensed he was working with a future Major champion, Garner replied that while he could see undoubted talent, his primary objective was simply to nurture the players in his care.

Around the same time, Michael Bannon, runner-up to Rafferty in the 1980 Irish Amateur Close at Royal County Down, was acquiring a reputation as a gifted coach at Holywood GC, several years before a youngster named McIlroy would become his most celebrated pupil.

When Garner moved on, the GUI appointed as his successor another English coach, Howard Bennett, who established such a close relationship with Harrington during the amateur years that the player retained him into his professional career until Bob Torrance took over in July 1998.

In the meantime, Ireland's six-man team won the European Championship in 1987 for a second time in five years. And future stars like Clarke, Harrington and Paul McGinley could look to new heroes, such as Seve Ballesteros, Bernhard Langer, Sandy Lyle, Nick Faldo and Ian Woosnam. Meanwhile, Tony Jacklin made these role models all the more heroic when captaining European Ryder Cup teams to victory over the once-dominant US.

With his appointment as head greenkeeper at Dungannon GC in 1983, Godfrey Clarke opened the door for participation by himself and his son in inter-club matches. As he pointed out last Sunday, the youngster's golfing future became a committed effort by a working-class family, who had to make sacrifices, just like Kenny and Marian McDowell and Gerry and Rosie McIlroy would have to do in later years.

Of those Dungannon days before his dad moved some years later to Ballycastle GC, the son recalled: 'We didn't really have a chance of winning a provincial pennant. The height of our ambition was to give the club a boost by winning a couple of rounds, but I looked upon it as terrific fun and great experience.'

Father and son played in both the Senior Cup and Barton Shield but never as partners in the foursomes event. 'Maybe we felt it would have put too much strain on family relations,' conceded Godfrey with a chuckle.

Though he was a scratch player at fourteen, young Clarke was more interested in rugby at Dungannon Royal. Which lent a certain irony to his golf club having to waive a regulation to permit him to play the Senior Cup and Barton Shield, given his status as a juvenile member. 'When the time came to choose between a physical-contact sport or a walking pursuit, the decision was effectively made for me,' Clarke recalled. 'As a fifteen-year-old, I broke my arm during rugby training and, on medical advice, golf became my sport of choice from then on.'

Ireland's young amateurs of the 1980s had the best of two worlds. With no lack of competition from their peers, they could also test themselves against gifted career amateurs such as McGimpsey, Pierse, Declan Branigan, Adrian Morrow, Mark Gannon and Barry Reddan. And as a priceless by-product, they were making their own special contribution to North–South relations some time before the peace process secured a treasured prize.

'I consider myself to have dual nationality, British on one hand and Irish on the other,' said McGimpsey. 'There's no way around that. But there was nobody more proud of playing for Ireland than I was. Through 226 senior international matches, I was proud to be part of winning Irish teams and never had a problem in standing for the Irish national anthem.

'I consider myself lucky to have had the opportunity of playing great courses throughout this island – places like Baltray, Lahinch, Portrush and Rosses Point – on an annual basis. Our courses are better than anywhere in the world, which must also be hugely influential in moulding top-class talent. Right now, after Darren's win, people are emphasising Northern Ireland because its smallness has the effect of magnifying the achievement all the more. It makes an attractive statistic. But an equally attractive statistic, in my view, is six Majors from Ireland in the last four years.[1] That's unbelievable – a cause for celebration throughout the whole of the island.'

Clarke's entirely predictable international debut for Ireland came at Lahinch on 11 September 1987, on the last day of the Home Internationals. And with a half-point in his singles against Scottish veteran George Macgregor, he contributed to Ireland's first Triple Crown triumph.

Three years later, he moved to the professional ranks with a manager, Chubby Chandler, who would become a lifelong friend. Though the 1991 Walker Cup at Portmarnock beckoned, there was nothing further to prove after a 1990 season in which he captured the Spanish Amateur, North of Ireland, South of Ireland and Irish Close titles, going through twenty-five matches unbeaten.

By that stage, the GUI production process was being fine-tuned year on year, while former amateur rivals found themselves playing side by side in the professional ranks. Like in the World Cup at Erinvale, South Africa, in November 1996, when Clarke and Harrington teamed up for the first time.

On the eve of battle, Harrington bowed to his partner's seniority, acknowledging Clarke's decisive victory over him in the Irish Close final of 1990. 'I was totally in awe of Darren at that stage,' he said. 'He was a fantastic player, totally unbeatable in my view.'

On a more recent eve of battle at Royal St George's, Clarke turned to Rotella and asked: 'How does Pádraig approach a Major?' The American replied: 'He has a very quiet mind. And you, Darren, have to have a very quiet mind.'

Clarke did what Harrington did, and won. Which suggested the image of this huge jigsaw in which Joe Carr put the first pieces in place, more than thirty years previously.

---

1   Pádraig Harrington won the 2007 and 2008 Open Championships, as well as the 2008 USPGA Championship; Graeme McDowell won the 2010 US Open; Rory McIlroy won the 2011 US Open; Darren Clarke won the 2011 Open Championship.

24

A TOUCH OF CLASS

ANTHONY CRONIN

Like his owner Charlie Haughey, Irish Grand National winner Flashing Steel is an inveterate legend creator.

23 APRIL 1995

Charlie Haughey's Irish Grand National winner, Flashing Steel, has had, like his owner on occasion, plenty of critics. The experts were dubious about whether he would ever jump well enough to land one of steeplechasing's great prizes. They said his pedigree was that of a flat racer rather than a jumper. Since the races he won had usually gone his way and he had fallen in the Cheltenham Gold Cup, they wondered how he might be in an eventful contest with plenty of runners, or if he had to fight out a stern finish. Before last Monday's race they pointed to the fact that the only horse to carry twelve stone to victory in an Irish Grand National in recent years was Desert Orchid. And whatever else he might be, Flashing Steel, they claimed, was no Desert Orchid.

Well, the great thing about racing – as opposed to politics, say, or literature – is that there comes a point where the experts are proved finally and indisputably to be either wrong or right. It is what happens out there beyond the white railings that matters, not what is said in the press room or in the bar.

And what happened out there on Monday last was a display of the utmost gallantry and resolution by a top-class steeplechaser who survived one of racing's stiffest tests to win a victory that was altogether memorable. Connoisseurs are not likely to forget in a hurry the way Flashing Steel got his head down in the last few yards to put the issue beyond doubt.

Of course what nobody ever doubted about him was that he shared something else with his owner, namely the almost indefinable characteristic known as 'a touch of class', something which even his bitterest political opponents never denied Charlie. Or that, as indeed was the case with his owner too, there had hung about him from the very beginning of his career the almost equally indefinable sense of being destined to do remarkable things. Flashing Steel, like Charlie, might well find a place in the record books. As soon as he had won his first hurdle race people were talking about Grand Nationals and Gold Cups.

The story, as far as his present connections are concerned, goes back to a day at Leopardstown when John Mulhern had a runner in a bumper called Buckboard Bounce. Buckboard Bounce was a pretty useful animal in the making, and his trainer thought he was well up to winning the bumper that day until, in the closing stages, a big, light-framed bay fellow called Flashing Steel went past him as if he was standing still.

Knowing how good Buckboard Bounce was, Mulhern made enquiries, and wound up buying Flashing Steel from his owner-trainer, Neil Parker, and passing him on to his father-in-law, Charlie Haughey.

As an owner Charlie had another characteristic which is worth noting and one which is pretty well indispensable to that activity anyway, whatever about politics or anything else. As an owner of racehorses he was plain lucky and had been so right from the time when, as a not at all affluent young man, he had sent a horse called Miss Cossie to be trained by Dick McCormick, who had once shared with Steve Donoghue the distinction of being the only two people ever to have ridden The Tetrarch.

Miss Cossie won five races off the reel for McCormick's eager young patron and she was followed by a remarkable number of other winners from what amounted to relatively few horses. They included Vulforo, who was trained by Tom Dreaper to win a Power Gold Cup, and Aristocracy, who won a Group race when trained by Dick McCormick's son, Richard, and a Curragh handicap under a welter burden after going to Vincent O'Brien, finishing his career by winning over hurdles for Edward O'Grady.

Right from the beginning Flashing Steel was regarded by his connections as something rather special. The present writer remembers his owner mentioning the purchase in the august surroundings of government buildings. Though he hadn't much time in those days to expatiate on the dreams of ownership, there was a light in his eye which suggested cheering crowds and historic occasions on the greenswards of the future.

But there have been times since then when those future events may have seemed rather distant. Flashing Steel won his winner's bumpers and followed up by winning twice over hurdles. But it became apparent that he needed a certain kind of going to be seen at his best – good but with a bit of a cut in it, the sort of ground he could get his toe into. An intelligent horse who takes full note of everything around him, he is also a bit of a worrier and his races seemed to take a lot out of him.

But the big problem to which John Mulhern had to address himself was his jumping. This involved long periods of schooling over various obstacles, usually riderless and on a long rein. During these sessions Flashing Steel was taught to measure his distance from the take-off point more carefully and, if he got it wrong, to put in the occasional short or long one.

How effectively it was all done can be measured by his performance at Fairyhouse. When the others were coming down all round him, he made only one serious error, and in fact Jamie Osborne's big problem was the loose horses. Being the sort he is, Flashing Steel was taking too much note of them and had to be eased back a few places on the far side and made to concentrate. But when Osborne had come over on the Thursday before the race to jump half a dozen fences on him as a final school, he had declared himself satisfied after three. Flashing Steel's jumping could not be improved.

Next year's plans will include, all going well, another attempt at the Cheltenham Gold Cup and another Irish Grand National. It may sound over-ambitious but there are at least two reasons why it could come true. One is that, as Eimear Mulhern points out, for a horse who is now ten years old, Flashing Steel has had very little racing – twenty-six races of which almost half have been victories.

The other is his owner. Charlie Haughey is not only a focus for myth and legend but an inveterate legend creator. As the scenes at Fairyhouse on Easter Monday amply witnessed, the most extraordinary things do happen where he is concerned. But if he never wins another race, Flashing Steel's place in the history books is, like his owner's, secure.

SPEAKING OUT

There's a magpie who lands in front of my front window every morning. I'm going to get him shot one of these days.

25

'MISTAKE COST KERRY THE TITLE'

KEVIN KIMMAGE

Páidí Ó Sé will rely on instinct to avoid a repetition of a disastrous loss to Armagh.

It was late one Tuesday evening in May of 1996 when I first set foot in Ventry. Five days before his first championship outing as Kerry senior football manager, Páidí Ó Sé had agreed to meet me in his pub after training, but hadn't arrived by the time I passed through the doors. I ordered a glass of orange and waited. Half an hour later, he arrived, shook my hand for the first time and looked me over.

As he called for a pint I could see him studying the contents of my glass. 'Jesus, Kevin,' he said, 'would you ever have a real drink, you're making us nervous on that stuff.'

He ordered a pint for me, introduced a few of the locals and we sat together into the early hours of the following morning. He told the stories, I supplied the laughter and it occurred to me that I was about to get the most colourful interview of my journalistic career. If, that is, we ever got to talk on the record.

It was sometime after 2 a.m., with the bar silent and the last punter long gone that he finally signalled it was time to get down to business. And it was then that the transformation occurred. Having sat with the anecdote-a-minute football legend all evening, I was now facing 'the manager'. His responses were truculent and monosyllabic. It was a short interview.

Seven years and two All-Ireland titles have done little to loosen Páidí's tongue within range of a tape recorder, so as I brush through his doors on this, the first Saturday after Christmas, the journey has been made more in hope than expectation. He sees me before I see him, ushers me over to where he's sitting with a friend.

We shoot the breeze for half an hour and he wonders whether the interview will be a big piece. That depends, I suggest, on how talkative he is. He smiles. 'You're lucky,' he says, 'you've caught me on a good day.'

The day isn't quite good enough for him to bring us into the bowels of the Kerry football team. Any query too close to what he considers the sacred turf of team matters brings down the shutters, but what follows is probably as candid an interview as Ó Sé will ever give as long as his name hangs over the dressing-room door in Kerry.

It begins with a query about their preparations following the return of the squad from their winter holiday to South Africa. 'We'll be straight back into training in mid-January, as soon as we return,' he says.

'I don't want to be hurtful or embarrass any of the teams in the Second Division but certainly this year we're getting quality games against the best teams. That will give us a great run-in to the championship. We'll be taking the league extremely seriously because it's a big year for Kerry … and Páidí Ó Sé … and I will be leaving no stone unturned to restore lost prestige in Kerry.'

Why do you consider you have lost prestige? There was hardly any shame in coming within a point of winning the All-Ireland title?

'We didn't win the All-Ireland last year, so it didn't matter whether we lost by one point or fifty. That's not acceptable to Kerry supporters. People will say that we're great losers and all that. We are gracious in defeat but, deep down, Kerry people don't like to lose. Being a Kerry manager is probably the hardest job in the world because Kerry people, I'd say, are the roughest type of fucking animals you could ever deal with. And you can print that.'

I would have thought that what other people think doesn't particularly bother you, whether they are from Kerry or otherwise, I suggest.

'Well, yes, but I discovered something this year and I'll tell you now, whether it be football, business or anything else, from here on in I'm going with my instincts. I'm not going to be dictated to, or told that I should do this or I should do that. That didn't happen with me this year. I made a mistake.'

What was the mistake?

'I'm not going to say any more about it than that. At the end of the day, I did not go with my instincts and I'm disappointed about that. I have a very good group of selectors in John O'Keeffe, John O'Dwyer, Eamonn Walsh and Eddie "Tatler" O'Sullivan. I'm comfortable with these people. They're very loyal to me but they don't let me get my own way all the time. I need people like that, because I have strong beliefs, and I get ideas into my brain that might be crazy, and whether it's my wife, my mother or my selectors, sometimes I need somebody to stand up to me. But from here on in, I'm going with my instincts whether they be right or wrong. Because, at the end of the day, I'm the one that's going to take the bullet.'

He has what he describes as a number of 'new, inventive ideas for the Kerry team' to put in place in 2003. He has not discussed these with his selectors yet, but they will sit down together in South Africa to hammer out an approach for the coming season. One of the most significant changes is likely to see Ó Sé take a greater hand in the physical preparation of the team, a role previously entrusted mainly to John O'Keeffe. It was at O'Keeffe's insistence that all the squad members completed the same rigorous training regime last year and this was seen as the prime reason for Maurice Fitzgerald's absence from the panel. An absence all too obvious in the dying minutes of the All-Ireland final when the team desperately needed a steadying hand.

Ó Sé has indicated to close colleagues that the future training regime should be more flexible – a move likely to ensure the return of Fitzgerald, who has received an invitation from the manager.

'I'd love to have Maurice back. All the team would. But that (whether he returns) is a matter totally for himself. I have invited him back but he's a very private person and I don't want this interview to be seen as an attempt to turn up the heat on him. But I do want to clear the air on this. There was a perception that a conflict between myself and Maurice was the stumbling block to his return. Not true. Maurice and myself have a very good relationship, there has never been a strain between us and I've never stood in the way of his return.'

To illustrate his admiration for Fitzgerald he mentions the three people in the world whose opinions he holds in the highest esteem. The first is his former boss. 'There was always one man who had the highest of confidence in me, and that was Mick [O']Dwyer. He knew deep down I wanted to be a manager. I remember one particular night in training, he forgot his whistle, and I had one in my bag and he said, "You fucker, you're looking for my job."'

That was near the end of his reign with Kerry?

He laughs. 'It was near the end of my reign, and his.'

The second is Fitzgerald. 'Maurice has a great feeling for the game, I love talking football with him.'

The third name is a little more unlikely: 'The Minister for Foreign Affairs, Brian Cowen, who has an absolutely great knowledge of football.'

His association with Cowen is a product of one of his other great passions. A self-confessed political animal, there are, he says, three 'f's in his life: 'Family, Football and Fianna Fáil'.

A lifelong friend of Charles Haughey and Bertie Ahern, his political affiliation last year prompted tourism minister, John O'Donoghue, to appoint him to the board of Bord Fáilte. Inevitably, for a man whose CV only shows terms as a garda and publican, the appointment prompted questions about his suitability for the post. Criticism which clearly hurt, for he talks at length about his ideas for the new role.

As he speaks, you are reminded about a passage from his autobiography. 'I live the life of a professional football manager. Maire (wife) and Beatrice (mother) provide that luxury for me. The pub, the shop, the kids. I spent seventeen years in the Kerry jersey and the last six ranting and raving about Kerry football. But you can't serve two masters; Maire has always picked up the slack.'

Yet here he is attempting to serve both Bord Fáilte and the Kerry footballers. Won't that present a conflict? 'No. Because I have a very, very active mind. I suffer from insomnia. I can't get anything more than three hours sleep per night, it's all I need, at any time of the year. I might go up for a nap during the day, but basically, I won't sleep. My mind never stops working.'

How do you relax? 'I never relax. I suppose I'm at my happiest this time of the year, when I'm having a few pints with the locals. I just can't relax. I'd love to tell you that I'm the cool, calm, calculated guy, but I'm not. I can't switch off.'

Do you feel more uptight during the season when the stakes are highest?

'Not particularly. Believe it or not, the time that I'm most relaxed is when I'm out on the field. And people think I'm wired to the moon. But I'm more relaxed because I'm concentrating totally on the game.'

He may feel comfortable monitoring events on the field, but he isn't prepared to talk about them. Questions about the All-Ireland final are rebuffed unequivocally. 'I'm keeping my powder dry. I'm not going to discuss anything that happened this year, because I hope the element of surprise will be there for Kerry next year.'

You take a different tack: his notorious superstition.

'There's a magpie who lands in front of my front window every morning. I'm going to get him shot one of these days.'

Why?

'I hate the sight of fucking magpies.'

Really?

'I do.'

In what way?

'You asked me about the All-Ireland before and I told you I don't want to discuss it.'

Not even the build-up to it?

'I don't want to discuss anything about that.'

What were the good points to come out of Kerry's year?

'In black and white, any year you don't win an All-Ireland is a bad year. End of story. Kerry have won thirty-two All-Irelands in the past because they set high standards for themselves. We didn't win it this year, so it was a disastrous year.'

Were there any pluses at all?

'I wouldn't say there were. I'd only be codding you if I said I thought there were.'

As the interview ends, his wife, Maire, brings out tea and biscuits. She apologises for not having something more substantial ready, but the family are busy packing for the holiday in South Africa. The team and families left the following day. With business to attend to, Páidí was due to join them the following Friday, 3 January.

'I'm not looking forward to fourteen hours inside an airplane,' he says. 'I'm afraid of my living shit of them.'

He prefers the sights around Ventry, and before you leave he shows you some. First, he brings you up the road to the home of nephews Darragh, Tomás and Marc. As Páidí summons the three boys, their mother, Joan, offers you a cup of tea. You decline, say your helloes and goodbyes and then Páidí brings you down the road to his mother's house. 'Have a look at the photographs when you go in,' he whispers.

Beatrice shakes your hand and also wonders if you would like a cup of tea. Páidí points at the walls, full of images of him in his playing days. As you take them in, he stands there, smiling. Pride in his mother's pride. Still burning, still driving him on.

26

'I'M THE BIGGEST ROGUE THAT YOU'LL EVER COME ACROSS; I'M A POLITICAL ANIMAL'

KEVIN KIMMAGE

It was a comment which was pure Páidí, but his sense of humour was somehow lost in translation.

12 JANUARY 2003

After the interview, Páidí Ó Sé poured a mug of tea for me and made a statement which, in the light of all that has transpired since, seems ironic. 'You,' he said, 'are a lucky journalist for me.' I was intrigued. 'Really,' I said, 'how's that?' He reminded me of the last time I had formally interviewed him. Early in 1997.

Ah yes, I remembered. Páidí was in ultra-cautious mode that day. Extracting meaningful words was well nigh impossible. Evidently, he remembered too. The following September Kerry won the All-Ireland title for the first time in eleven years and somewhere deep in the recesses of his superstitious mind, the manager connected the two events.

So here he was, almost six years later, sitting in his kitchen, *piseogs* doing a jig in his brain, thinking, 'With this fella here again, it's a good omen for Sam coming home.' Maybe it will next September, the centenary of Kerry's first All-Ireland success. Maybe Páidí will ride out the current storm and still be holding the reins. What is fairly sure, given the events of the last seven days, however, is that he'll reckon the luck has worn off this particular journalist's charm.

The interview that has dominated the sports pages this past week took place in the early afternoon of Saturday 28 December. It hadn't long been in progress when he made what has become branded as an infamous statement about Kerry supporters. I had asked him why he felt that Kerry had lost prestige last season, having come within a point of All-Ireland champions Armagh.

'We didn't win the All-Ireland last year, so it didn't matter whether we lost by one point or fifty. That's not acceptable to Kerry supporters. People will say that we're great losers and all that. We are gracious in defeat but, deep down, Kerry people don't like to lose. Being a Kerry manager is probably the hardest job in the world because Kerry people I'd say are the roughest type of fucking animals you could ever deal with. And you can print that.'

My immediate response was laughter. The tone and texture was pure pre-management Páidí. Exuberant and humorous.

One week later it was reproduced in print, unsanitised. Sure it looks cruder in cold print, but at a time when the sports pages are filled with clichés and waffle, here was a breath of candour I considered admirable. And all the more exceptional coming from a man whose strong and outgoing personality has suffered self-castration in his efforts not to reveal anything which could be used against the Kerry team.

During the interview, one of the topics which arose but didn't survive the final draft was the suggestion that he has never received the credit he deserves for his role in guiding Kerry to two All-Ireland successes.

'I get credit for nothing,' he replied. 'But that doesn't bother me. I'm at my happiest when I'm with my family. I have a great wife, Maire, three kids, Neasa, Siún and Páidí Óg; a fantastic mom, Beatrice. I have my brother, Tom, and I lost my other brother, Mícheál, during the year. And then there's the four lads (Mícheál's sons) – Fergal, Darragh, Tomás and Marc. Believe it or not, all of the rest of the Kerry team I treat as my own family. I treat them as if they were my own flesh and blood. And until I've finished with Kerry, that's the way it's going to be. I worry about them, I'd do anything for them. I'd get up in the middle of the night for them.'

Why?

'Because that's my make-up. I'm the biggest rogue that you'll ever come across; I'm a political animal, but I love my players.'

Loyalty is a big part of Ó Sé's make-up. As a child, he was driven by the lure of the green and gold. As a player, he would put his head in where others wouldn't dream of putting a boot. As an All-Ireland-winning captain, in deference to his home place, he made his acceptance speech *as Gaeilge*. As manager he endeared himself to few in the media through his constant refusal to allow them access to his players on all but the most controlled occasions.

For journalists, that makes Ó Sé and his Kerry team a nightmare to deal with. He has received relentless criticism, but remains impervious to it all. In his book it is the right thing to do because it protects his players.

He could have done with a bit of protection himself last week. When all hell broke loose it quickly became apparent that his regard for Kerry football is not reciprocated by those in high places. On Sunday afternoon all was quiet on the Gaelic games front. With a few preliminary O'Byrne Cup games in Leinster, one Dr McKenna Cup match up north and no inter-county action listed for Connacht or Munster, the *Irish Examiner*'s sports desk found itself with some space on its hands, so it lifted extracts from Ó Sé's *Sunday Independent* interview and printed them on Monday.

Between the two pieces, members of the Kerry County Board apparently began to receive complaints about Ó Sé's reference to their supporters. They could have pointed out to the complainants, as many neutral commentators have done since, that, yes, the language was crude, but the manager was simply pointing out how difficult it is to please Kerry supporters.

Instead, they opted for an act of breathtaking hypocrisy. Last August, Darragh Ó Sé was sent off on a straight red card in the first half of a senior club championship match in Gallarus. With the player facing an automatic month-long suspension and Kerry due to play in an All-Ireland semi-final a fortnight later, it was a controversial decision to say the least. At half-time, the county chairman, Sean Walsh, crossed the field and, in full view of the crowd, was seen to admonish referee Tom McCarthy. Here was the county board's highest ranking official openly undermining the authority of the match official. An act all the more serious at a time when counties all over the country are struggling to recruit referees.

Funnily enough, on that occasion there was no rush by the county board to disassociate itself from the actions of their own chairman; no suggestion that Walsh's position was on the line. Yet here, four months later, Páidí Ó Sé was being isolated over one quote in a newspaper.

To appreciate the inflammatory level of their intervention, it is instructive to understand how the wheels of the media turn. In journalism, old news is no news. By Tuesday morning, Ó Sé's statement would have been fading into the mists of time had the county board not given the story legs by providing a new and tantalising angle: the controlling body disassociating itself from its manager's actions was unprecedented. Manna from heaven for sports desks in the barren days of early January.

Immediately, the story outgrew the 'toy department', a rather unkind euphemism for the sports desk. On Tuesday, the *Irish Examiner* published a front-page story which was then taken up by *What It Says In The Papers* that morning. The controversy took flight to South Africa from where Ó Sé issued an apology – thus providing ample sports copy for Wednesday.

Thursday brought no respite, with many organs printing extracts from Radio Kerry's *Terrace Talk* programme broadcast on Tuesday night – an evidently lively debate involving Páidí's friend Liam Higgins, and Ger Power, a close associate of John O'Keeffe.

Another controversy which has arisen since last Sunday concerns Ó Sé's intentions on the training field and his relationship with team trainer John O'Keeffe. During my interview, I had picked up Ó Sé on his intention to leave no stone unturned next year. How many stones were there left to turn, I wondered? 'I have had a little bit of time to think and reflect,' he said. 'I have new ideas for the new year. New inventive ideas for the Kerry team which I intend putting in place.'

He didn't elaborate on these 'ideas'. I pushed him. 'In what areas,' I asked, 'preparation or training?'

'Preparation and training,' he replied.

Later he touched on the matter again. 'I have my own new ideas for the team in the new year. I want to bring in a bit of creativity, I believe there needs to be a new freshness there, but then again I'm not going to divulge any of that publicly. I don't want any of the country to know what I'm doing. Let other people milk their cows and I'll milk mine.'

Had he discussed his ideas with his fellow selectors, I wondered? 'I'll be meeting them in South Africa. We'll be having a meeting about that.'

From the interview, and armed with knowledge obtained elsewhere that he favoured a more flexible approach to the fitness regime to facilitate the return of Maurice Fitzgerald, I deducted that it was likely that Ó Sé would be taking a more active role in the physical preparation of the team – my words, not Páidí Ó Sé's. Others interpreted this as a suggestion that O'Keeffe's role would be diminished. Amid the controversy, it hardly helped matters that O'Keeffe's job as a teacher had precluded him from travelling to South Africa.

Perhaps the most interesting reaction to last week's interview was the 'shock horror' in some quarters of Kerry at the suggestion that Páidí Ó Sé might be looking for free rein when he announced he would be 'going with his instincts' this year. Why shouldn't he? He is the manager, after all, and instinct is what sets the great ones – Boylan, O'Dwyer, Heffernan – apart.

In the interview, Ó Sé agreed that he had been reluctant to go with his own intuition in the past. 'The problem,' he explained, 'was that there was always a consensus of opinion out there that I was volatile, that I was a maverick, I'd run in the wrong direction. That I wasn't balanced and that I couldn't be trusted. And I suppose I gave them plenty of ammunition for that as well. I drank porter late at night in houses. As a footballer, myself and certain mates of mine burned the midnight oil.'

Now Ó Sé is prepared to trust his own intuition in an effort to prove himself a great manager and bring Sam back to the Kingdom. He is, in essence, upping the ante. It's time for the Kerry County Board to clarify his role at the head of the team. Do they believe that Ó Sé really is the boss, the man who should call the shots next season, or is he considered merely a figurehead whose wildest impulses need to be controlled by those around him? If the answer to the former is 'yes', then they should back him as publicly as they disassociated themselves from him last week. If not, he'll hardly need to ask where the door is.

27

'YOU ARE ALWAYS QUESTIONING YOURSELF'

MARIE CROWE

The pain of Ryan McBride's death is still felt by Derry City and their manager Kenny Shiels.

8 OCTOBER 2017

From the window of Crawford's coffee shop in Maghera you can see the local cemetery. Kenny Shiels looks across as he speaks, pointing at the spot where his brother David is buried. David Shiels was killed by the IRA in a case of mistaken identity almost thirty years ago. He was shot four weeks after his son was born.

The firing started as he was outside feeding his dog. He was hit. A hail of bullets riddled the caravan the family was living in – a makeshift home while their new house was being built. His wife escaped unharmed but the baby received a ricochet mark above an eye. Luckily, it wasn't life-threatening.

It was a devastating time for the grieving Shiels family, something Kenny hoped never to experience again. But just last March, the Derry City manager found himself grieving once more when the captain of his team died suddenly.

'Come on down here quickly, Kenny.' These were the words uttered to Shiels in a phone call on that fateful Sunday evening when the news broke that Ryan McBride had died in his sleep. These are the words he will never forget. The team physiotherapist didn't want to deliver the news on the phone. He was concerned about Shiels racing down the road from Maghera to Derry knowing the tragedy that was unfolding a stone's throw from the Brandywell.

'When I got there and saw everyone it was like there was numbness about the whole place,' explains Shiels. 'You had twenty players there and the youth players were there too just looking at each other and no one knew what to say. I'm thinking I'm supposed to be the leader of this group of people. What do I do now? And you have to try and act like you are unaffected by it and you can't. That emotion is there and you think about all the things that are happening … it's really hard to take and no one can understand it.

'I've lost a brother, he's buried over there beside my father, and that was traumatic. This was different because a manager–player relationship has a close affinity to a father and son relationship. I speak to the team all the time about trying to be a family. I've always done that with players. I feel that builds up a good rapport, relationship and dynamic. Ryan was like that.

'Because he was so quiet it felt even worse. He wasn't an out-there guy. He was modest and quiet and it's just hard to understand why it happened. Even talking to you now puts me into that train of thought. It's hard to believe it was this season. This is October. In some reflections it feels like a couple of years ago and in other thoughts it feels like a couple of weeks ago.'

When trying to get on with life, Shiels thinks of McBride's family and how they might be dealing with things, how they get on with it. They have a foundation going in his memory and that helps; it's therapeutic and maintains a connection.

'You might think, you've only known him a short time, which is true, but it was a close relationship. He will never be forgotten that's for sure. Having football to play makes it both easier and harder. Easier because you have kept a connection, an invisible relationship there, where you feel there is a wee bit of purpose as well as the normal incentives that are there.

'You want to do well because you work for that club, every manager is the same. We have a bit of extra incentive because inside us we are doing it to try and connect with Ryan's legacy. It's harder then because that brings a wee bit of pressure. You want to try and help the players who are still there, you are more affectionate. It's a season where you compartmentalise; it will be next season before you have that closure, that mental closure. There are so many people who need an arm around their shoulder and you are looking around the dressing room and wondering where to start.'

Before McBride passed away, Derry were flying high in the league. They had the perfect start to the season – five straight victories. But after the tragedy they hit a poor run of form, embarking on a six-game winless run. This was to be expected given the huge emotional trauma of the team captain's death.

'The ensuing six weeks to two months were hard, you are trying to get normality back. Like every football team, we all have issues: Shamrock Rovers, Cork, Drogheda and you have to try and go back to your mentality of, "I'm here to win football matches at this club." This is cruel.

'You spend so much time thinking about what you could do and what you haven't done. You see someone who has had a dip in form and in a normal season if someone has a dip in form you are not thinking is it because of what happened? Now if they aren't playing well you are thinking that what happened is the reason and you can be so wrong. This season has had a big impact on my life, on how I am.

'I feel a wee bit damaged. You are always questioning yourself, we had really tough training that week and I think and hope that wasn't the cause. (The cause of) his death was inconclusive, you don't know why; he just went to sleep and passed away. You don't know why it happened; you hope that it's not because we worked him too hard. They are young, healthy people, what can you do, and we will never know. It makes it harder but it's not about it being hard for me, it's about their family, they come first. They are so quiet and so like Ryan. He was such a great fella.

'Every other player in the league came through an academy structure except Ryan. When he was fifteen he went to play in a pub league, a big strong boy, and he came to Derry from there, he was unique.'

There are so many layers to Kenny Shiels, so many emotions within the man that he is unable to contain. As the conversation bounces from topic to topic his demeanour reflects how he feels. He's animated and exhilarated when talking about football and youth development. He's troubled when talking about the past and perplexed when talking about the future.

First, the past. He grew up in a Protestant family just outside the village of Maghera. His father was football-mad and having eight sons meant he had the basis for a team. He was a chicken farmer and he called his band of boys 'Roy's Chicks'. They played football from dawn till dusk. He formed the football club in the village so they would have a team to play on. This was when the Troubles were at their peak and divisions were deep.

'At the time everyone on one side of the village was one religion and everyone at the other side was another religion. The only thing that connected it was my father and the football club he started. Both religions played on the team.

'At that time you couldn't play Gaelic and football, but the boys sneaked away and played with us anyway. We built brilliant friendships because of that. There were very few cars back then, so we went in a trailer to matches, or in the boot. They were fantastic times.

'What my father did was unbelievable; he would have went to the top of the town for a drink. He was on his own, he was the only one from his religion that did that and everyone liked him. He was a councillor and he would get Catholics houses and Protestants houses. He just loved people. I see a lot of that in myself, that passion for people no matter what. When I was in Coleraine, I signed players from

Shankill and the Falls and we all became friends. It was the whole embodiment of our sport.'

Before returning to Derry, Shiels, who has a degree in psychology, spent time managing in Scotland, most notably with Kilmarnock. He was appointed Derry manager in November 2015 and last season they finished third and qualified for Europe.

As to the future, it's a rewarding job being the Derry City manager but demanding too and there are lots of challenges that come with the role. Like trying to keep players and also trying to entice players to come and play for Derry City when they could realistically earn better money playing elsewhere.

'I go to countries that have poor economies, like Spain, Portugal, Eastern Europe or lower leagues in Scotland. I can't go to the market in Dublin, you have the twenty per cent VAT and the Brexit situation hasn't helped.

'All these things are against us. I'm loath to talk about it too much because it comes across as paranoia, excuses, all those things. It's hard to find the right age balance; we have a very young squad. When we lost 5–0 against Bray it was hard to take but we had three teenagers in the back four. We had six teenagers in the team. We had an inexperience and naivety, but there is so much learning from that. We lost 5–0 to Dundalk last year and we went twenty games unbeaten after that. It can be educational as long as it doesn't destroy you psychologically.'

Derry City are on the verge of qualifying for Europe again and if they achieve that, their season will have been a success. Having European football will help financially and also be a draw for potential new signings. But with only ten teams set to contest the Premier Division next season, the geographical landscape could be tricky.

'We have just lost Drogheda and if we lose Finn Harps and Sligo too that's three of our four closest teams. And you are bringing in Waterford and you have Cork and Limerick and Galway. If we lose them three, then that will cost us £30,000 extra in transport alone.'

As he ponders what lies ahead for both his team and himself, he's never sure what life will throw at him but he knows no matter what he will keep going and football will be with him every step of the way. There's some solace in that.

28

CUSACK'S GIANT LEAP FORWARD

EAMONN SWEENEY

It's been a good week for Irish sport; it's also been a good week for our gay friends, gay neighbours, gay brothers, gay uncles, gay sons and gay daughters.

25 OCTOBER 2009

Today's column will be about homosexuality so I must issue a warning that some readers will find some of its contents immoral, unnatural and downright disgusting. I know I do.

What, for example, could be more immoral, unnatural and downright disgusting than this statement? 'Sexual relations outside marriage constituted a violation of bodily integrity, and homosexuality did so in a particularly grave manner as being against the order of nature and a perversion of the biological function of the sexual organs ... it was important that the state should do all in its power to discourage the spread of homosexuality and in particular should not appear by the laws to condone sexual practices calculated to undermine the institutions of marriage and the family.'

That choice piece of hate speech was issued from one Rory O'Hanlon SC in 1980. At the time Mr O'Hanlon was representing the state as it defended the legal ban on homosexuality being challenged in the High Court by David Norris. He was not giving his personal opinion; he was giving that of the state. Or, in other words, us. This was being said in the name of the people of Ireland.

Justice Herbert McWilliam ruled against Norris, telling him 'it is reasonably clear that current Christian morality in this country does not approve of buggery, or of any sexual activity between persons of the same sex'.

This was the country that Donal Óg Cusack was born into.

Justice McWilliam did say that 'there was no foundation for any of the common beliefs that male homosexuals were mentally unbalanced, effeminate, vicious, unreliable, less intelligent or more likely to assault or seduce children, or young people, than were heterosexual males'. Very good of him. Though presumably anyone who had laboured under the delusion that homosexuals were, for example, less intelligent, had lived in blissful ignorance of the work of Oscar Wilde, Francis Bacon, Benjamin Britten, Ian McKellen, W. H. Auden, Marcel Proust, Tennessee Williams, E. M. Forster, John Gielgud and Truman Capote, among very many others.

David Norris fought on. In 1988 the European Court of Human Rights found that the Irish ban on homosexuality infringed the rights of gay people. The Irish government had no option but to repeal the ban, though it took five years to do so.

On the day the bill legalising homosexuality was passed in the Dáil, a Fine Gael TD from Louth named Brendan McGahon said, 'I believe homosexuality to be an abnormality, some type of psycho-sexual problem that has defied explanation over the years. I do not believe that the Irish people desire this normalisation of what is clearly an abnormality ... while they deserve our compassion homosexuals do not deserve our tolerance ... such people have a persecution complex because they know they are different from the masses of normal society. They endure inner torment.'

In a slightly less florid manner, some other politicians got in on the act back then. Three of them went on to hold ministerial rank.

'I do not often find myself in agreement with my constituency colleague Deputy McGahon but on this occasion I am,' said our current Minister for Justice Dermot Ahern.

'The problem is that this bill will be seen as sending a message that society regards buggery as a natural, healthy and acceptable act but I disagree totally with that. It would be irresponsible to send such a message to our young people at a time when AIDS is such a prevalent disease,' said future Minister of State and Taoiseach's brother Noel Ahern.

'I ask the house to pause and think whether the decriminalisation of homo-sexuality is the duty of the house or whether it would in fact adversely affect future generations ... if the argument is accepted that homosexuality is not morally wrong is there still a basis for a law to protect youth from corruption?' said future national laughing stock John O'Donoghue. These were our representatives. We voted for them.

This was the country in which Donal Óg Cusack grew up.

And that is why nobody should underestimate the bravery it took for the Cork goalkeeper to publicly come out as a gay man in his autobiography or what a huge step forward this represents for Irish sport. We should also understand what a huge challenge it is to the bigotry and prejudice which remain against gay people in this society.

Perhaps there are people reading this column and thinking, 'Why is there such a big deal being made about it? Why do gays have to go on about their sexuality so much?' But it's not gay people who make an issue of homosexuality, it's straight people. Most straight men have, for example, been in a pub with a woman and, suddenly overcome by affection, leaned across and kissed her.

If a gay man did this with his partner, he'd be regarded as looking for trouble in most of the country's pubs. There's even a chance he'd suffer physical violence. Do gay couples walk arm-in-arm down our main streets with the same unselfconsciousness and freedom as straight couples do? They don't, because straight people wouldn't stand for it. In most towns every pub is a 'Straight Bar'.

This is the country Donal Óg Cusack lives in.

The work of people like David Norris has made Ireland a better place for gay people. But it's far from ideal. Two years ago, Brian Lenihan, then Minister for Justice, told a meeting of the Gay and Lesbian Equality Network that they could forget about gay marriage. 'Gay marriage would require constitutional change and in my view a referendum on this issue would be divisive and unsuccessful and, furthermore, would jeopardise the progress we have made over the last fifteen years.'

You can read a lot into that simple sentence. Brian Lenihan thinks a referendum would be 'unsuccessful'. Why would it be? After all, it's no business of any straight person whether gay people want to get married. Well, is it? Yet apparently our leaders think they'd band together to deny them this right. The clue is in the word 'divisive'. Lenihan knows the bigots would come out of the woodwork were such a referendum held. And instead of doing the brave thing and facing them down, the government hadn't the stomach for that fight.

Ponder that bit about jeopardising the progress we have made over the last fifteen years. Brian Lenihan was warning GLEN not to make the straights angry or they might take away what they so grudgingly granted in the first place. In other words he's behaving as though gay rights are a gift dependent on the good mood of the majority, rather than something which should be granted as a matter of course.

This is the country in which one of our leading hurlers decided to unapologetically declare himself a homosexual man. He asked for no one's permission and he expressed no regret. This, he said, is who I am and if you've got a problem, that says more about you than it does about me. We needed to hear this.

Donal Óg's coming out coincided with the burial of Stephen Gately. There was a lot of hypocritical guff surrounding the presence of the former Boyzone singer's 'husband' at the funeral. We were told it showed how much we'd moved on, how much we'd 'matured as a nation' that Andrew Cowles was 'accepted' at the funeral.

But Stephen Gately's 'husband' wasn't his 'husband', he was his civil partner. They couldn't have got married in this country because the government feel this wouldn't be 'accepted'. I expect similar self-congratulatory nonsense to be written about Donal Óg. But we don't deserve any plaudits because he came out. It doesn't show that we've 'matured as a nation'. It shows that he's a mature individual. It is a credit to him, not to us. Were we to put in place legislation that meant Donal Óg Cusack might one day be able to legally marry, then we could start clapping ourselves on the back.

I'm sure there are people who feel the Cork keeper should have kept quiet about his sexuality. But that kind of silence has obtained for too many years. It's not too long since a well-known gay Irish public figure, who never left the closet, died, and the papers were full of stuff about how he'd never met the right woman, he wasn't the marrying kind etc., etc. In fact they went a bit OTT with this kind of stuff, as if this was in some way the most suitable posthumous tribute to the man. But we're always better off with the truth. And, above anything else, Donal Óg Cusack has made us face up to the truth.

It was not just a coming out, it was an honest coming out. There was no dissembling, no kowtowing to the straight prejudice which demands that gay men present themselves as sexless creatures. Instead he said that, like many a healthy young straight Irishman, he'd spent plenty of time trawling the pubs in the hope of a ride. And he didn't apologise for it.

What Donal Óg Cusack did at the weekend is important, too, because it challenges some of the myths peddled by the homophobic pressure groups Brian Lenihan and his cabinet colleagues run scared of. They tell us that homosexuality is 'a lifestyle choice' and that people can be 'influenced' towards it. The implication is that people become gay for the same trendsetting reasons that they might develop a passion for performance art or avant-garde cinema, or that they are suborned into the culture by listening to one too many George Michael albums, watching one too many episodes of *Queer As Folk*.

Well, Donal Óg Cusack grew up as a GAA-loving teenager in a small East Cork village. It is doubtful that gay culture played a big part in his teenage years, doubtful too that a young man whose big ambition was to play hurling for Cork thought, 'Do you know what? I'll become gay because that looks like a cool thing to do.' As he says, he knew he was different. He didn't make a sham marriage, he didn't go on for the priesthood, he didn't emigrate or do any of the other things which gay men once felt they had to do to stop the rumours and the sly questions of, 'No sign of you to get married then?'

Sometimes we kid ourselves that we're tolerant because we condescend to accept flamboyant gay men in the Julian Clary/Graham Norton mould. But we have more problems with accepting our gay neighbours, our gay relations, the gay mechanic, the gay bricklayer and the gay farmer. That's another reason why it's such a big deal that Donal Óg came out. Because one look at how the man plays the game is sufficient to destroy that old myth that gay men are uniformly effeminate, sissyish and, above all, instantly recognisable.

It's been a good week for Irish sport. It's also been a good week for the gay man I know who religiously travels forward and back from England every year to watch the Galway hurling team in action, and a good week for a friend of mine whose brother recently got married in England. It was a gay wedding and the family, dyed in the wool fans of GAA, soccer and Munster rugby, all went over. So did the children from the brother's previous marriage. When I see solid no bullshit country people reacting like this, I wonder if Brian Lenihan underestimates us a bit.

It's been a good week for our gay friends, our gay neighbours, our gay brothers, our gay uncles, our gay sons and daughters. And that means it's been a good week for all of us as we continue the struggle towards that day when we cast aside all the old bigotries and taboos, a day when our kids and grandkids will look on our hang-ups as relics of a darker, thankfully departed time.

And when that day comes one of the people we will have to thank is a very brave man from Cork. A very brave gay man.

29

TAKING A STAND AGAINST INEQUALITY

CLAIRE McCORMACK

Mayo's Sarah Rowe says women GAA players feel like second-class citizens.

She was known as 'the baby' of the team from day one. As a 'cheeky' newcomer, Sarah Rowe had no qualms about hopping on the team bus, marching down to the back seat and sitting beside her hero, Cora Staunton. She was just fourteen, but already training with the Mayo senior team.

Although she wouldn't be eligible to play at inter-county level for two more years, the Ballina player was like a sponge around her idols. She observed them, listened to them, looked up to them – and of course, had a bit of crack.

Despite the dedication, commitment and sacrifices the ladies made to grace the red and green jersey, Rowe, even as a teenager, saw the inequalities they, and their counterparts, faced within the GAA. The barriers became even more pronounced as the talented young sports star started playing soccer for Ireland at the same time. Six years later, Rowe has excelled in both sports and is now the senior player the younger Mayo girls revere.

Despite the ongoing success of the Ladies' Gaelic Football Association's current advertising campaign, sponsored by Lidl – the retailer has invested €1.5m in the women's game in the first year of a three-year deal – Rowe says teams are still battling many of the same obstacles. Although she is hopeful, deep down, Rowe doesn't know if women's sport will ever be on a level playing field with men's.

In terms of funding and structures, she says ladies' Gaelic football and soccer couldn't be more different. The disparities became particularly apparent to the attacker when she returned from the Republic of Ireland Under-19 women's soccer team's memorable campaign at the UEFA European Championship last year.

'We got to the semi-final and lost, but it was the first time an Irish team had ever done it, so I came home on such a high,' she said. 'I thought soccer is definitely the way: I got to travel, live with the girls, we were treated so well. Then I went back to Gaelic and back to training on really bad pitches, not getting food after training, not getting any support.'

She currently plays football for Mayo, Dublin City University and her home club in Ballina. She also plays soccer for Shelbourne and hopes to line out for Ireland later this year. She says the fundamental set-up for women's soccer is a lot better than the GAA. It comes down to one thing: finance.

'There is just more money involved in the soccer. Our Shelbourne team are treated really well; we still wouldn't get food after training, but you get nice gear, there is a very good structure in place, it's very professional,' she said. 'With Mayo at the moment, we are training on a pitch in Ballyhaunis where there are only two floodlights and we can barely see to the other side, and the pitch is absolutely in a heap.'

The Mayo ladies currently have a rota set up, so that one person brings food for training. 'It could be sandwiches or fruit or rice cakes, but it's not even anything proper that you should be eating after training,' said the aspiring PE and biology teacher, who is on a sports scholarship at DCU. 'Often times we have to arrange our own lifts because we can't afford to get a bus to the matches. It's very frustrating.'

Her friendship with Aidan O'Shea – the two were a couple for a while – has given her first-hand knowledge of the enormous gap between the treatment of the county's men's and ladies' sides.

'It doesn't even compare. MacHale Park is the main pitch in Mayo and we get to play on it once a year for the Connacht final, while the lads train on it day in and day out,' she said. 'They get after-training physio, access to any gym, they literally get whatever they want because they want to make them perfect – whereas we definitely don't get that.'

This year the Mayo ladies were able to use the men's gym, which she describes as being 'one step closer'. Although barriers continue to frustrate players and affect performance, Rowe believes sportswomen from all disciplines have almost accepted this attitude as 'the norm'.

'It definitely impacts on players, but we're nearly so used to it at this stage that it feels normal, we don't complain about it because it's not going to change anyway. It's not acceptable, definitely not. When I look at any boys' team – and I've talked to a few of them – I realise that I train more than them and they get way more than I've ever gotten. No lads team would put up with the conditions we train and play in, they would go nuts. The lads complain that the game isn't professional, while we'd settle for a bit of food.'

Although Rowe is thrilled and honoured to be part of the current LGFA campaign to raise awareness of the difficulties female athletes have in getting the same recognition as their male counterparts, she says a lot more money must be invested before they reap real and lasting dividends.

For instance, she wants to see All-Ireland double-headers in Croke Park, so the ladies and the men play their finals on the same day. The forward also believes if ladies' teams all over the country were treated better and got more respect, it would encourage younger girls to commit to the sport for life instead of falling away from the sport early.

'Even talking to Aidan, he would say that playing in front of 80,000 people is the best feeling in the whole world and I'd say, well I'm never going to get to experience that,' she said. 'If young girls saw us treated the same, so many more would get involved and we'd have better teams. They don't think we'll bring in the same money or the same crowd, but you have to put it in front of people.'

Despite the demands of playing soccer and Gaelic football at the highest level, the twenty-year-old remains fully committed to both, as her schedule can testify. The second-year student, who lives in a 'GAA house', trains nine or ten times a week. Her housemates are Aisling Sheridan, who plays for Cavan, Sligo's Grainne O'Loughlin and Longford's Michelle Farrell.

'We're very supportive of each other, if we're all lying on the couch, one will say, come on, we're all going to the gym, get up, whereas if we didn't have that push, we mightn't go,' she said, adding, 'there is a healthy competition between us.'

Despite her enviable figure, Rowe says she is trying to lose some body fat and is abiding by a strict diet of smoothies and porridge for breakfast, omelettes and salad for lunch and chicken, veg and sweet potatoes for dinner. However, she still allows herself small treats, such as rice cakes and peanut butter, and dark chocolate.

Her social life in college is also a lot different than her peers'. 'After January, I don't have much interest in going out. I just want to get fit, get in shape and eat well. It took a while to make my friends understand that sport is my priority and that I love them so much but I can't be there all the time,' she said.

As for men, she says she will always look for someone with an interest in sport. 'It doesn't matter if they're not brilliant at it, but it's just so they understand.'

Rowe has missed out on opportunities to travel and see the world like other students, but she has been offered an exciting opportunity to complete a masters in Atlanta on a one-year soccer scholarship.

'For me, all the sacrifices are worth it because what I gain from sport will stand to me forever. I have no intention of slowing down and I know I won't have any regrets. I'm a very ambitious girl and I'm only getting started.'

30

'SOME PEOPLE WRITE IT DOWN OR KEEP JOURNALS – I WRITE IT ON MYSELF'

AISLING CROWE

Camogie star Ashling Thompson has gained strength from adversity.

29 JUNE 2014

Ashling Thompson has been soaked to the bone by the heavy downpours that rained upon her following a day five years ago when that which came together fell apart. Not with the slow imperceptible pace that Buddha taught. When things fell apart for Thompson, it was with all the horrifying force of a car ploughing into the back of her vehicle at sixty m.p.h.

One moment the Cork camogie star was sitting in her car, stationary outside her home. The next she was unconscious, and when she woke up the neck and back injuries she had suffered left a scar on her psyche. Unable to eat because of the trauma, she no longer had the strength to play the game that consumed her life.

In a halting voice the twenty-four-year-old recalls the dark clouds that never seemed to part to let sunlight through and the questions nobody could answer for her. 'When you're playing sport since you were six or seven you can't understand, "Why can't I play? Why does this have to happen to me?" It was utter devastation.'

Her whole world and her family life is inextricably tied to sport. Her mother coached her at underage camogie, her father and her two brothers hurl for Newtownshandrum. Thompson excelled across many sports – camogie, football, athletics, soccer and basketball. Precocious and a fierce competitor, sport enriched her life until the moment when everything came to a sudden and violent halt.

Three years of frustration followed the accident, the pain of attending training sessions and the agony of watching from the sideline. Then Frank Flannery walked through the doors of Milford camogie club and Thompson and the team would be changed utterly.

By simply understanding there was a person behind the player, and through realising that Thompson was suffering, Flannery parted the clouds and let the light shine on the passionate sports fan again. It's not possible for every coach to have such a startling effect, but she believes coaches and managers have to realise players are people and although they dedicate their lives to the games they play, what happens in the world outside the four white lines can have a huge bearing on the games played between those lines.

The sports injury management graduate credits her Milford club's former manager with the final and hardest stage of rehabilitation and helping her arrive in a place that led back to the Cork senior team. Flannery took a side that had been beaten in a county final and a player who had been badly buffeted by fate all the way to the All-Ireland crown in 2012. When he had to move on, James McGrath continued to lead them in the same direction and to a second successive title. Three in a row is the aim for this year.

Mental health is the crisis this country refuses to confront head on. The GAA and GPA are attempting to fill a void they shouldn't have to fill. In light of her own experiences and suffering, Thompson, who hopes to gain a scholarship to Limerick IT to study sports nutrition or coaching, believes women should be offered the same supports to help them through whatever problems they may be faced with.

'There is nothing similar for women and there should be. There is definitely a need for it. Everybody has been through something traumatic in their lives. I've had a few traumatic experiences myself in the past and I think it is a massive thing. We are all equal, we are all human beings, we all go through similar things at times.

'People don't know what goes on behind closed doors and people would probably be absolutely shocked to hear of what some people go through. I think that it is a massive thing because if you're not mentally right in a game you are not going to play right, no matter how good you are. I'm a passionate believer in that.'

This is not the only area where Thompson sees inequality. As the daughter of a two-time All-Ireland winning Cork ladies' footballer, it is a battleground she knows has a long history.

'It's not an attitude reserved for camogie – it's every sport across the board that women play. I just don't think it is fair. We put all our time into it, it's a full-time job and our lives go into it, so we definitely deserve the same respect back. We are all human beings and we all should be treated the same.'

The story of her life is not locked away in a journal, stashed under the bed. It is written on her body – not just in the scars she bears from injury but inscribed in ink. Tattoos adorn her, and deciphering the meaning behind each symbol unlocks the code. The external reveals the internal.

A definite number eludes her but she thinks the tattoos number ten or eleven. The most visible and most prominent is an eye-catching sparrow on her left arm, intertwined with a flower and butterflies for her mother and two older brothers. A couple of stars have been added for her nephews. That tattoo was born out of the adversity of the crash and the devastation it wreaked on her life.

'Each one tells a story, they are not just there for the sake of it. Some people keep a journal or write it down, I write it on myself. That was part of the car crash – starting over, getting through the hard times. Turning over a new leaf and hopefully keeping it that way.'

But she draws strength from it too. 'If I look down at my arm if I'm in a bad place or even if I'm not playing well, I always look down and think, "Keep it fresh, this is your time so make the most of it because life is very short." I always look down and it reminds me to keep going and do the best I can.'

The lash extensions are as permanent a feature of her identity as the tattoos. Without them, she feels exposed, undressed, so under her helmet they are a part of her match-day armour. She breaks the rules we have for our female sports stars. Society created an image of how women in sport should look, but with her body art and false lashes, allied to her gift for hurling, Thompson challenges those assumptions of how camogie players should look.

'I love fashion. I love clothes. Rihanna would definitely be my main fashion icon. I love the way she is just different, an individual, and doesn't care what anyone thinks. I think that's a good way to be – being yourself and being comfortable with that. It's how I lead my life. I'm comfortable with who I am and if people want to accept me that's okay, and if they don't that's okay also.'

Like her idol, Ashling Thompson is walking tall against the rain, doing her own thing.

THE LONG AND WINDING ROAD

It was like I had been assaulted, and my attacker was now travelling in the ambulance with me, smiling.

THE LEGEND OF FRANKIE KERR, THE SWAGGER OF A BORN LEADER

DION FANNING

Hailed as a possible world champion and the most skilful boxer in Europe, Frankie Kerr quit the sport when he was twenty-two. Frankie's son, Brian, and boxing aficionado Ulick O'Connor came together to tease out the life story of Kerr senior.

18 JANUARY 2004

When Frankie Kerr took his son Brian into town, the young boy would be struck by the number of people who would greet his old man. 'Do you know him, Da?' young Brian would ask. 'No, but they know me,' his father would reply. As a boy Brian Kerr collected stamps and his father's friendships across the globe aided this pursuit. Frankie Kerr received postcards and letters from around the world and young Brian would acquire the stamps.

One day he received an exotic stamp. He studied it for a while and then showed it to his father. 'I used to play with that man when I was your age,' Frankie told his son, looking at the face on the stamp. His father didn't talk much about his crowded life, but when he did it intrigued his youngest son.

Much of it made little sense. He had heard about boxing titles, trips across America, encounters with Mussolini's family. He knew there was a glorious life, a hidden story concealed beneath the elegant pinstriped suit of Frankie Kerr. Sometimes it was all too much. He looked at the stamp again. Here was another mystery. 'How the hell did my da ever play with the Prince of Mesopotamia?'

* * *

Ulick O'Connor was concerned about Frankie Kerr. He used to see him in Trinity, spluttering and coughing his way across the college square on his way to the boxing club at the back gate, beside the Lincoln pub. Ulick had boxed for UCD but since

Kerr had taken control of the sport at Trinity, he had galvanised the whole place, although you wouldn't know it to look at him.

It wasn't that he was modest, Ulick felt, but there was a control and a discipline about him which deflected the attention of all but the most perceptive. There was also effervescence. Trinity Boxing Club was not only becoming the best university boxing club in the country, but the parties weren't bad either. Students from all over the world boxed for Frankie and they stayed to enjoy the revelry. It was the place to be. It wasn't just Frankie Kerr's achievements in the ring that made Ulick admire him. He was a great fella, he thought, particularly for a Belfast Orangeman.

But Ulick was anxious. He didn't think Frankie took care of himself and he was worried about his health, more worried than Frankie himself who, despite the coughing fits, never went to see a doctor. Ulick approached a couple of figures in Trinity, explained the situation. Surely, with all the medical expertise surrounding Frankie in Trinity, somebody could have a word? They knew what Frankie had achieved, one was a boxer himself, but nothing was done.

Frankie Kerr's bad health worsened and in January 1968, at the age of fifty-one, he died of pneumonia. Brian Kerr was fourteen.

In the foreword to *The Ulick O'Connor Diaries*, recently published in paperback, Richard Ingrams writes of his friendship with Ulick and the surprise in England that a literary man should come from a sporting background. It is, he says, another contrast with the English and a result, he suggests, of Ireland never becoming an industrialised country.

Ulick O'Connor's sporting achievements are exceptional. He boxed (the record for a knock-out in the National Stadium is four seconds, the holder is Ulick), played cricket, rugby, soccer and was an athlete of note (while at UCD he set an Irish pole vault record). 'It might seem a strange background for a writer to emerge from,' Ingram writes, 'but in Ireland, the combination of sport and literature (or sport and politics, for that matter), is by no means unusual.' Indeed, the only puzzling thing about it for an Irish reader is that people might find the broad interest remarkable in the first place.

While his achievements in both fields distinguish him, he follows in a great tradition. Kavanagh absorbed the language of horse-racing into his poetry and used the terms in his judgements of his peers – 'He's only an old handicapper,' he said of one writer, 'we are looking for Classic prospects.' Beckett appears in Wisden and John B. Keane arguably cared more for Kerry's All-Ireland prospects than the future of literature.[1] Brendan Kennelly may feel the same.

---

1   Wisden refers to the *Wisden Cricket Almanac*, a detailed reference book on the sport

Ulick's love of sport abides and he has followed the career of Kerr very closely – 'I admire him like billy-o' – and when a meeting was suggested, he agreed immediately. His memory is prodigious and he was immediately recalling various incidents in the wonderful life of Frankie Kerr.

But it was not just the life of Brian Kerr's father that united Ireland's football manager and its foremost man of letters. They share an understanding of a lost sporting world, a changed Dublin and the memory of a football education at the hands of Liam 'Rasher' Tuohy – 'Rasher is his hero,' Ulick reminded me a couple of days before the interview. 'Of course, Rasher is my hero too.'

* * *

When they came together for lunch in Chapter One on Parnell Square, the connection was immediate. They had never met before but they shared stories of mutual acquaintances and laughed when they remembered great Dublin men like Paddy Ambrose and his pigeons.

Kerr had, as requested, brought a couple of his father's boxing trophies, which were polished and cleaned as a Christmas gift from his family. The trophies are beautiful – one, Ulick says, resembles the Ardagh chalice – and his memory is sparked again. Kerr listens with fascination to his feats of recall.

The trophies are carried in a hat-box, which leads to a discussion about hats and then tailoring, which was Frankie's trade for most of his life in Dublin. 'All of the barristers in the law library who were in the boxing club were dressed by Frankie at Premier Tailors,' Ulick remembers. 'You could get a suit for a fiver and they were beautiful suits, equal to the best in the city. People would say, "Where did you get your suit?" which is saying something.'

There is a lot to say about Frankie Kerr, a lot he never said, and while the conversation during lunch touched on many subjects and characters, the central theme was a voyage around Brian's father. 'If he had turned professional, he would have been a millionaire,' Ulick says. 'He would have won a World Championship.'

Frankie Kerr quit boxing in 1938. He was twenty-two years old. Nobody knows if he was already suffering from the poor health that would end his life prematurely, twenty-nine years later, or whether the pressures of travelling while trying to raise a family brought an end to it, but it was a puzzling decision. Kerr had lost in the European Championships in Milan the year before. It was a decision so

---

which has been published annually for over 150 years, and is hailed as the Bible of cricket.

controversial and at odds with the view of everybody in the arena, bar the judges, that Mussolini's son-in-law had a medal commissioned commending Kerr as 'the most scientific boxer' at the tournament. It was another event in his life that Frankie Kerr rarely spoke about.

In 1939 the European Championships were due to take place in Dublin, the Olympics were scheduled for the following year. Sergo, the Italian who was awarded the European Championship decision ahead of Kerr, was Olympic Champion. Kerr would have fancied his chances for gold. Instead he stopped. But he never looked back, never boasted about what he had achieved or what he had lost. He never gave details of his privileged childhood as a boy in the Raj or playing with the future Prince of Mesopotamia. 'He never talked about anything he'd won or done,' his son remembers.

As far as the Kerr family know, Frankie Kerr's father was a high-ranking officer in the British Army. Ulick has heard he was a captain, but the Kerrs have seen the pictures, noted the servants crowding around in the background and think he was higher. 'A captain in the Raj would have had plenty of servants,' Ulick says.

A newspaper cutting records the fact that Frankie Kerr fought his first fight in Baghdad. The army took his father to Egypt and India as well as Mesopotamia. It was there, as a child, that Frankie befriended the future prince. The family developed a love of cricket and hockey too – Frankie would later play for Three Rock Rovers in the Leinster League.

Davey, one of Frankie's brothers, used to tell a story. There was a big parade in the barracks in Egypt. It was the British Empire at its most resplendent. The Governor General may have been there, generals were certainly in attendance. All was set for a splendid display when a donkey came charging through the barracks, on its back Frankie Kerr. The youngster was ordered to stop by the sergeant-major with the words 'Who goes there?' With a swagger detectable in pictures taken more than sixty years ago, the child saluted and said, 'Frankie Kerr, sir!' before trotting off on his donkey.

The Kerrs returned to England, moving from the Isle of Wight to Aldershot and then back to Belfast. 'As far as we know, his father was a Belfast man,' Brian says. 'Someone came from Scotland before that, and there was a change of religion in the family as well.'

'What religion was Frankie?' Ulick asks.

'We were all Catholics.'

'I know you were, but was he a Catholic too?'

'He was, yeah. There was a change. I think Mrs Kerr, the grandmother of the father changed and she was from a wealthy family. After that, they didn't want to know about her. He never talked much to us about the past but I knew he was never happy. He didn't want to go back to Belfast. He came here as a young man and I think he was annoyed about the whole business and the madness that went on. My eldest brother, Frankie, says they went up for his own father's funeral and they came back the same night.'

The boxing life was some story. After Baghdad, he kept on fighting. At the age of sixteen, Frankie won his first Irish Championship in the same year that he took the Ulster title. He had qualified for the Olympics. He fought in all the trials, but then was told that he had to be seventeen to fight in the Olympics.

'He came to Dublin then,' his son remembered. 'Fr McLoughlin, who went on to found Arbour Hill, brought him to Dublin, got him a job in Dunlop's in Abbey Street, where the VHI is now. His job was making footballs and stringing tennis racquets. He told me that he'd laced up the football for a match when Northern Ireland beat Wales, I think, nine–something. A fella called Joe Bambrick scored six goals.'

But there would be no Olympics for Frankie Kerr: Ireland didn't send a team in 1936, when he had a real chance of a medal, and by 1948, when the games were held again following the war, he was ten years retired.

Until he sat down to lunch, Ulick had been sure that Frankie Kerr was a Protestant. 'It's amazing how little these things actually mattered.'

'It was probably an issue in Trinity,' Kerr says, 'but it never mattered to him. Without saying it, I knew he had a hatred for discrimination or any kind of racism.'

The journeys of a travelling boxer, the childhood spent with the British Army and a sense that his birthplace was a fractious place probably bred tolerance in Frankie Kerr.

'What amazes me,' his son says, 'is the amount of travelling they did as boxers in the '30s. He was in America twice (Frankie won the Golden Gloves in 1933). His mother died when he was on his way to America – it must have been the '38 one – and they didn't tell him 'til he was on the boat back because there was nothing he could have done.'

On his way back from the European Championships in 1937, Frankie stopped off for a fight in France. 'We found a little postcard he wrote to my mother when they were preparing for the wedding. It just said, "Dying to see you, hope everything is ready for the wedding" and at the bottom he'd written, "Won easily last night, see you soon."'

* * *

In 1963 Frankie Kerr dragged his ten-year-old son Brian out of bed. Sonny Liston was fighting a young upstart from Kentucky called Cassius Clay and the father, the boxing man, wanted his son to see the fight. Like a lot of people in boxing, Frankie Kerr was unhappy with the antics of Clay.

'He was disgusted by Ali,' Brian Kerr says, 'by Cassius Clay at the time. The behaviour and the brashness.'

'None of us realised at the time that Ali was doing a put-on,' adds Ulick.

Frankie Kerr's feelings for Ali were not shared by his son, who invariably buys a book about Ali every year.

'I haven't read most of them. The ones I like most are the books of photographs; one of them is actually like modern history, not just Ali's history. The crowds that were around in Africa when he appeared in places. There's a great picture of him in a lift with four women and he actually married the four women in the lift with him.'

'He was lucky to survive that,' Ulick remarks.

Ulick, of course, had close encounters with many of the sporting greats. He wrote a sports column for *The Sunday Times* for many years and he had the fortunate knack of placing himself at the centre of events – when he went to interview Laurie Cunningham who was playing for Real Madrid, it happened to be the same week in 1981 as the attempted coup.

'I met Ali in the middle of his five years off fighting. If you give up your game for five years, to make a comeback is prodigious. That's real greatness. To give it up, not to lose your discipline, to keep the power and the hunger.'

Ali's fight in Dublin on his return to boxing was not, Ulick feels, a high point. 'It was a terrible fight. A fella let a roar in the middle of it, he was one of those fellas who had trained their voices at the stadium, you could hear it in the open air and he opened up, "Hit him, you have the wind behind you."'

The great American boxer Billy Conn was also in Dublin for that fight and Ulick spent some time with him. 'He was sent over by the mob, I think from Boston, and he wanted me to help him hijack the fight. He said to me, "Do you know anyone in the IRA?" and I said, "Well, I might." He said, "There's two million in prize money for this fight and I don't like the idea of two n****rs getting all that money, could you put me in touch with somebody and we'll organise a hijack?" He was quite serious about it too.'

The talk is easy now. Ulick remembers uproarious nights at the stadium, including one when his mother came to see him. 'She was so nervous that she turned around to ask someone for a cigarette and when she turned back the fella was knocked out.'

Or the time he caused a riot when he was introducing a fight. Forgetting that the microphone was still on he turned to Mickey Bowman, a featherweight, and muttered, 'Remember Shan Mohangi,' referring to the medical student who murdered a woman in Dublin and later returned to South Africa and became a politician. 'The fucking place exploded,' with umbrage being taken by Bowman's African opponent.

But their love of boxing is another connection. 'As a manager of a soccer team, your desire for things to go well would force you into disappointment or anger,' Kerr says, 'but in boxing, they had a dignity in defeat. That's particular to boxing, is it, Ulick?'

'It's the greatest of them all. The last gentleman's sport. It's like a Japanese religious ceremony at the end. The fella would go over and shake hands with the seconds, then the result would be announced and he'd have to go and shake hands again. I never saw a fella coming out of the stadium saying, "Fuck it, I should have won that." Boxing is the arena of natural gentlemen.'

* * *

Ulick and Kerr throw names across the table. Ernie Smith – 'Your father and him are generally regarded as the best ever' – Mick Coffey, Mick Meagan, Kevin O'Flanagan, whom they both regard as one of the greatest and most underrated of all Irish sportsmen, and, of course, Paddy Ambrose.

Ambrose was Shamrock Rovers' centre-forward in the 1950s but his devotions were elsewhere. 'He was a lovely man,' says Kerr. 'I was up at Rovers in '73 or '74, managing the youth team. I was about twenty. We were doing pre-season training and I was on my way home. I was living in Drimnagh and was walking down to Ranelagh to get the 18 [bus]. Paddy came out and asked me where I was going and said he'd drop me up as he was heading to Walkinstown. I knew he lived a good bit out on the north side so I said, "Why are you going to Walkinstown?" and he said, "I'm going to drop these lads off there." He pointed to the back seat and there were a load of pigeons. He dropped them off in Walkinstown and said, "They can make their own way home from here."'

Ulick remembers Paddy going on the lam for his pigeons. 'They were the reason he didn't stay in England. He got a trial for Norwich at eighteen but he said he couldn't leave the pigeons. He ran away and went to live in Cork for a year because he thought they wouldn't find him down there. He had the pigeons down there and he figured Norwich wouldn't look for him in Cork.'

Both men knew Ambrose through Liam 'Rasher' Tuohy. 'Tuohy and Ambrose were stuck together like God's glue.' Tuohy was a football visionary, who gave Kerr his grounding in the game and remains his mentor. In the early 1970s he picked Ulick for a game between Old England and Old Ireland. Paddy Farrell and Tommy Eglington were also on the team, while Stanley Matthews played for England.

'Were you picked on the basis of your ability,' Kerr asks Ulick, 'or were you influential with the selectors?'

'I could play well enough to justify my existence. Rasher was inside-left and I was outside. He just gave me the ball on my toe all afternoon and I got in all the crosses. At the end of the match, I was carried off on the shoulders of the crowd, not Rasher. He was a terrific guy.'

Ulick produces a picture of Stanley Matthews on the ball and a packed Dalymount watching as Ulick moves in to dispossess the great man.

* * *

In 1953, shortly before Stanley Matthews dominated the FA Cup final with Blackpool at the age of thirty-eight, Frankie Kerr, a couple of years younger than Matthews, was travelling to England with a university boxing team. News came from Dublin that Frankie's wife, Margaret, had given birth to a boy. Frankie gathered all the team around him and put their names in a hat. He pulled out the name of Brian 'Spud' Murphy. That was it, he would call his son Brian. (Thirteen years later Spud Murphy, on holiday from the Middle East where he worked in the oil business, would present young Brian with a fiver. With it, he travelled to England and saw every match but one in the 1966 World Cup.)

Frankie Kerr had moved from Dunlop's and started tailoring five years after he arrived in Dublin. Perhaps that was the reason he retired, as he had to work long hours and brought the same devotion to his new job as he had to the sport where he boxed with such grace. But Frankie could not let go of boxing and started training in Trinity almost immediately after he quit fighting. The club was where he spent most time with the boxers but, like his son in another discipline, another time, he was constantly looking after them, always making sure they could prosper.

'He would meet them off the bus in O'Connell Street and tell them, "Go up to Margaret in Drimnagh, you'll be fine." We had a small house but you could wake up in the morning and there could be anyone there, Chinese lads, African lads, all lovely lads, great lads.'

By the time Brian was born, the Kerr family had dispersed, with his eldest brother, Frankie, fifteen years older, living in England. 'Another brother, Davey, was in the army, while Mairead was at school. She was deaf and lost her speech and hearing from the whooping cough injection when she was a baby. It wasn't too often there was a full house of us.'

Frankie made sure it was filled. 'I met a fella out in Portmarnock recently when we were staying in the hotel with the team. His name was Tommy McCarthy, he was a bantamweight, a lovely guy. I hadn't seen him in about forty years. He said to me, "I lived in your house for a few months," and I said, "I remember Tommy. Me ma thought we'd never get rid of you."'

Apart from Trinity, Frankie trained at the Jewish Boxing Club, and in Drimnagh they used to fight at the St John Bosco. Frustrations over the ring – it had to be taken down on a Thursday night for the dance and put up again on a Sunday – led Frankie and others, including Austin Carruth, to plan their own boxing club. They collected around the houses and raised the money for Drimnagh Boxing Club. Frankie died before it was built. In 1992 Austin's son Michael, boxing out of Drimnagh, won gold at the Olympics.

Brian Kerr remembers visiting his father in St Mary's hospital. He would walk through the Fifteen Acres and watch the football with, even then, his manager's eye, before visiting his father. 'It was such a contrast. There would be roaring and shouting on the pitches when I'd go in and I've never forgotten the silence when I came out. The matches were over and you could have heard a pin drop.'

Ulick, too, visited him in hospital, but even at that point Frankie resisted the urge to talk about himself and his times. 'He didn't talk about any of that,' his friend remembers.

Frankie came out of hospital but he struggled through the winters. 'He'd be in Trinity and he'd come home and take out his little inhaler to get him going. His breathing used to be very heavy,' his son recalls.

In 1967 Frankie Kerr fell ill with pneumonia. It was his last fight.

'He's been dead so long, but it amazes me how many people come up and say to me they knew my father.'

'The history of Frankie Kerr is absolutely phenomenal. He was like Muhammad Ali, he was that good,' Ulick declares. 'I knew him very well, but I never knew quite what he had done. I see the similarities between Brian and Frankie. Well, the leader. Frankie was a leader in boxing. He completely resurrected Trinity and brought them right up to the top without apparently bossing people. I can't describe what he had, the place suddenly warmed up. It's an extraordinary story and I'm very pleased I got on with him.'

Later, in the Olympus Gym, Ulick steps up to the bag and hits it with expertise. Brian Kerr stands on the ring apron, looks around and says, 'It must be the loneliest place in the world,' imagining the thoughts of a boxer. It was a lonely place for his father, but it may well have been his only time of solitude in a life crowded with friendship, love and astonishing achievements.

32

THE GOOD AND THE BAD

EAMON DUNPHY

The 1980s brought out the best and the worst of the human condition.

31 DECEMBER 1989

Reflecting on the 1980s, as one has been obliged to do during this final week of sport's most turbulent decade, the two strong images belong to 1988. One of these images is good, magnificent indeed; one is bad, a desperate reminder of how evil can insidiously corrupt man's most innocent pursuit.

My first memory is of Severiano Ballesteros winning the British Open Golf Championship on the last green. Seve hadn't won a Major title for a few years. At Royal Lytham he'd been within striking range all day. The tournament had developed into a battle of nerve and talent between this great man and Nick Price, one of the world's best touring pros. Price had begun with a lead of a couple of strokes. He'd never looked like cracking. Seve covered holes 6, 7 and 8 in four under par to draw level. But, that apart, Price matched Ballesteros's superb golf shot for shot all the way to the fourteenth green.

On the fourteenth Price missed from six feet. The first chink in his armour, a sign that Seve's greatness, now manifested by magnificent golf, deep concentration and a determination that constituted an almost unearthly force, was getting to Price, who was, by comparison, merely human. Price played the fifteenth gloriously, the previous lapse seemed to be redeemed.

Price has never won a Major title, but he had been close once before, against another great golfer, Jack Nicklaus. Three shots behind with, I think, five holes to play, Nicklaus had outwitted Nick Price, proving that there is more to greatness than technique, showing us cunning, daring, ruthlessness, qualities that the masters of sport's finest crafts deploy in proper measure at the proper time.

Golf is sport's finest craft. When it comes to match-play, as the great championships often do at the end, you search for your own best game … and the weaknesses in your opponent's mind and spirit. It's a brutal business, inspiring to watch.

Men like Ballesteros and Nicklaus are tormented, obsessive in their great competitive years. Golf is not a game, it's their life. They are at their most deadly when they believe that it's over; that the great years are behind them ... when others, in reality or in their darkest imaginings, have 'written them off'. Thus Nicklaus the year he beat Nick Price. And Ballesteros in 1988.

Ballesteros had the honour on the last tee with the cushion of a shot gained on the sixteenth. He was lucky with his drive, which finished in the light rough, right of the fairway.

Nick Price cracked. His drive was sliced wildly right, a Sunday morning shot prompted, no doubt, by the tormenting thought that Ballesteros was going to do to him what Nicklaus had ... break him. Guys like Nick Price aren't obsessive, they are simply superb golfers, craftsmen for whom this is a job, not a life.

Price's second shot showed what a marvellous player he was, illustrated why he had twice come as close as you can to winning a Major title. In a moment of acute emotional distress Nick Price flew the ball straight as an arrow across gorse and heather to the edge of the eighteenth green, where the vast crowd waited for the final act of which – before he offered this courageous response to imminent humiliation – it had seemed he would be the victim.

Ballesteros had hit his second pin high but left, off the green into thick grass from which it would be – in any circumstances, much less these – virtually impossible to leave a simple final putt.

As Seve's ball lay he knew he would have to execute the perfect shot to ensure victory. He would have to strike the ball without hitting it. Played with too much force the shot would have scuttled ridiculously way beyond the hole. Played too gently it might stay where it was ... or plop harmlessly onto the green short of the target.

What was required was perfection – part stab, part caress, a contact that would be a fraction away from disaster. He had to flirt with the danger of being too long or too short, find the perfect touch that lay an inch either side of looking stupid, confirming all those assertions that he'd 'gone' as far as Major titles were concerned.

Does life depend on moments like this?

Yes, for men like Ballesteros it does. Seve was a poor caddy-boy from northern Spain. He began playing golf with makeshift clubs and cracked balls discarded by The Members. He grew up in Franco's Spain, where society was divided along lines more to do with caste than the relatively innocuous class system we know. He would have experienced scorn, indifference, outright hostility.

Seeing him now, a man of fierce, unbridled pride, one could understand how much he must have hurt as a youngster growing up amid indifference. Respect would matter; self-respect would come through mastering The Members' hobby.

If Ballesteros is driven – and he is – it is because the only Ballesteros that is respected is the one who wins championships, who plays the game of golf more compellingly than any other man. Besides Ballesteros the champion, there is no other Ballesteros; golf is self, golf is life. Thus, many of sport's greatest champions … everything they are is bound up in this performance art of craft.

The shot that won the British Open of 1988 was beautifully played. Television allowed us to see the club-head make perfect contact. As the ball reached mid-point on its twenty-five-yard journey, it was clear that the championship was decided … a roar, part wonder, part admiration, part respect, rose above the crowded greenside.

A look of indescribable pleasure lit Seve's face. He was defiantly content. This had been a great day for him, for those of us who'd watched, for sport in its purest, most enthralling form.

In theory Price still had a chance: sink a putt across a green that must have looked as long as a runway and force a play-off. Realistically the South African was dead.

He charged his putt yards past the hole. An impossible toll had been extracted from his emotions this past hour … it had happened slowly, he had resisted bravely with great skill. He was a tough professional, but this was no longer about the craft of golf, at least not that alone.

Sport is most punishing when your fingers touch the great prize, when the glorious moment you dreamed about as a child, the moment that everyone who has played sport imagines himself savouring, is suddenly starkly real. The moment realised will transform your life, the lives of those who love you, who have supported you, who ache now as they wait to see if you can do it.

This is an emotional moment … it's not about your game but about your mind and your spirit. You must remain in command of your craft and yourself, knowing – as Christy O'Connor Jnr would have at The Belfry – what shame awaits the professional who fails to deliver the shot that will secure the prize.

The professional knows he is capable of executing this shot – he has done so many thousands of times in competition when it didn't matter as it does now, and in practice. Nick Price would split the eighteenth fairway at Royal Lytham nine times out of ten in other circumstances. So, knowing that the shot is in his bag, he knows that if he fails now the flaw will be in him, in his character, not his craft. The moment in sport is about self-respect.

For those of us who love sport this moment is beautiful because, yes, it is a metaphor for life, for that other world – the real one – which exists, it often seems, to facilitate the things that are exposed and punished in the great sporting arenas: cheating – yourself or others, laziness, carelessness, self-indulgence, vanity, greed, complacency, all that is venal, all conspiracies designed to allow you and those who lie like you to take more out of the world than they put in.

In sport, quite simply, the truth wins out, the truth of the beautiful moment, the instant when Seve Ballesteros made contact with the golf ball in the thick grass, twenty-five yards from the flag fluttering innocently on the eighteenth green at Royal Lytham.

This was also the year of Lockerbie; sport's importance is as a civilising influence, an antidote to evil. For what one claims for men like Ballesteros is not that they are free of original sin but that they show us, in their most beautiful moments, what is possible without resort to venality. Theirs is a world, a workplace, free of can't, where problems are solved, fears dispelled by deploying the best resources of mind and spirit – discipline, imagination and courage – rather than the baser material deployed elsewhere in life as men try to come to terms with their existence.

Golf survived the 1980s, its ethos and traditions an inspiration still.

Two months after Seve's Open, the Olympic Games took place in Seoul. My second lasting image of the 1980s causes me to wonder about sport's future, its ability to survive in the material world.

Ben Johnson tested positive for drugs after winning the Olympic 100 metres title. One was hardly surprised. Who didn't know that drug-taking was endemic to athletics, had been for the past two decades? All those grotesquely-shaped bodies … men and women … there was something evil at the core of this sport.

Evidence existed of blood-doping, steroid consumption, pills given to young girl gymnasts to delay the onset of puberty. All of this was a long way from the golf course, from purity.

In the 1980s the Olympic movement ceased to represent anything that was worthwhile in sport. Who now looks forward to Barcelona 1992? The question isn't whether The Games will be a travesty, rather, how will the Olympic ideal be corrupted?

Will it be the politicians who exploit the next Games, as they did in 1980 and 1984, or the peddlars and consumers of drugs? Or will Barcelona be rendered incredible because the sports of track and field, which draw most of us to the Olympics, no longer engage the emotions?

Ben Johnson was caught and cruelly disgraced. But what about the others? Who can believe in a sport both of whose greatest exponents, Carl Lewis and

Flo-Jo Griffiths, have been accused by other athletes of consuming performance-enhancing drugs?

Which great achievement is real, which the product of pill-taking? We don't know ... ergo we don't care. This is the dark side of sport. Here, the ideal perverted by contemporary values, here worldliness squashing innocence with vile pervasive certainty.

Ben Johnson was a victim. Leaving Seoul in disgrace he looked haunted, bemused, bewildered, knowing the truth ... that he had committed no crime, other than to behave as most of his rivals behaved.

Athletics as once we knew it died in the 1980s, failed to make the transition from amateurism to professionalism. Even the sport's heroes can't be afforded unqualified admiration. In between great championships, men like Coe, Ovett and Saïd Aouita avoided each other ... preferred to run in exhibition races, for appearance money rather than medals, for gold rather than honour.

Sport without honour is mere vaudeville, its exponents mere vaudevillians. There is nothing wrong with showbusiness, but it should be promoted in theatres. Athletics failed to survive the 1980s because its administrators lacked competence and will.

Professional soccer may well be on the same desperate road. For the same reason. Football will remember the 1980s for the tragedies of Heysel, Bradford and Hillsborough. On each occasion death was caused by incompetence, the failure of those responsible for administering the game to come to terms with the times they live in. At Bradford, a Victorian grandstand was ignited by a discarded cigarette. At Heysel, tickets were stupidly allocated; at Hillsborough, the logistics of the occasion tragically misunderstood.

In 1980s England the blackguard ruled, a triumph of deadly conviction over administrative inadequacy. How definitive that victory has been is most despairingly reflected in FIFA's decision to accommodate the English and their hooligan mobs in Sardinia next June.

On the field, soccer has fared little better. Maradona was the decade's great player. His finest moment, victory in the World Cup of 1986, was symbolically tarnished when he illegally used his hand to score the decisive goal against England.

Sport reveals truths ... the truth of 1980s soccer is reflected in the person of its greatest player. He is a cheat. Spoiled too, by money and adulation, currently the redundant victim of both.

To understand what has happened to professional soccer in the 1980s one has simply to recall the great men of other decades and compare them to Diego

Maradona. Think of Pelé, as gracious as he was gifted … think of Bobby Charlton … think (and shed a tear) of Beckenbauer.

I prefer to say goodbye to the 1980s in a more optimistic vein. To do so I can, with pleasure and wonder, reflect on Irish sport. We have retained our traditions, our manners, much as the great sport of golf has.

We have Croke Park, Thurles, Killarney and Páirc Uí Chaoimh … Lansdowne Road … Portmarnock or Royal Dublin during Carroll's week … Galway Races … all our racecourses … all our shrines to sport, bastions of good humour and decency where friends, kindred spirits meet to engage in friendly conflict, to escape the desperate venality of the common week, of common experience, to refresh our spirits and remind ourselves of what is best in human nature.

We have, in this small place, heroes on the Ballesteros scale … so many that one dreads to name them for fear of leaving someone out. Roche, Kelly, Rafferty, Smyth, O'Connor, O'Brien, Staunton, Spillane, English, Coghlan, O'Shea, Jonjo O'Neill.

We cherish them as we must. We are lucky, and those who love sport must fight in the 1990s so that we may stay lucky, producing men like that to honour this society. I wish you all a happy and peaceful New Year.

33

JESUS WEPT; TRIGGS WALKED

EAMONN SWEENEY

An A to Z of the Decade (2000–09).

27 DECEMBER 2009

A is for Appropriately Named. No Hollywood scriptwriter would have dared to give the fastest man in the world as obvious a name as Bolt. Yet here he was, a young man who'd give lightning a run for its money. His sprint doubles, and double world records, in the 2008 Olympics and 2009 World Championships were the most viscerally exhilarating sporting achievements of the decade. The fact that Usain Bolt always seems to enjoy his sport at a time of much grim talk about 'focus' and 'being in the zone' is an added bonus.

B is for Basel, home town of Roger Federer who, like Bolt and Tiger Woods, redefined the nature of excellence in his chosen sport. In 2004, 2006 and 2007, Federer won three of the four Grand Slam titles with only the emergence of the magnificent clay-court specialist Rafael Nadal denying him victory in the French Open. An aesthetic joy to watch, the irony is that Federer may eventually be best remembered for his 2008 final defeat at Wimbledon by Nadal when both players hit extraordinary heights in maybe the finest match of all time.

C is for Cholesterol, the tackling of which by Pádraig Harrington seemed to have a phenomenal effect on his career. One minute he's extolling the joys of Flora ProActiv and the next he's winning his first Major. He obviously stuck at the FPA, because there were two more the following year. Modest, cheerful and hard-working, Harrington is as likable a sportsman as this country has ever produced. His British Open victory in 2007 was the emotional highlight because it was the breakthrough, his USPGA triumph the following year was perhaps his greatest performance.

D is for Dodgy, a polite way of describing ethics in the world of Russian business. But nobody at Stamford Bridge cared too much about commercial practices among the oligarchs when Roman Abramovich bought the club. The man from Saratov's deep pockets have enabled the Blues to replace Arsenal as Manchester United's chief Premier League rivals. They will exit the decade as Premier League leaders, though Carlo Ancelotti will be well aware that he's the team's fifth manager in five seasons. Had Abramovich been in charge of Manchester United, Ferguson would have been sacked before he ever won anything.

E is for El Guerrouj, the man from Morocco who proved to be one of the greatest runners of all time when in 2004 he became the first man in eighty years to win the 1,500m and 5,000m double at the Olympics. That he beat the almost equally great Kenenisa Bekele to win the longer half of the double shows the extent of his achievement. Hicham El Guerrouj's 1,500m world record of 3.26.00 has lasted eleven years, his world mile best of 3.43.13 has lasted ten.

F is for Foot and Mouth, the pesky disease whose general outbreak in 2001 denied Istabraq the chance to become the first ever four-time Champion Hurdle winner. It would perhaps have been the most emotionally satisfying of all Irish victories at the Cheltenham Festival but it was not to be. The bad luck story of the decade, made worse when the horse was knocked out of the running by an injury the following year.

G is for Gooch. In the spring of 2002 I went to see Kerry play a Division Two league match against Laois in Limerick. Less than a minute into the game, Colm Cooper collected a ball in the right corner. That was his first touch in inter-county football. His next couple of touches brought him past two defenders and a few seconds later he was planting the ball in the net. The most skilful player of our era never looked back after that.

H is for Hat-Trick, the three tries scored by a young Irish centre when we beat France in Paris in 2000, our first victory there in twenty-eight years. The twenty-one-year-old Brian O'Driscoll was telling us two things: that this would be a very different kind of decade for Irish rugby and that it would be his decade. His fingerprints are all over the Noughties.

I is for Invincible, as in Michael Schumacher, who made everyone else look like they were driving tractors as he won the first five Formula One world titles of the decade. His sheer dominance, winning eleven out of seventeen races in 2002 and thirteen out of eighteen in 2004, did, however, knock the fun out of the event, which has been far more exciting since he retired and gave everyone else a chance.

J is for Jockeys, the great home-grown trio of Johnny Murtagh, Michael Kinane and Kieren Fallon, who dominated the decade, winning seven of ten Derbies, seven of ten 2,000 Guineas, four Prix de l'Arcs, eight Ascot Gold Cups and seven King George and Queen Elizabeth Stakes among many others. Fallon battled his demons and often seemed to be losing, Murtagh battled drink and won, and the quiet man of the trio, Kinane, retired right at the end of the decade, universally acclaimed and respected.

K is for King Henry. As the decade began, Henry Shefflin was a promising young player on a somewhat underachieving Kilkenny team who'd just lost two All-Ireland finals in a day. Ten years later, the Ballyhale man is the one hurler who can justifiably be compared with Ring and Mackey, the most important player on the greatest team of all time. He may be surrounded by great hurlers but there were times when he put the team up on his back and carried it home.

L is for Lynch Mob, the one of the moral variety which has descended upon the outstanding sportsman of the past decade in the last few weeks. Since 2000, Tiger Woods has won twelve Majors and played golf of a sublime standard never previously witnessed, most notably in 2000 when he won three out of the four Majors and in 2005 when he won two and was second in one and fourth in the other. That is what matters about the man.

M is for Miracle Man, the dubious description of Lance Armstrong, whose wins from 2000 to 2005 completed a seven-in-a-row of Tour de France wins, which will probably never be equalled. Three years before his first victory the Texan had been given less than a fifty/fifty chance of surviving cancer which had spread to his brain. And then ...

N is for Neilstown, home club of Kenny Egan, Olympic silver medallist at Beijing and the figurehead of an extraordinary renaissance in Irish amateur boxing. The light-heavyweight was backed up by bronze medallists Darren Sutherland at middleweight and Paddy Barnes at light-flyweight. A host of international successes at underage and senior level since then have underlined Ireland's progression to the status of the European Cuba.

O is for Old Trafford and the old man in charge of the team there. It's hard to credit it now but at the start of the 2001/2002 season Alex Ferguson declared that this would be his last campaign in charge of Manchester United. Since he changed his mind United have racked up another four Premiership titles and a Champions League victory. He may be cranky and he may not be the world's best loser, but Ferguson's love of positive attacking football at a time when the game is too often ruled by fear enabled United to illuminate the Premier League all through the decade.

P is for Phelps, yet another miracle of sporting nature in a decade not short of them. Still just twenty-four, big Michael from Baltimore is already the most successful Olympian of all time with fourteen golds, eight from Beijing and six from Athens. Only eight countries in the world won more golds at Beijing than Phelps did. He's also set thirty-four world records.

Q is for Questionable Decisions in big games. Munster's Heineken Cup triumph might have come years earlier had a perfectly good John O'Neill try not been ruled out in the 2001 semi-final against Stade Français; Spain and Italy were blackguarded by the refs when they played host nation South Korea in the 2002 World Cup finals; Tipperary had reason to be aggrieved by the game-turning penalty in this year's All-Ireland hurling final; Tadhg Kennelly should have been sent off in the opening seconds of the football decider. But nothing provoked as much complaint as Thierry Henry's handball against Ireland in this year's World Cup qualifier play-off. It was the only time the aggrieved team suggested they deserved a replay. Most wonderful of all was the sight of Irish politicians raging against the dishonesty of it all. Expect Shane MacGowan to turn up at your house over the holidays and criticise your Christmas drinking.

R is for Rage against the Machine, also known as the Cork hurlers, who staged three strikes during the decade. Whether those disputes were an example of the will to win and passionate desire for excellence which brought them two All-Irelands, or a distraction which probably cost them more than that pair of triumphs remains an open question. Either way, they are the team most likely to sing along this Christmas with, 'Fuck You, I Won't Do What You Tell Me.' Their spiritual leader Donal Óg Cusack's decision to come out as the first openly gay Irish sportsman showed that, whatever you thought about his role in the strike, you couldn't deny his guts.

S is for Spin, weapon of the two greatest bowlers in the history of cricket. By the end of the decade, off-spinner Muttiah Muralitharan of Sri Lanka, with 756 wickets, and leg-spinner Shane Warne of Australia, with 706, headed the all-time rankings. Warne, paradoxically, was probably never better than when taking forty wickets when Australia lost the 2005 Ashes series. Muralitharan, who has taken five wickets in an innings sixty-six times, was ranked as the greatest cricketer of all time in 2002.

T is for Thomond Park, consistently the most exciting Irish sporting venue over the decade. Perhaps nothing will ever quite have the emotional resonance of the 1979 victory over the All Blacks, but Munster went close to matching it on a regular basis in the past ten years. The miracle match against Gloucester, the slaughter of Sale and the whaling of Wasps were highlights, but there was no such thing as a routine day out at Thomond. Then you had the away heroics in Toulouse and Leicester, and the final victories over Biarritz and Toulouse. No fans were better rewarded, or better deserved it.

U is for Ultimate Fighting Championship, and also for Ulster Football Champion-ship. Critics of football as played in the six counties sometimes maintained it was hard to tell one UFC from another. But that was the sourest of grapes – no team was as appealing when in full flight as the Tyrone side whose 2005 final victory over Kerry was the game of the decade. And no All-Ireland victory had the emotional charge of Armagh's football breakthrough in 2002.

V is for Vengeance as exacted by Leinster in this year's Heineken Cup semi-final. For years Leinster had been the subjects of almost universal derision concerning their lack of manliness when compared to the mighty men of Munster. (None of it, by the way, coming from Munster players.) The amusing quips about 'ladyboys' rang slightly hollow after Leinster gave Munster the kind of hammering no one thought we'd ever see our number one province receiving. What price a rubber match in next year's Heineken final?

W is for Williams, the two sisters who were the best players in women's tennis at any given time during the decade no matter what the official rankings said. Never mind the anonymous Belgians or the interchangeable Russians, when Venus and Serena wanted to win the big titles, they did so. The women from Compton combined for seventeen Grand Slam victories over the decade, despite taking time off from the game due to injuries (Serena) and occasional lack of interest (Venus).

X is for Xavi, player of the tournament as Spain won the 2008 European Football Championships, a star on the exceptional Barcelona team which passed Manchester United off the field to win this year's Champions League. And a bloody godsend to a journalist creating an A–Z.

Y is for Youngsters. There's a number of prodigious kids who might do great things for Irish sport over the coming decade. Watch out for Wexford's European junior swimming champion Grainne Murphy, World Under-17 silver medallist over 800m Ciara Mageean, European youth champion and outstanding boxer of the championships Jason Quigley from Donegal, and Moate's Joe Ward, who stopped three of four opponents on the way to winning the world schoolboy light-middleweight title this year.

Z is for ZZZZZZZ, the proper response to what happened in Saipan in 2002 when one man decided he didn't want to play for another man and people who normally weren't interested in sport suddenly decided football was a matter of national interest. A triumph for *Liveline.* A Nation Mourned. Jesus Wept. Triggs Walked.

34

SPORT STRIPPED NAKED

TOMMY CONLON

The plain people of Ireland descend on Clonmel for what was once the most controversial activity in the country, before muzzling muted 'the antis'.

10 FEBRUARY 2002

The hare comes shooting down this fenced-off corridor at the top of the hill, past the hut where the dogs are waiting, and out into the open field. He has 450 yards to the escape at the other end.

With about 100 yards gone the slipper releases the two greyhounds – the switch is tripped, the chase is on.

Compelled by instinct, propelled by speed, they devour the ground, eyes fastened on the quarry, hunting him down in a maddened burst of streamlined power. Up ahead, the hare scuttles through the rough grass, his miniature skips no match for the loping, elongated strides of the hounds behind. He knows they are closing in but he keeps a straight line, through the dip in the middle of the field and up the incline, his eyes fixed on the fence that represents his escape.

Fifty, eighty or 100 yards from the fence, the first dog pulls alongside and forces him off his line. In the eyes of the judge, and the watching public, he has won the race. But he is oblivious to their agenda – he sees only the hare. The other dog arrives and both combine to cut him off from his exit, facing him back down the hill. It is then that his natural assets kick in and with a manic series of twists and turns, dummies and darts, he eludes the dogs. Slavishly they follow his rapid-fire switches in direction, turning left when he shoots left, right when he shoots right, losing a microsecond with every turn, bewildered by the hyper-agile reflexes of their target.

When he has engineered enough room he will straighten and head for the fence again. If he is still too far from it they will reel him in and turn him again, forcing him into another sequence of stop-start runs, over and back, until he has gained enough time to straighten again and make another dash for safety.

Eventually he reaches sanctuary, disappearing through the gap at the bottom of the fence as the dogs are denied, left without a kill, panting from their exertions. The hare, meanwhile, is collected on the far side and returned to the paddock holding the 200 or so other hares, his work done.

The first time you see it, it is thrilling – nature in the raw for a pasty-faced city dweller whose only knowledge of wildlife comes through the television. The hundredth time you see it, it is monotonous – the hare wins virtually every time.

But that is missing the point. Coursing is not about the survival of the fittest. It is about hound against hound, not hound against hare. There is a predator and a prey but the predator is muzzled, the prey, by and large, is safe. The dogs can get to the hares but they can't get at them. It is a tease, a torment, excitement followed by frustration. They are eunuchs in a harem of hares.

Or at least they have been since 1993, when muzzles became compulsory and the bitter controversy over coursing more or less evaporated. At an infamous meeting in Clounanna, Limerick, in February of that year, fifty hares were killed over three days and the outcry finally forced the coursing authorities to act. Opponents argued at the time that it would destroy the sport. In fact it has thrived. 'The crowds have been going up steadily every year since '93,' says Jerry Desmond, secretary of the Irish Coursing Club.

At the national finals last week, held over three days in Clonmel, more than 12,000 turned up on the Wednesday. 'I think the fact that the kill has effectively been taken out of coursing has made people more comfortable with it.'

In 170 courses, one hare was killed, on the Tuesday. 'The dog pucked the hare up in the air,' said one observer, 'and she came down and broke her neck on the ground.' A few more were pinned down by the dogs but rescued. Some racing commentators believe that 'pinned' hares should also be included in the fatalities, given the damage they may have suffered. Others argue that it depends on the level of damage, if any, sustained.

The hares are gathered by members of coursing clubs from all over Ireland and brought to Clonmel (and every other meeting) about a month before the event. They are inoculated against disease and fed a diet of oats, fruit and vegetables. 'We have very extensive paddocks and they have plenty of space,' says Desmond. A few days before the meeting they are individually 'trained' to run in a direct line from the slipper's box to the escape. They are coursed once and taken away after the meeting, usually to a different part of the country in order to 'mix the breed'.

They are, says the Cork trainer Barry Lynch, tough and intelligent animals. He is sceptical about the level of psychic trauma that 'the antis' claim they suffer during a course. And given the hazards they face on a daily basis, it is tempting to consider that their month in captivity is a bit of a holiday camp, a break from the rigours of the real world – but no one has yet ascertained the hares' opinion on that.

'Any hare that's anywhere in Ireland tonight,' said Lynch on Tuesday, 'is under pressure of some kind, whether 'tis something out of the sky, or a tractor or a fox – anything wild, loose dogs, wild cats, anything. He lives in no burrow, he lives in a field, his young are reared there, he's doing that all his life, surviving all kinds of animals, urbanisation, everything. He survives – he's survived since Methuselah.'

One hare lucky to survive the week was the unfortunate chap picked from the pack for the Derby semi-final on Wednesday afternoon between Cillowen Harbour and Oncelovedalass. The Clare-bred and owned Cillowen won the race (or 'buckle') comfortably. But he caught the hare at full tilt and went flying, tumbling wildly to gasps of 'oooh' from the crowd. The hare was dazed and unable to make a clean break for the escape. It was still some 100 yards away from it and the dogs chased it relentlessly until they finally pinned it down. 'He's fucked,' said the man at the rail – and he wasn't talking about the hare. Cillowen Harbour had spent so much energy chasing the hare he would be depleted for the final.

Minutes later a crowd gathered round the dog and its handler as it sat panting on the walkway by the side of the field, utterly exhausted. 'He's flahed,' said a Cork punter – and he was. The decision was taken not to run him in the final. First prize of €31,700 went to the second finalist and favourite, Murtys Gang, part-owned by the Clare All-Ireland winning hurling captain Anthony Daly.

Both dogs were bred by the Gallery family in Ennis – they trained and owned Cillowen Harbour themselves. 'He was very tired after and we felt it would be wrong on the dog to ask him to go back up again,' said George Gallery Jnr. 'He hit the hare on the run and that took the good out of the hare, the hare was weak after it, he was disorientated, and he (Cillowen) got a bad tumble in the process. The hare couldn't get away as quickly as we would have liked and they were down on top of him and that excites a dog an awful lot as well, so it takes an awful lot out of him both mentally and physically.'

Not to mention what it took out of the hare. Gallery had been first on the scene. 'I passed the hare to yer man (a steward) when I caught up with them and he was grand. He was just a bit disorientated but when I handled him he was still good and strong and there were no cuts or anything on him and yer man took him away.' As for Cillowen, they brought him back to the kennels but, after consultation with vets and officials, it was decided to call the final off.

'He got his wind fairly fast but his legs were weakened.'

The legs. 'You could pay 12 or 13 or 1400 quid for a good pup,' says Lynch, 'and maybe more. You could pay up to 2,000 for a well-bred pup,' he adds as one of the neighbour's children gives one of his dogs, Mucky Rojo, a thorough wash-down. 'And one of the things you look for when you're buying is a good, straight back leg, as opposed to a bit of a cow-hock or a twist.'

But the basic requirement is speed. 'They actually have speed at a very young age. At four or five months old they have tremendous speed. When they're very young they can twist and turn, they can fly, and they love it. Like, they're born that way: four legs, (the) two back legs push on the two front legs and that's the way they go. All the importance is in the back legs, the front is only steering, the power is from behind.'

The training will put in the stamina and after that you're looking for a cool temperament and a competitive streak – 'what we call heart, good heart.'

The greyhound industry has a broad base at the bottom of its pyramid. A dog may have to win six races before it qualifies for Clonmel. To win the Derby or Oaks, he or she will have to win another six over the three days. In the Oaks, the locally-owned Limousine had an easy win in the final. Added to the abandoned Derby final, it made for an anti-climactic Wednesday.

The betting ring had heaved with punters all day. 'I'm told the volume of betting was huge,' said Desmond. English geezers in hats, with accents straight out of *Lock, Stock and Two Smoking Barrels*, mingled with punters from Northern Ireland, Europe, America and Australia.

But mostly it was the plain people of Ireland – and in fairness some were very plain. Loads of ould fellas with blood-pressure faces, country men with limps and gimps and trembles, shuffling and wheezing in big overcoats, the odd bottle of Powers in a pocket, or a punnet of chips in swollen, purple-red hands. Lots of young fellas too, rough rural diamonds some of them, or small-town shapers, sucking pints and fags in the dark shed underneath the stand, done up as a bar for the couple of days.

'It is very elemental,' says Desmond of the coursing: two dogs, one hare and an open field. In a way it is a throwback to another time and place, to a pre-processed, pre-pasteurised modern Ireland.

It is, of course, deeply unfashionable too, a sub-culture that has disappeared off the contemporary radar. But it's there and its roots are deep – a hidden life in the hidden Ireland.

35

THE LONG AND WINDING ROAD

PAUL KIMMAGE, JOE BROLLY, JOHN GREENE, DAVID CONACHY AND FERGUS McDONNELL

Paul Kimmage, Joe Brolly, John Greene, David Conachy and Fergus McDonnell took on one of cycling's toughest climbs, Mont Ventoux. It's a story of strength, stamina and swearing; a journey of drama, pain and friendship.

3 JULY 2016

PART 1: THE CYCLE OF LIFE
DAVID CONACHY

Five years ago, on a whim, I picked up an old bike that was lying around the house and went for a cycle. A friend joined me and we rambled around some roads in our area for a few hours, and I went home happy. I didn't know it then, but something had been awakened inside me.

Cycling has given me an energy for life – a positive energy I had not experienced before. For somebody whose only real taste of sport as a kid was golf, this was something totally new. I was in thrall to the freedom, the torture of the climb when there's nowhere to hide and the buzz when you are whizzing down a mountain, hitting high speeds on two wheels less than an inch wide.

There is no problem too big that cannot be parked for five hours once you escape to the open road. It allows you to take a step back and see things differently. Cycling has the power to heal. It takes you places you haven't been before; it teaches you more about yourself, and others.

It is not about who has the best bike, or the most expensive gear – it is about being comfortable with yourself. Yes, you are part of a group, but ultimately you are on your own and you learn to be okay with that because, you know what, it's okay to feel good about yourself.

So, the cycling craze which has swept the country might look like a lot of things to the outsider but really, when you strip away ego and machismo, in my experience it nearly always comes down to the same thing: everybody is on their own journey. Everybody is there for a different reason, and for the coping classes this is one of the great treatments for the trials and tribulations of everyday life. At least being on the bike allows you to take control.

We all have mountains to climb but, just like being on the bike, we get better at it.

There's always another mountain to climb. In May, that mountain was Mont Ventoux in the south of France in the company of mother hen Paul Kimmage, Tour de France cyclist, fluent French speaker and driver; Joe Brolly, the wee man from Dungiven; John Greene, who dropped two dress sizes to make the team; and Fergus McDonnell, the new kid scared shitless. Five men with very little in common, all looking for something.

PART 2: HARDEN THE FUCK UP
JOE BROLLY

It began, as cycles often do, like the opening scenes in *Deliverance*. Idyllic weather, sun beaming and the happy chatter of a bunch of free men rolling through Provence without a care in the world. But to be a cyclist is to be a student of pain.

In any cycle I have ever done, there comes a point where the only thing left is Rule 5. Your body may be a pillar of lactic acid. Your brain may have stopped working. All that remains is a primal instinct to keep pedalling. In *The Rules*, published by the Velominati, or 'Keepers of the Cog', each rule has its own chapter, with detailed explanations and anecdotes.

All except for Rule 5, which simply reads: 'Harden the fuck up'. The photograph that accompanies the rule is of an Italian cyclist, Fiorenzo Magni, the Lion of Flanders, perhaps the toughest motherfucker ever to take to a bike.

It was halfway through the 1956 Giro and he had just broken his collarbone. He carried on, but unbalanced, fell again two days later and smashed his humerus, the long bone running from shoulder to elbow. He could no longer pull up on his bars, so he tied a tube around the stem and pulled up on it with his teeth to control the bike. He finished second after an epic series of mountain attacks.

I don't like cycling. But I can't resist it.

Three hours in and I was bored. Me: 'Come on lads, let's find a bar.' Kimmage: 'Shut the fuck up, Joe.' After seventy-odd kilometres, we hit the foot of Mont Ventoux, the Beast of Provence. I wasn't bored any more. The conversation dried up.

After fourteen kilometres of the most notorious ascent in world cycling, the hailstorm came. No one had checked the weather and we were in summer gear. The temperature dropped below zero. The bikes were buffeted by the freezing gale, threatening to drive us off the cliff edge. We were pedalling to outrun hypothermia. At the summit, where the mountain is like the surface of the moon and you are above the clouds, John Greene collapsed, frozen. He passed out. Frozen myself, I took him in my arms and hugged and rubbed him frantically. There was no shelter and no way to get him back down.

As we contemplated the worst – a miracle. An ancient French couple appeared in their tiny old Renault. They had come up to take in the views from the top of the monster. Kimmage explained the problem in his perfect Dublin-French. We carried John into the back seat. *Les anciens* drove him down the twenty-one kilometre descent. Me and Dave followed. On the way down, hitting speeds of seventy k.p.h., body in spasms with the cold, I could hear a strange groaning sound and was surprised to realise it was coming from me.

The ambulance took John to hospital. Later that night, he appeared back at the hotel, like a ghost. 'Harden the fuck up,' I said. We all laughed. It wasn't mentioned again.

PART 3: A ROUGH RIDE
PAUL KIMMAGE

Coffee was taken at a small café in Mollans-sur-Ouvèze, a picturesque village in the rolling hills to the north of the mountain. Brolly was in flying form and regaled us with tattle from *The Sunday Game*, a sketch from *Après Match* and a hilarious impression of a supporter he had once observed during a game at Ravenhill: 'DRIVE ON, ULSTOR!'

We had three 'petit-col' (500/600m) to digest before the main course and adopted this as a rallying call when the gradient started to bite:

Fergie: 'Drive on, Ulster!'

Dave: 'Drive on, Ulster!'

John: 'Drive on, Ulster!'

But the tone wasn't right.

'This guy is a well-heeled Ulster Protestant,' Brolly explained. 'He lives in Bangor. He was educated at Belfast "Inst". He doesn't walk to Ravenhill with his tail between his legs – he puffs his chest out! He's there to win! It's "DRIVE ON, ULSTORRRR!"'

We laughed and tried again.

The first sense we had that things were getting serious was when Brolly stopped talking. An hour had passed since we had left the lavender fields at Sault and started climbing through the forest; a glacial wind was gusting across the mountain and we had just passed Chalet Reynard and caught our first glimpse of the summit.

The café owner had warned us about the conditions. 'Be careful,' he said. 'It will be wild up there this afternoon.' We were flanked by scree and rock and the full force of the Ventoux was suddenly upon us. The cold was the real surprise – my hands were starting to freeze – and I suggested turning around.

Getting to the top is no big deal when you've raced in the Tour de France. Or won an All-Ireland. But the challenge was different for the three boys. John and Dave were flying and had pressed on ahead so I offered the carrot to Fergie: 'The forecast is much better for the morning. It will be a lot easier if we start the climb fresh.'

But he wasn't buying, and said: 'I'm not going to spend another night wondering about it.'

So we pressed on … five kilometres … four kilometres … three kilometres … two … inching towards the memorial to Tom Simpson and the reward of hot coffee at the summit café.

'That's the hardest part, Fergie.'

'Keep going, Fergie.'

'Great stuff, Fergie.'

The final kilometre – a ramp with an average gradient of 9.5 per cent – is an absolute ball-breaker. Dave was waiting at the top with a smile that stretched to Avignon, but as we cheered Fergie to the top and posed for some photos, a terrifying reality suddenly dawned. The café was closed! The wind-chill was -10. We had to get out of here.

'Where's John?'

He was huddled in the doorway of the café and shaking uncontrollably. I nearly flipped. 'Are you out of your fucking mind? Why didn't you go straight back down?'

But he was pale as a ghost and in no state to argue.

An elderly French couple – the only others on the summit – were sitting in their car with the engine running. I tapped on the window and they agreed to take him to Bédoin, at the foot of the mountain. It was a huge relief to put him in the car but they had only just set off when there was a new problem.

What were we to do with his bike?

'Just fuck it over the wall there,' Brolly said.

'Are you serious?' I asked.

'Yeah.'

'A three-grand carbon fibre?'

'Och, sure nobody will touch it.'

'You're completely insane.'

But the words were only out of my mouth and he was halfway down the mountain with Dave.

'Drive on, Ulstor!'

I jumped onto my bike and descended gingerly around the first hairpin with my right hand on John's bike and my left on my brake. There was a café at Chalet Reynard, six kilometres below, and the plan was to put it in storage for the night if we could get there before it closed.

Fergie raced ahead to keep it open. There were a couple of hairy moments, but I managed to get it down. We ordered two large coffees and sat for twenty minutes, shaking with the cold, then descended at speed to Bédoin as John was being taken by ambulance to Carpentras.

Not quite what we'd signed up for, but an interesting day.

PART 4: A DAY IN PROVENCE
JOHN GREENE

'Just look at that. Would you just look at that, Greene.' It's almost twenty-four hours since the drama on top of Mont Ventoux and there has been little talk of the day before. Barred from the bike on doctors' orders, the plan for a second assault on the Beast of Provence has been scrapped. Joe Brolly is only too happy to stand down in solidarity.

We share a guilty secret.

Earlier the previous day, about fifty kilometres into our spin, Joe and I found ourselves talking furtively at the back of the group. Joe had been plying me with stories about the wonders of Provence, tempting me with talk of good food and even better wine. He knew he was close to turning me, he just needed to close the deal. 'Wait till you see Ménerbes,' he said. 'Come on, you've got to see this place.' Ménerbes is the hilltop town immortalised by Peter Mayle in his book *A Year in Provence*.

'Fuck it, I'm not cycling tomorrow,' I blurted out.

'Now you're talking, sir.'

We were bored.

Six hours is a long time on a bike, too long for Joe and I. Had fate not intervened it is likely I still would have found myself in the spectacular town of Ménerbes that beautiful May afternoon, lounging on the terrace of the Maison de la Truffe et du

Vin du Luberon, drinking a glass of red wine, peering over the old stone wall at the majestic landscape below and listening to Joe Brolly enthuse:

'Just look at that. Would you just look at that, Greene.'

But fate had intervened.

Twelve months earlier, I was in a café on the Col du Glandon in the Dauphine Alps with my three travelling companions, sharing good conversation and awful coffee. It was nearing time to go when one of the group said: 'Next year, John, you'll be with us.' He meant it. 'No chance,' I replied, 'absolutely no chance.' And I meant it.

We paid for our overpriced coffee and left. Dave Conachy, Paul Kimmage and Joe Brolly put their helmets back on, clipped in and set off on their bikes on the next leg of an epic journey which would eventually bring them all the way back to the notorious Col de la Croix de Fer, the Pass of the Iron Cross. I climbed back into our rental car and headed down to our next rendezvous point. The descent is famously fast and I hadn't driven far before I had to pull in and let them pass. I marvelled at their courage, fitness and mental strength, but did not have any urge to join in. After years of putting on weight this was the world as I understood it. I was the bag man.

A month after we returned home, the penny dropped. I started walking, a little at first, then more. Then I started jogging, a little at first, then more. Finally, in February, I relented and agreed to take part in this year's big adventure.

And it was all going so well too.

As we cruised out of town having broken bread in Sault, there was a nervous excitement in the air. Paul, of course, had been down this road before. So had Joe. The mountain held no fear for Dave, who last year overcame La Marmotte – a gruelling 175 kilometre slog with total climbs of over 5,000 metres. Fergie was nervous, but confident. I knew that the group would look after me, but I had never climbed before.

By the time we reached Chalet Reynard, six kilometres from the summit, Dave and I felt good and were clear of the others. We still had another 500 metres to climb. The lunar landscape is beyond intimidating. There is no shelter from the ice-cold wind, and the road stretches steeply in front of you to the weather station on the mountain top, towering above you with a giant one-fingered salute. Abandon all hope, ye who enter here.

Dave powered on, and I followed several minutes behind. We took some photographs while we waited for the others and I went to see if the café was open. It wasn't. The difference in temperature from when we left Bédoin that morning was around seventeen degrees. The rest is a blur … icicles on the building, shivering cold, Brolly trying to warm me up. Kimmage taking charge. A blanket, the back of a car, awake, asleep. A gentle old French couple, shivering cold. Cat hairs on the blanket, this couple must like cats. Dave flying by the car on a high-speed descent. 'Ça va?' 'Ça va bien.' And the cigar – oh, the smell of the driver's cigar. Awake, asleep, shivering cold.

As the ambulance pulled away from Bédoin the summit of Mont Ventoux loomed large. My body cried for sleep but the paramedics prodded me each time my eyes closed. 'Non, non, non.' I stared out the back window, transfixed by the mountain top. It stayed in view for most of the twenty-minute journey. It was like I had been assaulted, and my attacker was now travelling in the ambulance with me, smiling.

The next morning, Dave, Paul and Fergie set off to conquer the Beast again. Joe and I enjoyed a day in Provence.

PART 5: JOURNEY'S END
FERGUS McDONNELL

Journeys take many forms. The ones we embark on in our personal lives can last years and never reach a destination. And some can take less than a week and teach you more about yourself and your fellow travellers than you could ever imagine.

We had landed among the lavender fields of Provence and wondered at the monster of Mont Ventoux that towered above us. Our journey from Lyon's Saint-Exupéry Airport, in a big enough car which, at times, seemed far too small for the egos inside, had been one of wise-cracking and story-telling.

When Paul Kimmage first told me that Joe Brolly was on board for the trip I was delighted. 'Bring ear plugs,' he warned. Not for the first time in those few days, I would have reason to take heed of what Kimmage had to say.

But the chattering in the car fell strangely silent at that first sight of the mountain. Soaring impossibly high into its shroud of grey cloud, it represented an enormous challenge and one in which the journey would matter as much as the destination.

As it turned out, it mattered more.

My trip was double-edged. As well as the self-inflicted two-wheeled torture, I was staying on after the others came home to visit my eldest brother, Gerry, who has lived in the village of Monieux for sixteen years, and in France and other parts of Europe for close to forty years. Gerry is a child of the 1950s. Shaped in the image of the music and the carefree lifestyle of his youth, he busked his way around the continent before settling down in this wonderfully remote and tiny village in a house he shares with his thirteen-year-old daughter, Gina.

I had expected that reaching the summit would be the highlight of the trip, but it wasn't. It wasn't even second. The highlight turned out to be spending time with Gerry, who, having made what convention insists are the wrong decisions throughout his life, is content and healthy(ish) despite a recent heart scare, and living in a wonderful part of the world. The temptation was to ask, 'Where did it all go wrong?'

The second was the extraordinary generosity of Paul Kimmage. On both days, he cajoled, encouraged and almost carried me up that mountain. It must have been painful for him to ride at such a slow pace, but he never even suggested that he might push on.

On the second day, the pair of us began the ascent with the intention (or so I thought) of only going part of the way up, to meet Dave on his way back down after an early start. After a while he asked me how I felt, and proclaimed that the fact I could answer him meant I was all right.

After another few energy-sapping kilometres he announced that he had made an executive decision – we were going all the way to Chalet Reynard. It's an experience I'll never forget and one which, without his significant help, would have been much poorer.

The descent the three of us shared along the Gorges de la Nesque, from Monieux to Villes-sur-Auzon, is the most magical time I have spent on a bike.

THOSE IRISH HAVE EGGS

It is a law of life that stolen pleasures are sweeter – a law that admittedly gets some of us into trouble quite frequently, but a law nonetheless.

IN RUGBY HELL, THEY PLAY CROUCH, TOUCH, PAUSE, ENGAGE, COLLAPSE

NEIL FRANCIS

I have left this world and passed to the Underworld. This is my account of my first day in Hell.

There is a portal here in Hell where we can use a social networking site – would you believe it, it's called Hell-O.com. You should know a couple of things about Hades before we start. Hell is timeless; one day lasts about three or four earth months. Pain and fear is real and constant, even if you are torn to shreds by a gang of demons you somehow come back to life again. Hell, just like Heaven, is eternal.

When I got the bad news I just seemed to be in a queue at the River Styx. Mercifully, somebody had gone to the bother of putting two pennies in my eyes to get me across the river. Charon the Ferryman wasn't having any of it though.

'Yeh know the way there is a near depression/recession happening on Earth?'

'Yeah.'

'Same here! In most ordered societies the price of goods and services normally falls through the floor but our boys, the hedge funds and speculators, are doing a great job for us keeping the prices artificially high. They all end up in here though.'

'What are you saying?'

'Two pennies don't get ya on the boat, the price is a million euro – ya gotta swim.'

Five miles through molten lava hurt like hell. No skin only bone by the time I got to the other side. The pain was excruciating but after a while I was whole again.

I have to say Hell was a disappointment; from the wailing, screaming and moaning to the random attacks from machete-wielding demons, it was pretty stock stuff. Sunday drivers and DJs blaring boyband bilge twenty-four/seven onto the streets. In Hell, they too dig the roads up just as everyone returns to Hell school in September. The aesthetic of the great pit and the fires was cool but after a while …

Amazingly, I bumped into Lucifer.

'Hey Frano, welcome to Hell – I watched your career, loved your style.'

'Thanks.'

'If there was work in bed you'd sleep on the floor.'

'That's a bit uncharitable.'

'There is no charity here. What do you want?'

'Listen Your Evilness, it's a bit dull here, is there a rugby hell?'

'I'm surprised you weren't sent straight there. I'll get Old Ned to show you around.'

Ned took me in the lift and started showing me around.

'It's not a bad place down here Frano – in fact … hey look up over there.' Whooooooooosh. Suddenly my torso fell to the ground and my head rolled twenty yards past it. Ned fell around the place laughing. 'Gotcha! Sorry that was Courtney Lawes. We love him down here, in fact we have 100 Courtney clones running around here with scimitars and when you least expect it or you are unsighted, he'll come in and take your head off. Clean off.'

'Jesus, that hurt.'

'Don't say that down here,' said Ned as he put my head back on my torso.

'What next?' I asked.

'We are going to see a game.'

I have to say I was encouraged, until Ned explained the rules.

'Well, both teams are made up entirely of props and the referee is a prop as well. We call our game Crouch, Touch, Pause, Engage, Collapse. So the ball is kicked off and because they are all props they knock it on and we have a scrum. They get down in the scrum and it collapses. They all get up again shaking their heads and pointing at their opposite number. Then they get down for more scrums and more collapses.'

'But surely the ref gives a penalty?'

'He does but they are all props here and they don't know what to do so they decline the penalty and opt for the scrum.'

'Jesus, surely the ball comes out eventually.'

'Don't say that here. Yes, it does but the first receiver is a prop and he knocks it on and we start all over again. The game normally ends 0–0. They go away happy. Wait for it, now here's a scrum you have to roar … Heavvvve or Courtney comes along again.'

The game lasts twenty-four hours and they prod you with white hot pokers if you fall asleep.

After the game there was a press conference. To my amazement, they wheeled out Declan Kidney.

'What's the Monsignor doing down here?' I intoned.

'Ah no, he goes straight to Heaven but he drives them scatty up there so they kind of lease him to us from time to time. It's torture. If you've been good in Hell, they ritualistically disembowel you; if you have been bad, you get a two-week Declan Kidney post-match conference.'

Two weeks later, but still on the same day, Ned says, 'Okay, let's go on the beer.' I have to say the flicker of excitement was extinguished after two minutes when he had explained the rules.

'It's a weekend in Cardiff and you are going on the piss with Dylan Hartley. There is no Heineken or Guinness, it's just Welsh bitter to drink. You have to drink gallons of the stuff and when you fall over and get sick you have to start all over again immediately.'

'Well, after the post-match conference I need a beer – set them up.'

The beer arrived and it was warm, frothy and putrid.

'This isn't beer is it, Ned?'

'No! It's not! Do you see that demon behind the bar? That's Beelzebub's nephew; he is the foulest, dirtiest demon in Hell. Every beer you've had tonight came out of his foul bladder. You have to admit, though, it does taste nicer than Welsh bitter. We had to drink thirty kegs of the stuff, one for every Welsh Lion going to Australia.'

When they say the hangover from Hell – they don't really know what they are talking about. Ned took me to another room.

'Are you a Munster supporter?'

'No.'

'You are not going to like it around here so.'

'Why?'

'Well back in the Jurassic period we organised a match between Munster and the All Blacks and of course Munster won so even one hundred billion trillion years later they can still remind you that they beat the All Blacks.'

'Oh Jesus.'

'Don't say that here. Of course in Hell Munster have won the Heineken Cup for the last 913 seasons. We celebrate by singing "The Fields of Athenry" – one hour for every cup. All the nuances are observed, all the sssss's as they sing "we had dreams and songs to sing". Whispering "where once we watched the small free birds fly". They can sing it merrily for months at a go. The only break they get is when "American Pie" is introduced, you will have to lead that by the way.'

'Please, please, mercy.'

After four months of 'The Fields' – although it was all in the one day – I begged forgiveness.

'I am afraid we have a room full of IRFU committee men to get through before you can rest.'

'Wonderful, electrodes on my testicles or what?'

'No, no, they just want to sit down with you and tell you where you went wrong as a player, etc., etc. Don't worry, we have confiscated all of their pipes; it took away from the smell of methane we have here in Hell.'

The salties were flowing before Ned said, 'Only joking – we will do that tomorrow. You must be exhausted. C'mon we'll get you ready for some kip. We have a little house which you can share with the resident. He is not a bad bedfellow.' I sauntered in through the garden and froze as I saw 'Mick Doyle' on the nameplate over the door.

'I've been waiting for you Frano ...'

37

OUT OF THE BLEAKNESS, CATHERINA'S STAR SOARS

CLIONA FOLEY

McKiernan is not a lonely, long-distance runner; she is finding a way around Ireland's athletics brain-drain to do it her way – and at home.

10 FEBRUARY 1991

Inside, a seat runs around the wall, above the cement floor and below the hooks where the locals hang their kit. This is a man's room, flanked by a cement-floored communal shower and only men's urinals. The runner always brings her own mat, avoids the toilets and at least twice a week gets down to the business of training: running in and out from this ice-box for the next hour.

Her gym is the changing room in the car park of the local football pitch at the bottom of the lane to the family farm. It is a grey 8' x 10' glorified shed, unheated, with a corrugated roof.

This is where the current number three on the IAAF international cross-country Grand Prix circuit does half of her training. Last Saturday in Albufeira, Portugal, a twenty-one-year-old Cavan girl, Catherina McKiernan, won the sixth race in that series, to add to a previous second and fifths in what is basically her first senior international season. On Monday, it was back to basics in Cornafean.

Villanova and Santa Monica, yes. But Cornafean, no. It is hardly a club name that would strike fear into the hearts of international competitors. The only really famous sportsperson to ever come out of Cornafean before was typically a Gaelic footballer, by the name of John Joe O'Reilly, captain of Cavan's famous two-in-a-row All-Ireland champions in the late 1940s.

Today Gaelic football still takes pride of place over Catherina McKiernan. She gets an eight paragraph blurb on the front page of the local papers, while inside the county footballers, who have the dubious distinction of languishing pointless at the bottom of Division 2 of the National Football League, get two-page spreads.

In all honesty, Catherina McKiernan couldn't give a fiddler's.

Someone who spends an hour's training, which involves running in and out from a changing-room floor to a football pitch, interspersing power exercises like sit-ups and squats with bounding – a sort of exaggerated slow-motion sprinting action – is not bothered by who's watching her.

In the townland of Cornafean and in Cavan town, ten miles away, across some of the hairiest roads this side of Beirut, she is simply part of the landscape.

She's the wee girl who, every lunchtime, runs out the two miles from Cavan town centre to the golf club, her five-foot-six, seven-and-a-half-stone frame bouncing along, over the hedge, up the steep incline from the eighth green and around the deserted course.

Most days she laps it five times, except Tuesdays when she works on her adapted 'hills' circuit on the first nine holes. Then she returns over the hedge, back into the courthouse where she showers and returns to her work as a telephonist.

Catherina McKiernan thinks this the best possible of all worlds. A job that allows her a ninety-minute lunch break for training and will give her the occasional day off for races.

She adores the golf course, the peace, the ideal hilly terrain and the gorgeous spongy ground underfoot to which she attributes her lack of injury.

When she started training seriously, two years ago, it was on a circuit marked out across three fields behind the family home, a smallholding which overhangs a bleak and windswept valley between Ballinagh and Killeshandra, where dairy farming is an imperative, not an alternative.

'It took me about seven minutes to do a circuit of those fields and it did become fierce boring,' she admits. 'The golf course circuit takes me about thirteen to fourteen, depending on my pace and it's just ideal really.'

Her lifestyle, as the only senior runner of any note in what is just a fledgling club with primary school members, training alone in a county with one of the bleakest reputations in the country, has that quintessential image of a lonely long-distance runner.

But the youngest of a close-knit family of seven children, nestled in the bosom of a rural community, she does not appear lonely. Late in her secondary schooling, at a time when she was stuck into every sport possible, especially camogie, the BLE National Middle and Long Distance coach, Joe Doonan, took her under his wing after unsuccessful attempts to get her a coach locally.

Now he is the man who guides her progress doggedly. 'What we've done this year is planned her move into the international scene and she's done well,' Doonan says. 'She has the right body type, she's dedicated and she's a quick learner.'

Doonan travels the eight miles from his home in Carrigallen several times a week to join her on the bizarre training nights in Cornafean. Another of his charges, Patricia Griffin, trains in the garage of the local priest's house. And once a week if possible, they drive to a cinders track in Lanesboro, a full six-hour trip all told. Come April, they make a weekly visit to the tartan track in Tullamore Harriers.

No, she is not lonely. America; now that would have been lonely, she feels.

'They were ringing me up to go on scholarships before I left school and stuff, but I never had time to reply, nor wanted to go. Can you imagine it? Out there they seem to run so many races, whenever their coach or college wants them, and they don't seem to get much rest. Here I can progress at exactly my own pace. And I have my friends and family here too. There's a lot to be said for that.'

She won a schools cross-country title in 1988, came third in the national seniors a year later. Last year she won it and surprised many by beating American-based Valerie McGovern for the national 3,000m track title.

The cold or the recent snow, which interrupted most of our lives, especially in the week before she ran a second to Jane N'Gotho in Plassey, Limerick, doesn't affect her.

'I just jogged out from town as usual, changed into my spikes, jumped over the stile and ran on. It was gorgeous, really dry snow and fluffy. You don't slip with the spikes.'

Two years ago she was seventy-third in the World Cross-Country in Norway. Last year she improved thirty-three places. On her current Grand Prix form she's being tipped for greater things; the inevitable, dangerous media hype that follows precocious success.

Doonan says tipping her for a medal in the World Cross-Country at the end of March is more a hindrance than a help. The big guns, like Negura (Romania), Dandova (Italy) and the good Chinese and Norwegians haven't appeared on the Grand Prix circuit yet. Catherina, he says, will just be looking to move up to the top twenty placings.

Progression and enjoyment are Doonan's underlying themes, two things which he claims are so often absent for those who go away. Yes, facilities could be better, but Catherina will perhaps, at last, prove that home-based coaches and athletes can do it.

The current one-who-didn't-get-away is herself remarkably stoic. 'I'm in no hurry. Sure I don't even know what I'll be doing in the track season yet. I just take one race at a time.'

No, she insists, there's nothing else she could ask for right now. But, when pressed, she says, 'Time. I'm doing very well at what I'm doing right now, but if I'm to do well at the next Olympics or two I'll need more training time next year.'

She looks at you, this clear-skinned, unblinking, cherubic young face and nods. 'Oh, yes. I'm working for an Olympic medal. I think I've proved on this Grand Prix circuit that I can do it if I keep it up.

'Running is brilliant. I never get bored because every day I have something different to concentrate on in training. And I'm never overworked. In fact, if anything I tell Joe that I feel I could be doing more. Honestly, my day isn't complete if I don't get out training.'

In Cornafean they don't get Eurosport. So no one in the community saw her winning run in Portugal, though they have a tape of her second place three weeks previously in Limerick. Tonight the young local priest, a family friend, calls to see what he teasingly calls 'the video'.

No, Catherina McKiernan is not a lonely, long-distance runner. With the help of her coach, employers, family and BLE, she is finding a way around what some describe as Ireland's athletic brain-drain.

But she does hesitate when asked about what else she would like most to help her; a tartan track, a weights room, a proper indoor facility nearby?

'No, nothing, honestly. They'd be nice but they're not crucial and anyhow they're not feasible.'

Then she stops. 'Well … you would like support, d'you know. No not money, just … well, you'd like more people to come and watch you and cheer you on, d'you know … that'd be nice.'

38

OPEN OUR GROUNDS

RAYMOND SMITH

There are no hang-ups in the GAA about playing on a soccer pitch, but soccer on a GAA pitch? Never.

28 JANUARY 1990

The GAA stands accused of a lack of credibility in the controversial and emotive area of permitting its grounds to be used for soccer and other games seen to be in direct conflict with hurling and football.

Rule 42A should go, or at least be amended in such a manner that will allow Central Council to give the green light, where it thinks fit, to the staging of selected soccer matches or, indeed, any other 'foreign games'.

I know I will be berated by the 'traditionalists', the guardians of the 'national ethos' and those who, at the moment, are very concerned about the challenge that the march of 'Jack's Army' presents to the national games in maintaining and winning the allegiance of young people.

The GAA is being hypocritical in its retention of Rule 42A as it stands. The era when there was a case for having such a rule in the Official Guide is long since past. It is insular and isolationist in the extreme. Worse still, it smacks of fear – a fear born of the fact that the higher echelons of the GAA now admit that if they allow even one soccer match to be played at Croke Park or any other venue, the thin end of the wedge will be in place.

To put the rule in its historical perspective, it was devised to prevent garrison games being played at GAA grounds. The rule was formulated before independence when there were British Army units garrisoned in towns throughout what is now the Irish Republic. The GAA was closely identified then with the national struggle and many leading players and personalities were in the front rank of those fighting for 'The Cause'.

With the coming of the Treaty and freedom for the twenty-six counties the need to talk about 'garrison games', in the Republic at any rate, became an anachronism. And as time went on and Ireland entered the European Community and the youth did not see emigration in the same light as in the past, it became a greater anachronism still.

I accept, however, that there are GAA people in Ulster, especially in counties across the border, who still set their faces firmly against the use of GAA grounds for 'garrison games', especially soccer and rugby, on the basis that there is a continuing British Army presence in the North.

But these people no longer count in the argument as it is being presented from Croke Park. And if they are angry with me for writing this, then let them ask Danny Lynch, the Association's press officer, who voices the feelings of the president, John Dowling, and the director general, Liam Mulvihill.

Danny Lynch went on record in Birr last week to state quite clearly that the GAA has no 'ideological hang-ups' about providing facilities for soccer matches. The fundamental reason, he stressed, for the Association's refusal to allow soccer on its pitches was because it would effectively be assisting its competitors.

And soccer – as the Republic of Ireland team heads for Italy – is seen to be the main competitor.

As Mr Lynch put it: 'If you had two supermart chains in direct competition for the same custom, you would not find one handing over its warehouse to another.' The 'custom', in this instance, is the youth of Ireland.

We are down, then, to the essential issue of straight competition. Cut out all the waffle and the bottom line is that the Republic of Ireland's achievement in reaching its first World Cup finals has resulted in the GAA digging in.

I believe the GAA cannot have it both ways. It cannot enter the modern era – one of commercialism when much that it held sacred has been thrown out the window in the amassing of millions – and at the same time dig in its heels in one area against the wishes of so many of its rank-and-file members.

For example, there is a rule in the Official Guide that directs the GAA to advance the cause of Irish music, song and dance. The GAA is happy, though, to reconcile this with allowing pop concerts (bring on Prince and let Denis Conroy enjoy his act) at major stadia for the express purpose of raising money.

A private commercial concern with satellite television in mind is staging a repeat of the Cork v Mayo All-Ireland senior football final of last year at the Brentford soccer stadium and the GAA authorities here are only too happy to take their 'cut'. No hang-ups whatsoever about playing on a soccer pitch. Commercialism rules, okay.

I could go on, but let's concentrate on the essential argument and on why the Limerick Convention has sent a motion to Congress asking that Rule 42A be altered in such a way as to permit Central Council to deal with applications as it deems fit. It's planned to stage a Republic of Ireland v USSR international next year in Limerick when Treaty 300 will commemorate the Siege of Limerick and subsequent treaty. Limerick want it to go on at the Limerick Gaelic Grounds – the only suitable venue – and it would bring in between £100,000 and £150,000 in rental for the GAA.

Limerick see this as a special application, they emphasise that people who follow different games in the city and county participate in the Development Committee's draw – that it wasn't GAA followers alone who helped build the new Mackey Stand. They argue that the GAA should show that it has moved with the times and be able to take the magnanimous approach; one befitting the country and its future.

I think the Limerick argument is reasonable. Central Council would, if the Limerick motion were passed, still call the shots. It could accept or turn down any application it wished.

The very youth the GAA is seeking to win over or retain simply cannot understand its outmoded attitude. Television has broadened their horizons to the extent that they are catholic in the games they follow. Would one soccer match a year – like the Liam Brady benefit game – in Croke Park make any real difference, stop an avid Dublin fan, for example, following the Dubs?

Would an Ireland v USSR match at the Limerick Gaelic Grounds – the only one in 1991 to be staged there – turn a keen young hurling enthusiast against going to Munster hurling finals? I very much doubt it.

Finally, the money that would be available to the GAA from renting Croke Park and other grounds for soccer and other games could go to subsidising hurleys for our aspiring young players. I would make no apologies for taking every penny that could be amassed in that way if it saved hurling for future generations.

Even though it has now been confirmed that there will be government money for the GAA to aid its Croke Park development plans, the real millions that could accrue from National Lottery funds are being tossed away because the Association will not allow soccer to be played in the stadium. Of course, the government would also like a running track at Croke Park in a major reconstruction that could make it akin to a National Stadium. The GAA, again seeing soccer as its main competitor, prefers to say 'NO' and work mainly from its own resources, which on its own admission will be stretched to the very limit.

The millions that will have to be spent by the GAA could so easily have gone to the development of hurling and football among the youth.

A democratic debate has been opened because Limerick have sent a motion to Congress. It's the delegates at Congress who must make the final decision. They have the opportunity to show that the Association is moving with the times and is ready to enter the next century without fearing a challenge from any quarter. Let them grasp it and give a two-thirds majority to the motion.

Deep down, though, I fear that the traditionalists and the guardians of the 'national ethos' (will we ever get away from it?) will have their way once again.

39

EPSOM'S SUPREME TEST NO LONGER RELISHED

ANTHONY CRONIN

There was a time when there was only one 'Derby'. Has that time now passed?

18 JUNE 1995

Is the writing on the wall for the Epsom Derby, for over 200 years Europe's premier Classic and the greatest horse race in the world? In spite of Epsom's new ownership and new sponsors, in spite – or perhaps partly because of – the move to Saturday, this year's race, the 215th renewal of the Derby Stakes, was in some respects anyway, a bit of a flop.

There was a time when even to call it the 'Epsom Derby' was regarded as *lèse-majesté*. There was only one Derby. It was the other races, whether at Chantilly, Churchill Downs or the Curragh, which had to have a geographical prefix. The real Derby was run at Epsom. The other middle-distance colts' Classics were imitations.

But it is precisely the fact that it is run at Epsom which is part of the real Derby's trouble. The mile-and-a-half course at Epsom is not so much a switchback as a roller-coaster, entirely unsuited to three-year-old Classic colts at the stage of development at which they are called upon to race there. The hill down to Tattenham Corner is the steepest on any English racecourse except Brighton. At the corner the ground falls alarmingly away from the rails, a camber which has no sooner been adjusted to than it tilts up and goes the other way, towards the far side of the course.

In the old days people used to speak about Epsom approvingly as 'the supreme test of a thoroughbred'. And it is still that. It tests not only a horse's speed and stamina but its courage and conformation, particularly its ability to gallop at full stretch up hill and down dale, against the collar for the first four furlongs and against – as you might say – the grain for the next four, before encountering the tricky finishing straight, with its demands on stamina and the steep inclination towards the far rail which makes it difficult to get balanced.

Add to all this that a fierce pace is usually set early on because the first bend is to the right and the second to the left, which makes it easy to get chopped off – as Walter Swinburn on the winner actually did this time – and that there is constant jockeying for position coming down the hill, which makes it a sometimes very rough race.

A supreme test indeed. But modern-day owners don't want their horses to be supremely tested if that means running the risk of perhaps fatal injury, or at least of the termination of a career before it has properly begun. Willie Carson was right when he said some weeks ago that half the horses involved came back unsound after Epsom and many (now transmogrified to 'most' by some of the hacks) were never the same again that season.

Money is more important to the modern breed of owner than it was to the aristocratic owner-breeders of Epsom's and England's golden age. And the modern breed of thoroughbred does not exist to win races at all hazards. It exists to make as much capital as possible out of a cleverly juggled season, as Peter Savill, whose juggling so far has been superb, is evidently hoping Celtic Swing will do.

Signs on, over half the runners this year were Arab owned – seven out of fifteen by the Maktoums and one by Prince Fahd Salman. But even though he has now been elevated by some of the hacks into a supremely wise, great and far-seeing sage and racehorse trainer – a sort of cross between Bertrand Russell and Vincent O'Brien – even Sheikh Mohammed may begin to have his doubts about Epsom after a few more Pennekamps. And if it gets to the stage where he owns all the horses and trains all the winners it won't really be much fun for him either. Nor would public interest in the race long survive such a state of affairs.

It was in the hope of increasing public interest that the event was switched to Saturday this year. It was a tawdry, pseudo-democratic, television-oriented hope and it was tawdrily rewarded. Attendance figures, despite much creative revision of previous counting methods, were actually down; and so, lo and behold, were the supposedly more important viewing figures.

The Derby on Wednesday used to be a public festival of a unique kind. Uncounted – and now seemingly uncountable – thousands took a day off for it. And if they were not entitled to, so much the better. As somebody should have told the organisers, it is a law of life that admittedly gets some of us into trouble quite frequently, but a law nonetheless.

That there was something wrong with the atmosphere this year, all hands were agreed. It was easy to move about and there was a huge police and security presence. The hacks were well treated, the early arrivals among them, including the present writer even being offered breakfast, but there was still something missing apart from the long march to the old paddock, now replaced by a rubber-surfaced monstrosity.

From the top of the grandstand the atmosphere on the Downs on what was admittedly a cold, overcast day seemed positively funereal, but unless they bring back the vanished attractions of the post-war decades and the raucous 1960s, the dubious bookmakers and still more dubious tipsters, the jellied eels, the boxing booths and the strip shows, there may be nothing they can do about that.

And though the absence of Celtic Swing undoubtedly lessened the attractions of the race in the popular imagination, neither can they moan about Mr Savill and his kind if they are not willing to run for the considerable money on offer. What those who love the Derby – of whom the present writer is unashamedly one – must hope for now is that the winner turns out to be an outstanding horse. A few years of bad winners would certainly speed the still great race's decline.

All we know about Lammtarra so far is that with the favourite having broken down and Celtic Swing having dodged the issue, he did not beat them in a remarkable time and manner. He is not very imposing to look at, but then chestnuts of his golden colouration never are. He was backed at long odds to take very large sums out of the ring, but by whom and why remain unanswered questions.

I thought there was something in the wind when I saw the Dubai contingent paying particular attention to Swinburn and his mount as the runners sorted themselves out for the parade. It appears now that he was tremendously fancied – and it's now they tell us – even to beat Pennekamp.

Many tears were shed over his former trainer's role in the winner's career, but who really believes that if poor Alex Scott were still alive the horse would have come back to him? On the previous day Henry Cecil had had the galling experience of seeing Moonshell, who never came back to his yard after being in Dubai, win the Oaks. She too is now trained by Saeed bin Suroor – who, in spite of the doubts expressed in some quarters, is a real person, as I can vouch, for I actually (I think) spoke to him. But since it is now acknowledged (if that is the word) that Sheikh Mohammed himself does the training while three other people, including Saeed bin Suroor, merely do the 'conditioning', I still was not talking to the real trainer.

But whatever the Sheikh and his three conditioners do in Dubai, Lammtarra was only the second horse this century to win the Derby without a run as a three-year-old, the other being Grand Parade, who was bred by 'Boss' Croker at Glencairn and won it in 1919 with Donoghue up, when he was Lord Glanely's second string and was trained by Frank Barling at Newmarket, the mere mention of some of those names bringing back Epsom's great traditions and glories.

So what is the answer to the question many people are now asking, which is whether Lammtarra will beat Celtic Swing at the Curragh? I am inclined to think that the real question is whether they will meet. The fact that the race was run at a cracking – as it turned out, bone-cracking – pace from the start, demonstrates that Lammtarra stays. What the manner of his victory would seem to show is that he has speed to burn. Although somewhat round-actioned, it was no trouble to him to race on good ground, but he will probably go in the soft as well.

Tamure had looked all over a winner until Lammtarra swooped and then he was made to look suddenly very ordinary. However much the Curragh management waters, they should not be surprised if Mr Savill takes his big black horse once again to Paris, this time for the Grand Prix de St Cloud, which, fortunately for his training schedule, is to be run on the very day of the Irish Derby.

40

MONEY-RIDDEN ATTITUDES SHOULD NOT PREVAIL

MICK DOYLE

It is high time for rugby to switch from defence to attack to save the sport from the march towards the money god.

11 NOVEMBER 1990

Ask not what I can do for my country,
Ask, rather, what playing for my country can do for me.

Anonymous Modern Rugby Player

A far, far cry you will agree from the tear-jerking, chest-swelling exhortation of John F. Kennedy to his fellow Americans during his inaugural presidential address in the early 1960s. An innocent, proud era when many strove to reach for the ultimate … for the honour and glory of country and fellow man.

In Irish rugby terms it was the era of Elvery, O'Neill, Fitzgibbon and Nestor; of Blackthorn boots, Law made-to-measure boots, Bukta knicks, indeterminate-origin jock straps, Higgles scrum caps and wayward sweatbands.

Back then there was no adidas, no Puma, no Le Coq Sportif and definitely no money.

As a player you dreamed your dreams and trained your guts out; you played till you dropped and hoped you would get on the 'firsts' or your provincial team. A final trial was 'something else', but the big prize was a green jersey with a little shamrock nailed onto it.

You bought your own boots, you paid your own bills and you washed your own gear. Why? Because you played a game you loved and did your best at whatever level you were selected and, when the ultimate beckon came to play for Ireland, you were ten feet tall and there was nothing you wouldn't do to honour your country and the people and place you came from.

Money? You would be ashamed to even think of it, ask for it or accept it. You were proud to represent yourself and honour those who depended on you. You were proud to be an amateur, to play the game because you loved it.

A few Irish players felt obliged to be remunerated for their abilities and did the honourable thing. They became professionals, joined the ranks of rugby league in England and worked hard for recognition in that code.

But it wasn't for them and none adapted to it: happily they are back in the amateur ranks again as if they never had to go away. They again enjoy the camaraderie and ethos that is peculiar to rugby union – especially the game in the four home unions.

I consider myself fortunate to have been 'current' in the 1960s as a player and to have been honoured each of the twenty times I played for Ireland. I was equally fortunate and privileged to have played for the Wolfhounds, the Baa-Baas and the Lions. Serving as Leinster and Irish selector and coach brought my personal life and rugby career to a pinnacle that I never dreamed of on the Eller (Under-13) pitch in Newbridge College in 1953, when I saw and handled my first rugby ball. I had to work hard for all the things I achieved – nothing came easy and competition was fierce and formidable.

The rewards were indescribable. The sacrifices were many and costly but worth every penny – even in hindsight.

I am not unusual but I am in the minority in that I was self-employed for all my major rugby involvements and I know what being short of money is about. I know also the monetary cost to me of my rugby career as a player, coach and selector. Nobody paid me to take time off and nobody paid me to play. Some offered but I wouldn't accept it.

I reckon therefore that I have the right to take issue with some of the selfish, presumptuous copy-cat attitudes that seem to prevail among some of our glamour players at present and the inexplicable stupidity of some 'senior' rugby administrators from other countries, who seem hellbent on foisting their 'money-ridden' attitudes on the rest of us.

Currently expressed opinions articulated ad nauseum on behalf of and by the privileged but irrelevant few in the hope of galvanising the majority view into action to prevent some 'fate worse than death' for amateur rugby, are registering zero in my reception centres.

My antennae detect sound waves of selfishness, greed, exploitation and crass, self-centered elitism. I pride myself on open-mindedness and a liberal dash of tolerance. I also value my own judgements and trust my instincts when I perceive what I can only describe as a 'con' being perpetrated on rugby union by players and officials who seem to be conduits and verbal stormtroopers for the exploiters.

The rape of rugby is being planned in a cynical, concerted and familiar fashion and it is high time for the relevant personnel to switch roles from defence to attack. Get off the pot!

In case some readers are confounded by rhetoric at this stage I will be more specific. Let us examine some of the persuasive propositions on offer.

1   'Rugby union players are no different from Aussie Rules or rugby league players. To claim otherwise is bullshit.' This is a currently expressed Australian viewpoint.

Response: Friend, I have news for you. They are totally different, particularly because Rugby Union is played, by choice, for the love of the game and not for reward. Like our Gaelic footballers out there at present. For 'Rugby Union players' read 'The Privileged Few' and not the 99 per cent who play the game day in and day out, referees, administrators or just supporters who unselfishly give their time.

2   'Current Irish players give up a lot of time to train, attend squad sessions, etc. and should be able to make some extra money to compensate them, to give them a little extra income.'

Response: For those who are interested you can now pay a player, any player, not just a prima donna, to speak, write or otherwise communicate for you provided it doesn't take money from the game itself, or words to that effect. So roll up! Roll up! Take your pick and pay your money. As it happens I believe that this is a human right anyway with which I have no difficulty.

3   'The day that rugby union began to charge money into grounds was the day the whole ball game changed.'

Response: I am not an apologist or a spokesman for the IRFU but I have been in the front line long enough to know they have administered the game very well. They can do even better. They collect money to run the game for ALL players and spectators – not the frantic few.

4   'Us Irish international players feel like rank amateurs when we see the level

of preparedness and professionalism of teams like Australia, New Zealand and France.'

Response: I agree with that. At present we are about the worst team of the seeded unions and probably the unseeded as well for the forthcoming World Cup. The IRFU are backward in their awareness and apparent appreciation of what it takes to prepare a team capable of taking on international opposition.

Just compare England's and our performance against the representatives of the 'Disappearing Green Goose' and you will appreciate what I mean.[1]

Our All-Ireland League is a start – only a start. It will take probably five years to translate into meaningful, measurable benefits, where the top players congregate in fewer clubs and develop into real world-class competitive players and not cardboard cut-outs.

However, our present structure of AIL fixtures from 6 October to 24 November – Argentina intervening – and interprovincial games on 1, 8 and 15 December, followed by quick sunburn on the Costa with no final trial, to be followed by further league matches on 5, 12 and 26 January, which are then superseded by a round robin draw on 9 and 23 February and 9 March, is unacceptable.

By the way, for those of you interested, there is an odd match against France, Wales, England and Scotland on a few free weekends between 2 February and 16 March – Jack Charlton permitting.

In 1986 I tried to introduce a respected sports nutritionist to the Irish team squad to advise players on their eating habits in relation to training and playing but I was 'blown out of the water' for being too professional. I really experienced the 'not wanted here' syndrome in all its glory.

I fear the wrong attitudes prevail at committee meetings when decisions are made. That is my gut feeling. Trouble is, I know most of the people responsible. Irish team players and potential team players need far more organisation and opportunity to build a team. Ask Fitzie.[2]

---

1   The 'Disappearing Green Goose' refers to the Argentina rugby team that toured Ireland and Great Britain in 1990. Ireland narrowly beat the Pumas 20–18, while England won 51–0.

2   Ciaran Fitzgerald captained Ireland to the Triple Crown in 1982 and 1985. After retiring, he served as head coach from 1990 to 1992.

I would resist strongly any suggestion of players making money for playing rugby at the exalted levels. However, players are losing money during training and other preparations. Might I suggest that they each receive worthwhile mileage and food allowances which leave them their dignity and allow them to bring along their wives and loved ones to share in their sporting life.

In the name of everything that is worthwhile in rugby union I would ask the IRFU to grab the 'bullet train' and join us in the 1990s. We can still preserve our game and ethos.

Willie Duggan must have been the most inexpensive self-employed player Leinster and Ireland ever had: he didn't come to training sessions. Training took the edge off his game – or so he told me. He didn't send in a bill for expenses either.

I will leave you with a simple thought. If we were to remunerate our top players for their performances in the green jersey over the past few years how much do you reckon they would owe US by now? Image my elbow.

'In great attempts, it is glorious even to fail.' – Anonymous.

41

THOSE IRISH HAVE EGGS

TOMMY CONLON

Boxing's honourable history in this country was further enhanced at the World Championships in Belfast.

After a punishing five fights in six days the Irish captain James Moore rested on the seventh and received his World Championship bronze medal at the Odyssey arena in Belfast yesterday.

Sharing the podium with a Cuban, an American and an Uzbek, the Arklow welterweight was Ireland's sole representative among the global array of medal winners who had made it this far after a week in the company of amateur boxing's elite performers.

Some 340 boxers from sixty-six nations had converged on Belfast last weekend for the first world senior championships to be held on this island. The championships, inaugurated in 1974, had yielded four Irish bronze-medal winners over the years before Moore made it five with a heart-stopping victory against his Turkish opponent, Firat Karagollo, on Thursday afternoon.

It was the pinnacle in a week of peaks for Irish boxing, when the sport's honourable history in this country was further enhanced by an unprecedented team performance – six of the twelve fighters made it to the quarter-finals, one fight away from medals. Damien McKenna, the Drogheda bantamweight, made it through on Tuesday and the other five joined him on Wednesday in what became a procession of Irish victories on the day.

'We were flying that day,' said Jim Moore, head coach of the Irish team and father of James. 'We were on a high, it was electric.'

But it couldn't last. On Thursday all but Moore the younger fell to earth. His clash with Firat was unbearably tense, the Irishman trailing by two points with just seconds remaining – it finished 24–24, Moore taking it on the countback of punches thrown, 110–82. The twenty-three-year-old electrician bounded onto the ropes with joy, the big home support in raptures. 'Sheer ecstasy,' he said, 'unbelievable.'

A dedicated trainer with a tunnel vision approach to his sport, Moore came into these championships in superb physical condition, beating a Latvian, a Lithuanian and then a very tough Italian before facing the Turk for a medal. He was Ireland's captain for a good reason.

'The most important thing about him,' said Breandán Ó Conaire of the IABA [Irish Amateur Boxing Association], 'is his mental toughness. He is completely focused, he never lets anything distract him and that of course feeds into his physical preparation – he doesn't skimp on anything.'

Firat, a factory worker from the Black Sea region, cried in his dressing room afterwards, according to one Turkish official. 'Firat leads by two points last few seconds!' said Saim Eskioğlu, in broken English, 'I saw no punches thrown but still the match finished square, twenty-four to twenty-four.' But this is boxing and the Irish camp saw it completely different: 'I couldn't believe the scoring,' said Jim Moore, 'if he had lost it would've been brutal.'

On Friday Moore returned to the ring to face the American Anthony Thompson for a place in the final. He was beaten decisively, 36–24, but it was a fierce encounter, Moore getting off the floor twice, Thompson once. The American coach visited him in his dressing room afterwards to praise him for his heart – Thompson meanwhile was getting his arm strapped up.

'It was very physical,' said Moore yesterday, 'but I love fighting, I love a good ould tear-up, toe-to-toe, that suits me down to the ground. Irish boxers are famous all over the world for their fighting spirit and if you didn't see fighting spirit out there (on Friday) you'll never see it. There's no way I would have given up out there, they would have had to nail me to the floor cos there was no way I was staying down.'

'Actually he loves fighting,' chipped in his father, laughing, 'more than boxing, which sometimes annoys me a little bit, that he has skills that he may not show.'

Jim Moore senior has been involved with the Arklow boxing club since the 1960s. On Wednesday, shortly after James won his third fight, they heard that the club had received a £30,000 government grant to replace the rotting floor.

'James has been coming to the club since he was seven, he's been tippin' and tappin' ever since. He's probably the most focused and committed boxer that I've ever come across, not because he's my son, but I know by him, he's one-tracked, he gets really intense before fights and if you say anything negative to him at all he'll blow you out of the water.'

It was an emotional week as head coach, he admitted, watching all the Irish fighters go about their work with varying degrees of success. And it would be stupid to pretend that he doesn't feel it more when his son is involved. 'Because you do, it hurts, and when he got hit and put down I felt really – it was like taking the punch myself, worse even, I'd rather have taken it. But I knew he wasn't hurt because he'll always let you know, wink at you or something, that everything's okay.'

The team trained full-time for the championships at the National Coaching and Training Centre in Limerick, starting on 3 May. Members of the Great Britain team were brought over to spar and work with them, facilities were top class and a strong team spirit evolved. 'It was the best prepared team ever,' said Coach Moore.

And it showed in the performances. Among the highlights was John Paul Kinsella's furious battle with the excellent Romanian Marian Velicu in the light-flyweight quarter-final on Thursday afternoon. It was an unrelenting show of guts and stamina by the tiny twenty-year-old from Dun Laoghaire. 'He gave everything,' said Moore, 'I thought he was magic.'

Damien McKenna left Belfast with his two eyes black and blue, a cut on the bridge of his nose and a slit under his left eye. A Chinese opponent accounted for some of the damage in the first round. 'And then,' recalled the twenty-six-year-old, 'I had a very tough fight with the guy from Tadjikistan and in the last round he caught me with a very good right hand over the top and I've two black eyes from it and a cut underneath.'

Known as a skilful boxer, McKenna proved this week that he could fight as well. 'The Chinese fellow was very tough,' said Moore, 'but he went toe-to-toe with him and banged him out, he was brilliant. Kenneth Egan (middleweight), absolutely brilliant as well, only a young boy, had two great wins.'

The light-heavyweight Alan Reynolds survived a pulsating second round battle with a Turkish opponent who rocked him with some early shots before succumbing to a late surge from the Sligoman. Michael Kelly from Dundalk also had two wins before losing, like Reynolds, to a formidable Frenchman.

'How many athletes,' asked a delighted Ó Conaire on Thursday night, 'do we have in the top eight in any other sport in the world? We have twelve weights in boxing and this week we had a boxer in the top eight in half the weights in world boxing. You look at the competition, the whole world of boxing is here this week, all the professional amateurs as well as the real amateurs, like us.'

The 'professional amateurs' are the ones who are paid to train full-time in academies, like the almost mythical Cubans, who again dominated this week with their power, technique and hardness. The French, Russians, Germans, Ukrainians and other East European countries are also organised along full-time lines. 'They stay in the amateur ranks because they get paid, it's their profession and also, a lot of them get educated as well and that's the way to the future.'

Ireland is improving but, as ever, it's a distance behind and, as ever, they relied on their bravery and spirit, along with their skill, to make a mark this week.

'I was talking to the Mexican guys on Thursday,' said Ó Conaire, 'and one of them said, "They're great fighters, the Irish, *tienen huevos*," which literally means "They have eggs." I speak Spanish and I knew what he meant. I said to him, "You mean they have balls," and he said, "Yes, I mean balls." And he was right, they do. *Tienen huevos*.'

GAME OF WINNERS

How many people would have believed that Paul O'Connell was walking home with a Superman T-shirt under his arm?

LAST HURRAH FILLED WITH EMOTION FOR GOLDEN BEAR

DERMOT GILLEECE

Jack Nicklaus will say goodbye to the British Open on a course he fell in love with.

10 JULY 2005

It has been a long goodbye. After bidding farewell to the US Open at Pebble Beach in 2000, the feeling was that Jack Nicklaus had also played his last Open at St Andrews a few weeks later. But the irresistible lure of the Old Course has brought him back for what now seems certain to be a last hurrah, starting on Thursday.

The occasion will be hugely emotional for the Nicklaus family in that the great man's bag will be carried by his son Steve, who, with his wife Krista, lost a seventeen-month-old son, Jake, in a tragic accident earlier this year.

'Krista is not going to make the trip because she's expecting in the first week of August,' said the Bear last week. 'Though Steve is caddying for me, he obviously plans to be back well ahead of delivery. And she's going to have a little girl. And hopefully she'll help heal some of the wounds.'

Meanwhile, the Royal Bank of Scotland have taken the extraordinary step of placing his likeness on a five-pound note to mark the occasion. And a unique print of the Road Hole, measuring 76cm by 135cm, has also been produced to commemorate the Bear's final bow.

'When I played there in May, the Old Course looked like it was ready for the British Open,' Nicklaus continued. 'I'm kind of a sentimentalist, I suppose, but it was the same course. They've changed a few tees, but in the middle of May, when you'd expect it to be soft, it was as hard as a rock. And I thought of all the people who played there and how it's still a competitive challenge after all the years.'

Ireland already has six players in the field – Pádraig Harrington, Darren Clarke, Paul McGinley, Graeme McDowell, Peter Lawrie and British Amateur champion, Brian McElhinney – and Todd Hamilton will be defending the title which he won unexpectedly at Royal Troon last year. But it is hard to escape the feeling that this could be the one to bring Tiger Woods's Major championship tally into double figures.

Woods likes the notion of Nicklaus farewells – and with good reason. 'I've been pretty good on them so far,' he said with a mischievous grin. 'Let's see, I won this year's Masters which was his farewell. I won at Valhalla (2000 USPGA) and I won at St Andrews. Now that he's on his second go round at St Andrews, maybe I can do it again.'

Curiously, Woods overlooked Pebble Beach, where he was no fewer than twenty strokes ahead of the great man after two rounds. That was when Nicklaus departed the scene six strokes outside the cut, but not before producing a memorable parting shot in the form of a glorious three-wood second to the heart of the green at the long 18th.

He is unlikely to play another Major championship after this, though there must still be a chance he might return to the Masters. So his target for next weekend is clear. 'I certainly want to finish my career on Sunday and not on Friday,' he said. 'That's my big goal and my swing actually feels a little bit better after a few recent changes.'

Though tributes will flow freely next weekend, two Irish players saw fit to honour Nicklaus in advance. McGinley recalled having dinner with him, his son Gary and Roddy Carr in Spain some years ago, when he asked Nicklaus how confident he was when at his best.

Pausing to give the matter some thought, he turned to McGinley and said, 'It's like this. On the morning of a tournament I would go to the practice ground and I'd look up and down the line of players. And I knew I was better than every single player on that range. But I also knew that each one of those players knew I was better than them.'

'That,' said the Dubliner, 'summed up his remarkable superiority, though he never came across as an arrogant person. Self-belief was the key.'

For Harrington, there were memories of watching the Bear's sixth Masters triumph on television in 1986. And a much closer view of him at Augusta, two years ago. 'I played with Tom Watson for the first two rounds and Jack was ahead of us and you could see he was still very special by how the people reacted around him,' he said. Harrington went on: 'Play was backed up when we got to the tee on the short fourth and he was hitting when Tom walked on. And you could just see the two of them puffing up their chests. They were trying so hard it was unbelievable.

And it was great to witness the enduring rivalry between them. That's probably what Jack is missing most: the rivalries he had in his heyday.'

Though Peter Thomson never shared a tee with Nicklaus in the Open, his respect is undiminished. When I asked him if he felt sympathy for Doug Sanders over the crushing loss to Nicklaus in 1970, he replied: 'I think it would have been inappropriate if Sanders had won, because the championship was set up to produce the best winner. And Nicklaus was the best.'[1]

Five new tees will increase the overall length of the Old Course by 164 yards to 7,279 yards for this week's Open. They are: 2nd hole – tee moved back forty yards and slightly to the right into an unused area of the Himalayas putting green. This will bring Cheape's bunker into play. 4th hole – additional sixteen yards will force choice of line to left or right of central mounds; 12th hole – extra thirty-four yards will bring hidden fairway bunkers back into play; 13th hole – carry over Coffins bunkers extended from 250 to 285 yards; 14th hole – extra thirty-seven yards makes this the longest hole on any Open Championship course at 618 yards. It brings the Beardies bunkers and Hell bunker back into play and increases the out-of-bounds threat on the right.

The most significant change is unquestionably at the 14th. 'For the life of me, I haven't figured out where the average driver is going to hit the ball,' said Nicklaus, who made a ten there in 1995. 'When I played in May, I hit it short of the Beardies and over the junk, which was an area of no more than twenty yards. That's a pretty small area. So I think it will certainly make a difference.'

It seems remarkable that a course of such length could be fit into only eighty-three acres, but this is possible because of the double greens and shared fairways. Since being closed to general play on 18 June, divots have been filled and green-speeds have been gradually increased to 10.5 on the Stimpmeter.

We're informed that it takes ninety minutes for eleven greenkeepers to cut all the greens, with each man walking an average of four-and-a-half miles. For this week, however, the staff of fourteen will be augmented by nearly fifty greenkeepers, mainly from other links courses in the Fife region. Work will start at 4.30 a.m. and they are expected to have the course ready for play in three hours.

Nicklaus was introduced to links golf in the 1959 Walker Cup matches at Muirfield. That was when his father, Charlie, and three of his friends, made the relatively short journey to play St Andrews. 'When they came back, my dad said you won't believe it,' he recalled. 'That's the worst golf course I've ever seen.'

---

1   Sanders only needed to par the final hole to win, but missed a putt from three feet.

'When I asked why, he said it was so hard and bumpy that things bounced all over the place. And you couldn't make any putts on the greens. I later found out he and his pals three-putted thirteen or fourteen greens. And, you know, they just had a horrible time. So I wasn't prepared for much when I showed up in '64 (the Open which Tony Lema won).

'But when I got there, I looked at it and I immediately liked it for what it was. In fact I fell in love with it right from the first day. And when I returned in 1970 and won, the galleries basically took me as one of theirs. It was like a Scot winning. That's the way they treated me, both times I won at St Andrews.'

He continued: 'I've loved the British Open, the challenge of it; the fun of it. I've always loved going over there to play on the different golf courses, getting a break from the heat of our summer. I loved planning for the different conditions and the type of golf you had to play. Every year would be totally different. I mean it would be dry some years. Others would be wet. And sometimes it would be windy. There's so much variety, even though the golf courses, to all intents and purposes, have stayed relatively the same throughout most of that time. You knew what was going to be there.'

Then, of course, there was a constant awareness of what St Andrews had meant to Bobby Jones. 'Growing up, all I heard was Bobby Jones, Bobby Jones and his thirteen Major championships. And how he played the Old Course and walked off and tore up his card. But he later said that if you're going to be a player people will remember, you have to win the Open at St Andrews. That thought was always in my mind.'

Which would explain why, on that trip in May, Nicklaus sat at the 18th while his eyes filled with tears – 'Just because of what it is; what it has meant to the game of golf, and what it's meant to me.'

Here's hoping his final leaving is delayed until Sunday.

43

PHENOMENON IN THE GAME OF WINNERS

DAVID WALSH

Aidan O'Brien may be lucky, but luck has played a minor part in his extraordinary achievements.

Ten minutes before 7 a.m., well over an hour before dawn, the day begins. Stable doors click open, lads arrive with saddles, horses are tacked up for work. 'Easy there, fellow,' someone whispers but the first moves of morning are made in silence.

Soon the horses are ready and led from their boxes, the clip-clop of their hooves on the pathway kills the silence and foretells the business about to begin. Behind the lamps which light up the yard, the young trainer stands in the darkness. Away from the glare of the lights, he is comfortable. From here he has become a phenomenon in the game of winners.

In Dublin, at an awards banquet the previous evening, he had suggested to his wife Anne-Marie that they stay the night, but she knew that wasn't what he wanted. They left a little after midnight and were home around 2.30 a.m.

Now, less than five hours later, he watches each horse, looking for hints of lameness, for runny noses, listening for coughs. Reassured, he nods in the direction of the gallops and the horses leave the yard. He jumps into his four-wheel drive and follows.

The gallop at Owning in Co. Kilkenny is cut from the side of a hill and it winds its way upwards for a mile. Up here it is bleak and cold, but he talks of it as fresh.

Out on the gallop, he again scrutinises as each horse is walked past him. 'Steady swinger John,' he says to the rider of the first, indicating the pace at which he wants the horse galloped. 'Steady swinger Shay; steady swinger P.J.; good steady Ross; steady swinger Barry, steady swinger Colm, you can take them along Colm; good steady Ted ...' They nod knowingly.

Twenty minutes after 7 a.m., this is where they are found most mornings. They walk to the bottom of the gallop, the trainer drives almost to the top and from this position he will watch the horses come round a turn and gallop towards him up the long, steeply rising hill.

This morning the view is bleak. All he can see are the lights of Carrick-on-Suir away to the south, but as he waits, the sky over Slievenamon tinges with red and the darkness gives way to gloomy grey.

His eyes are now trained on the corner down below, waiting for the rush of thoroughbreds. When they come it is a strange sight for, bunched together, they move like a black blanket over the ground.

'You don't see much at this hour, do you?' he says. But the effort of the animals animates him. He drives on towards the top of the gallop and watches as riders dismount and loosen girths. 'They have done their work and the riders jump off to make the walk back to their boxes a bit easier. We loosen their girths to let them relax a bit better. It is a way of rewarding the horses, of saying well done. You can't keep their noses to the grindstone all the time.'

Many of the riders tell him how strong and well their horse felt. Good, good, he replies. This life, he says, he would never want to swap it. He is trying to remember if he's ever taken a holiday in his life. He thinks not.

This isn't a complaint, nor is it said to foster the notion of his dedication. It is just that he wouldn't voluntarily want to be away from this; not for a fortnight, not for a week, not for a night.

'You see all this,' he says pointing out into the stretch of semi-darkness, 'I have been so lucky. To have married Anne-Marie, to have this place, great lads working here, training horses to win, being right on the pulse the whole time; I must have the best job in Ireland. Lucky man, that's what I am.'

Lucky he may be, but luck has had a minor part in the extraordinary achievement of the last two and a half years. Since the first day of last January, Aidan O'Brien has trained 237 winners in Ireland.

There is nothing to set this mark against, no old trainer who sent out 250 winners in his best year. O'Brien hasn't so much picked up where others left off as started from a different point.

He is now in his kitchen, the first part of the day's work is over. Puts on the kettle, fills a bowl with cornflakes, it is getting close to 8 a.m. and he's explaining that he doesn't think in numbers. He didn't set out to train 100 winners this year, nor 200. 'It would be foolish to set targets.'

Foolish, he is not.

It's very simple, he says. He wanted to train racehorses, to have enough of them to make a living and to be competitive when he brought them to the racecourse. That was the starting point and everything he has done since then has been an extension of fundamentally simple ideas.

Twenty-six years of age, he looks less. Through his conversation there is a seam of incredulity, almost as if there is no explanation for this extraordinary success. Almost.

It is now 8.25 a.m. and he is again in his place high on the gallop at Owning. From here he can see for miles but his eyes are again on the corner down below. As he waits, the phone in his four-wheel drive rings. Mark, one of his head lads at Ballydoyle, wants to know the instructions for each horse in his first lot. He reads out the horse's name, the trainer tells precisely what he wants.

Once the phone is put away, he refocuses on the corner. This group is less together than the first and one horse loses his position halfway up the final rise.

Heaving, panting, recovering, the horses file past the trainer. He again enquires from every jockey and they tell how good their horses felt. Until the last one, the one who struggled. 'He's no good, is he?' asks the trainer.

'What?' replies the rider.

'No good, is he?'

'No. No good.'

'We'll give him another week, if he doesn't show a lot of improvement he'll go home.'

As the horses return to their boxes, the trainer explains his philosophy. 'That horse you just saw, he struggled to keep up this morning. In races he would be asked to go faster and he wouldn't be able to. Here, he's only taking up a box and as a racehorse, he's no use to his owner and no use to me.

'I could tell the owner that he might win a race in six or eight months but everything would have to go right for him. With very few horses does everything go right and that's why you'd be only codding yourself. A lot of times it is better to make the hard decision early. It saves the owner money and another horse can be put into that box.'

This pragmatism underpins the O'Brien approach. His horses are fit, well-fed, happy and properly assessed. Judging the horse's potential correctly is one of the key elements.

'We see whether they have the ability to be a top novice, hurdler or chaser, and if one of them has, we train him to be that. Five or six runs in a season, not much more. A horse like Hotel Minella or That's My Man, you don't want to run him any more than that.

'With an ordinary horse, it's different. If we can get out of an ordinary horse in one season as much as others might get out of it in four seasons, then I think that's the way to do it. The owner gets the most out of his investment in the shortest time.'

Balyara, a good ground horse, ran twenty-three times for O'Brien this year. Eight times the horse won. The alternative was to race the horse less this year, to try to win eight races over three or four seasons. 'That,' says Aidan O'Brien, 'would be harder to do. The chances of a horse staying sound for four seasons are not great and even if he does, the owner ends up paying a lot of training fees.'

The O'Brien view of things has been well vindicated. Wonderfully well. 237 winners. Again confronted with the numerical total, he brushes it to one side. But not with the modesty which generally infects his response to praise.

'I don't want to sound cocky,' he says, 'but when you are doing something and you think you know what you're doing, you are hopeful of getting results.'

At 9.30 a.m., he goes inside for breakfast. The first two lots at Owning have been worked and watered. He has seen all of his Christmas runners and is generally satisfied. Anne-Marie's breakfast is quickly taken and, within fifteen minutes, he is on the road to Ballydoyle.

Arguably the world's most famous training centre, Ballydoyle was once home to the world's finest trainer, Vincent O'Brien.

The offer came like a bolt from the blue. Paul Shanahan, racing manager for Coolmore, approached him at Goffs' October Yearling Sales fifteen months ago. 'Would you be interested in training at Ballydoyle?'

At the time Aidan was just a few days short of his twenty-fifth birthday and making a name for himself as a trainer of jumpers. Ballydoyle was another sport, another world; he needed time to think it through.

John Magnier, boss at Coolmore, was sure he was right for the job. In O'Brien, Magnier saw a bright trainer, full of ambition and utterly dedicated. As well as that, Magnier had long believed in quickly giving responsibility to young people. Magnier would also have reckoned that if O'Brien turned him down, he was probably the wrong choice anyway.

'Vincent O'Brien was going to be a hard act to follow,' says Christy Grassick, manager of Coolmore Stud, 'but Aidan was the obvious successor to us. Since M.V. himself, no young Irish trainer has made a comparable impact on the game in such a short time.'

On the road to Ballydoyle, P.J. calls from Owning and gets instructions for the fourth lot. Mark calls from Ballydoyle, wanting instructions for his second lot. The trainer knows exactly what he wants and the organising takes less than five minutes.

He stops in Clonmel for *The Racing Post*. This journey, he says, from Owning to Ballydoyle, gives him time to think. On the road, he works things out. The drive, he says, is like a breath of fresh air. The extra responsibility of Ballydoyle has, he thinks, made him sharper. What he enjoys most is the natural rhythm of his year. Winter is for the jumpers, now he wants them right for the hectic week which begins on Tuesday, then Leopardstown in January, and finally Cheltenham and Punchestown.

But he enjoys the different pace of the Ballydoyle winter too, seeing the yearlings ridden for the first time, watching them make progress slowly. 'The one mistake you can make is bringing horses on too quickly. You can never bring them on too slow. Because I am training jumpers to win next week, I can be patient with the flat horses and make sure they get the right foundation.'

At 10.15 a.m. he arrives at Ballydoyle and heads straight for the enormous indoor facility where many of the yearlings are mounted and ready for their morning's work. 'A nice-looking bunch, aren't they?' he says.

Coolmore's satisfaction with his first season performance is shown in these yearlings, for they look better and are better bred than the pretty successful group he had last season. It is also seen in the construction of an equine swimming pool, which will add significantly to facilities that are about the best in the world.

So much evidence that A.P. O'Brien shall be around for a long time to come? 'I don't think of it like that. You do your best and you see what happens.'

In this way, he refuses to be burdened by the enormity of the operation. Better to think of it as an opportunity.

At Ballydoyle there is a roadway which runs parallel to the all-weather gallop. So he can watch the yearlings as they canter, every stride of the way. 'Look at how healthy they are, so well developed, so much potential to work on. That filly's a lovely mover. Some of these could be very serious horses ...'

He is watching from his four-wheel drive as they walk back to their boxes when, again, the phone rings. Ballyhire Lad's owner is on the other end of the line. Straight to the point. 'Will he win the Sun Alliance Chase or not?' O'Brien laughs at the notion of giving an opinion on a race three months down the road.

Here he is in Ballydoyle, watching 1997 Classic hopefuls and feeling in charge of something wonderfully exciting. Then, one phone call, and one of his owners is putting a Cheltenham dream into words. 'There is nobody,' he says, 'who has a job like mine.'

Lunchtime at Owning, his two-year-old Joseph on his lap, *The Racing Post* beside his food, the Racing Channel on the kitchen television. Food, shelter, family and horses: the essentials of his life.

You wonder what he has got? What it is that others haven't? The horses are fit, they are well trained, there is the uphill gallop, the insistence that when they turn up at the racecourse they are ready to compete. What else is there about this horse trainer? It is a question he will not entertain. 'The things we do down here are nothing more than simple, common sense things.'

As he says this, Joe Crowley walks into the kitchen. A successful trainer before joining forces with his son-in-law, common sense comes easy to Joe. He picked things up in the old way and he reckons he's now learning a lot from the young fellow. 'But I'm learning from you,' says Aidan, 'two heads are better than one.'

Bantering away with Joe, there is a reminder of how well he relates to people. You think of something he once said of his own father. 'When I started with a few point-to-pointers at home, I could hardly get one of them fit enough to race. But my father always believed I could do this. Knowing that made some difference to me.'

The legacy is apparent in his own relationships with people. 'I am an encourager because I have always known what it meant to me. When you are encouraged, you work harder to do the right things. Don't you? If you're getting knocked down, you're going to be that bit sour all the time. And it's exactly the same with the horses.'

Tea-time at Owning. Back at the table, young Joseph again on his lap. He is talking about the jumpers. Hotel Minella could develop into a Champion Hurdle contender. That's My Man should be a serious challenger for the Supreme Novices, Gaeltollah is another good horse and you could take your pick from Theatreworld, Shaunies Lady and Magical Lady for the Triumph Hurdle.

As he speaks, young Joseph plays with tractor, trailer and horses. He is at that point in his game when the horses need to be nourished and he quietly pours some milk from his cup into the trailer. Then he dips the horse's head into the milk, until the head is completely submerged.

'Ah Joseph,' says his father, 'that's not the way a horse likes to drink.' So Dad takes one of the horses, walks it to the tractor and gently tilts the horse until its mouth touches the milk.

Encouraged by his father, young Joseph follows on with another horse. This time, doing it the right way.

44

'I'M BETTER AT CONTROLLING MY TEMPER'

BRENDAN FANNING

He may not be a captain, but a more mature Paul O'Connell is a real leader on the field.

The interview is all wrapped up and as the photographer moves in for his slice of the action, this seems like a good time to slip out the door. You know what's coming. With a bit of luck you might be in the car before he gets to the punchline and runs the risk of getting, well, punched. This reinforces the adage that it's never a good idea to work with children, animals or photographers.

I remember standing outside the changing rooms in Young Munster's ground in Derryknockane some sixteen years ago while negotiations opened on an unlikely deal. Different snapper but same dilemma. Back then the artist wanted to get the Clohessy brothers to take a shower together, which he would then capture on film. Great idea. It didn't help that the younger of the two brothers wasn't prepared to talk to us never mind get his kit off. It was a long drive home.

Now we are back in Limerick, though in the plush surroundings of the Marriott Hotel, and the window through which I had hoped to escape has just closed. 'Sure you may as well hang around,' says the snapper. 'You can hold the reflector for me.' In the circumstances, you would sooner hold a live snake.

He then launches into his sales pitch to Paul O'Connell. The idea is this: O'Connell takes off his sports top and replaces it with a white shirt – prop number one – under which would be prop number two. As he outlines the image, he starts to slide prop number two out of the brown paper bag. It is a blue T-shirt with a logo on the front, only part of which would be visible in the photo with a shirt button or two left open. You can just see the top of the 'S' on the T-shirt when O'Connell intervenes with a horrified look on his face.

'Ah Jaysus, you've got to be joking.'

* * *

The speculation started before summer was out. As Declan Kidney faced the media for the first time as Ireland coach, he was asked about the captaincy for the coming season and he said it had yet to be put to bed. From what had been billed as nothing more than a meet and greet session at the end of the first training spin of the new era, the media went away with more than a free lunch.

This was something that could sustain us in the couple of months before the coach picked his captain, and then we could turn our attention elsewhere. For the November series, Brian O'Driscoll was named as that man. It seemed that what had been put to bed would now be put to sleep.

Then it woke up with the announcement of the Six Nations squad. No sign of a captain. We went into reverse mode to pick up the threads of the story from the close of summer. Surely this was the end of the era of O'Driscoll as captain, for why else open the door on an issue that had been closed in November?

Declan Kidney explained last week that the only question had been over seeing whether or not O'Driscoll still had the appetite for doing the job. You would have thought that had been squared away in the autumn when he had been named as captain. Maybe it had and it came up again? Maybe Kidney doesn't want O'Driscoll as his captain but steered clear of it for fear of being seen to be Munsterising Ireland. Or perhaps in the way that he liked to get the best out of Munster players by making them sweat for their place, he was doing the same with O'Driscoll.

Whatever the reason, it is easy to conclude that O'Driscoll was not enamoured of the process. And equally it makes sense that despite having ditched the Leinster job last season he wasn't ready to do the same with Ireland, not least because he didn't want an horrendous World Cup and Six Nations as the last files opened on his laptop. And it is certain that some of his colleagues were surprised that the preamble didn't lead to the gig going to O'Connell. So what does O'Connell think?

'I said in an interview the other day it had never been a goal of mine to captain any team. It's something that if it's right for the team, it happens. It's something that I would like to do, sure, but I enjoy my role with Ireland at the moment and I don't speak any less or any more or do anything different – I hope, anyway – than if I was captain. I'm happy with where I am in the Irish camp. Everything Brian has brought to the team – his experience – he deserves everything I can give him now in the Six Nations. I said it was a non-issue and it really was for me.'

He is hosing down this fire before it spreads any further and you have to admire the clarity of his delivery. Genuinely he wants it all to go away. Whether you believe him or not, about the degree of his ambition, doesn't matter, for he will do as he says and he has conducted himself with dignity.

Some may have interpreted this as a blow to O'Connell's chances of leading the Lions in South Africa this summer, having been in the running behind O'Driscoll four years ago in New Zealand. It won't do him any damage at all. And if he gets it, then surely it will be a more uplifting experience than the last time.

He was home from that tour no more than a week in July 2005 when he took off to a friend's wedding in Derrynane beach, beyond Waterville. It was a lovely day and while the guests were quenching their thirst outside Bridie Keating's bar, they were treated to some theatre by some of O'Connell's buddies. One took on the role of hooker Shane Byrne, the other of O'Connell. In a re-enactment of the shambles that had been the first Test in New Zealand, when the Lions lost more lineouts than they won, the Byrne character would throw the ball far over the head of the fella playing O'Connell – who would then start remonstrating with his teammate over his crap throwing. Anybody in the congregation who didn't know Paul O'Connell before the show certainly knew who he was after it.

You show him a line from a newspaper column of a few weeks ago and ask for a reaction.

Four years ago in New Zealand, we expected O'Connell to take on a Johnson-esque role for the Lions. Instead, the Munsterman failed to be even Paul O'Connell.

'Yeah, I didn't play well down there but I don't think anyone played well down there. Even when I look back at the second Test where I gave away a silly penalty – and I think I may have dropped two kick-offs as well – apart from those few incidents, and they were really glaring incidents, I played really well.

'Donners (Donncha O'Callaghan) always slags me that I didn't enjoy that tour but I actually did. Like, I never worked so hard on my rugby in my life. You know when you're not playing well and you go out and you try and drag some bit of form out of yourself from nowhere. I found that tour tough but I enjoyed it in terms of mentally sticking there to the end and being there fighting to the end no matter what and that's certainly what I did. That's what I think I did anyway.'

The adversity appeals to him?

'Yeah, I think it does. Yeah. I suppose it's a persecution complex or something. I did enjoy it and I was playing with Donners as well in the second row for the last two Tests which was great. I find him unbelievably motivating. So we were kind of in it together, like. It was tough though, don't get me wrong. Whenever anyone asks me about things like that, no one's career is always up and up and up. There are big ups and big downs and these things happen.

'I look back on the Lions now – it's part of my career. Would I be sitting here after winning two Heineken Cups if I hadn't gone through that? I probably wouldn't be. So people say have I any regrets? I'd have regrets but I'd understand that these things happen for a reason and you learn from them and you get better and you mature and you become a better player because of them.

'I think I mellowed a lot after that tour. I got a lot of perspective and things like that – with stuff like giving out to people. Lads will probably read the article now and laugh when I'm saying this but it definitely gave me a lot of perspective in my rugby, and life and everything.'

* * *

We are almost done with the first quarter of the Munster versus Clermont European tie in Thomond Park and already there is an undercurrent. Second row Thibaut Privat is looking for afters at every get-together and he is the catalyst for a fight that kicks off a few metres from the touchline. It is close enough for us to feel the heat.

It's his Canadian buddy Jamie Cudmore who plays the lead role, however. So quick is he to get his gloves off that you'd imagine he served his time on the ice before leaving for Europe. Rapidly it develops into a one-on-one where he is going for a quick knock-out of O'Connell before the officials can step in. O'Connell has taken a couple of slaps and has looked to the touch judge who's raised his flag.

'I just assumed that would be the end of it – your man would think: "I'm going to the bin now for ten minutes," or whatever, but when I turned around he hit me another one and then I think he loaded up another one so I had to start fighting back at that stage. It was so close to the touchline that if I'd started throwing punches straight away I'd be gone on a yellow or red straight away. And I didn't want that like.

'It's a hard one because those little incidents are important psychologically for a forward pack and for yourself individually that you can't be standing for that type of thing. So while it was probably good that I didn't get sent off with him at the same time … you know, should I have been diggin' straight away? There's a happy medium there that you've got to weigh up in terms of standing up for yourself and for the pack and for the team and trying to keep your discipline to stay on the pitch. I didn't get the red but then they did dominate us in the second half. Sometimes you'd look back at little incidents like that and wonder.'

This sounds like a gunslinger questioning the wisdom of staying out of the saloon on a Saturday night. Particularly if someone is going to draw on him walking down the street minding his own business.

Post-match, Clermont coach Vern Cotter made some effort to suggest both men should have seen red but he was simply supporting his man. His heart wasn't in it. In the seconds O'Connell had to weigh up what was the best course of action, he got it absolutely right. First, he showed real discipline and then he displayed magnum force in making up the lost ground.

As a kid making his way in senior club rugby, that wasn't always the running order. He rode in on the back of his brother, Justin, who had a reputation as a good player. Physically, Paul was bigger and he brought a couple of extras in his kitbag: his years of competitive swimming added to his athleticism and the dedication he had given to golf had taught him something about drive, if not discipline.

'I still have a bad temper,' he says. 'I'm getting better at controlling it but back then, you know, I probably made a lot of mistakes. Silly things. You know the AIL and that level of rugby, you had to intimidate or be intimidated really. And growing up in Young Munster, where we traded on being hard and never taking a backward step.

'Playing for Ireland people often ask me who were my favourite players for Ireland growing up. All of my favourite players would have been Young Munster fellas. Ger Earls and Peter Meehan and Peter Claw and all those guys and the stories that went with them. They weren't better than a lot of the teams they beat, but they beat the crap out of them.'

He starts naming them off. The Gers: Clohessy, Copley, Earls; Paco Fitzgerald, Peter Meehan, Ray Ryan, Mark Fitz and Deccie Edwards.

'They were incredible, that pack. They were everything that rugby can be about. You could look at some teams that would throw the ball around and that's one way of winning rugby games, but they were sheer physicality and intimidation.'

By the time O'Connell got into the second row on the senior team, most of them had moved on. Their AIL winning team of 1993 was to have a reunion at yesterday's league fixture at home to St Mary's, now postponed. You get the impression that for all his achievements higher up the line, he would love to number himself among that group.

For consolation, though, first there was Munster and then Ireland, and in the season of his international debut as a twenty-two-year-old he was off to New Zealand on tour. You show him a picture taken from that trip and he recalls it as a carefree experience, if a trip down there can ever be anything like that.

'That's when rugby was no pressure and you'd just go out and play. And if you lost, (Anthony) Foley got the blame or Woody (Keith Wood) got the blame. Any young guy at that age playing – you just go out and make sure you enjoy it. That's one thing I find a lot now – the pressure of losing. There's a core group of us has to make sure the atmosphere is right, that our game is right during the week. Then there's other young guys who just have to get out and play. When that photo was taken that's what I was: I used to just go out and play as hard as I could.

'I remember playing in the game against the New Zealand Divisional XV and it was really enjoyable, a really relaxed game. We whupped them by fifty points, but I can imagine that Woody, who would have been captain that day, was thinking that we could be on a hiding to nothing. Maybe he'd be thinking this could be very sticky. I was going out just to try and get the ball as much as I could.'

He has a lot of nostalgia for those days but in the interim he has grown into something close to the full package. O'Connell was always quick to highlight his shortcomings on the skills front, but the amount of time Tony McGahan has put into Munster's handling has paid off for his captain more than anyone.

He has grown into the role of leader, from beating himself up initially after every defeat to toning down the criticism of others now when a ball is dropped in training. The days when Munster needed to harangue each other to develop a serious attitude are over. With two Heineken Cups in the cabinet, they're not trying to figure out how it's done.

Is he happy with his lot?

'Yeah, but I'd like to have achieved a lot more with Ireland. You know, I laugh at people who say they've no regrets when they look back, but the regrets are probably what shaped you in terms of what happened later on in your career, so at the moment while I'd like to have achieved a lot more with Ireland, I'd like to think I've a lot more time with Ireland as well. But in terms of the life it's given me it's incredible. I can't speak for anyone else but I've never once felt like I'm going to work. Even on the worst days you still feel one hundred times more alive than someone working in an office behind a desk.

'There's a very good atmosphere around the team (Ireland) at the moment and no matter what we did it was always going to be tough. But the best thing for any team morale is winning. There's no team that loses games like we did that has great team morale. I look around our place for the last few weeks – Enfield and here (Limerick) and there was a very good atmosphere and I suppose the form of some of the young guys is very exciting for a lot of us older fellas maybe. Yeah, I like the way we're going now. I liked the way we were going before the World Cup as well, so we'll see in a week's time.'

* * *

The non-runner status on the snapper's idea is confirmed as such. Negotiations open on a new front. With great reluctance, O'Connell tries on a white shirt complaining that it makes him look fat. He's right. The snapper shoots a few more frames but he's not happy with the look. This has the potential to explode. That it doesn't is probably down to O'Connell's humility. He doesn't consider himself a star and so doesn't behave like one.

A long time ago, a man who you would hope knows more about rugby than he does about media relations advised him to adopt a Death by Boredom approach to interviews, so that the journalist wouldn't come back. Mercifully, he ignored that nugget of wisdom. He seems to understand that everybody has a job to do and while it may be painful to co-operate, it's often the best policy, whatever that job may be.

In the end, the compromise is a reversion to the sports top with the hood up. When the green light comes, he springs out of the chair, free at last. As he leaves, the white shirt is left lying on the table, but he accepts the brown paper bag with prop number two folded neatly inside.

And as he shuffles off up Henry Street, you wonder how many people would have believed that Paul O'Connell was walking home with a Superman T-shirt under his arm.

45

'IF YOU'RE BOTHERED BY ME, DON'T WRITE ABOUT ME'

DION FANNING

From Tallaght to Hollywood, Robbie Keane has always divided opinion.

28 AUGUST 2011

Robbie Keane isn't the first person to arrive in Los Angeles thinking he can leave everything behind. The city was built on reinvention. Los Angeles is a place where so many go looking for the impossible. Many more arrive on the west coast fleeing impossible lives to dream it all up again.

'If you come to live in LA and don't like it,' a man said to me last week, 'go back to where you came from. You'll soon realise why you went to LA.'

Robbie Keane went to Los Angeles for many reasons. There may have been a multi-million dollar contract, although Galaxy sources suggest it is less than the $9 million reported, but there would have been millions wherever Keane went.

There was undoubtedly the lifestyle, but there was something else as well. Keane moved to Galaxy to avoid the inevitable, or at least make the inevitable feel different.

'I don't have one ounce of regret about the Premier League,' he told me last week. 'I scored over 100 Premier League goals. What more can you do? You can win the Premier League but the chances of that now are pretty slim.'

Keane could see his future in England and he didn't like it. LA Galaxy, by offering something different, offered him a chance to forget. We have all joined in the criticism of Keane and it is baffling sometimes even as we do it. He is Ireland's record goalscorer, yet he is always only one wrong move away from running straight into the posse.

When he chose Sunset Boulevard over Sven's Leicester, he was said to have given up on the challenge. There is no question that he grew weary of what was left for him in Britain and wondered what his career there had become. Three years ago, he joined a Liverpool side challenging for the title but left them six months later peripheral to that title challenge.

There would be no more title challenges in England. He faced the prospect of relegation battles, promotion possibilities or simple mediocrity. Instead, two weeks ago, he took a decision that offered change and hope.

Keane admits to very few doubts – 'When I make up my mind, I'm strong' – but the move to Liverpool, the return to Spurs and the loan moves and attempts to move him on have clearly ground him down. He left England ten days ago, no longer a target for the big clubs and simply a wage burden at Tottenham Hotspur.

Keane may have avoided the sense of painful decline, fading powers and the inevitable hurtling towards retirement by travelling to a league which will make him feel young.

He is one of Galaxy's three designated players, signings that fall outside the salary cap of MLS. He will have to assimilate in many ways, playing alongside teammates who, in some cases, will earn in a year a little more than he earns in a week.

Those who felt he was ducking out of top-level football when he agreed to join LA Galaxy ignored the restorative effect on Keane of doing something different.

'I've played in England for so long, you know,' he said, sheltering from the sun in the Home Depot Center tunnel on Wednesday. 'What do you do? Do you stay in the Premiership and just play for the sake of playing? Just to try and score a few more Premiership goals or something. It's not like I'm going to go to a team like Chelsea or Man U who are going to win something.'

This was the reality Keane faced as the summer went on and he looked for a club. He admits to being jaded with that routine and if a move to LA excites him, it's hard to see how it will damage his international career. He has played his best football under Giovanni Trapattoni, despite three years of uncertainty and injury. A reawakening in California can only help.

'He's not going to get any easy afternoons,' LA Galaxy coach Bruce Arena says. 'I don't think you're going to be disappointed with the kind of form Robbie will have with Ireland.'

Keane has entered a league of questionable quality but one of vigorous physicality which is intensely competitive.

'Listen, it's a challenge for me because the teams are quite even, you know,' he says. 'It's not as if one team is like Man United and then a Wigan, that kind of gap, without being disrespectful to them. Obviously you get two or three players who are designated players but the rest are quite even.' He will be tested in a league that wants to test itself, that asks those who arrive the same question. 'We've had a number of guys on different teams throughout the years who've come in and thought it was going to be easy, that the pace is going to be slower,' Galaxy's captain Landon Donovan says. 'They're in for a rude awakening.'

Spend a week talking to fans, reporters, players and those who work in MLS and you begin to hear the same things. They look for one thing in players because they sensed for so long that players looked for something different from them. The MLS makes it hard because some have thought it's going to be easy.

Bruce Arena recalls one of his first conversations with Keane: 'Robbie told me "I'm here to play, not to retire."'

* * *

Preview of LA Galaxy's Concacaf Champions League game in the LA Times, *25 August*: 'The Galaxy and Costa Rican champion Alajuelense are 1–0 in Champions League Group A play after home victories. A win Thursday would put the Galaxy atop the group. Parking will be free for this game.'

* * *

Tuesday morning in parking lot 6 of the California State campus in Carson City. Five adults and four children are sheltering from the sun. All the children wear Galaxy jerseys with 'Beckham 23' on them. Suddenly a group of fifty or sixty teenagers emerges as if from nowhere. They shatter the stillness with their collective noise of the carefree.

The Galaxy fans are worried. They scatter and assume defensive positions. Their niche market is under threat. They spread out as if under command. It looks as if they are protecting a set of concrete steps that seem to lead only to a basement. From these steps, their quarry will emerge.

But the schoolkids are unaware and uninterested. Their leader addresses them and they march happily away towards some other pursuit on campus in their meandering summer.

Seconds later, the most famous footballer in the world and a man who has cost more than £70 million in transfer fees climbs the steps. They belong to the nine fans and the nine alone.

Beckham spent longer posing for pictures on Thursday night than he did on his way to training on Tuesday. He was pestered as he tried to leave the Home Depot Center and he moved mechanically from one picture to the next. It was as if he was clearing his desk. This was office admin for his job of being famous.

There was only one difference on Thursday night – those who queued up for his picture had spent the last ninety minutes playing against him. The players of

Alajuelense had no professional reticence and asked Beckham to pose, which he did every time. This is the impact Galaxy expected Beckham to make; it's not what they're expecting from Keane.

'You do some things because the off the field is just as important as the on the field – and that's David,' Tom Payne, LA Galaxy's president, told me. 'David had to do the business for us on the field but also had to help drive business for us, for the league, for every club in the league. Robbie's a different case. We thought about it. I had long talks with Tim Leiweke [head of AEG] who ended up doing the deal about the business ramifications of it … Obviously we hope he helps us off the field but more importantly we need his help on the field.'

Players don't pose for pictures with Beckham in MLS any more. On Thursday, Galaxy won their Concacaf Champions League game easily. It's a competition that everyone at Galaxy concedes has yet to make an impact, but they are as quick to say that it doesn't represent football in the US.

Not many fans want to make the journey through LA rush hour to make a 7 p.m. kick-off for a competition they don't understand. The Galaxy ultras, the LA Riot Squad and the Angel City Brigade are there but, unlike Keane's debut against San Jose, the stadium isn't engaged. On nights like these, it is easy to agree with those who worry about Keane's choices. Under a beautiful sky and in a gentle breeze, he could be playing for the entertainment of billionaires in the desert. As Eduardo Galeano once wrote, 'The stadium of King Fahad in Saudi Arabia has marble and gold boxes and carpeted stands, but it has no memory or much of anything to say.'

* * *

Alexi Lalas arranges the meeting for the Hangar Bar in Manhattan Beach. 'I've met a lot of football people here,' he says. There are six men sitting at the bar drinking beer and watching two baseball games on five TVs. A short-order cook fries lunch at the end of the bar. You never took Beckham here, I suggest. 'No,' he says, 'this isn't David's kind of place.'

Lalas was general manager of the Galaxy when Beckham arrived. He describes the effect of dealing with the Beckham Corporation as a 'hurricane'. He was among those scattered when AEG decided that it wasn't working and fired Ruud Gullit, who failed to appreciate what was required during his short time as the Galaxy's coach, and Lalas, who maybe appreciated it too much.

Lalas is a missionary for MLS. He sees his own dismissal as a necessary part of the process to get Galaxy to where they are today. They might be a club known around the world because of David Beckham but they have to get ready for a time without Beckham.

Keane's signing demonstrates that the Galaxy are doing that. It has to have football merit, he argues, because it doesn't make business sense.

'In that respect, I like it,' Lalas says. 'This was done purely out of competitive reasons. A lot of decisions we made over the years balanced business and competitive. Make no mistake about it, this was a competitive decision.'

Keane has been signed to win the MLS Cup, the final of which will take place in the Galaxy's stadium. They will have to negotiate the play-offs to get there and then win a final to demonstrate that they are, as most observers agree, the strongest team in the US. 'We're expected to win championships,' Tom Payne says. 'I make the argument that our club is a bigger brand around the world than our league.'

Clive Toye, who was general manager of the New York Cosmos, says it would have made business sense for an east coast club to sign Keane. The Galaxy may have laid on corned beef and Guinness for Keane's unveiling, but there isn't the same Irish community in LA as there is in Boston or New York.

Galaxy had offers to play in Ireland during their close season before Keane's signing. His arrival might change things in one respect – 'We might ask for a little bit more,' Tom Payne says of the money on offer from the promoters who want to put on the game. But there are as many as fifteen different proposals from around the world that the Galaxy will consider. 'I don't know if we'll have the opportunity or not.'

Keane wasn't signed for that, he was signed to score goals. Bruce Arena arrived when Lalas and Gullit left. He changed the culture of the club and he made the side hard to beat. Under Gullit, they had leaked goals. Arena fixed that while Beckham continued to drive the business.

Lalas and Gullit didn't agree on much but they both knew that Beckham made business sense. For too long, David Beckham has known that he makes business sense.

The struggle to assimilate the perfect business logic of signing Beckham with the passive aggressive anarchy Beckham brings to all accepted codes of dressing-room behaviour was chronicled in Grant Wahl's book *The Beckham Experiment*. Central to the story was the tension between Landon Donovan and Beckham. Donovan would hand over the captaincy with some reluctance to Beckham. Donovan is captain again now and the player who demands most from his teammates. He's an unusual footballer ('Thank you for your time,' he said to me at the end of our interview) and one who understands what's required.

'I love playing here, I love being a part of this,' he says. 'I don't think people give it enough credit. I'm a realist and I know we're not anywhere near the Premier League or La Liga or the Bundesliga, but it's a league that's growing. I promise you, ask Robbie in a couple of months and he's going to have high praise for it.'

Donovan says it will require hard work to succeed in America. 'To be honest, it's often times harder to play here. Not from a quality standpoint, but the games are harder sometimes. You don't necessarily get the same service you'd get in the Premier League, you don't have the same talented players around you. Robbie playing in the Tottenham side doesn't have to do a whole lot. He just has to get in front of the goal and hit the target. Here he has to do more, he has to help out, he has to defend, he has to help us move the ball. It's not as easy as people think and often times it's more difficult.'

Keane, through his trademark displays of encouragement and a goal on his debut, has overcome any initial problems. Arena and Donovan both praised his work ethic and honesty last week.

'There have been instances, not in our franchise but in other teams, where people have come in and haven't taken it seriously and they've failed,' Tom Payne says. 'One thing about this league, and sports over here, is that there are athletes. If you're not here ready to work, you won't make it. It doesn't matter how good you are.'

* * *

On his first day, the Galaxy staff asked Keane was there anything he needed at the training ground. He wanted one thing: a kettle.

Now there is a kettle at the Galaxy complex as well as PG Tips and Barry's Tea. Galaxy are going to be asking Keane for a lot more. He seems ready for the challenge.

'Robbie, we've got a meeting in two minutes.' Landon Donovan sprints past the new signing, who is leaning against the tunnel wall at the Home Depot Center, talking about the week he's had. Donovan offers a reminder of the quality that can be glimpsed in the MLS and of the changing face of football in America.

There was a time when it was a very different game. MLS was a 'Wild West' when Lalas came back to play – under Frank Stapleton – at the New England Revolution, but before that there was NASL.[1] Clive Toye was the man who signed Pelé for the New York Cosmos. He compares the approach of the two.

---

1 The North American Soccer League was the forerunner to the MLS. In the 1970s it attracted big names like Pelé, George Best, Franz Beckenbauer and Johan Cruyff to play in it, but went out of business in the early 1980s.

'The NASL was akin to getting on the wagon train and hoping we could build a nation,' he says. 'The MLS is akin to getting on a plane and complaining if it's a bit late.' Toye says Pelé was the man 'who made so much possible'. When asked via email about Beckham, he replies, 'Who? Oh the chap who turns out for LA sometimes when he isn't off making personal appearances.'

Beckham has played twenty times for Galaxy this season, but few could deny Toye's essential point. Galaxy once needed Beckham more than he needed them.

Keane will have to prove himself on both sides of the Atlantic. Everyone I spoke to dismissed the concerns about travelling, pointing out that Americans, north and south, do similar journeys all the time.

If anyone will be worried about jetlag at the moment it will be Galaxy. Keane misses a game against Kansas next Monday as he'll be in Moscow with Ireland, and the club are trying to get him straight back from Russia so he's fresh for their home game against Colorado three days later.

The football world Keane enters is different from anything he has known and that's what he wants. He has a few friends playing for the New York Bulls and they told him to expect a physical challenge.

Keane gives the sense that nothing excited him about playing in England any more.

'Sometimes you need different things in life, you need different challenges that will give you that little boost. To be going through the same routine again in England that I've done since I was seventeen, it was repetitive stuff for me. This is all new. It's a great place to live. Great town, great team.

'It's not the Premiership, of course it's not – what is? The Premiership is the best league in the world but you've got people like Beckham and Landon Donovan, who could play in the Premiership. (Thierry) Henry came over, although maybe he was a bit older than me. I think David was the same age, maybe a year older than me. It's a thing that's growing and I want to be a part of that.'

There was nothing he wanted to be a part of in England. 'I'd have been going to a team that maybe would be top ten or mid-table or something like that. I was in the Premiership a long time and it just came at a good time for me. I had one year left on my contract at Spurs. I wouldn't want to come here when I was thirty-four, thirty-five, when I was kind of finished. I still have a lot to offer. I could have stayed in the Premiership but I've got a lot to offer. I want people to say, "He's done really well over here", rather than, "He's at the end of his career. He's thirty-four and his legs have gone."'

He has no plans to quit international football. 'I'm committed to Ireland, which

I've always been. You know that, I always have been since I've been seventeen. I don't pull out of games for the sake of pulling out, unless I'm out of a game with a genuine injury. For me, it's more or less the same. I'll play for the club and if we've got an international game I'll go back for it. For me, it's as simple as that unless somebody tells me otherwise.'

Keane knows that even on the new frontier, there are old truths. Above all else, no matter what he does, he will be criticised. He knows what has been written about the move.

'I've been aware of a few little things. One or two people writing about it but ten people saying different things so it's not really ... I've been playing since I was seventeen,' he shrugs his shoulders and wonders if he can say what he really thinks. 'It's just like, I don't really ... to be honest ... I don't really care.'

Does he ever ask himself why he gets the flak? He shrugs again, then he stretches his arms out wide, his palms in the air, almost as if he has reached the point in one of his longer goal celebrations when he stands to accept the acclaim. He is signifying apathy but doing it with grand gestures. 'It doesn't really bother me, that's being totally honest with you. As long as I keep scoring for Ireland, that's the most important thing.'

He smiles. There are no doubts right now. Landon Donovan wants him in a meeting and then there is another day of LA sun, promising a land forever young. There is eternity here and the critics aren't among the chosen.

'As I said, if they're that worried about it and I'm not interested ... If they're that bothered by me, then don't write about me. Simple.'

Right now it's simple and new in California. He will face more questions and he will be tested physically in a league that may lack many things, but not the intensity of its examination. At this moment it all makes sense. But Keane soon will face the setting sun and that can never be eluded.

No matter what Los Angeles tells him about reinvention and endless youth, he can't avoid the truth that the sun always sets in the west.

THE BACK YARD

Everyone always tells me off for interviewing stars – why don't I interview 'real' people?

THE SECRET GEORGE BEST

EAMON DUNPHY

Once George Best's intelligence was applied to football. Now his mind is redundant.

9 DECEMBER 1990

We were to meet in a pub in Mayfair. He was late, but I knew he'd come this time. Mary had promised. You're a friend, she'd told me; he won't let you down. Don't worry, I told her … letting me down isn't the issue. Is he okay? That's the issue.

Mary loves George Best. They've been together since 1987. That year she came back to London from Beirut, where she'd known personal tragedy of her own. She's an attractive woman who must have been beautiful once. She's beautiful now in a different kind of way … the way people who care, who sacrifice to care, are beautiful. A certain light shines in their eyes … the light of love.

Mary cares for George. She nurses him, does his business deals, tries to make sure that no more bastards steal his money.

Waiting for him, we talk. The early afternoon winter sunshine casts a melancholy light on the bar, which is now shedding its lunchtime customers. Since his recent appearance on *Wogan* George is back in the news. He was drunk. He used bad language. The newspapers wrote of his shame. The watching world shook its head. Tut, Tut. Bad Boy George Sins Again.

George has an image problem. He has always had an image problem. Girls and booze. Oh yes, a great footballer, but wild, crazy, unreliable. Sages nod their heads, football's Sensible Tendency tell us, more in sorrow than in anger, that they understand George. His problem is that he couldn't handle fame. He had too much money, too much of everything desirable in this world. He was indulged by Matt Busby and thus ruined by the evils of our age: drink, sex, money, fame. Now he's paying the inevitable price. That's the image, the impression. The truth is a different matter.

The whole truth, the reason why George is now fighting for his life, has to do with football, with the nature of a great footballer's short life and how a man like George, consumed by a passion for playing, must adjust to another life when the glorious day of youth has passed.

The unfolding tragedy of George Best's life is part of the Manchester United story. In a book to be published next year I hope to tell the story in full. For now all one can do is write about the consequences, the George Best I spent a couple of days with in London this week.

Mary talks of the man behind the notorious image. He is easily bored. He reads books late into the night. Watches television quiz shows – the better ones, like *Mastermind* – and sport. He'll go to bed at one o'clock and wake up at five. Restless. He's always been restless. The image suggests a playboy.

The truth is that George is highly intelligent, always has been. Once that intelligence was applied to football. Now his mind is redundant, his spirit too. People don't understand that when your legs pack up, when you are too old to play any more, all the other faculties that made you great still function: your mind, your soul. Your legs didn't make the difference. Your body withers, your spirit remains alive. Redundant. But alive, and if football means as much to you as it did to George Best, the sense of being disabled is painful, cruel … ever-present.

Lester Piggott and Muhammad Ali belong to the same exclusive club as George. Ali took the extra fights that left him maimed for life. He couldn't stay away from the gym, there was no other life, no other game, no other means of self-expression. Lester Piggott's return to race-riding was ostensibly for money, but anyone who saw the smile on this great man's face after Royal Academy won the Breeders' Cup saw happiness defined. There was more than money at stake. Lester's was the smile of a child on Christmas morning, the smile of innocence, delight, contentment.

Contentment is what George Best will never have again. Hence the restlessness, the long dark lonely night of a spirit denied self-expression. Booze is an anaesthetic, girls a distraction.

The phone rings in the pub. The call is for Mary. George is on his way. He's just stopped for a quick drink, consumed anonymously in some crowded bar across town.

'Hell is other people,' Sartre wrote. Hell for George is facing another day of fame, another hazy day of notoriety. After the first couple of drinks the senses are dulled, he can cope with the boredom, forget the vibrant genius he used to be – the beautiful ghost that haunts him – and come to terms with his other self, the old footballer who is now merely famous.

To those who saw him on *Wogan*, George is famous for being drunk, for the girls and the goals he scores on old videos. He is a celebrity. These days that's his job. On working days he travels around Britain earning up to £1,000 a night speaking at sportsmen's dinners. Diners pay £20 a head to see notoriety in the flesh, to hear about the great games, to ask questions about the actresses, beauty queens and models he has known. George obliges. Not the real George. The *Wogan* George.

On non-working days like last Tuesday the real George goes to the pub. He arrives, slipping quietly in the door, moving quickly, head down, to his favourite corner seat. The handshake is strong, warm, the affection real. He is heavy now, the once sallow skin pale, the beard covering most of his face.

I remember him at fifteen: slim, dark, graceful and shy. He's still shy … and gentle … the boy still visible behind the swollen body and greying hair and beard. Mary thinks – and hopes – he's mellowing. She prays that the fires of youth will cool, that the restlessness will cease, that he will be peaceful. Stop killing himself … stop grieving for the game he once played … played as no one ever did before or ever will again.

George laughs at the notion of grief. We open a bottle of champagne, the first of many we will consume this afternoon. George is a quiet drinker. This is not a hell-raising scene. Just a way of passing time. This pub is a safe place. The landlord is Irish, protective of his celebrated customer. As the day passes, we talk about things of little consequence … old times, old friends, funny things that happen to the other George Best – the celebrity – in taxis and pubs and on the after-dinner circuit.

George understands what has happened to him. Much of it has to do with the difference between Ireland and England … between *Wogan* and *The Late Late Show* … between Terry Wogan and Gay Byrne. Between good and bad, decency and indecency, a concern for the man and a desire to exploit him. The shame of George's *Wogan* appearance was to some extent mitigated by his recent spot on *The Late Late*.

Television is for glib men, not for George. Wogan is quintessentially glib, ten minutes of idle chatter. Gay Byrne was different, more sensitive, more discerning of the real George, allowing time for a conversation. Showing some respect.

'Words,' George smiles ruefully. He's no good with words. He is inarticulate. That is a crime in the television age. If you can't spiel you're dead. After *Wogan* his father, Dick, phoned him to ask what the hell he was at. After *The Late Late* his dad rang again to say he'd been proud of him.

His father's approval means everything to him. He is still a boy, a great sportsman, but a boy who remains sensitive, decent, vulnerable. That Gay Byrne enabled some sense of this to be conveyed mattered. To George and his father. And to Mary.

A friend of theirs came into the pub late in the afternoon. The sun had set, twilight bringing the early evening drinkers in from offices and shops. Mary's girlfriend had been Christmas shopping. She'd bought a copy of the BBC's *Mastermind* book. George opened it at the General Knowledge section. We had a quiz.

Who invented the bouncing bomb?

Barnes Wallis.

Who succeeded Khruschev at the Kremlin?

Brezhnev and Kosygin.

Who shot Lee Harvey Oswald?

Jack Ruby.

We had great fun for an hour or so. George was incredible. He won the quiz hands down. All the above answers are his. Mr Thinking Footballer here was well and truly exposed.

'Words,' George smiled.

You bastard, I replied. Why do you hide behind the playboy mask? Why don't you let them know you as you really are?

Why not learn to play the game ... be a Trevor Brooking, a Bob Wilson, a Jimmy Hill? Why pretend to be just another lush, pretend so convincingly that even I was fooled? He ordered another bottle. And opened the book again at the section containing some sample questions from the Mensa Test. There were four questions. He answered three. When he went to prison for some drunken indiscretion they'd given him a list of sixty questions, to assess his intelligence. He'd answered them all. The secret George Best.

No wonder he can't sleep.

There's too much happening; his spirit is, as it's always been, alive; he has more intelligence and imagination than he can dispose of. He is inarticulate. Football was the way he articulated, giving magnificent expression to the precious gifts of mind and spirit he possesses.

Football was the source of respect ... his self-respect and other people's. Football made him proud, allowed him to be himself. Up to a point, the point where the great club he belonged to began to disintegrate and he began to self-destruct in despair.

Others, like Bobby Charlton and Denis Law, survived, adjusted, learned to cope with the real world, where words, however banal, will suffice. They had wives and children, mortgages on homes to which they retreated when the game was over. But George was wedded to the game, fatally, like Piggott and Ali.

One of the Mensa questions we tackled the other day was poignantly relevant: reduce (. . . .) agreement, fill in the missing word which means the same as the ones either side of the brackets.

I couldn't. George answered: contract.

The George Best of common currency has frequently been reduced these past few years. The contract he was unable to enter was between the footballer and the man. In his case such a coming to terms, such an agreement, was impossible; the footballer was the man, beautiful, courageous, inspiring. The stage was the world. The world of words and deals, glib assertions, lies and banal celebrity was a problem he was ill-equipped to deal with. No poet could deal with Wogan.

The image in which George is imprisoned is pathetic. The reality I glimpsed this week was strangely comforting. Sitting at the bar all afternoon was another great old sportsman who offered hope: that you could be a free spirit, take your drink and play life's game to your own set of rules and survive to mellow old age.

Denis Compton was to cricket what George was to football, a genius fond of life's distractions. George sent Denis a drink which was soon returned. They raised their glasses to each other, exchanging knowing looks, a silent toast that only they would understand completely.

Compton joined us for a while before moving off into the night. The old cricketer's contempt for the modern version of the sport he once graced – the doctored wickets, the helmeted heroes, the banal clamour of the hospitality tent – was an echo of George's view of contemporary soccer and its heroes. To hear them talk thus was sad. To know they were right even sadder. Their respect for each other, though unspoken, was clear. As precious to one as the other. Poets in a prosaic world.

Privately George is alive and well for much of the time. The days and nights are a battle, boredom the enemy. He must trade on his notoriety, do *Wogan* and the sportsmen's dinners, recount his dalliances with empty beauty queens, be George Best as the world understands him to be. That's what people want. That's what he delivers. And every time he does it he squanders some respect, self-respect, the kind that really matters.

Pleasure, a measure of fulfilment, is an afternoon passed quietly in a pub showing off to friends, being Mastermind – *himself* – for an hour or two.

I went back to my hotel. He went off with Mary to get some fish and chips and a reasonably early night. This week he is going to a health farm to dry out. The battle continues … to be understood and respected for what he is as much as for what he was … to survive and try to play the game on the world's terms rather than his own. To reach a measure of agreement between what he is and what we will pay him money to be. If he does that he will survive. If he fails he will die. Of boredom rather than drink.

47

IN SEARCH OF THE REAL GIOVANNI TRAPATTONI

DION FANNING

Cusano Milanino is the furnace that forged the Ireland manager, and the working-class hero stays close to his roots.

The crowd had gathered in the town square on a Monday night. It was late summer, the last days of the holidays, and the children were restless, convinced, as always, that there was something better to do, someplace else they could be. With the return to school now a real and present danger, these feelings were getting urgent.

In the main square of Tipperary town on a drizzly August evening, there was unlikely to be anything to do and the parents knew this. They resisted as the children pulled on their arms, as they wanted to pay attention when the man with the silver hair ended the night by getting up to address the crowd.

Then, even the children seemed to fall silent when Giovanni Trapattoni stepped to the microphone and began to cry.

They had put on a civic reception in Tipperary when they heard that the Ireland team were coming to stay nearby. It was the kind of ceremony that comes naturally to towns across Ireland. The dignitaries were gathered on the back of a truck to listen to speeches and music. It could have been a slightly less than ordinary night in a midlands town but Trapattoni, as he has done so often, transformed the humdrum into something memorable.

He saw something in the three or four thousand people standing before him that evening that he has been able to see all his life. He saw himself and he saw possibility.

The mayor made a speech welcoming Trapattoni to Tipperary and welcoming John Delaney home. She read out Trapattoni's achievements in football. It took some time. And when the CJ Kickham Brass & Reed band played the Italian anthem,

Trapattoni was moved, sitting down when it was over and grabbing Delaney's arm. He later told the crowd that he was emotional because it was the first time he had heard his anthem on foreign soil outside a football ground in fifty years.

Wherever he goes in Ireland, Trapattoni reminds the audience of where he came from. It is not a hack act because he still calls it home, still worships at the local church and eats at the restaurant off the main square in the town where he was born.

Any examination of Trapattoni's life reveals a simple but profound truth. Few football men in the modern era have held such a unity of purpose between their philosophy of life and their philosophy of football management. For Trapattoni, the worker has always been king.

As a willing traveller to all corners of Ireland, Trapattoni always remarks that he was once a boy who was visited by the 'famous', who would make him think of a world beyond his small town, but one which would not have been possible without it.

When he stood up to speak last August, Trapattoni thanked the people for their welcome, looked out over the main square of Tipperary town and said to them: 'I grew up in a town just like this.'

* * *

Cusano Milanino is a town that Giovanni Trapattoni has never forgotten because he has never left it. He was born on Via 24 Maggio, a small side street. He now lives in a villa less than half a mile away.

Last Wednesday evening, I arrived in Cusano Milanino and it wasn't hard to find people to talk about Giovanni Trapattoni. There was no reluctance to open up to an Irish journalist. Italy may be a football and fashion sophisticate but it is a provincial country too. My friend Francesco, who was acting as translator, pointed out that 'everybody is proud that a foreign journalist is coming to talk about a man they love'.

In the main square, we approached two men who pointed out the Trapattoni landmarks and directed us to I Vini di Mariu's, Trap's local restaurant. Ask for Mariu, they told us, he can help you. It was just before 7 p.m., too early for anyone to be eating, but a man stood behind the counter, his back ramrod straight. He looked a bit like Roger Moore.

We asked if he was Mariu and he said no.

Francesco explained who we were and what we had come for. The man began to talk. He knew Trapattoni well, he came to his restaurant often. He was a great customer and a great man, humble, and proud of Cusano Milanino. This was good stuff, but we felt we should talk to Mariu, who, according to the men in the square, knew Trapattoni even better.

'Would it be possible to talk to Mariu?'

'I am Mariu.'

'You just said you weren't Mariu.'

'I thought you were trying to sell me something.'

Soon we were joined by Pino, one of the men from the square, who wandered in to check on the action. Mariu directed us to a wall with pictures of Trap everywhere. There was also a bottle of wine with his face on the label. Beside it, Mariu had a bottle with Mussolini's image on it. I pointed this out.

'Guys, if this bothers you,' Mariu said, 'I really couldn't care less.'

Mariu really couldn't care less. As he hunted for photographs, Mariu pulled out an Italian flag, but one from Mussolini's time with an eagle across the front of the tricolour. He laughed again, not caring less.

Mariu knows Trapattoni's story and the story of Cusano Milanino. The town is divided by a main road with Cusano historically being on one side and Milanino on the other. Cusano was the original town where workers and farmers lived. Trapattoni's parents moved from Bergamo to find work and they lived on this side of town when his father found work in the Gerli wool-dying factory.

Milanino was built at the beginning of the twentieth century, a paradise for the upper-middle classes outside Milan on the other side of the street from Cusano. Trapattoni may live across the street now, but he is most comfortable with those who understood where he came from and where they came from too.

He grew up playing football with Cusano boys, not seeing in football a way, as others had, to escape, but to implement what he believed in. He has talked to Mariu about the tales of his career, of marking Pelé. 'Pelé didn't want to play the second half against Trapattoni,' Mariu says, 'because Trapattoni was like a jellyfish and he wouldn't let him go.'

In Italy, Trapattoni is loved, but it is not just in Ireland that they have difficulty understanding him. When speaking Italian, he would sometimes revert to Milanese dialect, which would make him hard to understand, especially for those from the south. His phrases became part of football culture in the country.

'*Se la và, la g'ha i gamb,*' was Trap's favourite – 'If it goes, it's got legs,' suggesting a fondness for the end rather than the means. His malapropisms were famous too.

There is an Italian saying '*Non dire quattro se non ce l'hai nel sacco.*' It comes from the fields, where they would collect grain in bags of four and means, 'Don't say four unless you've got it in the bag.' When Trapattoni uttered it, he said '*gatto*' instead of '*quattro*', 'cat' instead of 'four' and now 'Don't say cat until you've got it in the bag' has become part of the lexicon, although it has no meaning.

When he talks about Ireland to Mariu, he talks about how well he has been treated. He took the delegation from the FAI to eat in the restaurant, introducing them to Mariu and his favourite wine, Caipizze.

Mariu got to know Trapattoni when he was managing Juventus, and when he was Italian manager Trapattoni would spend more time in his home in Cusano Milanino and often invite Mariu to his house for the traditional Italian aperitif at 6 p.m. Mariu would bring the wine and they would talk. What does Trap talk about? 'He always talks about football.'

On the wall beside the wine with Trap's face on it, there are plenty more pictures. Pino points out one with Lothar Matthäus, Andreas Brehme and Nicola Berti from the Internazionale team that won Serie A in 1989 with Trapattoni as manager.

One evening Trap brought the players to Mariu's. The boys from Cusano Milanino came to the restaurant to see the famous players and have their picture taken. Pino's son Fabio was seven and was one of the boys who had their picture taken.

'Trapattoni has an incredible memory,' Pino says. 'The other day he met my son at the bar and he said, "You are Fabio, Pino's son. I remember you having your picture taken with the team in '89, sitting on Matthäus's lap."'

The men are relaxed now, talking politics and football. Francesco works for a radio station in Milan and Mariu tells him that he likes the music they play, but they are a little left-wing.

Mariu expresses more private views, which again are not necessarily those of Trapattoni, stating that with the players Trapattoni has, what he has achieved with Ireland is a 'miracle'.

There may be more miracles to come.

* * *

Before the draw for the play-offs, Trapattoni walked into the Reeg Caffè in Cinisello Balsamo and told his friend Raffaello, who runs the bar, that Ireland would be drawn against France or Portugal, but he was almost certain it would be France. Trap wasn't happy about it. 'You will see,' he told Raffaello, 'we will get France.'

Raffaello's bar is not the kind of place, as Raffaello himself points out, where you would find Fabio Capello or Marcello Lippi hanging out. On the night we went in, there were four men in there, one wedded to the slot machine, the others wedded to the other familiar consolations of Raffaello's bar. These are ordinary men, poor ould fellas, and Trapattoni often sits among them in this working-class place, talking about one thing: football.

Cinisello Balsamo is the industrial heartland that rebuilt Italy after the war. It is three kilometres from Cusano Milanino and it is here that Trapattoni famously has an office in the garage of his friend Pasquale Piccolo.

There used to be three great employers in Cinisello Balsamo – Falck, Ansaldo and Breda – and at their peak they employed 120,000 workers in their iron works as Italy was rebuilt after the war. Before that, trams and trains were built in this area, giving the poor families who came north from Southern Italy work and dignity. There was then, as there is now, a Milanese philosophy that is embodied in Trapattoni, a belief that only through hard work can you succeed.

Cinisello Balsamo used to be known as Italy's Stalingrad, as the communist party drew support from these workers. Now it is a different place. The industries have gone and so have many of the young, but the older men remain, spending their days in places like Raffaello's.

Raffaello isn't eager to talk at first. This is a private sanctuary for Trap, he says. He likes to come in here and when he sits down, he talks with Raffaello about tactics and individual players. We mention a couple of Irish players and Raffaello smiles. He knows them, knows Trapattoni's views and he says a few things that make it clear he knows about Ireland, although he never gives too much away.

The traditional aperitif is Campari and sparkling wine (it is known as the bicycle because you get two drinks – two wheels) but that is too much for Trap, who will usually have a Campari with bitter orange and talk football, always football, with Raffaello.

Raffaello is a Juventus fan, which makes it even easier to talk to Trap, but it would never be difficult. 'He will talk to anybody who comes in here and he treats everybody with respect.' Raffaello goes to a backroom and he returns carrying a Juventus wallet. In it is an English £5 note autographed by Trapattoni, a gift to Raffaello's daughter. 'He hasn't changed all the time I have known him. He is strong and principled and devoted.'

* * *

Every week a package arrives at Pasquale Piccolo's Autobatti's garage across the road from Raffaello's. It contains DVDs from the weekend's matches in England and Trapattoni will collect them and take them to an office upstairs to watch them. He was here, too, the day of the play-off draw and was, according to Claudio, one mechanic working in the garage, 'depressed for half a day' after he knew Ireland would be playing France.

There are lots of garages in Cinisello Balsamo – the main drag in the industrial quarter, Via Lincoln, has at least twenty – but it is easy to know you are in the right place. On the desk in the office beside the workshop there is an FAI media guide, and a pennant from an Ireland game hangs from the wall.

He has used this place as a retreat for longer than that. 'He is at home here; after difficult moments he can get some tranquillity here,' Claudio says.

The FAI came here, Claudio says, to sign the contracts and it is here that Trap conducts interviews as well as watching DVDs.

'He has the same passion now as when he was managing Juventus, Internazionale or the Italian team,' Claudio says.

They have seen him through all these times in this garage, the elimination from World Cups and European Championships when Italy looked for answers and scapegoats.

These people, his friends, sheltered him through those storms. Sometimes they look at him and wonder if he will take it easy, unwind, but they know the answer, know that the melancholy from a bad result or a bad draw will quickly be replaced by enthusiasm.

'His friends would love to see him a bit calmer but it is impossible,' Claudio laughs.

They know now that he will not change. He is stubborn and passionate, loyal and committed to this area and to the philosophy he learned here.

'When he was young he wasn't a super-talented footballer, so to get where he was he had to work a lot,' says Claudio. 'He worked hard when he was a kid and he has passed on that philosophy to his children.'

If Alex Ferguson learned about loyalty in Govan, Trapattoni discovered the principles of his life in the hearts of these men. 'After the war here, it was very hard and that is the world he grew up in.'

'He will always have passion, that is why people love him,' Claudio says. 'For people to love you, you have to give.'

* * *

As he travels around Ireland, Trapattoni hasn't stopped giving. There is one more gift he would like to present to the people: if Ireland qualify for the World Cup, he will again have proved that his philosophy is timeless.

On the wall of Mariu's, one newspaper cutting has edged in among the pictures.

It is a story from a November 2000 edition of *Corriere della Sera* when Trapattoni was Italy manager. 'How does one become a Trap?' the headline asks. The answer is there, too: 'Work, work and never give up.'

Trapattoni knew the answer long ago and in Cusano Milanino they wouldn't even see the point in asking the question.

48

'WE'RE NOT IN THE BUSINESS OF RUINING PEOPLE'S LIVES'

PAUL KIMMAGE

What doesn't make it into print can be at least as interesting as what does.

Kieren Fallon has left The Westbury and has almost reached Grafton Street when I spot him coming towards me. He pauses and looks at me curiously, his mind working overtime.

This guy knows me.

'I hope you're going back,' I smile, nodding towards the hotel. 'I'm supposed to be interviewing you in five minutes.'

'Yeah, yeah. I just popped out to get some cash,' he replies.

He turns around and leads me back to the hotel and a table in the dining room that would be fine for old friends catching up for a chat. But we're not old friends, and this isn't a chat.

Should I ask about the room? (I'd been assured a room had been booked for the interview.) Perhaps not, he seems fidgety and unsure.

A waiter arrives and we order coffee (me) and sparkling water (him). Two couples are gabbing loudly in the corner and together with the piped music it's a struggle to fix his voice.

I place a copy of *Form*, his just-published autobiography, on the table and tap the photograph on the cover: 'They've added a bit of blue to your eyes?'

'Yeah, I hate having my picture taken,' he replies. 'I hate the camera. I hate interviews.'

This is a story about some of the people who made my year, and the ones who got away.

1 RORY REDUX

Then there's the story of the lunch, which spread throughout the Naval Special Welfare community. Guys still tell it, almost a decade later: Tiger and a group of five or six went to dinner in La Posta. The waitress brought the check and the table went silent, according to two people there that day. Nobody said anything and neither did Tiger, and the other guys sort of looked at one another.

Finally one of the SEALs said, 'Separate checks, please.'

The waitress walked away.

'We were all baffled,' says one SEAL, a veteran of numerous combat deployments. 'We are sitting there with Tiger f—ing Woods, who probably makes more than all of us combined in a day. He's shooting our ammo, taking our time. He's a weird f—ing guy. That's weird s—. Something's wrong with you.'

Wright Thompson,
The Secret History of Tiger Woods

When a friend invites you to dinner with Rory McIlroy, and there are wives and girlfriends involved, work is off the menu. So there was no talking about golf that night, or the state of Rory's game. The venue was a fish restaurant in the Algarve in August 2016, and after five years of watching in wonder from afar, I was in a holding pattern above Planet Rory, hoping for permission to land.

Then the phone rang.

'He's coming.'

What!

'Bring Ann.'

What!

'No golf talk.'

What!

'He's on holiday.'

The first thing that struck me was how comfortable he was conversing about stuff – current affairs, education, tourism, politics – my wife loves. ('He's not at all like I expected.') And I spent the evening mostly observing until he mentioned a piece that had just been published about Tiger Woods.

'The Wright Thompson piece?'

'Yeah,' he replied.

'You read that?'

'Yeah.'

Now that was impressive.

Four months later, on an icy December morning a week before Christmas, everything was on the menu when he agreed to an interview during a brief visit to Dublin. 'The Essential Rory' ran for two weeks in January and was more than 15,000 words. But there was some stuff that got left out.

PK: Tell me about Conor McGregor. You've met him, obviously, and been to a couple of fights. A lot of people say: 'It's not a proper sport.'

RM: I've always been a fight fan. I've always been a boxing fan. MMA (Mixed Martial Arts) probably took me a while to get into and it's not nice to watch people taking knees to the head. But the more you watch it, the more you become desensitised, I guess. And they work hard – Jesus! I mean, imagine putting yourself through that stuff. You're in a cage and not getting out until you've either knocked the other guy out, or been knocked out. So it's brutal. I mean five five-minute rounds! Do you know how tough that is?

PK: Sure.

RM: So I've a lot of respect for them, and as brash as Conor is in his public persona, he's a great lad when you actually sit down with him. And we got on really well. It's a great story – this is a young guy from Crumlin who was a trainee plumber four years ago. And he has definitely captured the imagination. I mean, who would watch UFC, especially in this country, if it wasn't for him?

PK: We wouldn't know anything about it.

RM: No, and that's why when he talks about wanting a slice of the company ... yes, it's all a bit of a show but at the same time you're like: 'He's on to something there.'

PK: When did you first meet him?

RM: After his second fight against Diaz in Vegas – I sat and had a chat with him at the after-party and he couldn't have been nicer. And (his partner) Dee couldn't have been nicer. I wouldn't be comfortable doing what he does in terms of his persona but that's an act of sorts. He's got another three or four years at this and has to make the most of it while he can, and I think that's a thing that people need to understand.

Five months later, as Rory wrestled with a back injury that would compromise his year, Wright Thompson was making plans to travel to Dublin for a piece on McGregor. 'Crossing Crumlin Road', published in August, would be one of the most talked-about features of the year.

2 'THAT'S A PROMISE'

Nobody is forced to give an interview: I don't doorstep anyone or pester them; I put in a request and accept the answer, yes or no. Moreover, the people I interview are not novices. They know the media game and have usually benefited from it for most of their careers. They don't give interviews out of the kindness of their hearts – they are usually trying to plug whatever new film or book or record they are launching. The wisest among them count the column inches and recognise that four pages in a national newspaper is certainly big publicity, whether favourable or not.

Lynn Barber,
Demon Barber

Three decades ago, before the Internet and smartphones, when newspapers were king, whenever you told someone you worked for a Sunday paper the response was invariably: 'What do you do the other six days of the week?' But there's more to this business than meets the eye.

Take X.

A national icon and veteran of the media game, he was a great subject for 'The Big Interview', so I called him a year ago and sent a text when he didn't pick up: 'Hi X, have just left a message. Was hoping you might sit down with me to talk about your life.' I called again an hour later and eventually managed to track him down. 'I'll do it,' he said, 'but not now. Come back to me in the summer.'

Six months later, on 6 May to be precise, I spent three days reading his autobiography and making notes before phoning and sending a text: 'X, "come back to me in the summer", you said. It's the summer. And I know you're a man of your word. Would Wednesday or Thursday work?'

He replied two hours later: 'Paul, apologies for the delay. Yes, I will do the interview but I'm tied up until July. I'll have plenty of time to sit down with you then, if that's okay?'

'That's fine, X,' I said. 'See you in July.'

'Perfect,' he said. 'That's a promise.'

July was two months later. I phoned and left a message, then sent a text. 'X, have tried calling several times. Could you give me a suitable time/place/date please? Or if you don't want to do it at least let me know.'

He did not respond.

3 THE BEST OF JAYO

Canavan scored a class goal on the stroke of half-time from a Mulligan knock-down, then Harte took him off for a breather before sending him on again to close the deal. More evidence of how they were rethinking the game. Improvising. Setting different standards. We ended up chasing the game, and in the dying seconds Canavan pulled me down with a virtual rugby tackle as I sprinted to take a return pass. Their best player doing whatever it took. Not giving a shit what anyone might say on that evening's Sunday Game. *He'd been blackguarded himself enough across the years, so could you really blame him?*

Colm Cooper,

Gooch

The biggest interview I've ever done was with Floyd Landis, the disgraced former Tour de France winner, in November 2011. It took a week to transcribe, ten days to write and five years of being chased through a Swiss court. No two interviews are ever the same, but the big hits these days are a bit more manageable – three days to transcribe, five days to write and (hopefully) no summons from the 'wigs'.

John Kavanagh was a big hit.

We spent a morning together in October 2016 and covered every aspect of his life from childhood bullies, his affection for tarantulas and wrestling with Kieran McGeeney, to his nurturing of Conor McGregor and life in the fast lane with Ronaldo and J-Lo.

It was one of my favourite interviews of the year, but you can't please everyone and within an hour of it going online I was getting abuse from a guy on Twitter who clearly wasn't a fan.

To summarise:

'You didn't ask Kavanagh about doping in MMA?'

'I did ask him.'

'You didn't.'

'I did.'

'You didn't. I've read the piece again.'

'I asked him. I chose to leave it out.'

And so it was with Jason Sherlock.

His autobiography, *Jayo*, was about to hit the shelves, but our shot at securing an interview had been complicated by a column ('Is winning all that matters?') I'd written about Jim Gavin and his post-All-Ireland press conference. Sherlock was an integral part of the Dublin coaching team. Jim was his friend.

I sent him a note, expecting the worst: 'If you're under pressure, I'll understand.'

He sent a reply reflecting his best: 'I'd be happy to do it.'

We met a week later at a Dublin hotel – private room, no noise – and spent a fascinating afternoon reflecting on his complicated childhood and remarkable life. But that wasn't enough for the assholes on Twitter:

'Can't believe Jayo gave that wanker an interview!'

'Why didn't he challenge him on his views?'

But what if he did?

PK: I asked Jim at the press conference: 'Is winning the only thing?'

JS: Well, I wasn't at the press conference.

PK: I know that.

JS: So are you asking what I think?

PK: I'm interested.

JS: I think there are examples of winning at all costs in other sports but I don't think you could associate that with Dublin in terms of what they've done over the last three years.

PK: There's a line you use about Jim in the book: 'He holds true to our values and culture.' What about the last minute of the All-Ireland this year? Where does that fit with winning the right way?

JS: Well, we don't talk about winning, so that's not something that's part of our values or culture.

PK: So the culture is what?

JS: We empower the players to perform and to be the best that they can be.

PK: So throwing (David Clarke's) kicking tee away is okay? The grabbing of the

Mayo shirts is okay? If winning isn't the only thing, how is it acceptable for a player to take out a GPS unit and throw it at a free-taker? How is that acceptable? And you're going to say: 'It's not acceptable.' But it is acceptable because any Dublin player who was asked about it said they'd have done the same thing.

JS: Listen, things happen in games, and there are loads of examples of games that finished ugly. The two most talented players of my era were (Peter) Canavan and the Gooch, and Canavan rugby-tackled the Gooch to win an All-Ireland. So what's changed?

PK: Sure.

JS: What's the deterrent? How do we ensure it doesn't happen? That's the challenge because I think, to a man, if the roles were reversed Mayo would have done the same. They wouldn't give a shite. And we wouldn't have an issue with it. And whether that's right or wrong …

PK: Don't tell me that Ciarán Kilkenny will have a photo on his mantelpiece in 20 years' time of him walking to the sideline with a black card pointing at him. That's not going to happen.

JS: Yeah, probably (not).

PK: I understand doing-what-you-have-to-do has become part of the game. I get all that. But it was still ugly to me. Is there no part of it that was ugly to you?

JS: Well, at the time we were consumed by the game, so it wasn't something I was focused on. We had a black card. We were a man down. I know where you're coming from but I think the bigger picture is: how can we protect the game so we can have better endings? Because ultimately we want the game to bring out the best in our players, and to show their best qualities. So I don't agree that it's winning at all costs but I think the administrators have a responsibility to ensure that doesn't happen. And that's where the debate has been lost.

4 THINGS THAT GO BUMP IN THE NIGHT

People's backyards are much more interesting than their front gardens.

John Betjeman

The month is November, 1999. I'm sitting in the lobby of the Kervansaray Termal Hotel – no crowds, low music – in Bursa with Tony Cascarino, before the second leg of a European Championship play-off with Turkey. We've been drinking coffee and shooting the breeze and I'm just about to leave when the conversation turns.

'This may seem an odd question, but what do you know about me?' he asks.

'I know you're a good player but not a great player,' I laugh.

'No, I'm serious. What do you know about me?'

'You're right, it is an odd question,' I reply. 'What do I know about you? I know you're thirty-seven years old and Ireland's most-capped player. I know you're a goal shy of the all-time scoring record. I know you've played in two World Cups and for Aston Villa, Celtic and Marseilles. I know you named your first son Michael after your Irish grandfather and your other son Teddy after Teddy Sheringham. I think you're possibly divorced but I'm not sure, and that you may have remarried a French girl, but I'm not sure about that either. I know you're well liked by your peers and by the media. A typical streetwise cockney, I'd say; one of the nice guys.'

He looked at me and smiled.

That's my front garden.

The month is May 2016. I'm sitting in a car with another man I've been writing about for twenty years. It's a cool, bright evening in Dublin and we're stuck in a line of slow-moving traffic on James's Street.

'Have you been?' he asks, nodding towards the Guinness Storehouse.

'Once, with a friend,' I reply. 'You?'

'Yeah, with my father, not long before he died.'

I nod and pretend the words have washed over me, but it's a job to suppress my alarm.

His father!

Really?

The guy in his autobiography?

Surely not?

We meet again the following morning. I cite some passages from the book and read from some notes I've made about things that appear odd to me; the references to his father, holes in the narrative, the curious inconsistencies, the almost perfect graph of his career.

But the penny has already dropped.

This is his front garden.

The interview is scheduled to run a week later but the holes are bothering me and I decide to put it on hold. A month later, he sends me a message: 'I hope you're keeping well. What's the story on the piece we did? I've had a good think about it and feel that I wasn't being totally open. If you want to do it properly then I think we could do better.'

'Let's do better,' I reply.

We meet a week later.

'You've been doing some thinking?' I say.

'Yeah, it's lack of sleep,' he replies. 'I'm a terrible sleeper.'

'Since?'

'I have spells where I'm all right, and spells when I'm up thinking all sorts of things.'

'I didn't read about this in the book?'

'I didn't talk about it in the book.'

'So what is it that keeps you awake at night?'

'Christ!' he says. 'I'm in a sweat just thinking about it.'

This was his back yard.

A few days later, still fretting over the interview, he asks to meet again.

'A few things haven't sat right with me,' he says.

'Trust me,' I reply. 'I'll take great care.'

But now we're both tossing and turning.

'It's not a problem for me to drop it if you're not happy?' I suggest.

'I'm sorry for wasting your time,' he says, 'but I don't want to be defined by what we've spoken about. I just feel uneasy about it all.'

The interview does not appear.

Betjeman was right: back yards are much more interesting than front gardens. And there's no greater thrill for a writer than going deep. But we're not in the business of ruining people's lives.

5 HOW DO YOU MEASURE THAT?

Everyone always tells me off for interviewing stars – why don't I interview 'real' people? They always know a fishmonger in Kensal Rise who is a million times more interesting than Rupert Everett. Well, fine – but who would read it?

Lynn Barber,
Demon Barber

Ed Joyce has never sold fish in Kensal Rise but he's rarely been described as a star, which is odd and pretty unfair given that he's considered by many to be one of the greatest sportsmen Ireland has ever produced. The problem, of course, is cricket, a sport where you have to play for England to make your name.

But that's probably what makes him so interesting.

Consider the facts of his breakthrough season in the summer of 2006. He scores a hundred playing for Middlesex in a four-day game against Yorkshire and is informed that night that he's been selected for England. The month? June. The opposition? Ireland. The venue? Belfast. 'Their' opening batsman? His brother, Dominick.

'It was crap,' he says. 'I hated that game. I absolutely hated it. It was a great day for Irish cricket – the first ODI (One Day International) between England and Ireland. There was a big crowd and it was on TV but it was the worst possible game for me to play in. It was just a weird experience.'

Joyce was a great story, and a cracking interview, but like Kavanagh, and Sherlock, there was some stuff that was left out. And like Kavanagh and Sherlock, there was a reason. Kavanagh's life was much more interesting than his views on doping; Sherlock's life was much more interesting than his views on Gavin; and there was a lot more to Joyce than whether CJ Stander or Bundee Aki should be playing rugby for Ireland.

Which is not to say his views on the subject weren't interesting …

PK: We've had this fierce debate here about CJ Stander and Bundee Aki playing for Ireland and I've been wondering if it's just an Irish trait to get excited about it? I don't remember the French getting excited when they picked Scott Spedding, or much debate when it happens in England.

EJ: The Tuilagis and all that?

PK: Yeah, although I think Manu went there quite young.

EJ: Right.

PK: And it's obviously interesting with cricket and the path you've taken.

EJ: I think (in cricket) we've generally welcomed people.

PK: I'm against it.

EJ: Are you? Okay.

PK: I'm not sure it's the same as cricket – and you can tell me otherwise – but we've got kids who've grown up playing rugby here and what we're saying to them is: 'We want these better guys. It doesn't matter that they're Samoan or South African – we just want a better team.' Because it's a pro game and a better team generates money.

EJ: Do you really think that will affect kids growing up?

PK: I do.

EJ: Do you?

PK: And I think 99.9 per cent of Irish rugby internationals agree with me and are just terrified to say it.

EJ: You'd say they're against it?

PK: I'd say they're totally against it. Luke Fitzgerald said it (first) and got so much abuse that he ran for cover. He lost caps because of the New Zealander …

EJ: Jared Payne?

PK: Yeah. So is it not natural in that scenario that you would resent that?

EJ: Well, obviously it's difficult for me to debate this because I'm on the other side in terms of cricket and that. But I've never seen any effect on … the England cricket team is a good example. There's always a South African or an Aussie (on the team) – Dawid Malan at the moment, Geraint Jones and KP (Kevin Pietersen) in the past – and I've never seen it do anything other than attract people to the game if the team is doing well.

PK: Right.

EJ: CJ Stander has come here to live. Clearly he is South African, not Irish, but he is making our team a better one and that's going to benefit everyone. Because I've seen it in cricket – if the team is doing better, it will benefit the sport in the long run; kids will want to play it; people will want to go and see it; sponsors will want to put money into it. And if a few people like Luke Fitzgerald fall by the wayside … well, I'm sorry for them, but they have to get better to get ahead of the other guy. That's my opinion and it's harsh, but that's professional sport. The fault is with the rule not the player.

PK: Absolutely.

EJ: This three-year thing is an absolute farce. The four-year thing for me (he qualified for England after spending four years at Middlesex) was an absolute farce as well – I didn't have to do anything to achieve that. But if it's a long-term commitment like seven years which it is now in England, that's a tough decision. And that's the way it should be.

PK: I totally agree.

EJ: Maybe make it six for rugby – because it's such a short career. But that would be a proper commitment.

PK: And it would take the mercenary aspect out of it.

EJ: Yeah. Because Bundee Aki had no intention of coming here and playing for Ireland, he came here to play for Connacht and it's certainly not his fault. He's come out and said: 'I'm not Irish. I'm not from here.' But he has been convinced by people from within the game. But I'd be surprised if 99 per cent (of his fellow internationals) were against it because that's not the way it is in cricket. No one in cricket begrudges the lads coming over – well, maybe one per cent of players – because it's just a fact of life.

PK: Sure.

EJ: If someone is better than me, they're better than me. No one can argue that CJ Stander and Bundee Aki aren't good rugby players.

PK: I'm not arguing that. And I don't have a problem with them playing for Munster and Connacht, but I do have a problem with them playing for Ireland. I mean, what are we? Who are we? Ireland or the fucking Barbarians? Because that's what it can become. We could have five on the team for the next World Cup!

EJ: And would you have a huge problem with that?

PK: I would have a problem with it.

EJ: Is the football team not the same?

PK: No.

EJ: Why?

PK: Because there's a connection – a parent or grandparent who was born here.

EJ: Not all of them.

PK: All of them.

EJ: Cascarino?

PK: Well, I understand why you would say that but what's his mother's maiden name?

EJ: I don't know.

PK: Theresa O'Malley.

EJ: (laughs) Really?

PK: He grew up with an Irish grandfather and a sense of his Westport roots. So there was a connection there.

EJ: Do you think that matters?

PK: I think it does matter.

EJ: I just think it's so … tenuous. Okay, so you grow up in an Irish household but how do you measure that? It's impossible. I think you just have to accept that people travel and play but I don't like it. I'd prefer it was an (all) Ireland team.

PK: That's what I'm saying.

EJ: I'd prefer, I'm not against it.

PK: It's a good debate.

EJ: Yes, it is a good debate.

6 'HEY! YOUR MONEY!'

Disaster is a dirty word in the sporting context but Ciara Mageean uses it herself, and with some justification. Everything about her race, her result and the immediate after-math clearly left her badly shaken and understandably so. It certainly wasn't pretty, or even close. Last to finish in her 1,500m heat killed all of Mageean's qualification hopes, and made for a worrying start for the Irish team at these World Athletics Championships.

Ian O'Riordan,
The Irish Times

Twenty-one years have passed since my first interview with Pádraig Harrington. I've spent more time watching him, listening to him, and transcribing him than any other sports star, but every time I go back to him a sobering reality bites: 'I haven't even scratched this guy!'

In February, a week after following him to California for the AT&T Pro-Am at Pebble Beach, I had this crazy idea to sit him down with Shane Lowry to talk about fame, money and life on Sunset Boulevard … crazy because poor Shane hardly got a word in, and because the discussion inevitably turned to the usual suspect.

'Is the Harrington we see on the golf course the same person as the Harrington we meet off it?' I asked.

'I couldn't tell you the difference,' Harrington replied.

'What would you say, Shane?'

Lowry paused and thought about it.

'Do I need to leave the room?' Harrington asked.

'No, I think he's pretty similar,' Lowry said. 'He's obviously …'

He paused again.

'I obviously do need to leave the room,' Harrington laughed.

I spent a lot of time with golfers and golfing people this year: Rory at the Merrion – private room, no music – in January; Harrington and Lowry at a JW Marriott – private room, no music – in Santa Monica in February; Dermot Gilleece, Graeme McDowell, Dermot Byrne, Colin Byrne, Ronan Flood, JP Fitzgerald, Jude O'Reilly and Roddy Carr, for a two-part feature on the Irish at the Masters in April. And Paul McGinley – another all-time favourite – at the Irish Open in July.

The British Open was looming but it was time to take stock. How about going back to the Tour de France? What about the hurling championship? And the football? There's a great piece to be written about Stephen Cluxton. Or Cathal McCarron and Tyrone. And when is the last time you interviewed a woman?

I wasn't sure about Ciara Mageean. She was five years too young (I avoid people under thirty), insisted that I clear the interview with her 'agent' and suggested we meet at a God-awful coffee shop – piped music, much noise – in Rathfarnham. She was also, horror of horrors, a runner, and I'd never met a runner who wasn't in denial about their dope-riven sport.

But this one was different.

'What can I do about it?' she said. 'If I'm told I'm running against a girl that I strongly suspect is doped, what can I do about that? Absolutely nothing. So what I say to myself is this: "I'm going to walk off this track knowing that I gave it everything out there."'

'Is that enough?' I asked.

'It has to be,' she said. 'I put a lot of trust in anti-doping. I believe they are going to catch the cheats – I have to. Okay, so the reality is that's not happening but I can't get bogged down with that. I can't do anything to change that. And I'm never going to cheat.'

'Why not?'

'There was this fella in Rathgar who cycled past me once and 20 quid fell out of his pocket. I picked it up and ran after him: "Hey! Your money!" But he kept going – he must have thought I was insane. So I gave it to Jerry (her then coach, Jerry Kiernan) that night, and told him to give it to the Guide Dogs for the Blind.'

You're laughing, right? I mean, you couldn't make it up. A 20 quid note! She tries to give it back! The fucking Guide Dogs for the Blind!

I had found a new hero.

Two weeks later, as she was lining up in the heats of the 1,500m at the World Athletic Championships in London, I was walking down Oxford Street after spending the day with Dan Martin. And though I'd rather scratch Newtownmountkennedy on my scrotum with a rusty nail than watch athletics on the BBC, I ducked into Selfridges (electrical department) to watch her race.

The performance didn't matter to me but it was tough to watch her upset. I reached for my phone and sent her a message: 'To my hero, from Samuel Beckett: "Ever tried? Ever failed? No matter. Try again. Fail again. Fail better."'

JOE BROLLY

An outspoken Gaelic football pundit, the Belfast-based barrister is also known for his advocacy work for several charities. Joe is a gifted writer and storyteller whose views on the GAA regularly polarise opinion. He joined the *Sunday Independent* in 2015. As a player, he was a free-scoring corner-forward and an integral part of the Derry team which won the county's only All-Ireland title in 1993.

TOMMY CONLON

Author of *The Couch* column, which has been appearing in the *Sunday Independent* sports pages since 2000, Tommy has a particular talent for finding an angle to a sporting event that others have overlooked or failed to realise the significance of, and bringing it to life for the reader. Conlon's column covers all sports from snooker and darts to Gaelic football, hurling and soccer.

ANTHONY CRONIN

Cronin was a regular contributor to the news and feature pages of the *Sunday Independent* but he could write brilliantly and knowledgeably on horse racing. He was a heavyweight in the Irish literary world, both through his own writings and as a critic. He also wrote significant biographies of Samuel Beckett and Flann O'Brien.

AISLING CROWE

Few writers are able to bring the deep background knowledge of their subjects to the page in quite the same meticulous way that Aisling can. Her interest in people and her love for sport are clear from the first line to the last, and she particularly shines when writing about horse racing.

DERMOT CROWE

Originally from Co. Clare, Dermot's love of hurling shines through in his writing, whether an interview, feature or match report. His forensic and wonderfully descriptive style means that no stone will be left unturned, no matter the subject. Dermot has been with the *Sunday Independent* since 1997.

MARIE CROWE

Marie joined the *Sunday Independent* fresh out of college after impressing during a stint on work experience. She quickly built up a vast network of contacts and her interviews with sports stars were notable for her ability to coax from them personal and honest insights into their lives. The Co. Clare native, who played Gaelic football, camogie and soccer, still contributes regularly to the paper.

MICK DOYLE

A legendary – but controversial – figure in Irish rugby, his straight-talking approach landed him in trouble occasionally, and for a time in the 1990s his columns were widely read. He played for Ireland, then coached his country to a triple crown and Five Nations title in 1985, and was also in charge of the team at the first Rugby World Cup in 1987. He died tragically in 2004, aged sixty-two.

EAMON DUNPHY

One of Ireland's most respected and controversial journalists, Eamon penned what many believe to be one of the greatest football books ever written, *Only a Game?*, about his life in professional football. Dunphy was capped by Ireland and, after retiring, embarked on a career as a writer and broadcaster, displaying a wide breadth of knowledge on sport and current affairs.

BRENDAN FANNING

Brendan began reporting on rugby in the mid-1980s, at the end of his playing career. He continues his involvement in the game as a coach and has been rugby correspondent of the *Sunday Independent* since 1996. His book, *From There to Here*, published in 2007, tells the story of Ireland's stormy transition from amateur rugby to the professional game. There are few, if any, more knowledgeable commentators on the Irish game.

DION FANNING

Dion was the football writer for the *Sunday Independent* for almost twenty years and is noted for his beautiful, flowing style of prose. His column, 'That Was The Week', showed the full range of his talents as he would regularly branch beyond the football world, demonstrating an in-depth knowledge of modern culture.

CLIONA FOLEY

At a time when female sports reporters were almost unheard of, Cliona blazed a trail. It would be incorrect, however, to pigeonhole her as a woman in a man's world. Cliona succeeds in sports writing for the simple and unglamorous reason that she is a very good writer.

NEIL FRANCIS

The towering, talented second-row forward played thirty-six times for Ireland and has since carved a name for himself as one of rugby's most astute and colourful columnists. His writing is edgy and witty … and informed.

DERMOT GILLEECE

Few writers in any sport command the respect afforded to Dermot by the golf community. A wealth of experience covering the greats of the game gives him the ability to entertain and inform his many loyal readers. He has been ever-present in the Irish newspaper scene since the late 1950s and his enthusiasm for his craft has never waned. He has also published several books on golf.

JOHN GREENE

John Greene succeeded Adhamhnán Ó Súilleabháin as sports editor in 2006. He is also a regular columnist, writing on a range of sporting issues. He began his career in the *Longford Leader* before joining the Independent group in 1998, working first with the *Irish Independent*.

KEVIN KIMMAGE

Younger brother of Paul, Kevin had a fine amateur career in cycling and represented Ireland at the 1992 Olympics. He was a noted Gaelic games writer whose interview with Páidí Ó Sé in 2003 – which features in this book – caused a stir in Kerry and beyond.

PAUL KIMMAGE

A former professional cyclist who first lifted the lid on doping in the sport through his book *A Rough Ride*, Paul's determination in pursuit of truth and fair play has set him apart; he has never been content to follow the herd. No subject has ever been too big or too small. His probing interviews remain a feature of Irish sports writing and he is one of the great exponents of long-form journalism.

CLAIRE McCORMACK

A native of Co. Westmeath, Claire started out as a general news reporter but quickly proved that she had several strings to her bow, not least as a talented sports writer. With a particular passion for Gaelic games, she is part of a new breed of writers who have maintained the strong tradition of chronicling life in rural Ireland.

TOM O'RIORDAN

The Kerryman is best remembered as a Gaelic games journalist, but his first love has always been athletics. He competed in the 5,000 metres in the Tokyo Olympics in 1964 and was a dominant figure on the domestic track and cross-country scene. He enjoyed a long and successful career with the Independent group, in the *Irish Independent* and the *Sunday Independent*.

COLM O'ROURKE

A true giant among Gaelic footballers, Colm won two All-Ireland titles with Meath and is an insightful, sharp and often mischievous commentator on the game he loves. He began working as a newspaper columnist while still playing, and has been writing for the *Sunday Independent* since the early 1990s. O'Rourke gets his point across in a gentle, often witty style.

SEAN RYAN

Sean was deputy sports editor of the *Sunday Independent* for a staggering thirty-two years until he retired in 2007. But he also was a highly respected commentator on the Irish soccer scene and has written a number of important books on the domestic game. He is still an occasional contributor to the paper.

RICHARD SADLIER

When his professional football career ended prematurely due to injury, Richard quickly turned his attention to media work. It soon became apparent that he had a talent for analysing the game and while he never got to fulfil his potential on the pitch, he is certainly making the most of his talent as a shrewd observer off it.

RAYMOND SMITH

A prolific writer and author, particularly on Gaelic games, Raymond also wrote extensively about politics, a subject he was deeply passionate about. For years, his *Complete Handbook of Gaelic Games* was the only credible reference book for Gaelic football and hurling. A hurling fanatic, in his varied career he also covered the war in the Congo. He died in 2000.

EAMONN SWEENEY

Pick a sport, any sport, from the smallest local battle to a major international event, and Eamonn has a remarkable ability to deliver an insightful and thought-provoking view. The Co. Sligo native, who now resides in West Cork, is informative, emotive, humorous and a master in his field. His 'Hold The Back Page' column has been a continuous presence in the paper since 2006.

DAVID WALSH

One of Ireland's most famous journalists, best known for his role in uncovering Lance Armstrong's doping programme, David began his career with the *Leitrim Observer*, but quickly rose to prominence on the national scene. In the late 1980s and early 1990s he became associated with Irish cycling's golden era, but his weekly pieces in the *Sunday Independent* delved into all areas of sporting life.

ACKNOWLEDGEMENTS

I've been fortunate in my career to have worked under some brilliant editors, beginning in the 1990s in the *Longford Leader* with Eugene McGee, to my mind one of the greatest provincial newspaper editors the country has ever seen. He has a rare understanding of local life, which he brought to bear in the paper. Aengus Fanning, who was the editor of the *Sunday Independent* from 1984 until his death in January 2012, was an extraordinary man who transformed the paper – and the Irish newspaper landscape. He believed in people, those who worked for him and those who bought and read the paper. His infectious spirit permeated the pages. He promoted good writing; he challenged the consensus; and he always looked for the other side of the story.

The influence of Eugene and Aengus is everywhere in how I chose the pieces which I thought best reflected the *Sunday Independent* sport section over the last three decades.

Aengus was succeeded as editor by Anne Harris, and she by Cormac Bourke, and both helped keep the flame burning.

When I first mooted the idea for this book to Patrick O'Donoghue of Mercier Press, he was enthused by it and worked hard to make it happen. He and the team at Mercier deserve enormous credit for the work they have done not just on this book, but in promoting Irish writing and Irish writers.

Adhamhnán Ó Súilleabháin became the paper's sports editor in 1988. He had a vision, and with the backing of Aengus, created an environment that allowed good writers to flourish, to question, to probe and, most importantly of all, to tell stories. The sport section of today is as much his legacy as anyone's. Adhamhnán was of enormous help with this book, as was Fergus McDonnell, the current deputy sports editor at the *Sunday Independent*, who encouraged the idea from the start, pored over drafts and offered invaluable feedback through the whole process.

Thanks to Cormac Bourke, *Sunday Independent* editor, David Courtney, group Head of Sport Content, and Ed McCann, the Managing Editor at INM, for believing in this idea and providing the necessary support.

And a final thank you to the writers who have made the sport section what it is over the last thirty years. My starting point was Euro '88, my finishing point the 2018 World Cup. In the initial trawl through the archives, I set aside almost 700 articles by forty-six different writers before beginning the task of whittling those down to what appears on these pages. There is a rich archive of material in the *Sunday Independent* vaults, and hopefully the pieces chosen give a fair and accurate reflection of the standards which I believe have been consistently maintained by the paper.

John Greene

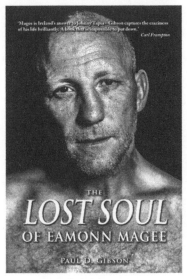
'Raw, riveting, beautifully written … an unforgettable book.'

Donald McRae, *The Guardian*

'Magee is Ireland's answer to Johnny Tapia – Gibson captures the craziness of his life brilliantly. A book that is impossible to put down.'

Carl Frampton

Eamonn Magee is widely regarded as one of the most gifted fighters ever to emerge from Ireland. Yet, despite becoming a world champion in 2003, such was his genius that it will always be considered a career unfulfilled. Women, drink, drugs, gambling, depression and brushes with the law all took Eamonn away from his craft. Then there was the violence: a throat slashed; an IRA bullet in the calf; a savage, leg-shattering beating. Wherever Eamonn went, trouble was never too far behind.

The Lost Soul of Eamonn Magee is a uniquely intimate telling of a barely believable life story. A compelling read filled with heartache and laughter, violence and love, unthinkable lows and fleeting, glorious highs, Eamonn's is a story for which the term 'brutally honest' might have been coined.

www.mercierpress.ie